The
Canadian Writer's
Workplace

Seventh Edition

The
Canadian Writer's
Workplace

Seventh Edition

**by Gary Lipschutz, Sandra Scarry,
and John Scarry**

NELSON / E D U C A T I O N

NELSON / EDUCATION

The Canadian Writer's Workplace
Seventh Edition

by Gary Lipschutz, Sandra Scarry, and John Scarry

Vice President, Editorial Higher Education:
Anne Williams

Executive Editor:
Laura Macleod

Senior Marketing Manager:
Amanda Henry

Developmental Editor:
Jacquelyn Busby

Photo Researcher:
Carrie McGregor

Permissions Coordinator:
Carrie McGregor

Content Production Manager:
Claire Horsnell

Production Service:
MPS Limited, a Macmillan Company

Copy Editor:
Elizabeth D'Anjou

Proofreader:
Maura Brown

Indexer:
Edwin Durbin

Senior Production Coordinator:
Ferial Suleman

Design Director:
Ken Phipps

Managing Designer:
Franca Amore

Interior Design:
Liz Harasymczuk

Cover Design:
Gary Blakeley

Cover Image:
Stephen Strathdee/Getty Images

Compositor:
MPS Limited, a Macmillan Company

Printer:
RR Donnelley

Library and Archives Canada Cataloguing in Publication

Lipschutz, Gary, 1964-

The Canadian writer's workplace / Gary Lipschutz, Sandra Scarry, John Scarry.—7th ed.

Fourth ed. written by: John Roberts, John Scarry and Sandra Scarry.

Includes index.
ISBN 978-0-17-650327-7

1. English language—Rhetoric—Textbooks. 2. English language—Rhetoric—Problems, exercises, etc. 3. English language—Grammar—Problems, exercises, etc. 4. Literature—Collections. I. Scarry, Sandra, 1946- II. Scarry, John III. Title.

PE1413.C355 2012   808'.042
C2011-905069-2

ISBN-13: 978-0-17-650327-7
ISBN-10: 0-17-650327-7

Brief Contents

Contents

UNIT IV: Readings   347

FRIEND/UNFRIEND   348

In this review of the movie *The Social Network*, Peter Howell of *The Toronto Star* discusses how world-popular Facebook got started and how ironic it is that the notion of "friends" is a big reason for its success.

NO GREAT SACRIFICE   352

People spend a great deal of time claiming to be environmentally conscious. But do they "walk the walk"? Suzuki and Moola, in this piece from their "Science Matters" column, strongly claim that people generally could do more than they do.

SATISFIED STRAGGLER   355

How often have you dedicated yourself to something that you know you're not good at? Is there something to be said for challenging yourself in this way? Nova Scotian Ashleigh VanHouten narrates her personal story about running a marathon, which she had never tried before.

THE $2-MILLION COMMA   358

Rogers is a leader in the communications industry. So it seems ironic that this company would make a mistake with a punctuation mark that would end up costing a fortune. Grant Robertson tells this uncommon story of the common comma.

CANADA, MY CANADA   360

Born and raised on the Brochet Reserve in Northern Manitoba, Tomson Highway paints a proud and vibrant picture of the country he calls home.

MY BODY IS MY OWN BUSINESS   364

Naheed Mustafa explains why she wears the traditional Muslim headscarf, the hijab.

writer Julia McKinnell about ways to combat this habit that seeks to sabotage
your plans.

If threats of terrorism weren't enough, fraudulent marriage is now another fear many
Canadians face. Cameron Ainsworth-Vincze explains how more people are getting
married just to get into Canada and to start a more prosperous life. And they do this in
spite of the harm to the people they are marrying.

Preface

It's been said that the first casualty of war is truth. Well, the first casualty of writing is often clarity. Writing without clarity is bad writing. *The Canadian Writer's Workplace*, Seventh Edition, is an easy-to-use textbook that aims to inspire and guide students on the road to achieving clarity in their writing. With this book, students are expected to develop the solid paragraph- and essay-writing skills needed not only in English courses, but also in many other courses taken in college and/or university and, subsequently, wherever written communication is required. *The Canadian Writer's Workplace* can help students get the most out of any endeavour that calls for the ability to write clearly and effectively.

EVERYTHING YOU NEED BETWEEN TWO COVERS

The Canadian Writer's Workplace is a **three-in-one textbook of grammar, rhetoric (writing steps and strategies), and readings.** When you use this book, there is no need to look for a supplemental book containing work on grammar or a book to teach writing skills or a reader providing material that inspires the students to generate thoughtful and well-written composition. Everything you need is already between two covers.

STRUCTURE OF THE TEXTBOOK

The Canadian Writer's Workplace is made up of five units:
- Unit I.   Grammar
- Unit II.   The Writing Process
- Unit III. Writing Strategies for the Paragraph and Essay
- Unit IV.   Readings
- Unit V.   Appendices

EIGHT TYPES OF EXERCISES, QUESTIONS, AND ASSIGNMENTS

With examples and figures, *The Canadian Writer's Workplace* offers constant reinforcement of every definition stated and every writing technique taught at every step of the way. Numerous practice exercises and writing assignments throughout the entire book offer further reinforcement of what is being learned. The format of *The Canadian Writer's Workplace* features flexibility in that the book enables an instructor to work on different exercises with an entire class, gives individual students opportunity to work by themselves or with a tutor in a lab, and encourages students to work in groups. Certain sections can be skipped if the material is not needed for a particular class—or a class might begin with a later section, with the earlier chapters being used as a review. Eight types of exercises, questions and assignments in this textbook are as follows:

1. Quick Quiz

Each chapter in Unit I begins with a Quick Quiz, designed to assess students' skills in the material in that chapter. Based on the results of this quiz, the instructor can choose either to skip over the material in the chapter, or to spend extra time on the material in question if the students' skills in this area are shown to be weak.

2. Practices

The answers for these are provided in the Answer Key at the back of the textbook. Practices enable students, therefore, to work independently by checking their work without having to consult an instructor.

3. Exercises

Answers to the Exercises are not at the back of the textbook. The main reason for the deliberate absence of these answers is so that instructors can assign these exercises for in-class testing or homework. Answers to the Exercises are provided, however, in the Instructor's Manual that accompanies the seventh edition of *The Canadian Writer's Workplace*.

4. Review Practices and Exercises

These are often found at the end of the chapter in Unit I. They are cumulative so that they test the students not only on a particular point of grammar, but rather on a number of points discussed within the chapter at hand. Similar to the Practices and Exercises earlier in the chapter, the Practices in the Review section have their answers in the back of the book while the Exercises in the Review section do not.

5. Working Together

A valuable and popular feature, "Working Together," can be found at the end of every chapter in the book. This feature promotes group work, an approach that provides opportunities for the peer-mediated activities that many instructors use to make their classes more fun and at the same time to reinforce concepts from a chapter they have already discussed in their classes.

6. Questions for Analysis

Several questions for analysis follow every model essay found in Unit III: Writing Strategies for the Paragraph and Essay. They prompt the student for short answers on either content or form. Sample questions include "Is the author's argument effective? Why or why not?"

7. Assignments

Throughout Unit III, the reader will find chapters on the various rhetorical modes or writing strategies, such as description, comparison, and/or contrast and process. For each chapter, there are "Assignments" listing several topics relating to the chapter from which the student can choose to write a paragraph or essay on something the student finds of interest to him or her.

8. Four Types of Questions Following Major Readings in Unit IV

Every major reading in Unit IV is followed by four sets of questions. The four sets are 1. Comprehension Questions, 2. Questions about Form, 3. Questions for Discussion, and 4. Writing Ideas. Often students ask professors if they can do practice writing in preparation for major writing assignments done in class. The number 4 type of questions in particular can be used for this purpose, and sometimes, so can questions from number 3. Regardless, all of these questions are designed to foster further understanding and appreciation for the reading they follow and the issues, in general, under discussion.

THE READINGS

Students often require inspiration to help motivate them to learn how to write better. In the interest of further inspiration and stimulation, the reading content in this edition has been expanded to include more cutting-edge essays with particular appeal to post-secondary students. Overall, the readings throughout the text are extremely varied: they include model paragraphs and essays (including a model research essay about cell phones and their potential harm to our health in Chapter 20: "Documentation") in Unit III and new major readings in Unit IV. Some of the works in Unit III are by student writers; others are taken from a wide range of novels, essays, short stories, and books of nonfiction by world-famous authors. Unit IV contains mostly nonfiction and some short fiction and poetry—all carefully chosen to evoke thoughtful and well-structured written responses from students. The writers of the readings in Unit IV are exclusively Canadian, and they are all seasoned writers and/or academics. The strong Canadian flavour of the text offers the post-secondary student in Canada an insight into various aspects of Canadian culture.

FEATURES OF THE SEVENTH EDITION

Many features of the first six Canadian editions of the book have been retained. As mentioned earlier, they include the comprehensive package of grammar, rhetoric, and readings. This seventh edition, however, offers some exciting and innovative changes:

- Chapters 15 and 16 in the previous edition on the paragraph have been combined in the seventh edition into one big chapter entitled "The Paragraph." Consolidation of material from the previous two chapters makes it easier to find items in the textbook that are related to paragraph development in general.
- A chapter introduced in the sixth edition (Chapter 20) entitled "Research and Documentation" has been divided into two separate chapters, Chapter 19: "The Research Paper" and Chapter 20:"Documentation" to allow for expansion of the content. Chapter 19 features tips on research, especially in the electronic world in which we now live, while Chapter 20 demonstrates

how APA and MLA documentation is applied to the research paper. Chapter 20 showcases a model research paper on the timely and controversial topic of cell phones and their potential long-term effects on our health.

- Six major readings in Unit IV have been replaced by more timely cutting-edge pieces that promise to engage the reader. Among the new readings are "No Great Sacrifice" by David Suzuki and Faisal Moola, which discusses how people are not going far enough to protect the environment, and Sarah Boesveld's "Gadget-Savvy, But Socially Inept?" about the negative consequences of having too much technology at our disposal.

- Chapter 16: "The Essay" (formerly Chapter 17) has been expanded to include a section called "Moving from the Paragraph to the Essay." This section introduces a new format called the "Preliminary Essay" that helps the students deal primarily with the organization of an essay before having to write a full-fledged one.

- The section dealing with the issue of euthanasia in Chapter 28: "Argumentation" has been revamped. The American piece in the previous edition has been replaced by a more current Canadian piece by McGill professor Margaret Somerville. Somerville's article is accompanied by two sidebars featuring an Angus-Reid poll, which examines the opinions of Canadians regarding euthanasia, and a report on Parliament's response to the bill that called for its legalization.

ANCILLARIES

Enriched Instructor's Manual and NETA PowerPoint® Presentation

The Nelson Education Teaching Advantage (NETA) program delivers research-based instructor resources that promote student engagement and higher-order thinking to enable the success of Canadian students and educators.

Instructors today face many challenges. Resources are limited, time is scarce, and a new kind of student has emerged: one who is juggling school with work, has gaps in his or her basic knowledge, and is immersed in technology in a way that has led to a completely new style of learning. In response, Nelson Education has gathered a group of dedicated instructors, from across a variety of disciplines, all of whom are recognized for their commitment to teaching, to advise us on the creation of richer and more flexible ancillaries that respond to the needs of today's teaching environments.

In consultation with this editorial advisory board, Nelson Education has completely rethought the structure, approaches, and formats of our key textbook ancillaries. The result is the Nelson Education Teaching Advantage. The key components created for *The Canadian Writer's Workplace,* Seventh Edition, include NETA Engagement and NETA Presentation. Each component includes one or more ancillaries prepared according to our best practices, and a document explaining the theory behind the practices.

NETA Engagement presents materials that help instructors deliver engaging content and activities to their classes. NETA Enriched Instructor's Manuals (EIMs) provide genuine assistance to teachers. The EIMs answer questions like the following: What should students learn? Why should students care? EIMs also describe techniques and resources to help students master key concepts. Dr. Roger Fisher's *Instructor's Guide to Classroom Engagement* (IGCE) accompanies every Enriched Instructor's Manual.

NETA Presentation has been developed to help instructors make the best use of PowerPoint® in their classrooms. With a clean and uncluttered design developed by Maureen Stone of StoneSoup Consulting, NETA Presentation features slides with improved readability, more multi-media and graphic materials, activities to use in class, and tips for instructors on the Notes page. A copy of *NETA Guidelines for Classroom Presentations* by Maureen Stone is included with each set of PowerPoint slides.

Test Bank

The Test Bank for *The Canadian Writer's Workplace,* Seventh Edition, contains an extensive selection of exercises corresponding to every point of grammar discussed in Unit I and the first three appendices in the back of the book. The test bank, along with the Enriched Instructor's Manual and NETA PowerPoint® Presentation, is available online and in CD format.

Aplia

Also new to the seventh edition is an online homework solution created by Aplia. Founded in 2000 by economist and Stanford professor Paul Romer, Aplia is an educational technology company dedicated to improving learning by increasing student effort and engagement. Currently, Aplia products support post-secondary-level courses and have been used by more than 650,000 students at more than 750 institutions. For students, Aplia offers a way to stay on top of coursework by providing regularly scheduled homework assignments. Interactive tools and additional content further increase engagement and understanding. For instructors, Aplia offers high-quality, auto-graded assignments that ensure students put forth effort on a regular basis throughout the term. These assignments have been developed for a range of textbooks and are easily customized for individual teaching schedules.

ACKNOWLEDGMENTS

For their advice and/or personal support, the author is indebted to John Artibello, Ben Labovitch, Denvil Buchanan, Karen Naidoo, Eric Wilding, Andrea Jacobs, Susan Whitzman, Dan Gaze, Caroline Stephens, Ron Schafrick, Martha Shephard, Michael Countryman and Tamina Basarab.

Kudos and thanks go to the winning team at Nelson—Laura Macleod, Jacquelyn Busby, and Claire Horsnell. Their hard work and dedication have helped make this edition what it is.

The comments and advice from the following reviewers were invaluable:

Veronica Baig, Athabasca University

Marilyn Boyle-Taylor, Seneca College

Scott Bunyan, Mohawk College

Neil Carter, Sault College

Rhonda Dynes, Seneca College

Jo Ann Foote, Lambton College

Lori Gauthier, Cambrian College

Karen Hebb, Southern Alberta Institute of Technology

Chandra Hodgson, Humber College

Christina Horgan, Southern Alberta Institute of Technology

Jim MacDonald, Humber College

Linda Maloney, Humber College

Sandi Mills, Centennial College

Jean Mills, Conestoga College

Nina Pyne, Sault College

To the student essayists who have generously given permission to publish their work in this edition of *The Canadian Writer's Workplace,* the author and editors wish to extend most sincere thanks. They are Margo Fine, Zack Goodman, Donald Pianissimo, Alexandra Savage-Ferr, Leila Sayeed, Leanne C. Southall, Akis Stylianou, Cara Watters, and Jenny Yuen.

Your Feedback or Questions Are Invited

If you have any feedback or questions you would like to send regarding this edition of *Canadian Writer's Workplace*, please do so via the following email address:

glips@centennialcollege.ca.

I look forward to your responses.
Gary Lipschutz

Unit I **Grammar**

© Gary Blakeley, Shutterstock

Chapter 1 Parts of Speech: Overview

The Canadian Writer's Workplace begins with an overview of grammar to ensure that you have an understanding of basic terms. Such an understanding will help you succeed with the rest of this text.

Words can be divided into nine categories called **parts of speech**. Understanding these categories will help you work with language, especially when it comes to revising your own writing.

Quick Quiz Test your knowledge of the various parts of speech. Determine the correct part of speech for the underlined words in the following sentences. There is no need to actually write the answers in the blanks; this Quick Quiz is primarily for self-assessment. The answers to the questions are upside down beside the quiz.

1. By installing the service, you agree to the following conditions.
   <u>Noun</u>   <u>verb</u> <u>article</u>

2. Follow the instructions on the screen to uninstall the older version of the program.
   <u>Verb</u>   <u>prop.</u>   <u>adj</u>   <u>prep</u> <u>noun</u>
   command.

3. Running the program is easily handled if you pay attention to the next part of
   <u>Noun</u>   <u>adverb</u>   <u>Pronoun</u>   <u>adjective</u>
   the video.

4. Everything you need to do is explained in ten easy steps.
   <u>noun</u>   <u>verb</u>   <u>prep</u> <u>Noun</u>

5. If you have any questions, call our toll-free number.
   __   _____ __   ____

Answers:
1. noun, verb, article
2. verb, preposition, adjective,
   preposition, noun
3. gerund (-*ing* word acting as a noun),
   adverb, pronoun, adjective
4. pronoun, infinitive (*to* + a verb),
   preposition, adjective
5. conjunction, noun, verb, adjective

Parts of Speech		
1. Nouns	4. Verbs	7. Conjunctions
2. Pronouns	5. Adverbs	8. Interjections
3. Adjectives	6. Prepositions	9. Articles

1. What Are Nouns?

> **DEFINITION**
>
> A **noun** is a word that refers to a person, place, or thing.
> **Example:** The *student* is doing her *homework*.
> Both *student* and *homework* are nouns.

Types of Nouns

There are two types of nouns: common nouns and proper nouns.

Types of Nouns	
Common Nouns	**Proper Nouns**
officer	Michael Johnson
station	Union Station
magazine	*Canadian Geographic**
university	Centennial College

* When a title is that of a major publication such as a book or a magazine, the title should be italicized or underlined (underlining in a handwritten text is the equivalent of italics in a printed text).

Common nouns are nouns that are not names or titles. For this reason, common nouns do not begin with a capital letter (unless, of course, the word begins a sentence):

> I plan to attend *university* next fall.

The word *university* is a common noun in this sentence because it is not part of a specific name or title. The *u* must not be capitalized.

Proper nouns are names or titles. Every significant word of a proper noun must start with a capital letter.

> *Carleton University* is in *Ottawa*, our nation's capital. *The University of Cape Breton*, on the other hand, is in *Sydney, Nova Scotia*.

In the above two sentences, the *U* in University (the word immediately following *Carleton* and the second word in the second sentence) must be capitalized because the word *University* in both cases is now a proper noun; it is part of the title of a specific university. (See Chapter 12: "Capitalization.") The University of Cape Breton includes the word *of*, whose first letter is not capitalized because *of* is a *preposition* (see p. 8), and a preposition is not considered a significant word in a title.

Concrete vs. Abstract Nouns

Nouns are said to be **concrete** if they represent things you can see or touch.

window	river
paper	finger

Nouns are said to be **abstract** if they represent things you cannot see or touch. These words can be concepts, ideas, or qualities.

meditation	carelessness
honesty	fearlessness

To test for a noun, it may help to ask these questions:

- Can I put the article *the* in front of the word?
- Is the word used as the subject or object of the sentence?

A noun may be the subject of the sentence it is in (the performer of the action). But it may not be. All subjects are nouns, but not all nouns are subjects. For example, a noun might be an object (the receiver of the action) instead.

> *Marissa* gave a book to her daughter.

The noun *Marissa* is the subject of the sentence. The noun *book* is a direct object (it receives the action directly). The noun *daughter* is an indirect object (it receives the action indirectly).

Countable vs. Non-countable Nouns

Countable nouns, quite simply, can be counted.

> There are three *marbles* on the floor.

Non-countable nouns, just as simply, cannot be counted.

> The *water* spilled onto the floor.

Do not put an indefinite article (*a* or *an*) in front of a non-countable noun. For example, the following is not correct: A water spilled onto the floor.

2. What Are Pronouns?

DEFINITION

A **pronoun** is a word that takes the place of a noun. Like a noun, it can be the subject or object of a sentence. Pronouns come in several cases (*see next page*).
Example: *He* is dating the girl next door.
(The pronoun *he* can replace a noun such as *Johnny* or *the boy*.)

Pronoun Cases

Depending on how it is used in a sentence, a personal pronoun will be in one of three cases: subjective, objective, or possessive. Possessive adjectives (last column) are not pronouns because they do not replace nouns; they modify them instead.

| | Personal Pronouns | | | Possessive |
	Subjective	Objective	Possessive	Adjectives
Singular				
1st person	I	me	mine	my
2nd person	you	you	yours	your
3rd person	he	him	his	his
	she	her	hers	her
	it	it	its	its
Plural				
1st person	we	us	ours	our
2nd person	you	you	yours	your
3rd person	they	them	theirs	their

Relative Pronouns	**Demonstrative Pronouns**	**Indefinite Pronouns**
who, whom, whose	This	all, both, each, one
which	that	nothing, nobody, no one
that	these	anything, anybody, anyone
what	those	something, somebody, someone
whoever, whichever		everything, everybody, everyone

3. What Are Adjectives?

> **DEFINITION**
> An **adjective** is a word that modifies a noun or pronoun.
> **Example:** The *red* car is hers.

An adjective usually comes before the noun it modifies, but it can also come after a verb.

> The *unusual* letter was delivered to my house.
> It felt *heavy*.

4. What Are Verbs?

> **DEFINITION**
> A **verb** is a word that indicates an action, state, or occurrence; its form also indicates the time at which the action, etc., takes place.
> **Example:** The Vancouver Canucks *advanced* to the Stanley Cup Finals in 2011.

Verbs can be divided into three classes: action verbs, linking verbs, and helping verbs.

Action Verbs

An action verb tells us what its subject is doing. Most verbs are action verbs.

> The athlete *cycles* 20 km every morning.
> (The action takes place in the present.)
>
> The crowd *applauded* the sax player.
> (The action takes place in the past.)

Linking Verbs

A linking verb joins the subject of a sentence to one or more words that describe or identify the subject.

> She *is* a jazz musician in her twenties.
> He *seemed* excited about getting married.

Common Linking Verbs		
act	become	look
appear	feel	seem
be (am, is, are, was, were, have been)	grow	taste

Helping Verbs (also called Auxiliary Verbs)

A helping verb, or auxiliary, is any verb used before the main verb.

> It could show the tense of the verb:
> > It *will* rain tomorrow.
> > (shows future tense)

> It could show the passive voice (see pp. 38–41 for more on active and passive voice):
> > The new concert hall *has been* finished.

> It could give a special meaning to the verb:
> > Avril Lavigne *may be* singing at that concert.

The most common auxiliary verbs are forms of the irregular verbs *do, have,* and *be.*

A *modal* auxiliary is a helping verb that comes before the main verb and expresses probability, obligation, ability, or necessity.

Common Modal Auxiliary Verbs
can, could
may, might, must
shall, should
will, would

See Appendix C at the back of the text for more on irregular verbs.

5. What Are Adverbs?

She is sure to succeed *eventually*.

- The adverb *eventually* answers the question "When?"
- It ends in *-ly*, and it modifies the verb *succeed*.

It will be *very* cold tomorrow.

- The adverb *very* answers the question "How?"
- It modifies the adjective *cold*.

Winter has come *too* early.

- The adverb *too* answers the question "How?"
- It modifies the adverb *early*.

Here are some of the more common adverbs:

Common Adverbs		
Adverbs of Frequency	**Adverbs of Degree**	
always	even	quite
ever	extremely	surely
never	just	too
often	more	very
seldom	much	
sometimes	only	

6. What Are Prepositions?

Common Prepositions			
about	below	in	since
above	beneath	inside	through
across	beside	into	to
after	between	like	toward
against	beyond	near	under
along	by	of	until
among	down	off	up
around	during	on	upon
at	except	outside	with
before	for	over	within
behind	from	past	without

7. What Are Conjunctions?

> **DEFINITION**
>
> A **conjunction** is a word that joins or connects other words, phrases, or clauses.
> **Examples:** I was sick, *but* I still came to work.
> She had eggs *and* pancakes for breakfast.

Connecting two words

> <u>Sooner</u> *or* <u>later</u>, you will have to pay.

Connecting two phrases

> The story was on the radio *and* in the newspaper.

Connecting two clauses

> Dinner was late *because* I had to work overtime at the office.

> Since one word can have several meanings, and words can function differently depending on their forms, you must study the context in which a word is found to be sure what part of speech it is.

> The parent makes sacrifices *for* the good of the children.

In the sentence above, *for* is a preposition.

> The parent made sacrifices, *for* the child needed a good education.

In the sentence above, *for* is a conjunction meaning "because."

Conjunctions

Coordinating Conjunctions	Subordinating Conjunctions	
and	after	provided that
but	although	since (meaning "because")
nor	as, as if, as though	unless
or	because	until
for (meaning "because")	before	when, whenever
yet	how	where, wherever, whereas
so	if, even if	while

Correlative Conjunctions	Adverbial Conjunctions	(also known as "conjunctive adverbs")
either . . . or	To add an idea:	furthermore
neither . . . nor		moreover
both . . . and		likewise
not only . . . but also	To contrast:	however
		nevertheless
	To show a result:	consequently
		therefore
	To show an alternative:	otherwise

TIP

You can use the acronym FANBOYS as a way to remember the coordinating conjunctions: *F* for *for*, *A* for *and*, *N* for *nor*, *B* for *but*, *O* for *or*, *Y* for *yet*, and *S* for *so*.

For
And
Nor
But
Or
Yet
So

8. What Are Interjections?

DEFINITION

An **interjection** is a word that expresses a feeling (often a strong one) and is not connected grammatically to any other part of the sentence.
Example: *Darn!* I lost my wallet. *Well*, that means I'll have to borrow cash from a friend.

9. What Are Articles?

DEFINITION

An **article** is a word that identifies a noun in a general sense.
Example: *The* dogs were mistreated for years by *a* previous owner.

Articles are considered to be adjectives. There are two types of articles: definite (*the*) and indefinite (*a, an*).

> She read *the* magazine (a particular magazine).
> She read *a* magazine (some magazine not identified).

Do not use *a* or *an* with non-countable nouns (things that can't be counted separately, such as *water*).

> Water leaked under my roof during the rainstorm.

Use an indefinite article (*a* or *an*) before countable nouns when you don't specify the particular thing referred to.

> *An* open window allowed the fresh air in (any one of a number of windows).

Use *a* before a noun that begins with a consonant or with a *u* pronounced as *y*. Use *an* before a word that begins with a vowel or a silent *h*.

> *a* vacation
> *a* unit, *a* eulogy (*u* and *eu* in these words are pronounced "*yu*")
> *an* automobile
> *an* hour

Working Together: Puzzle Pieces and Sentence Parts

Review the names for sentence parts by doing this crossword puzzle. Feel free to look back through the chapter for the answers.

Grammar Terms Crossword Puzzle

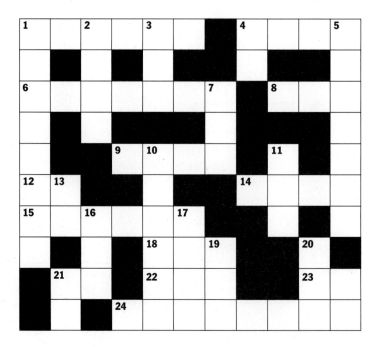

Across

1. Verbs like *hop, sing,* and *play* are called
   _____ verbs.
4. A helping verb
6. Every sentence has a _____ and a verb.
8. A helping verb
9. Which of the following is a preposition?
   must, upon, they
12. A preposition
14. *Word, witch, wall,* and *willow* are examples
    of this part of speech.
15. Most nouns are _____ nouns. They are
    not capitalized.
18. In the following sentence, which word is an
    adjective?
    His pet theory was disproved.
21. A preposition
22. In the following sentence, which word is an
    abstract noun?

    The era was not economically successful.
23. A preposition
24. A word that can take the place of a noun

Down

1. *Joy, confidence, and peace* are examples of
   this kind of noun, which is the opposite of a
   concrete noun.
2. Which word is the subject in the following
   sentence?

   Here is the tube of glue for Toby.
3. An indefinite pronoun
4. A plural pronoun
5. *Look, appear, feel,* and *seem* are examples
   of _____ verbs.
7. Which word is the object of the preposition
   in this sentence?
   He made sure to call her before ten.
10. The opposite of a common noun
11. A pronoun
13. A preposition
16. A helping verb
17. Which of the following is a proper noun?

    king, Nero, hero, teen
19. Which of the following is an adjective?

    net, tan, Nan, man
20. Which word is the verb in the following
    sentence?

    Run down to the car for our bag.
21. A common linking verb

Chapter 2 Recognizing Subjects and Verbs

Quick Quiz Test yourself on your knowledge of subjects and verbs. In each of the following sentences, find the subject of the sentence and the verb that goes with it. Write your answers in the spaces provided. The answers are upside down beside the quiz.

Subject   **Verb**

_____   _____   1. The definition of marriage has become a major issue in Canada.

_____   _____   2. Studies show that many people are getting married later than their parents did.

_____   _____   3. In Quebec, a large proportion of people have chosen to live in common-law relationships.

_____   _____   4. Researchers have given more attention to divorces than to successful marriages.

_____   _____   5. A positive attitude toward the partner appears to be the most important quality in a successful marriage.

Why Should We Use Complete Sentences When We Write?

If you walk up to a friend at noon and say "Lunch?" you are expressing only part of a complete thought. Your friend probably understands your meaning: "Would you like to join me for lunch?" Even though we do not always use complete sentences in daily conversation, we usually have complete thoughts in mind. We say and hear words and phrases such as "Lunch?" every day, and these words and phrases seem to be complete thoughts because both the speaker and the listener supply the missing words in their own minds.

You are free to use language in this way when you speak casually with friends, but you must use a different approach in more formal speaking and writing situations. When writing down your thoughts, you cannot assume that another person will finish your thoughts for you. Each of your written thoughts must be a complete expression of what is in your mind.

The purpose of writing is to communicate something that is of value to a reader. Once you understand how the parts of a complete sentence work, you will be able to focus as much attention on *what* you are saying as on *how* you are saying it. You can take control of the sentence. You will have the power to make words work for you.

What Is a Complete Sentence?

> **DEFINITION**
>
> A **complete sentence** must contain a subject and a verb, as well as express a *complete thought*.
> **Example:** The cat drank. → Simple past → "its over" idea
> (*Cat* is the subject; *drank* is the verb. You need not know what the cat drank in order for the sentence to be complete.)

A *complete thought* is difficult to describe. It may be best understood by means of an example:

1. If you want an "A" in this course.
2. If you want an "A" in this course, you should do all your assignments and homework, attend all your classes, and communicate to your professor any difficulties you're having.
3. You want an "A" in this course.

The first thought is incomplete. The second thought is complete. So is the third. Obviously, length does not determine completeness.

How Do You Find the Subject of a Sentence?

The subject of a sentence is the person or thing about which the rest of the sentence makes an assertion. Any sentence must be about someone or something; therefore, every sentence must have a subject. To find the subject of any sentence, ask yourself this question: Who or what is the sentence about?

When you have answered this question, you have found the subject of the sentence. Try to zero in on one word that is the subject—sometimes this is not possible, but it is possible most of the time. The subject in sentence #3 on page 13 is *you*. The words *"A"* and *course* are also nouns, but neither is the subject of the sentence.

Exercise **Recognizing Subjects**

Examine each of the following sentences and ask yourself who or what it is about. (Choose only one word where possible.) Underline the subject. Answers and explanations are provided below.

1. The student graduated in the spring.
2. The unemployed Rick Daniels spent the summer looking for work.
3. He took a job as a security guard.
4. The building was near the waterfront.
5. The warehouse grew bitterly cold.
6. Cowardice was not the issue.
7. Tina and Margot listened to his complaints whenever they got together.

Since the subject of a sentence is made up of one or more nouns (or a word, phrase, or clause that functions as a noun), it is helpful to learn some of the terms used in traditional grammar to describe different kinds of nouns.

1. **The student graduated in the spring.**

The sentence is about the *student*. In this case, the subject is a common noun.

> **DEFINITION**
>
> **Nouns** refer to people, places, and things. Most nouns are common nouns.
> **Common nouns** are the general terms for all the people, places, and objects around us. They are not specific names; therefore, they are not capitalized.
> **Examples:** woman, city, cola

2. **The unemployed Rick Daniels spent the summer looking for work.**

The sentence is about *Rick Daniels*. In this case, the subject *Rick Daniels* is made up of the two words in his name, both of which are proper nouns.

> **DEFINITION**
>
> **Proper nouns** name particular persons, places, or things. Proper nouns are always capitalized.
> **Examples:** Juanita, Calgary, Pepsi

Notice that words such as *unemployed* can be put in front of nouns to describe them further. These words are called **adjectives**. *The, a,* and *an* are called **articles.** An article is also a form of adjective because it modifies a noun (***Example:*** *the* cat).

3. He took a job as a security guard.

The sentence is about *he*.

> **DEFINITION**
> Words that can be used in place of nouns are called **pronouns**.
> **Examples:** she, he, it, we, I, you, and they

to have, to be, to go
4 infinitives

4. The building was near the waterfront.

The sentence is about the *building*, a common noun. Can you replace this noun first with a proper noun and then with a pronoun?

_____ was near the waterfront.

_____ was near the waterfront.

5. The warehouse grew bitterly cold.

The sentence is about the *warehouse*. Here the common noun is not about a person or place but a thing. What pronoun could take the place of *warehouse*?

_____ grew bitterly cold.

6. Cowardice was not the issue.

The sentence is about *cowardice*, another common noun.

7. Tina and Margot listened to his complaints whenever they got together.

The sentence is about *Tina* and *Margot*. The subject is made up of two proper nouns joined by *and*. This sentence provides an example of a compound subject.

> **DEFINITION**
> A **compound subject** is made up of two or more nouns joined together by *and, or, either/or,* or *neither/nor*.
> **Example:** Neither the *teacher* nor the *students* know the answer.

Not every noun or pronoun functions as a subject. Nouns and pronouns can also function as **objects.** Can you find a noun in the following sentence that is not the subject of the sentence?

Marc bought a ticket.

The word *ticket* is a noun, but not a subject. It does not perform the action of the verb, *bought*—it receives the action. It is an object. (The subject, *Marc*, does the action.)

Guide to Finding the Subject of a Sentence

Definition: The subject of a sentence is who or what the sentence is about.

How to find the subject: Ask yourself, "Who or what is this sentence about?" or "Who or what is doing the main action?"

- Subjects usually come early in the sentence.
- Subjects can be modified by adjectives.
- Subjects can be compound.

Look for these two kinds of words as your subjects:

1. **Nouns:** the names of persons, places, or things

Common	or	Proper		Concrete	or	Abstract
aunt		Aunt Giselle		face		loneliness
country		Ghana		people		patriotism
watch		Timex		jewellery		time

2. **Pronouns:** words that take the place of nouns

Personal	Indefinite	Relative	Demonstrative
I	one	who	this
you	each	that	that
he, she, it	some, someone, somebody, something	what	these
we	any, anyone, anybody, anything	which	those
they	nobody, nothing		
	everyone, everybody, everything		
	all		
	many		
	several		

📁 **Practice   Finding the Subject of a Sentence**

Underline the subject in each of the following sentences. An example has been done for you. Check your answers against those in the Answer Key on page 451.

The seat belt <u>sign</u> switched on.

1. The plane landed.
2. Michelle Bates gathered her bags.
3. She was so excited.
4. Strange sounds filled her ears.
5. A mother and her three children shared a lunch.
6. The battered red taxi idled outside.
7. A light rain had fallen recently.

Finding the Subject in Sentences with Prepositional Phrases

The sentences you worked with in the Practice on page 16 were short and basic. If we wrote only such sentences, our writing would sound choppy. Complex ideas would be difficult to express. One way to expand a simple sentence is to add a prepositional phrase.

He put his suitcase on the seat.

On is a preposition. *Seat* is a noun, used here as the object of the preposition. *On the seat* is a prepositional phrase.

> ### DEFINITION
>
> A **prepositional phrase** is a group of words containing a preposition and an object of the preposition with its modifiers. Prepositional phrases contain nouns, but these nouns are never the subject of the sentence.
>
> **Example:** The dog buried the bone *under the porch.*

In sentences with prepositional phrases, the subject may be difficult to spot. Consider the following sentence:

> In the young woman's apartment, paintings covered the walls.

In the sentence above, what is the prepositional phrase? Who or what is the sentence about?

To avoid making the mistake of thinking that a noun in a prepositional phrase could be the subject, it is a good practice to cross out any prepositional phrases in a sentence where you are looking for the subject.

> ~~In the young woman's apartment~~, paintings covered the walls.

With the prepositional phrase crossed out, it now becomes clear that the subject of the sentence is the noun *paintings*.

> ### TIP
>
> When you are looking for the subject of a sentence, do not look for it within a prepositional phrase.

You can easily recognize a prepositional phrase because it always begins with a preposition. Study the following list so that you will be able to quickly spot all of the common prepositions.

Common Prepositions

about	below	in	since
above	beneath	inside	through
across	beside	into	to
after	between	like	toward
against	beyond	near	under
along	by	of	until
among	down	off	up
around	during	on	upon
at	except	outside	with
before	for	over	within
behind	from	past	without

In addition to these common prepositions, English has a number of prepositional combinations—groups of words that function together as prepositions.

Common Prepositional Combinations

ahead of	in addition to	in reference to
at the time of	in between	in regard to
because of	in care of	in search of
by means of	in case of	in spite of
except for	in common with	instead of
for fear of	in contrast to	on account of
for the purpose of	in the course of	similar to
for the sake of	in exchange for	with regard to

TIP

Notice that when a prepositional phrase begins a sentence, a comma usually follows the phrase. (Sometimes, if the prepositional phrase is short, the comma is omitted.)

Examples: In the corner, the dog buried its bone.

Before lunch they left.

Exercise 1 Creating Sentences with Prepositional Phrases

Use each of the prepositions in the list below to write a prepositional phrase. Then write a sentence containing that prepositional phrase. Two examples have been done for you.

Preposition	Prepositional Phrase	Sentence
before	before breakfast	My cousin called before breakfast.

Preposition	Prepositional Phrase	Sentence
between	between the two barns	Between the two barns, the old Buick lay rusting.

Preposition	Prepositional Phrase
1. in	_____

Sentence _____

2. with   _____

Sentence _____

Preposition   **Prepositional Phrase**

3. of   _____

Sentence _____

4. from   _____

Sentence _____

5. during   _____

Sentence _____

6. by   _____

Sentence _____

 Exercise 2 **Finding Subjects in Sentences with Prepositional Phrases**

Remember that you will never find the subject of a sentence within a prepositional phrase. In each of the following sentences, cross out any prepositional phrases. Then underline the subject. An example has been done for you.

~~On the circus grounds~~, <u>Lisa</u> wandered ~~among the elephants, horses, and camels~~.

1. <u>Young people</u> in the circus search for travel, adventure, danger, and romance.
2. However, after a few weeks of pulling cages and sleeping on hay, most of these <u>people</u> get tired of the circus and go back home.
3. The art of <u>clowning</u>, for instance, is very serious work.
4. Today, a circus <u>clown</u> must graduate from Clown College in Venice, Florida.
5. The <u>staff</u> of Clown College looks across the country for applicants.
6. <u>Admission</u> to the college is not easy.
7. Only 60 <u>people</u> out of 3000 applicants are admitted.

What Are the Other Problems in Finding Subjects?

Sentences That Are Questions

Some sentences begin with words indicating that a question is being asked. These words, such as *why*, *where*, *how*, and *when*, give the reader the signal that a question will follow. This kind of sentence-opening question word is not the subject. The subject will be found later on in the sentence.

The following sentences begin with question words. The subjects are italicized:

> Why is *he* going away?
> How did *he* find his sister in the city?

Notice that the subject is not found in the opening part of either sentence. To make the subject in a question easier to spot, try answering the question or changing it into a statement.

> *He* is going away …
> *He* found his sister …

Using *here* and *there*

The words *here* and *there* can never be the subject of a sentence.

> There is a new teacher in the department.

Who or what is this sentence about? It is about a teacher. *Teacher* is the subject of the sentence.

> Here is the book.

The subject of this sentence is *book*.

Commands

Sometimes a sentence contains a verb that gives an order:

> Go to Halifax.
> Help your sister.

In these sentences, the subject *you* is not written, but it is understood. This is the only case where the subject may be left out when you write a sentence.

Sentences That Contain Appositive Phrases

In the example above, the words *the retired chemist* make up the appositive phrase because they give you extra information about Don Koyama. Notice that commas separate the appositive phrase from the rest of the sentence. If you leave out the appositive phrase when you read the sentence, the thought will still be complete.

> Don Koyama sat at his desk.

Now the subject is clear: *Don Koyama*.

The word *chemist* in the example in the box above cannot be the subject because it is in an appositive phrase.

Subjects That Look Like Verbs

Words that end in *-ing* but have no helping verb in front are called *gerunds*. They act as nouns, not verbs. A gerund, therefore, can be the subject of a sentence.

Jogging is good for your health.

Practice **Finding Hidden Subjects**

Each of the following sentences contains an example of a special problem in finding the subject of a sentence. For each sentence, first cross out any prepositional phrases and appositive phrases. Then underline the subject. An example has been done for you. Check your answers against those in the Answer Key on page 451.

What can we learn from the study of an ancient civilization?

1. Look at a map of South America.
2. Where is the ancient city of Chan Chan?
3. Here on the coastal desert of northern Peru stand the remains of this city of the kings.
4. Chan Chan, once the fabulously wealthy centre of the Chimor, is situated in one of the driest, bleakest regions in the world.
5. It was the largest pre-Columbian city in South America.
6. In the ruins of this city, scientists have found fragments to piece together the mystery of the past.
7. How could this civilization have survived this hostile environment and become so advanced?

How Do You Find the Verb of a Sentence?

Every sentence must have a verb. Verbs can be divided into three classes:

1. Action: An **action verb** tells what the subject is doing.
   Canada's Cassie Campbell *played* hockey in the Olympics.
2. Linking: A **linking verb** indicates a state of being or a condition.
   The crowd *seemed* exhausted during the triathlon.
3. Helping: A **helping verb** combines with a main verb to form a verb phrase; it indicates the time of the main verb or gives it a special meaning.
   Canadians *can* expect strong performances from their Olympic athletes in the future. The gold medal *might* become a tradition.

Verbs tell time. Use this fact to test for a verb. If you can put a word into different tenses, it is a verb.

Present:	(Today) he *runs*.
Past:	(Yesterday) he *ran*.
Future:	(Tomorrow) he *will run*.

Action Verbs

> **DEFINITION**
>
> **Action verbs** tell us what the subject is doing and when the subject does it.
> **Example:** The woman *studied* ballet.

Look at the example in the box above.

What was the woman doing?   studying

What is the time of the action?   the past (*-ed* is the past tense ending)

Action Verbs			
Most verbs are action verbs. Here are a few examples:			
arrive	learn	open	watch
leave	forget	write	fly
enjoy	help	speak	catch
despise	make	teach	wait

Practice **Finding Action Verbs**

Find the action verb in each of the following sentences. First cross out any prepositional or appositive phrases; then underline the subject of the sentence. Finally, circle the verb (the word that tells what the subject is doing). Note also the time of the action: is it past, present, or future? An example has been done for you. Check your answers against those in the Answer Key on page 451.

Many <u>people</u> (begin) hobbies ~~in childhood~~. (present)

1. Some people collect very strange objects.
2. One man saved the fortunes from fortune cookies.
3. A group of people in Alberta often met to discuss their spark plug collections.
4. People in Brandon will gather many types of barbed wire.
5. Collectors take pride in the possession of unusual items.
6. A collection, like odd rocks or unique automobiles, will let a person express his or her individuality.
7. Collections keep us entertained from childhood to old age.

Exercise **Finding Action Verbs**

Each of the following sentences contains an action verb. Find the action verb by first crossing out any prepositional or appositive phrases and underlining the subject of the sentence. Then circle the verb (the word that tells what the subject is doing). Note also the time of the action: past, present, or future. An example has been done for you.

<u>Attitudes</u> ~~toward medical practices~~ (will change.) (future)

1. Traditional Chinese medicine harnessed ancient healing techniques in the practice of "qigong" (pronounced *chee gong*).

2. Masters of this Chinese practice claimed the ability to cure many diseases.
3. The master will project a mysterious force into his students.
4. The hands of the Chinese qigong practitioner will pound at the air above a patient.
5. Many patients respond to this invisible force.
6. Some patients sway their bodies with the power of the force.
7. Some doctors conducted research in China in hopes of finding the secrets of this ancient art.

Linking Verbs

> **DEFINITION**
>
> A **linking verb** is a verb that joins the subject of a sentence to one or more words that describe or identify the subject.
>
> **Examples:** The girl is a constant dreamer.
>
> She seems distracted.
>
> We feel sympathetic.

In each of the examples above, the verb links the subject to a word that identifies or describes the subject. In the first example, the verb *is* links the noun *girl* with the noun *dreamer*. In the second example, the verb *seems* links the pronoun *she* with the adjective *distracted*. Finally, in the third example, the verb *feel* links the pronoun *we* with the adjective *sympathetic*.

Common Linking Verbs	
act	feel
appear	grow
be (am, is, are, was, were, have been)	look
become	seem
	taste

Exercise 1 Finding Linking Verbs

Find the linking verb in each of the following sentences. First, underline the subject of the sentence. Then draw an arrow to the word or words that identify or describe the subject. Finally, circle the linking verb. An example has been done for you.

Dreams are very important to the Aboriginal peoples of Canada.

1. My dream last night was wonderful.
2. I had become middle-aged.
3. In a sunlit kitchen with a book in my hand, I appeared relaxed and happy.
4. The houses were empty and quiet.
5. In the morning light, the kitchen felt cozy.

6. I seemed to have grown calmer.
7. The ice cream tastes very chocolatey.

Exercise 2 **Finding Linking Verbs**

Each of the following sentences contains a linking verb. Find the linking verb by first underlining the subject of the sentence. Then draw an arrow to the word or words that identify or describe the subject. Finally, circle the linking verb. An example has been done for you.

Colds <u>can be</u> miserable.

1. Monica is afraid of catching a cold.
2. She felt healthy.
3. Everyone in her family became sick.
4. Her brother looked horrible.
5. She seemed immune to the cold.
6. Soon Monica's head grew stuffy.
7. The chicken soup from the deli down the street tasted delicious.

Helping Verbs (Also Called Auxiliary Verbs)

Helping verbs (verbs that come before the main verb) can help the main verbs express a particular time and/or a special meaning.

Sentence Using Helping Verb	Time and/or Meaning Expressed
He *is* sleeping.	right now
He *might* sleep.	maybe now or in the future
He *should* sleep.	ought to, now or in the future
He *could have been* sleeping.	maybe in the past

A **modal auxiliary verb** is a helping verb that comes before the main verb and expresses probability, obligation, ability, or necessity.

Modal Auxiliary Verbs
can, could
may, might, must
shall, should
will, would

Be, do, and *have* are the most common auxiliary verbs. Remember that *be, do,* and *have* can also be used as main verbs of sentences. (When used as a main verb, *be* is a linking verb while *do* and *have* are action verbs.) All other helping verbs are usually used only as helping verbs.

Watch out for adverbs that may come in between the helping verb and the main verb.

The word *often* is an adverb that comes between the two words in the verb phrase *can frighten*. For a list of common adverbs, see page 7.

Exercise   Finding Helping Verbs

Each of the following sentences contains a helping verb in addition to the main verb. In each sentence, first underline the subject. Then circle the entire verb phrase. An example has been done for you.

In some writing classes, <u>students</u> (must keep) a diary of their work.

1. Keeping a diary could have several advantages.
2. In a journal, a person can safely express true feelings without fear of criticism by family or friends.
3. You will be able to capture your memories before they fade.
4. Important, too, would be the development of a writing style and the improvement of language skills.
5. A journal might awaken your imagination.
6. It may unexpectedly bring pleasure and satisfaction.
7. You should seriously consider the purchase of one of those lovely fabric-bound notebooks.

Chapter Review Exercises

Practice   Finding Subjects and Verbs in Simple Sentences

In each of the following sentences, cross out any prepositional phrases or appositive phrases. Then underline the subject and circle the complete verb. An example has been done for you. Check your answers against those in the Answer Key on page 451.

The modern <u>family</u> (has been disrupted) ~~by many negative outside influences~~.

1. Mother and Dad always blame me for any trouble with my sister.
2. My sister, the most popular girl in her class, is two years older than I.
3. Yesterday, for instance, she was trying on her new graduation dress.
4. Helpfully, I took out her new shoes and purse for her.
5. Margaret instantly became furious with me.
6. I was only sharing Margaret's excitement about her new clothes.

Exercise 1   Finding Subjects and Verbs in Simple Sentences

In each of the sentences in the following paragraph, cross out any prepositional or appositive phrases. Then underline the subject and circle the complete verb.

Go West! Western Australia, one of the remaining great boom areas of the world, constitutes one-third of the Australian continent. Why did people by the tens of thousands go to western Australia in the late 1800s? In 1894, Leslie Robert Menzies jumped off his camel and landed in a pile of gold nuggets. In less than two hours, this man gathered over a million dollars in gold. He eventually took 5 tonnes of gold to the bank by wheelbarrow! Kalgoorlie and Boulder, the two boom towns that grew up there, boast the richest golden mile in the world. With all the gold seekers, this surface gold did not last very long. Now the only bands of rich ore lie more than 1200 metres down under the ground. There are many ghost towns with their empty iron houses and rundown chicken coops.

 Exercise 2   Composing Complete Sentences

Below are two lists, one of subjects and one of verbs. Compose ten complete sentences, each one using any subject from one list and any verb from the other list. Use each subject and each verb only once. Try to vary the position of the subject in the sentence. An example has been done for you. (Do not use it as one of your own sentences.)

The dentist looks very tired today.

1.	dogs	is
2.	nose	chased
3.	she	are
4.	dentist	was
5.	Saskatchewan	singing
6.	fishing	has
7.	problems	screams
8.	obeying	see
9.	mailbox	approaches
10.	storm	looks

1. _____

2. _____

3. _____

4. _____

5. _____

6. _____

7. _____

8. _____

9. _____

10. _____

 Working Together: Singling Out Subjects

Student Profile: On a separate piece of paper, answer the five questions about yourself that are listed below. Write on every other line to make your writing more readable. Write freely for twenty minutes. Then exchange papers with another student. Using a pencil, circle the subject in every sentence in your classmate's writing (you should be able to narrow it down to one word in most cases). Try not to confuse subjects (nouns that do the action) with objects (nouns that receive the action). Be prepared to share examples with the class.

1. Tell about the first book you remember looking at or reading.
2. Who was your most memorable teacher in elementary school? What is it about this teacher that you remember?
3. What person outside of school has taught you the most?
4. What magazines do you subscribe to or would like to subscribe to, and why?
5. When you have a day or half a day to yourself, how do you spend that time?

Chapter 3 **Solving Verb Problems**

Note: For problems involving subject-verb agreement, see Chapter 4.

Quick Quiz Test yourself on your knowledge of verb forms. In each of the following sentences, choose the correct verb tense for the verb in parentheses. Answers to the questions are upside down beside the quiz.

1. The soccer game will continue only after the lightning and rain _____ . (stop)

2. Since he was poor and unappreciated by the music world when he died in 1791, Mozart did not realize the importance that his music _____ (have) in the twenty-first century.

3. My aunt told me yesterday that she _____ (buy) a new condo the day before that.

4. Hemingway wrote only about subjects that he _____ . (like)

5. I _____ (see) the woman buy the purple hat yesterday.

Answers:
1. have stopped, OR stop
2. would have
3. had bought
4. liked
5. saw

Since every sentence contains at least one verb, and verbs can take many forms, it is worth taking some time and effort to understand these forms and their uses. In Chapter 2, you learned to recognize verbs. In this chapter, you will study several other aspects of verbs that often cause difficulty for writers:

> Irregular verbs
> Verb tense consistency
> Sequence of verb tenses
> Present perfect and past perfect tenses
> Active and passive voice
> Subjunctive mood

What Are the Principal Parts of the Irregular Verbs?

The English language has more than 100 irregular verbs—that is, ones that do not form the past tense or past participle with the usual -ed ending. When you listen to young children, you often hear them utter expressions such as "Yesterday I cutted myself." Later on, they will learn that the verb cut is unusual, and calls for the irregular form: "Yesterday I cut myself." The best way to learn these verbs is to listen to how they sound. Say the irregular forms out loud over and over until you have learned them. If you find that you don't know a particular verb's meaning, or you cannot pronounce a verb and its forms, ask your instructor for help. Most irregular verbs are very common words that you will use often in both writing and speaking. You will want to know them well.

For more on this topic, see Appendix C: "Irregular Verbs."

> **DEFINITION**
>
> An **irregular verb** forms its past tense and/or past participle in a different way from the usual -ed ending of regular verbs.
>
> **Example:** Yesterday, he cut himself. (The word *cut* is the past tense form of the irregular verb *to cut*.)

Practising 50 Irregular Verbs

These are the three principal parts of irregular verbs:

Simple Form (also called **Bare Infinitive Form**)	Past Form	Past Participle (used with perfect tenses after *has*, *have*, or *will have*, or with passive voice after the verb *to be*)

I. The following verbs do not change their forms: (Notice they all end in -t or -d.)

Simple Form	Past Form	Past Participle
bet	bet	bet
cost	cost	cost
cut	cut	cut
fit	fit	fit
hit	hit	hit
hurt	hurt	hurt
quit	quit	quit
spread	spread	spread

II. The following verbs have the same simple present form and past participle:

Simple Form	Past Form	Past Participle
come	came	come
become	became	become

Exercise 1 **Using Irregular Verb Forms**

Fill in the correct form of the verb in the following sentences.

(cost)   1. Last year the tuition for my education _____ 7 percent more than the year before.

(quit)   2. I have_____ trying to guess my expenses for next year.

(spread)   3. The message has_____ that college costs continue to spiral.

(hit)   4. Most parents have been_____ with large tax increases.

(become)   5. Financing a child's higher education has_____ a difficult task.

III. The following verbs have the same simple past form and past participle:

Simple Form	Past Form	Past Participle
bend	bent	bent
lend	lent	lent
send	sent	sent
spend	spent	spent
creep	crept	crept
keep	kept	kept
sleep	slept	slept
sweep	swept	swept
weep	wept	wept
catch	caught	caught
teach	taught	taught
bleed	bled	bled
feed	fed	fed
lead	led	led
speed	sped	sped
bring	brought	brought
buy	bought	bought
fight	fought	fought
seek	sought	sought
think	thought	thought

Exercise 2 **Knowing the Irregular Verb Forms**

Fill in the correct form of the verb in the following sentences.

(buy)   1. Last year the school district _____ new chemistry texts.

(spend)   2. Some parents felt they had_____ too much money on these new books.

(bleed)   3. They claimed the taxpayers were being_____ dry.

(keep)   4. These parents argued that the school should <u>have</u>_____ the old books.

(think)   5. The teachers _____ the old books were worn out.

IV. The following verbs all have different forms:

Simple Form	Past Form	Past Participle
blow	blew	blown
fly	flew	flown
grow	grew	grown
know	knew	known
throw	threw	thrown
begin	began	begun
drink	drank	drunk
ring	rang	rung
shrink	shrank	shrunk
sink	sank	sunk
sing	sang	sung
spring	sprang	sprung
swim	swam	swum
bite	bit	bitten (or bit)
hide	hid	hidden (or hid)
drive	drove	driven
ride	rode	ridden
strive	strove	striven
rise	rose	risen
write	wrote	written

Exercise 3   **Knowing the Irregular Verb Forms**

Fill in the correct form of the verb in the following sentences.

(grow)   1. Adventure holidays _____ in popularity during the last decade.

(fly)   2. Years ago, travellers _____ to Spain to see bullfights.

(throw)   3. Today, some clients dream of <u>being</u>_____ by the bull.

(ride, swim)   4. As part of adventure trips, people <u>have</u>_____ horseback, <u>have</u>_____ across rivers, and have walked for days to get to their destinations.

(shrink)   5. Clients of a new trend called "reality tours" do not even _____ from visiting jails.

Exercise 4 Using Irregular Verb Forms

Supply the past form or the past participle for each verb in parentheses.

Ever since people _____ to write, they have _____ about the great
                          (begin)   (write)

mysteries in nature. For instance, no one _____ why the dinosaurs
                                              (know)

disappeared. Scientists now have _____ on one strong possibility.
                                     (bet)

That possibility is that 65 million years ago, a chunk of rock 10 km wide _____
                                                                            (hit)

the earth and _____ up a thick cloud of dust. The dust _____ the
                 (throw)   (keep)

sunlight from the earth; therefore, certain life forms disappeared. Some

scientists have _____ that this could also have _____ the earth's
                  (think)   (shrink)

animal population by as much as 70 percent. Other scientists are not so sure

that this is the answer. They believe time has _____ the real reason for the
                                                   (hide)

disappearance of the dinosaurs.

 Exercise 5 Using Irregular Verb Forms

Supply the past form or the past participle for each verb in parentheses.

Medical researchers have _____ a cure for the common cold,
                            (seek)

but so far they have _____ without success. The cold virus has _____
                        (fought)   (spread)

throughout the world, and the number of cold victims has _____ every
                                                             (rise)

year. Past experience has _____ us that people who drink plenty of
                             (teach)

liquids and take aspirin get over colds more quickly than those who do not,

but this remedy is not good enough. People have also believed that

you _____ a fever and starved a cold, but recent research has _____
       (feed)   (lead)

to a refutation of this belief. It has _____ a lot of time and effort to search
                                          (cost)

for a vaccine, but so far the new knowledge has not _____ a cure.
                                                       (bring)

Avoiding Unnecessary Shifts in Verb Tense

Do not shift verb tenses (move from past to present, for example) as you write unless you intend to change the time of the action.

> **Shifted tense:** The customer asked (past tense) for the prescription, but the pharmacist says (present tense) that the ingredients are being ordered (present tense).
>
> **Revised:** The customer asked (past tense) for the prescription, but the pharmacist said (past tense) that the ingredients were being ordered (past tense).

Practice 1 Correcting Unnecessary Shifts in Verb Tense

Each of the following sentences has an unnecessary shift in verb tense. Revise each sentence so that the tense remains consistent. There may be more than one correct answer for each sentence. Check your answers against those in the Answer Key on page 452.

1. After I complete that writing course, I took the required history course.

   _____

   _____

2. In the beginning of the movie, the action was slow; by the end, I am sitting on the edge of my seat.

   _____

   _____

3. The textbook gives the rules for writing a Works Cited page, but it didn't explain how to use parenthetical references.

   _____

   _____

4. I was walking in the park when all of a sudden I see her running toward me.

   _____

   _____

5. The encyclopedia gave several pages of information about astronomy, but it doesn't give anything about black holes.

   _____

   _____

6. The invitation requested that Juan be at the ceremony and that he will attend the banquet as well.

_____

_____

7. That website gives you excellent information, but it was too cluttered.

_____

_____

 Practice 2 **Correcting Unnecessary Shifts in Verb Tense**

The following paragraph contains unnecessary shifts in verb tense. Change each incorrect verb to past tense. Check your answers against those in the Answer Key on page 452.

Doctor Norman Bethune grows up in Gravenhurst, Ontario. He was educated in Toronto and serves as a stretcher bearer in World War I. He contracted tuberculosis and thereafter devotes himself to helping other victims of the disease when he practises surgery in Montreal. He also invents or redesigned twelve medical and surgical instruments. Bethune travelled to Russia in 1935, joined the Communist party, and goes to Spain in 1936, where he organized the first mobile blood transfusion service during the Spanish Civil War. After returning to Canada, he shortly left for overseas again, this time to China, where he helped the Chinese Communists in their fight against Japan. "Spain and China," he writes, "are part of the same battle." While there, he contracted an infection and died. Mao's essay "In Memory of Norman Bethune," prescribed reading during China's Cultural Revolution, urges all Communists to follow Bethune's example of selfless dedication to others. Bethune is the best-known Canadian to the Chinese, and many Chinese visit his Canadian birthplace.

What Is the Sequence of Tenses?

Sentences often contain two or more verbs that carry different tenses according to the times at which the actions take place. The type of sentence in which this happens is a complex sentence: one that contains both an independent clause and a dependent clause. (Note that the dependent clause might come before the independent clause.)

Before explaining the **sequence of tenses**, which refers to the proper order of verb tense when a sentence contains more than one action, it is first necessary to introduce the terms **independent clause** and **dependent clause**.

> **DEFINITION**
>
> An **independent clause (IC)** is a group of words that can be a simple sentence. _Independent_ means that the words can stand alone as a sentence, and _clause_ means there is a subject and a verb. An _independent clause_ is a **complete thought.**
> **Example:** The students worked on their papers all night long.

> **DEFINITION**
>
> A **dependent clause (DC)** cannot stand alone as a simple sentence. It is an **incomplete thought**. Even though it has a subject and a verb, it depends on the rest of the sentence for completeness.
>
> **Example:** Because their assignments were due in the morning
>
> The word *assignments* is the subject of the verb *were*, so this group of words is a *clause*. But it is not a complete sentence. It is a **dependent clause (DC)**.

> **DEFINITION**
>
> The term **sequence of tenses** refers to the proper use of verb tenses in complex sentences (sentences that have both an independent clause and a dependent clause).
>
> **Example:** The students had worked on their papers all night long because their assignments were due the following morning.
>
> The verb *had worked* in the independent clause is in the past perfect tense, and the verb *were* in the dependent clause is in the past tense. The first action (the students working) takes place before the second one (the papers being due).

The verb tense in the independent clause determines the tense of the verb in the dependent clause. The guide below shows the relationship between the verb in the independent clause (IC) and the verb in the dependent clause (DC).

Sequence of Tenses

Independent Clause	Dependent Clause	Time of the DC in Relation to the IC
If the tense of the independent clause is in the **present** (he *knows*), here are the possibilities for the dependent clause:		
	that she *is right*.	same time
He knows	that she *was right*.	earlier
	that she *will be right*.	later
If the tense of the independent clause is in the past (he *knew*), here are the possibilities for the dependent clause:		
	that she *was right*.	same time
He knew	that she *had been right*.	earlier
	that she *would be right*.	later
If the independent clause is in the future (he *will tell*), here are the possibilities for the dependent clause:		
	if she *goes*.	same time
He will tell us	if she *has gone*.	earlier
	if she *will go*.	later

Practice Using the Correct Tense

In each of the following sentences, choose the correct tense for the verb in the dependent clause. Use the guide above if you need help. Check your answers against those in the Answer Key on page 452.

1. The golf tournament <u>will continue</u> only after the thunder and lightning

    _____ .

    (stop)

2. Since he thought that he was buying a well-maintained car, Enzo <u>did not realize</u> the problems that this car _____ in the months to come.
   (have)

3. I <u>will know</u> when I get my next paycheque whether or not I _____ a stereo next week.
   (buy)

4. Albert Einstein <u>failed</u> the entrance exam at the Swiss Federal Institute of Technology because he _____ a very disciplined student.
   (be) + never

5. Jacob <u>ate</u> only those foods that he _____ .
   (like)

6. Sasha <u>believes</u> that with a lot of hard work and a little luck, she _____ successful.
   (be) + soon

7. I <u>know</u> that my best course of action _____ to tell the truth.
   (be)

How Do You Use the Present Perfect and the Past Perfect Tenses?

Forming the Perfect Tenses

Present perfect tense: has or have + past participle of the main verb
has worked
have worked

Past perfect tense: had + past participle of the main verb
had worked

What Do These Tenses Mean?

> **DEFINITION**
>
> The **present perfect tense** describes an action that started in the past and continues to the present time.
> **Example:** Elena *has worked* at the hospital for ten years.

The example in the box above indicates that Elena began to work at the hospital ten years ago and is still working there now.

Examine the following timeline. What does it tell you about the present perfect tense?

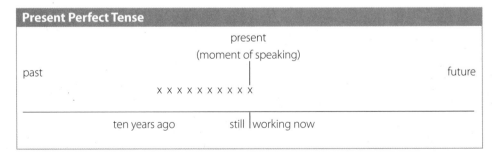

The following sentences include examples of the **present perfect tense:**

> She *has studied* French since 2004.
>
> I *have* always *despised* that television show.

DEFINITION

The **present perfect tense** can also describe an action that has just taken place, or an action whose exact time in the past is indefinite.

Examples: *Has* Elena *found* a job yet?

Elena *has* (just) *found* a new job in Moncton.

Have you ever *been* to Kapuskasing?

Yes, I *have been* there three times.

If the time were definite, you would use the simple past:

> Elena *found* a new job yesterday.
>
> Yes, I *was* there last week.

DEFINITION

The **past perfect tense** describes an action that occurred before another activity or before another point in the past.

Example: Elena *had worked* at the hospital for ten years before she *moved* away.

In the example in the definition above, there are two past actions: Elena *worked*, and Elena *moved*. The action that took place first is in the past perfect (*had worked*). The action that took place later, but was also completed in the past, is in the simple past (*moved*).

Past Perfect Tense

present
(moment of speaking)

past   future

first action   second action
in the past   in the past
x x x x x x x x x x

had worked   moved

The following sentences include examples of the **past perfect tense:**

> I *had* just *arrived* when the alarm *rang.*
>
> She *said* that Marty *had told* the class about the essay deadline.
>
> He *had provided* the report long before last week's meeting.

Exercise Using the Correct Verb Tense

Complete the following sentence by filling in each blank with either the present perfect tense or the past perfect tense of the verb given.

1. Yolanda told us that she _____ in Fort Smith before she moved to Mexico City.   (live)

2. Mexico City _____ visitors for many years.
            (fascinate)
3. This city _____ the largest city in the world, and people _____ it
            (become)   (watch)
   grow larger every year.
4. The suburbs of the city _____ old villages that _____ peacefully
                           (overwhelm)   (exist)
   since the days of the Aztecs.
5. Today, Mexico City _____ a computer-controlled subway system to deal
                      (build)
   with its huge transportation problem.

What Is the Difference between Active and Passive Voice?

In the active voice, the subject does the acting. In the passive voice, the subject is acted upon. (See examples in the box below.) But which one is usually better to use? And does this mean the other should never get used at all?

Active Voice Is Generally Best

Stylistically speaking, using the active voice most often produces a stronger sentence:

Active: The dog buried its bone.

Passive: The bone was buried by the dog.

The first sentence is stronger not only because it is shorter, but because the subject does the action, so more focus is placed on it. In the second sentence, *the bone* is the subject. But the bone does not do the burying. The dog has still done the burying, but *the dog* is not the subject. (In fact, it is part of a prepositional phrase, so it cannot be the subject. See the definition of a prepositional phrase on page 17.) So the focus is taken away from the action and its doer.

The Place for Passive Voice

Although active voice is generally better than passive voice, there are situations in which passive voice is more appropriate:

1. You are in a position of authority and, in an official capacity, you are required to give bad news to someone. In such a case, it is sometimes advisable to speak deliberately vaguely about what the cause of the bad news is. Using the passive rather than the active voice helps to do this.

   Unfortunately, it was decided that the job go to an internal candidate.

   The above sentence is in the passive voice. The person who made the decision is not mentioned. This wording might have been chosen to protect whoever did the deciding. Since the passive voice takes the focus away from the performer of the action (deciding), the recipient of the bad news is less likely to ask specific questions that the employer would prefer not to discuss.

2. It is also better to use the passive rather than active voice when the subject that has been acted upon is more important than the doer of the action.

> The Conservatives have been given more seats than the Liberals in the House of Commons.

Who is the doer of the action here? Who actually gave more seats to the Conservatives? The answer is *the people of Canada who voted in the election*. So why aren't these people mentioned at all? Well, it's obvious, since that's how elections work. What isn't obvious is who won, so that's why the word *Conservatives* becomes the subject of the sentence even though it does not refer to the doer of the action. The sentence, therefore, is better in the passive voice, which places the focus on the most relevant information.

3. Putting a sentence in the passive voice is also a good idea when the action itself is more important than the doer of the action. People in the sciences and in legal affairs often report events this way.

> Ice was found on Mars today.
> Michael Jackson was acquitted today.

In the first sentence above, there is no need to report that scientists found the ice. Nor is there need to mention, in the second sentence, that Jackson was acquitted by a jury of his peers.

Active and Passive Voice

In the **active voice**, the subject does the acting:

> The committee made the decision.

Choose the active voice generally in order to achieve direct, economical, and forceful writing. Most writing, therefore, should be in the active voice.

In the **passive voice**, the subject is acted upon:

> The decision was made by the committee
> or
> The decision was made.

Notice in these passive sentences that the actor is de-emphasized since it is not the subject. In fact, it may be omitted entirely from the sentence.

Choose the passive voice to de-emphasize the actor or to avoid naming the actor at all.

Study the two sentences below. The first is in the active voice and the second is in the passive. Which one is more appropriate in this case and why? What are the disadvantages of each?

> Chris Hadfield orbited the earth in 2001.
> The earth was orbited by Chris Hadfield in 2001.

How Do You Form the Passive Voice?

The passive voice of a verb consists of a form of *be* (*am, is, are, was, were, being, be,* or *been*) plus the past participle of the main verb.

> Cars and trucks *are built* in Oshawa.

1. Use the past participle, not the base form or past tense of a verb, to form the passive voice.
2. Identify the subject, and make sure the form of the auxiliary verb *be* agrees with it.
3. Use only transitive verbs (verbs that can take a direct object) in the passive voice.

Subject Acted Upon	+ Verb *to be*	+ Past Participle	+ *by* Phrase (Optional)
The race	was	won	(by the runner)
The fish	was	cooked	(by the chef)
The books	are	illustrated	(by the artists)

 Practice Choosing the Right Voice

Rewrite the following sentences, changing the active voice to the passive, and the passive voice to the active. Then decide in each case which one is best and why. Check your answers against those in the Answer Key on page 452.

1. No policy or funding announcements were made by the Canadian health minister at the International AIDS Conference in Toronto.
2. Six hundred and fifty million dollars (U.S.) was given by Microsoft founder Bill Gates to the war against HIV/AIDS.
3. Canadian authorities allowed the foreign minister of Zimbabwe into Canada for the international conference despite a ban on visits by senior officials from that African country.
4. The audience was told by former U.S. president Bill Clinton that many mistakes were made during his presidency, but that underfunding AIDS research was not one of them.
5. The International AIDS Conference in 2006 was attended by 22 000 delegates and 8000 journalists, exhibitors, volunteers, and staff.
6. The impact that poverty has on HIV and AIDS in developing countries was discussed in great detail at the conference.
7. Actor and activist Richard Gere stressed the importance of the role of media in spreading the word about HIV/AIDS.

 Exercise Choosing the Right Voice

Fill in the following chart by making all sentences on the left active voice and all sentences on the right passive voice. Then discuss with your classmates and instructor why you might choose the active voice or the passive voice in each case.

Active Voice	Passive Voice
1. _____ _____	1. The wrong number was dialled by the child by mistake.
2. _____ _____ _____	2. We went to the store where many shoes were available to be purchased.
3. The tornado struck Cherry Creek last spring.	3. _____ _____
4. The wind blew the leaves across the yard.	4. _____ _____
5. _____ _____ _____	5. In the 1970s, platform shoes were worn by many fashionable young men and women.

What Is the Subjunctive?

> **DEFINITION**
>
> The **subjunctive** is a verb form used to express untruths, desires, or demands. It is found in some dependent clauses.
> **Examples:** If I *were* a millionaire, I would travel around the world.
> She demanded that he *arrive* on time.
> Verbs in italics are in the subjunctive form.

Recognize these three situations that call for the subjunctive:

1. Unreal conditions using *if, wish, as if, as though*

> *If he were* my teacher, I would be pleased.
> He *wishes he were* in France.
> Try to act *as though you were* proud.

Note that *as if* and *as though* don't always call for the subjunctive. It is correct to say: "It looks as if it is snowing." In this case, the speaker is simply describing what is very likely true. The difference is in the degree of doubt.

The subjunctive of the verb *be* has the form **were** whether the subject is plural or singular. Use it to show that what is being wished for or considered is not (or not yet) a fact. For example:

> If I *were* you . . . (I can't be you.)
> I wish I *were* rich. (I'm not.)
> He acts as if *he were* the boss. (He's not.)

2. Clauses starting with *that* expressing demands, resolutions, or requests (after verbs such as *ask, command, demand, insist, move, order, recommend, suggest,* or *urge*)

> I *demand* that *she work* harder.
> Sullivan *insisted* that *Jones report* on Tuesday.

The subjunctive uses the simple form of the verb (see page 31) whether the subject is singular or plural.

3. Clauses starting with *that* after adjectives expressing urgency (as in *it is necessary, it is imperative, it is urgent, it is important,* and *it is essential*)

> *It is necessary* that *she wear* a net covering her hair.
> *It is essential* that Robert *understand* the concept.

Again, the subjunctive always uses the simple form of the verb.

Other Problems with Verbs

Do not use more than one **modal auxiliary** (*can, may, might, must, should, ought*) with the main verb.

> **Incorrect:** Ethan *shouldn't ought* to drop that course.
> **Correct:** Ethan *ought* not to drop that course.
> or
> Ethan *shouldn't* drop that course.

Do not use *should of, would of,* or *could of* to mean *should have, would have,* or *could have.*

> **Incorrect:** Alana *would of* helped you if she *could of*.
> **Correct:** Alana *would have* helped you if she *could have*.

See more on helping verbs in Chapter 1, pages 6–7.

Chapter Review Exercises

 Practice **Solving Problems with Verbs**

Revise each of the following sentences to avoid problems with verbs. Check your answers against those in the Answer Key on page 453.

1. He hadn't ought to drive so fast.

   _____

2. It is essential that Lynn takes her dog to the vet.

   _____

3. I wish I was a chef.

   _____

4. She sung for a huge crowd Saturday night.

   _____

5. I was shook up by the accident.

   _____

6. The hill was climbed by the skiers.

   _____

7. My father ask me last night to help him build a deck.

   _____

 Exercise **Solving Problems with Verbs**

Some of the verbs in the following paragraph are incorrect. Find the errors and correct them.

I knowed I was in big trouble in chemistry when I took a look at the midterm exam. My semester should of been a lot better. The first day I had my new textbook, I put it on the back shelf of a taxi and forgot it when I got out. Then I catched a cold and miss the next two classes. When I finally start off for class, I missed the bus and walked into the classroom half an hour late. The teacher scowls at me and ask to speak to me after class. I use to always sit in the front row so I could see the board and hear the lectures, but now that I am late I have to take a seat in the last row. I wish I was able to start this class over again the right way. No one had ought to have such an unlucky start in any class.

Working Together: Verbs, Not Verbiage

Student Profile: On a separate piece of paper, answer the following five questions about yourself. Double space or write on every other line to make your writing more readable. Write freely for twenty minutes. Then exchange papers with another student. Using a pencil, circle each verb in your classmate's writing. Are any of the verbs incorrect in their form or in their tense? Be prepared to share examples with the class.

1. Tell about the first car you remember owning or driving.
2. Who was the first person you were ever attracted to? What is one thing about this person that you remember?
3. Who was the person in school who taught you the most?
4. What is one television program you enjoy and why?
5. When you go away for the weekend, where is one place you like to go?

Chapter 4 **Subject-Verb Agreement**

Quick Quiz Test yourself on your knowledge of subject-verb agreement. On the line before each sentence below, write the correct form of the verb. Answers to the questions are upside down beside the quiz.

_____ 1. The history of humankind's attempts to fly (goes, go) back hundreds of years.

_____ 2. An ancient myth that describes men trying to fly with wings made of feathers and wax (has, have) been passed on.

_____ 3. The famous inventor Leonardo da Vinci made designs for a helicopter that (was, were) very detailed.

_____ 4. Every aviator who set a new flying record in the early years of flight (was, were) treated as a hero.

_____ 5. Not only helicopters but also the jet engine (was, were) among the advances that occurred during the Second World War.

Answers:
1. goes
2. has
3. were
4. was
5. was

For your sentences to be logical, all parts of each sentence must agree. Agreement is the correspondence between words in number, gender, or person. Subjects and verbs agree in number (singular or plural) and person (first [*I* or *we*], second [*you*], or third [*he, she, it*, or *they*]).

Since many students have problems with agreement in their writing, you should work through this chapter carefully so that you will be able to identify and deal effectively with these trouble spots in your own writing.

Subject-Verb Agreement within the Sentence

DEFINITION

There is subject-verb agreement in a sentence when a verb agrees with its subject in **number** and in **person**.

Examples: The girl plays.
The girls play.
I am here on Thursdays.

The verb *plays* in the first sentence is singular. It agrees with the singular subject *girl*.
The verb *play* in the second sentence is plural. It agrees with the plural subject *girls*.
The verb *am* in the third sentence is in the first person. It agrees with the first-person subject *I*.

If the subject is singular, the verb must also be singular. Notice how singular and plural subjects are handled in the following chart:

He
she
it
any singular noun
} sleeps

I
you
we
they
any plural noun
} sleep

Example: The baby *sleeps*.

Example: The babies *sleep*.

TIP

Remember that a singular verb (in the present tense) that goes with a singular noun or pronoun (except *I* or *you*) needs a final *s*.

Practice 1 Making the Subject and Verb Agree

Underline the correct verb in the following sentences. Check your answers against those in the Answer Key on page 453.

1. My uncle (cycle, cycles) 30 km a day.
2. He (amaze, amazes) the family.
3. His routes (varies, vary) with his mood.
4. Friends (cheers, cheer) him on.
5. I (hopes, hope) I'm that energetic at his age.

Special Problems in Making Verbs Agree with Their Subjects

RULE 1

The subject is not always the noun closest to the verb. Remember, you will not find the subject of the sentence within a prepositional phrase.

In the example that follows, the subject is underlined, the prepositional phrase is crossed out, and the verb is circled.

The hairline cracks in the engine (present) a serious threat to passengers' safety.

Practice 2 **Making the Subject and Verb Agree**

Underline the correct verb in the following sentences. Check your answers against those in the Answer Key on page 453.

1. The rules of the game of chess (is, are) very complicated.
2. The pawns on the board (moves, move) only one square at a time except on the first move, when they can move up to two squares.
3. The rooks on the four corners of the board (moves, move) in straight lines, not diagonally.
4. Several versions of the musical about the game and with the same name— *Chess*—(is, are) being performed throughout the world.
5. If all the pawns on, for example, the white side (is, are) gone from the board, no white pieces can any longer be retrieved.

Exercise **Making the Subject and Verb Agree**

Underline the correct verb in the following sentences.

1. The marbles from the box (is, are) multicoloured.
2. The box of soup cans in the kitchen (was, were) delivered from the charity.
3. The fees for riding public transportation (has, have) been lowered for the first time in the city's history.
4. The three students from English class (go, goes) to Tim Hortons together every day.
5. Over the bridge, through the tunnel, and across the meadow, the cats from the farm (travel, travels) daily.

RULE 2

Many indefinite pronouns take a singular verb.

Indefinite Pronouns

Indefinite Pronouns Taking a Singular Verb:

–one	everyone	someone	anyone	no one
–body	everybody	somebody	anybody	nobody
–thing	everything	something	anything	nothing
	each	another	either	neither

Everyone is expecting a miracle.

Indefinite Pronouns Taking a Plural Verb:

	both	few	many	several

The talks between the two countries failed.
Both were to blame.

Indefinite Pronouns Taking a Singular or Plural Verb Depending on the Meaning in the Sentence:

	any	all	more
	none*	some	most

The books are gone.	All were very popular.
The sugar is gone.	All of it was spilled.

*in informal usage

The English language is constantly evolving. The word *none*, for example, is in transition. The letters *one* inside the word *none* suggest that this indefinite pronoun should be singular. In formal usage, this is so, and *none* takes a singular verb in accordance with the subject-verb agreement rule:

> None of my pens *is* working.

In general (less formal) usage, *none*, like the other indefinite pronouns listed with it in the box above, can be either singular or plural depending on the noun that it refers to (this noun usually follows the preposition *of* after the word *none*).

> None of the sugar *is* wasted.
> None of the people *are* here yet.

This may be a case where you, the individual, have to make a decision. Do you go with formal or general usage? Your decision might depend on the audience for your composition and on its purpose (see pages 161–162 in Chapter 14: "The Four Stages of Writing for a Paragraph or Essay"). You might also want to ask your instructor what he or she prefers.

Practice 3 **Making the Subject and Verb Agree**

Underline the correct verb in the following sentences. Check your answers against those in the Answer Key on page 453.

1. Everyone in the four classes (is, are) studying for exams.
2. Neither book (has, have) the answer to her question.
3. Everybody in all programs (is, are) expected to bring a student card to the exam.
4. Each question on all exams (specifies, specify) how many marks the question is worth.
5. No one, except for emergency purposes, (is, are) allowed to leave the exam until it is over.
6. Both the English exam and the math exam (is, are) on Tuesday.
7. None of these pencils (is, are) sharp enough for the SCANTRON portion of the math exam.

RULE 3

When a pair of conjunctions is used, the verb agrees with the subject closer to the verb.

> *Neither* the textbook *nor* my lecture <u>notes</u> the meaning of the term "tidal wave."

Textbook and *notes* together make up the compound subject. Since *notes* is closer to the verb, the verb agrees with *notes*.

Pairs of Conjunctions		
neither…nor	either…or	not only…but also

Practice 4 Making the Subject and Verb Agree

Underline the correct verb in the following sentences. Check your answers against those in the Answer Key on page 453.

1. Neither the students nor the teacher (is, are) smoking on the patio.
2. It was obvious that not only the automotive students but also their dean (was, were) noticeably outraged by the college president's decision to shut the campus down.
3. Neither the police officer nor the firefighters (seems, seem) afraid in spite of people's continuous screams.
4. Not only the children but also their mother (takes, take) the bus every day.
5. Either the buses or the subway (has, have) resumed service, but not both.

RULE 4

In some sentences, the subject can come after the verb. In these cases, be sure that the verb agrees with the subject.

Here (is) the <u>surprise</u> I promised you.

Who (were) the <u>people</u> with you last night?

Practice 5 Making the Subject and Verb Agree

Underline the correct verb in the following sentences. Check your answers against those in the Answer Key on page 453.

1. In the room, there (is, are) two windows.
2. If they are ever late, there (is, are) always a good reason.
3. Who (is, are) her real friends, as opposed to those who just want things from her?
4. There (is, are) plenty of marbles on the floor.
5. Here (is, are) some salt for your fries.

RULE 5

A group noun in Canadian English usually takes a singular verb if the group is acting as a unit. (The test is to substitute the word *it* in place of the group noun.)

The town <u>council</u> (is planning) a Canada Day celebration.

In this sentence, the council is acting as a unit. *It* is planning a celebration. Therefore, the verb is singular.

RULE 6

A group noun takes a plural verb if the members of the group are acting as individuals.

(The test is to substitute the word *they* for the group noun and see if it sounds right.)

The town <u>council</u> are preparing their speeches for this event.

In this sentence, the council members are individually preparing speeches. *They* substitutes for the group noun in this sentence. Since the individuals are acting separately, the verb is plural.

Common Group Nouns				
audience	class	committee	council	crowd
family	group	jury	number	team

Practice 6 Making the Subject and Verb Agree

Underline the correct verb in the following sentences. Check your answers against those in the Answer Key on page 453.

1. The class (is, are) performing their presentations this week.
2. The family (is, are) all eating at separate times throughout the week.
3. The committee (has, have) decided to go ahead with the construction of the public swimming pool.
4. The group (has, have) voted 5–4 in favour of joining forces with their opponents.
5. The crowd (claps, clap) whenever the "applause" sign lights up.

RULE 7

The verbs *do* and *be* are often troublesome. Remember that standard English uses *s* for the third person singular in the present tense (*he, she,* or *it does*) and for the verb *to be* in the past tense (*he, she,* or *it was*).

Verbs *do* and *be*				
The verb *to do*			**The verb *to be* (Past Tense)**	
I do	we		I was	we
you do	you (plural) } do		you were	you } were
he }	they		he }	they
she } does			she } was	
it }			it }	

She *does* the signage for the Christmas pageant every year.
They *do* everything they can to help others.
You *were* at the scene of the crime.
He *was* elected to the position.

Practice 7 Making the Subject and Verb Agree

Underline the correct verb in the following sentences. Check your answers against those in the Answer Key on page 453.

1. The boy and his date (does, do) the samba every time they go to a Latin dance club.
2. She and he (was, were) the first ones to arrive.

3. It (does, do) feel like 40 degrees outside today.
4. Jake and Amelia (does, do) their homework together every weekend.
5. Cameron and she (was, were) here for three hours before they talked to each other.

Chapter Review Exercises

Practice 1 Making the Subject and Verb Agree

Underline the verb that agrees with the subject. Check your answers against those in the Answer Key on page 453.

1. He (doesn't, don't) study in the library anymore.
2. We (was, were) hoping to find him there.
3. The library (doesn't, don't) close until eleven o'clock.
4. (Was, Were) you late tonight?
5. Ann (doesn't, don't) care if you stay until closing time.

Practice 2 Making the Subject and Verb Agree

In the blanks next to each sentence, write the subject of the sentence and the correct form of the verb. An example has been done for you. Check your answers against those in the Answer Key on page 453.

	Subject	Verb
The eleven proposals for the development of a new building at Laurier Circle (has, have) been submitted to the city.	proposals	have
1. The price of airline tickets to England (has, have) remained fairly reasonable.		
2. His decision (requires, require) much thought.		
3. She (doesn't, don't) know the answer to any of the test questions.		
4. Either the guide or the security guard (see, sees) every visitor.		
5. The committee (agree, agrees) to the fundraising projects for this year.		
6. Potato chips and cola (is, are) most of her diet.		
7. One of the people in the audience (is, are) my brother.		

Exercise 1 Making the Subject and Verb Agree

In the blanks next to each sentence, write the subject of the sentence and the correct form of the verb.

	Subject	Verb
1. Included in the price of the trip (was, were) five nights in a lovely hotel and all meals.	_____	_____
2. None of the members (wants, want) to go.	_____	_____
3. Jerry and Aldo (works, work) well together.	_____	_____
4. The number of essay questions on the apprenticeship exam (seems, seem) to be increasing.	_____	_____
5. When (does, do) your parents return from their holiday?	_____	_____
6. In the whole town there (is, are) only two good restaurants.	_____	_____
7. Neither a piano nor Jim's guitar (was, were) available.	_____	_____

Exercise 2 **Making the Subject and Verb Agree**

Take your answers from the blanks in Exercise 1, and use them as the main subjects and verbs in your own sentences. For example, if the subject in the first column is *cars*, and the verb in the second is *perform*, your own sentence might look something like this:

Cars from Japan generally perform better than cars from the United States.

Note that the sentence *I prefer cars from Japan because they perform better than cars from the United States* would not work in this exercise because in this sentence, the subject is not *cars* but *I*, and the main verb is *prefer*.

Exercise 3 **Making the Subject and Verb Agree**

The following paragraph may have several occurrences of subject-verb disagreement. Rewrite the paragraph making sure all verbs agree with their subjects.

Going to the movies are a favourite thing for me to do on the weekends. If I don't have someone "special" in my life, I still go to the movies either with friends or even by myself. I like all kinds of movies: horror flicks, comedies, drama, adventure film, etc. And not all the movies I watch comes from Hollywood. I also like independent film, foreign films with subtitles, and Bollywood movies. When I go with my friends, they often want to see something I've already seen. They can't believe I see so many on a regular basis. But because I like movies so much, I sometimes sees them twice, especially since sometimes it's more fun to see the same movie with friends than a brand new one by myself. Except for the astronomically high prices the cinema charge for popcorn, pop, and candy, there's not many more exciting things to do than go to a great movie on a weekend night. For two hours or so, the problems of the world disappears, and I'm very content to be lost in a world outside of myself.

Working Together: Magazine Mayhem

To the Instructor: Bring a magazine (that you don't mind destroying) to class. If your class is made up of students from one particular program, you might want to bring a magazine in which there is related subject matter. Circulate the magazine among your students along with a pair of scissors. Announce to the students how much time they have for the following activity. Students may use their text if they think it can help.

To the Students: Cut out any one paragraph of at least five sentences long that looks interesting to you, then pass the magazine and scissors on to the next person.

In your paragraph, underline the subject of every sentence, and circle the verb that goes with each subject. Then rewrite the paragraph on a separate sheet of paper, but deliberately make every verb that you have circled disagree with its subject. Write as legibly as possible and double space your work, so that someone else can easily read it.

Now trade your rewritten paragraph with that of someone else who is sitting close to you. Keep your original paragraph with the underlined subjects and the circled verbs. On the separate sheet of paper you now have from someone else, underline the subject of every sentence and circle the verb that goes with each one, correct or incorrect. Write in corrections above the incorrect verbs, making sure all verbs now agree with their subjects. Trade back sheets of paper back with your classmate when you're finished.

Now compare the subjects and corrected verbs on the separate sheet of paper your classmate gave you to the answers on the original paragraph you cut out. Discuss any discrepancies with your classmate.

Chapter 5 Coordination and Subordination

Quick Quiz 1 Test yourself on your knowledge of combining sentences using **coordination** (a comma and a coordinating conjunction). The following pair of sentences could be combined into a single sentence. Among the four choices given, place a check mark in front of the example that joins them correctly using coordination. The answer to the question is upside down beside the quiz.

Chocolate became a popular drink throughout Europe. It was thought to be good for your health.

_____ 1. Chocolate became a popular drink throughout Europe, it was thought to be good for your health.

_____ 2. Chocolate became a popular drink throughout Europe because it was thought to be good for your health.

_____ 3. Chocolate became a popular drink throughout Europe, for it was thought to be good for your health.

_____ 4. Chocolate became a popular drink throughout Europe and good for your health.

Answers:
Sentence 3 is correct.
Sentence 1 is a run-on and sentence 4 is not parallel.
Sentence 2 is grammatically correct, but it shows subordination rather than coordination.

Quick Quiz 2 Test yourself on your knowledge of combining sentences using **subordination** (a subordinating conjunction or a relative pronoun). Combine each of the following pairs of sentences using either a subordinating conjunction or a relative pronoun. More than one correct answer is possible. Sample answers are upside down beside the quiz.

1. I live alone with two cats.
   They sleep on the braided rug in my bedroom.

   _____

2. The police stood by the door.
   They blocked our entrance.

   _____

3. She wore high heels.
   They made marks in the wooden floor.

   _____

4. My aunt is my favourite relative.
   Her name is Bharati.

   _____

5. He wore expensive designer clothes.
   He claimed to be struggling financially.

   _____

Reading the above sentences, you can see that writing only simple sentences would result in a choppy style. Also, it would make it difficult to express more complicated ideas.

You will therefore want to learn how to combine sentences. You can do this by using particular marks of punctuation and special connecting words called **conjunctions**. The two major ways of joining sentences together are called **coordination** and **subordination**.

What Is Coordination?

DEFINITION

The pairing of similar elements—words, phrases, or clauses—to give equal weight to each pair is called **coordination**. Coordination can link two independent clauses to form a compound sentence.
Example: I was sick. I went to work anyway.
I was sick, but I went to work anyway.

Combining Sentences Using Coordination

You can use coordination whenever you have two sentences that are related and that contain ideas of equal importance. There are three ways to combine such sentences. All three ways result in a new kind of sentence called a **compound sentence**. Before you study these three methods, however, it is important to understand the term *independent clause*. The **independent clause** is a group of words that can be a simple sentence. We can say that a compound sentence combines simple sentences, or we can say we that it combines independent clauses. Don't let this term confuse you. *Independent* means that the words could stand alone as a sentence, and *clause* means a group of words that includes a subject and predicate (what is said about the subject). IC will mean *independent clause* in the work that follows.

Use a Comma Plus a Coordinating Conjunction

TIP

The first way to combine independent clauses (or complete thoughts) is to use a comma plus a coordinating conjunction. A conjunction is a connecting or joining word.

IC	, and	IC
He spoke forcefully	, and	I felt compelled to listen.

Connectors: Coordinating Conjunctions

For easier remembering, spell FANBOYS.

Conjunction:	Logical use:
For	to introduce a reason
And	to add an idea
Nor (negative of "or")	to add an idea when the first clause is in the negative
But	to contrast two opposing ideas
Or	to show a choice
Yet	to contrast two opposing ideas (like but)
So	to introduce a result

Used in Pairs (correlative conjunctions)

either … or
neither … nor
not only … but also

TIP

Whenever any of the above coordinating conjunctions ("FANBOYS") is used to separate two independent clauses, always place a comma before it.

When the sentence is short, the comma before the coordinating conjunction becomes less necessary, but to be safe, it is wise to leave the comma in every time.

I arrived late, **and** most people had already finished the exam.

Practice Recognizing the Comma and Coordinating Conjunction

Each of the following compound sentences contains two independent clauses. Draw a single line under the subject and two lines under the verb of each independent clause. Then circle both the coordinating conjunction and the comma. An example has been done for you. Check your answers against those in the Answer Key on page 453.

The <u>speaker</u> <u>rose</u> to his feet the <u>room</u> <u>became</u> quiet.

1. The audience was packed into the room, for this was a man with an international reputation.

2. He could have told about all his successes, but instead he spoke about his disappointments.
3. His words were electric, so the crowd was attentive.
4. I should have brought a tape recorder, or at least I should have taken notes.

Did you find a subject and verb for both independent clauses in each sentence?

Now that you understand the structure of a compound sentence, you need to think about the meanings of the different coordinating conjunctions and how they can be used to show the relationship between two ideas, with each idea given equal importance.

Exercise   Combining Sentences Using Coordinating Conjunctions

Each of the following examples contains two simple sentences. In each case, join the sentences to form a new compound sentence. Use a comma and one of the seven coordinating conjunctions. There can be more than one correct answer for each example. Be sure the conjunction you choose makes sense in the sentence. An example has been done for you.

Two simple sentences: Many farmers are desperate. They are going bankrupt.
Compound sentence: Many farmers are desperate, for they are going bankrupt.

1. The farmers in Canada want to work.
   Some are experiencing severe financial difficulty.

   _____

   _____

2. Some people are losing their farms.
   The banks are refusing to make further loans.

   _____

   _____

3. Many government programs have not been effective.
   The public cannot do anything.
   (Use *nor.* You will have to change the word order in the second sentence.)

   _____

   _____

4. The farmers feel neglected.
   They are protesting against the government.

   _____

   _____

5. There is an increased need for farm products.
   The government pays farmers not to grow food.

   _____

   _____

6. Everyone needs what the farmers produce.
   We should be concerned about their problems.

   _____

   _____

7. In the future, fewer people will become farmers.
   The problem is likely to become increasingly serious.

   _____

   _____

Coordinating Conjunctions That Do Not Combine Two Independent Clauses

Remember that a coordinating conjunction such as *and* is not always used to combine two independent clauses. Often, it is used simply to combine two items. When this is the case, do not place a comma before the coordinating conjunction.

> I had bacon *and* eggs for breakfast.

The word *and* does not separate two independent clauses, so there is no comma before it.

> I had bacon and eggs for breakfast, *and* then I had a salad for lunch.

In this sentence, the second *and* does combine two independent clauses. Therefore, the comma is required.

The coordinating conjunction *but* is the exception here. It is always a good idea to put a comma before *but* regardless of whether it combines two independent clauses or not. This is because *but* is a strong indication of an opposite point of view. The comma gives the reader a chance to focus on this abrupt shift in thinking.

> He is short, *but* powerful.
> He is short, *but* he exudes a powerful aura.

Use a comma for both situations involving the word *but*.

Use a Semicolon, an Adverbial Conjunction, and a Comma

TIP

A second way to combine independent clauses (or complete thoughts) is to use a semicolon, an adverbial conjunction, and a comma.

IC	; adverbial conjunction,	IC
I had worked hard	; therefore,	I expected results.

Adverbial conjunctions (also called conjunctive adverbs) are another set of connecting words. They have similar meanings to the common coordinating conjunctions, but give the compound sentence more emphasis. They may also sound slightly more formal to you than the shorter conjunctions *and* and *but*. If an adverbial conjunction connects two independent clauses, place a semicolon before it. If it does not, use a comma before it instead.

> **TIP**
>
> Unlike the combination of a comma and a coordinating conjunction, the combination of a comma and an adverbial conjunction *cannot* connect two independent clauses.

Incorrect: I had worked hard, therefore, I expected results.

The above is a run-on sentence (see Chapter 7.)

Correct: I had worked hard, so I expected results.
Correct: I had worked hard; therefore, I expected results.

Connectors: Common Adverbial Conjunctions

Addition (and)	Alternative (or)	Result (so)
in addition	instead	accordingly
also	otherwise	consequently
besides		hence
furthermore		therefore
likewise		thus
moreover		

Contrast (but)	Emphasis	Time
however	indeed	meanwhile
nevertheless	in fact	
nonetheless		

 Practice 1 **Recognizing the Semicolon, Adverbial Conjunction, and Comma**

The following compound sentences each contain two independent clauses. Draw a single line under the subject and two lines under the verb of each independent clause. Then circle the semicolon, adverbial conjunction, and comma. An example has been done for you. Check your answers against those in the Answer Key on page 454.

The jet was the fastest way to get there (; moreover,) it was the most comfortable.

1. The restaurant is always too crowded on Saturdays; nevertheless, it serves the best food in town.
2. The land was not for sale; however, the house could be rented.

3. The lawsuit cost the company several million dollars; consequently, the company went out of business a short time later.

4. The doctor told him to lose weight; furthermore, she insisted he also stop smoking.

Practice 2 **Combining Sentences Using Adverbial Conjunctions**

Combine each pair of sentences below to make a compound sentence. Use a semicolon, an adverbial conjunction, and a comma. Be sure the conjunction you choose makes sense in the sentence. There can be more than one correct answer for each pair of sentences. An example has been done for you. Check your answers against those in the Answer Key on page 454.

Two simple sentences: Our family would like to purchase a computer. We must decide on which computer best serves our needs.

Compound sentence: Our family would like to purchase a computer; however, we must decide on which computer best serves our needs.

1. People once preferred to write with a pen or pencil.
   The computer has now become a favourite writing tool. (Show contrast.)

   _____

   _____

2. Computers provide a powerful way to create and store pieces of writing.
   They make the editing process fast and efficient. (Add an idea.)

   _____

   _____

3. Computers have revolutionized today's offices.
   No modern business is without them. (Show result.)

   _____

   _____

4. Computers have become relatively inexpensive.
   Most people own a computer. (Show result.)

   _____

   _____

5. Many children know more about computers than many adults.
   Many children are teaching adults how to operate computers. (Add an idea.)

   _____

   _____

6. Professional writers have become enthusiastic about the use of computers. There are still some writers who will use only a ballpoint pen. (Show contrast.)

_____

_____

7. We have many technological aids for writing.
   Let us not forget that the source of all our ideas is the human brain. (Show contrast.)

_____

_____

 Exercise **Combining Sentences Using Adverbial Conjunctions**

To each independent clause below, add the suggested adverbial conjunction and another independent clause that makes sense. Remember to punctuate correctly. An example has been done for you.

Adverbial conjunction + Simple sentence: (in fact) I was early for the exam
Compound sentence: I was early for the exam; in fact, I was able to study for an extra half hour.

1. (however) I'll be at the library for a few hours

_____

_____

2. (therefore) James asked to borrow my notes

_____

_____

3. (otherwise) I'm thinking about taking a part-time job

_____

_____

4. (instead) Marcus is not going home for reading week

_____

_____

5. (in fact) They haven't won a game this year

_____

_____

6. (furthermore) Suzie has given up coffee and cigarettes

_____

_____

7. (consequently) My computer keeps crashing

_____

_____

Use a Semicolon

> **TIP**
>
> The third way to combine two independent clauses is to use a semicolon by itself (that is, without an adverbial conjunction).

Remember, do not capitalize the first word after a semicolon (unless the word is one that is always spelled with a capital letter).

IC	;	IC
He arrived at ten	;	he left at midnight.
He arrived at ten	;	I left at midnight

This third method of combining sentences is used less often. No connecting word is used. The semicolon takes the place of the conjunction.

Two independent clauses: I used to watch the Toronto Blue Jays play baseball at Exhibition Stadium. Tonight, I'm going to see them play at Rogers Centre.

Compound sentence: I used to watch the Toronto Blue Jays play baseball at Exhibition Stadium; tonight, I'm going to see them play at Rogers Centre.

The semicolon was used in this example to show that the content of the two clauses is closely related and, therefore, belongs together in one sentence.

When sentences are combined by using a semicolon, the grammatical structure of each independent clause is often similar:

Gasoline prices increased; *vacations* became less frequent.

Both independent clauses above begin with a subject. (See Chapter 8: "Parallel Structure.")

 Exercise **Combining Sentences Using the Semicolon**

To each of the independent clauses below, add another independent clause that expresses a related idea with a similar grammatical structure. Join the two clauses with a semicolon. An example has been done for you.

Independent clause: He wrote the speech.
Compound sentence: He wrote the speech; she gave it.

1. The apartment was light and airy.

   _____

   _____

2. Many students decorate their rooms wonderfully.

   _____

   _____

3. I plan to learn two foreign languages.

   _____

   _____

4. I tried to explain.

   _____

   _____

5. This rain will never stop.

   _____

   _____

What Is Subordination?

When you use coordination to combine sentences, the ideas in both of the resulting clauses are given equal weight. However, ideas are not always equally important. Subordination allows you to show which idea is the main idea.

> **DEFINITION**
>
> **Subordination** is the method used to combine sentences whose ideas are not equally important. It is a combination of an independent clause and a dependent clause.
> **Example:** I stayed home today   because I was sick.
>   Independent Clause   Dependent Clause

Combining Sentences Using Subordination

When you combine sentences using subordination, you make the more important idea an independent clause and the less important idea a dependent (subordinate) clause. The sentence that results is called a **complex sentence**. Each idea contained within a complex sentence is called a **clause**. Various methods of subordination are discussed below; the method you choose shows the relationship between the main idea and the secondary one.

In a complex sentence, the main idea is called the **independent clause** because it could stand alone as a simple sentence. The less important idea is called the **dependent clause** because, even though it has a subject and a verb, it is dependent on the rest of the sentence for its meaning. Consider the following clauses:

> **Independent clause:** That girl leaves.
> **Dependent clause:** If that girl leaves

Notice that each clause in the example above has a subject and a verb. (In both cases, the subject is *girl* and the verb is *leaves*.) The difference is that the dependent clause has an additional word, *if*, which is an example of a special kind of connecting word (a subordinating conjunction—see below) that makes the clause "dependent" on an additional idea. A dependent clause contains a thought that is not complete; it cannot stand on its own. Here is the same dependent clause presented above but with an independent clause added to it:

> If that girl leaves, then I can finish my homework.

Now the thought is complete.

In your writing, you will want to be comfortable creating sentences with dependent clauses. For this, you will need to practise using two kinds of these special "connecting" words: **subordinating conjunctions** and **relative pronouns**. First, let's look at subordinating conjunctions.

Use a Subordinating Conjunction to Create a Complex Sentence

Following is a list of the most common subordinating conjunctions. These connecting words signal the beginning of a dependent clause. It is a good idea to memorize them, especially for the purpose of preventing fragments (see Chapter 6: "Correcting Fragments").

Connectors: Common Subordinating Conjunctions		
after	if, even if	unless
although	in order that	until
as, as if	provided that	when, whenever
as long as, as though	rather than	where, wherever, whereas
because	since	whether
before	so that	while
even though	though	

You might have had teachers in elementary school who told you never to begin a sentence with *because*. If so, they might have said this because they were afraid you wouldn't finish the sentence.

> **Incomplete:** Because the child was sick
> **Complete:** Because the child was sick, she stayed home yesterday.

With the addition of an independent clause to the dependent clause, the sentence is now complete.

Function of Subordinating Conjunctions

To introduce a <u>condition</u>: if, even if, as long as, provided that, unless

> I will go *as long as* you go with me.
> I won't go *unless* you go with me.

To introduce a <u>contrast</u>: although, even though, through

> I will go *even though* you won't go with me.

To introduce a <u>cause</u>: *because, since*

> I will go *because* the meeting is very important.

To show <u>time</u>: after, before, when, whenever, while, until

> I will go *whenever* you say.
> I won't go *until* you say it is time.

To show <u>place</u>: *where, wherever*

> I will go *wherever* you send me.

To show *purpose:* in order that, so that

> I will go *so that* I can hear the candidate for myself.

You can choose between two ways of writing the complex sentence. You can begin with either the dependent clause (DC) or the independent clause (IC).

First way:	DC	,	IC
Example:	If Barbara leaves	,	we can finish our homework.

First way:	IC		IC
Example:	We can finish our homework		if Barbara leaves.

> **TIP**
>
> Use a comma when you begin a sentence with a dependent clause. Do not use a comma when the independent clause comes first.

From the above examples you can see that when a sentence begins with an independent clause, a comma may not always be needed. For example, the comma is omitted if the dependent clause is essential to the main idea of the speaker.

Practice 1 Recognizing Dependent and Independent Clauses

In the blank to the left of each group of words below, write the letters *IC* if the group is an independent clause (a complete thought) or *DC* if the group is a dependent clause (not a complete thought, even though it contains a subject and a verb). Check your answers against those in the Answer Key on page 454.

_____ 1. while the photographer was getting ready

_____ 2. before the guests arrived

_____   3. I've been a bridesmaid for two of my friends

_____   4. even though we're all in our teens

_____   5. this one was more fun than most

_____   6. whenever I see you

_____   7. since I did not take the subway

Practice 2 **Combining Sentences Using Subordination**

Combine each pair of sentences below using subordination. Look back at the list of subordinating conjunctions if you need to. There may be more than one correct answer for each of these exercises. Check your answers against those in the Answer Key on page 454.

1. He was eating breakfast.
   The results of the election came over the radio.

   _____

   _____

2. Simon gave up his plan to launch a dot-com company.
   He felt it was too risky.

   _____

   _____

3. I will see my teacher tonight.
   She is speaking at the university this evening.

   _____

   _____

4. The designer hoped for a promotion.
   Not one person in the department was promoted last year.

   _____

   _____

5. The designer hoped for a promotion.
   She made sure all her work was done accurately and on time.

   _____

   _____

Exercise 1 **Combining Sentences Using Subordination**

Below are three pairs of sentences. Combine each pair by using the subordinating conjunction given. Write each new complex sentence two different ways: first, begin the sentence with the dependent clause and use a comma; second, begin the sentence with the independent clause and use a comma only if necessary.

1. (Use *since*.)   Wildlife habitats are being destroyed.
    Many species are in danger.

    a. _____

    _____

    b. _____

    _____

2. (Use *after*.)   He won the wrestling match.
    He went out to celebrate.

    a. _____

    _____

    b. _____

    _____

3. (Use *when*.)   Halyna returned from Europe this spring.
    The family was excited.

    a. _____

    _____

    b. _____

    _____

 Exercise 2 **Combining Sentences Using Subordination**

Rewrite the following paragraph using subordination to combine some of the sentences wherever you feel it would be effective. Be prepared to discuss the reasons for your choices. You may also want to discuss places where coordination might be a good choice. More than one correct answer is possible.

Many Canadian communities collect refuse from its source. Waste is delivered to a waste disposal site. Very little waste is recycled. Very little waste is burned. Many smaller towns and villages cannot afford a waste collection service or a proper waste disposal site. Smaller communities are prevalent in Canada. Improperly operated dumps outnumber the better-operated facilities used by larger communities. Over the next few years, many of our landfills will close. They are getting full. Some places in Ontario already truck their trash to the United States. The garbage continues to pile up. The newspapers print stories about it every week. Trash is not a very glamorous subject. People in every town talk about the problem.

Here is a summary so far of how clauses (dependent and independent) can be combined to form complete sentences.

Remember: IC stands for *independent clause* (complete thought).

DC stands for *dependent clause* (incomplete thought).

IC	, coordinating conjunction	IC
IC	; adverbial conjunction	IC
IC	;	IC
DC	,	IC
IC		DC

Note the absence of any comma when an independent clause comes before a dependent clause, as in the last row above.

Use a Relative Pronoun to Create a Complex Sentence

Often, two sentences can be combined using a relative pronoun.

Common Relative Pronouns		
who whose whom that	refers to people	**Note:** "whose" can also refer to things. **Example:** They performed a play whose two acts were only 15 minutes each.
which that whose	refers to things	**Note:** "that" can also refer to people when a class or type of person is meant. **Example:** The teacher I prefer is one that offers help outside of class.

Two simple sentences: The researcher had a breakthrough.
He was studying diabetes.

These sentences are short and choppy. To avoid this choppiness, a writer could join these two related ideas using a relative pronoun.

Combining sentences with a relative pronoun: The researcher who was studying diabetes had a breakthrough.

Now join a third idea to the sentence (use *which*).

Third idea: He reported the breakthrough to the press.

TIP

Remember to put the relative pronoun directly after the word it refers to.

	Incorrect:	The researcher, which he reported to the press, had a breakthrough who was studying diabetes.
	Correct:	The researcher who was studying diabetes had a breakthrough, which he reported to the press.

The relative pronoun *who* and its clause *who was studying diabetes* refers to *the researcher*, not to *a breakthrough*. See more on the relative pronoun *who* (vs. *whom*) on page 108. The relative pronoun *which* and its clause *which he reported to the press* does refer to *a breakthrough,* so this clause should follow the noun *breakthrough.* (See Chapter 10 for more on modifiers.)

Practice **Combining Sentences Using a Relative Pronoun**

Combine each of the pairs of sentences below into one complex sentence by using a relative pronoun. Do not use commas. More than one correct answer is possible for each pair of sentences. An example has been done for you. Check your answers against those in the Answer Key on page 454.

> That woman created the flower arrangement.
> She visited us last weekend.

Combined: That woman who visited us last weekend created the flower arrangement.

1. The chemistry lab is two hours long.
   I attend that chemistry lab.

   Combined: _____

   _____

2. The student assistant is very knowledgeable.
   The student assistant is standing by the door.

   Combined: _____

   _____

3. The equipment was purchased last year.
   The equipment will make possible some important new research.

   Combined: _____

   _____

How Do You Punctuate a Clause with a Relative Pronoun?

Punctuating relative clauses can be tricky because there are two types of relative clauses.

1. One type of relative clause is basic to the meaning of the sentence:

> Never eat fruit that hasn't been washed first.

The basic meaning of the sentence is not "never eat fruit." The relative clause is necessary to restrict the meaning. This clause is called a **restrictive clause** and does not use commas to set it off. *Note:* Clauses beginning with the pronoun *that* are usually in this category.

2. The other type of relative clause is not basic to the meaning of the sentence:

> Kim's famous salad, *which included spinach and almonds*, was delicious.

In this sentence, the relative clause is not basic to the main idea. In fact, if the clause were omitted, the main idea would not be changed. This clause is called a **nonrestrictive clause**. Commas are required to indicate that the information is nonessential. Note: Clauses beginning with the pronoun *which* are usually in this category. Remember, the relative pronoun *which* always refers to things.

Note: While *which* refers to things in a nonrestrictive clause and *that* refers to things in a restrictive clause, the relative pronouns used to refer to people (*who*, *whom*, and *whose*) are used for both nonrestrictive and restrictive clauses. Remember, restrictive clauses do not take commas to separate them from the rest of the sentence while nonrestrictive clauses do. (For more on commas, see Chapter 11: "Punctuation.")

Practice   Recognizing Restrictive and Nonrestrictive Clauses

Choose whether or not to insert commas in the sentences below. Two examples have been done for you. Check your answers against those in the Answer Key on page 454.

> The man who is wearing the Hawaiian shirt is the bridegroom.

(The relative clause is essential. There are no commas.)

> Al, *who was wearing a flannel shirt*, arrived late to the wedding.

(The relative clause is nonessential. Commas, therefore, are necessary.)

1. Canada's first census which was taken in 1667 showed 3215 non-Native inhabitants in 668 families.
2. Most of the families who lived near the St. Lawrence River were French Canadians.
3. By the time of Confederation, the population of the country had risen to 3 463 000 which was an increase of 1077 percent over 200 years.
4. If the population of Canada which is about 30 000 000 persons now increases by a similar percentage over the next 150 or so years, we'll have a population of 280 200 000 by the year 2167.
5. Where do you think we will we put everyone who lives in Canada then?

Exercise 1 Combining Sentences Using Relative Pronouns

Add a clause that begins with a relative pronoun to each of the sentences below. Use each of these possibilities at least once: *who, whose, whom, which, that*. Be sure to punctuate correctly. An example has been done for you.

Simple sentence: The leader was barely 1.5 metres tall.
Complex sentence: The leader, who was always self-conscious about her height, was barely 1.5 metres tall.

1. The figure skaters _____ began their program.

2. The music _____ had a Latin beat.

3. Their first figure _____ was a triple toe loop.

4. The crowd _____ cheered wildly.

5. Even the judges _____ seemed impressed.

6. Her triple axel _____ was a little ragged.

7. Their coach _____ was thrilled by the final score.

 Exercise 2 Combining Sentences Using Relative Pronouns

Combine the following pairs of sentences using a relative pronoun. There may be more than one correct answer for each example.

1. Stress can do a great deal of harm.
   We experience stress every day.

   _____

   _____

2. People often use food to help them cope.
   Some people work long hours at demanding jobs.

   _____

   _____

3. The practice of eating to cope with stress is often automatic.
   The practice of eating to cope often goes back to childhood.

   _____

   _____

4. Foods can actually increase tension.
   People turn to foods in times of stress.

   _____

   _____

5. One of the biggest mistakes people make is to use alcohol as an aid to becoming calm.
   Alcohol is really a depressant.

   _____

   _____

6. People should eat three light meals a day and two small snacks.
   People want to feel a sense of calm.

   _____

   _____

7. Eat a good meal at regular intervals to help reduce stress.
   Binge eating puts on pounds, drains you of energy, and increases your stress level.

   _____

   _____

Chapter Review Exercises

 Practice Combining Sentences Using Coordination and Subordination

Look over the following paragraph, which is made up of simple sentences. Then rewrite the paragraph, combining sentences where you think it would improve the meaning and style. Be creative, and don't be afraid to alter the wording to accommodate the changes you want to make. Check your answers against those in the Answer Key on page 455. (The Answer Key will give you one possible answer, but there are many ways of revising this passage.)

> The wind is strong. The waves are choppy. They are growing larger. I paddle my kayak harder. My arms are getting tired. The energy is draining from them. They grow limp and heavy. The other side of the harbour seems distant. The glow of the setting sun is behind me. It spreads orange and purple fingers across the sky. A wall of rocks lies offshore. It picks up the last light of the setting sun. It is a silver beacon. I focus on that wall and paddle harder. The sea smashes against my bow. It seems to push me away from shore. Flecks of spray hit my face. I taste the salt on my lips. With that taste of the sea, the beauty of the sea and shore strikes me. I am distracted from my labour and absorbed by the world around me. My kayak finally glides past the rocks to the sheltered beach beyond. I am exhilarated and exhausted.

Exercise 1 Combining Sentences Using Coordinating and Adverbial Conjunctions

Combine each pair of sentences below to make a compound sentence. Use a coordinating, subordinating, or adverbial conjunction, but be sure that the conjunction clearly shows the relationship between the ideas. There can be more than one correct answer for each example.

1. For many people, mathematics is a necessary evil.
   To a few, mathematics provides a lifetime of challenge and fun.

   _____

   _____

2. Most Canadians have studied math only to Grade 12.
   This limits their ability to understand new scientific developments.

   _____

   _____

3. Their knowledge extends to little more than basic arithmetic.
   People in the seventeenth century knew as much about math as most
   Canadians today.

   _____

   _____

4. Few Canadians study math at the university level.
   Many promising mathematics graduates are offered employment in the
   United States.

   _____

   _____

5. Many schools form math teams to compete in area contests.
   Other schools encourage interest in math with math clubs.

   _____

   _____

6. Some schools suffer from a lack of science and math teachers.
   Mathematicians can find well-paid employment in industry.

   _____

   _____

7. It is important to increase the number of mathematics graduates.
   Canadian students may continue to trail behind those of many other
   countries in math and science ability.

   _____

   _____

Exercise 2 Combining Sentences with a Subordinating Conjunction or a Relative Pronoun

Combine each of the following pairs of sentences using either a subordinating conjunction or a relative pronoun. Be sure that the word you use makes sense in the sentence. There can be more than one correct answer for each example.

1. People have been fascinated for centuries by the problem of stuttering. Modern science is only beginning to understand some of the underlying causes of the problem.

    _____

    _____

2. For some people, stuttering disappears by itself. For others, stuttering continues into adulthood.

    _____

    _____

3. Stutterers usually keep their condition. They seek professional help.

    _____

    _____

4. It is true that there is some psychological basis for stuttering. It is true that psychologists have not been able to solve the problem.

    _____

    _____

5. All kinds of scientists have looked at the problem from all different angles. There is no single answer to stuttering.

    _____

    _____

6. Stuttering runs in families. Children of such families have a greater chance of becoming stutterers.

    _____

    _____

7. You often hear someone say he or she knows the causes of stuttering. You know that person cannot be speaking scientifically.

    _____

    _____

Working Together: Practising Coordination and Subordination

A controversial issue today concerns the wide gap between the wages earned by people in some professions and the wages earned by people in other professions. For instance, some sports figures and entertainers earn millions every year. How are wages determined in our society? How do you think wages should be determined? Should there be a minimum wage in Canada? Should everybody earn the same salary? Divide into groups and discuss the subject for fifteen minutes.

Following the general discussion, practise using coordination by writing ten compound sentences on the subject of wage differences. If you like, you may try to summarize the ideas of your group. Try to use each of the following ten coordinating conjunctions to combine two independent clauses:

> **F**or, **A**nd, **N**or, **B**ut, **O**r, **Y**et, **S**o (FANBOYS)
> either/or, neither/nor, not only/but also (correlative conjunctions)

Now, revise each sentence you've written so that the two independent clauses are combined with a subordinating conjunction instead. Consult the list of subordinating conjunctions on page 63.

After working on these sentences for fifteen minutes, exchange papers with another student and answer the following questions about the sentences on the paper you have:

1. In each case, has the writer combined two independent clauses?
2. In each sentence, does the coordinating or subordinating conjunction carry the correct meaning for the sentence?
3. Is the punctuation correct?

Chapter 6 Correcting Fragments

Quick Quiz Test yourself on your knowledge of fragments. Some of the examples below are complete sentences; some are fragments (only parts of sentences). Write *C* if the example is a complete sentence. Write *F* if the example is a fragment. The answers to the questions are upside down beside the quiz.

_____ 1. Whale watching is a popular tourist activity in British Columbia.

_____ 2. Although its effects are being studied.

_____ 3. Whales coping with heavy boat traffic.

_____ 4. The noise from engines can disturb the whales' communication.

_____ 5. Which may be changing their habitat.

Answers:
1. C
2. F
3. F
4. C
5. F

Recognizing and Correcting Sentence Fragments

Once you have learned that a sentence must have a subject and a verb, and that a sentence must also express a complete thought, you are on your way to correcting one of the most frequent errors in student writing: the fragment. A fragment is an incomplete sentence. Although many of our daily conversations are informal and sometimes contain fragments, standard writing is always more formal and requires complete sentences.

Although you will occasionally spot incomplete sentences in professional writing, such as newspaper writing, advertising, novels, and so on, it is hoped that the writer is using these fragments intentionally. In such cases, the fragment may capture the way a person thinks or speaks, or it may create a special effect. A student developing his or her writing skills should be sure to use only standard sentence form (complete sentences) so that thoughts will be communicated effectively. Most of the writing you will do in your life—papers in school, business correspondence, or reports in your job—will demand standard sentence form. Fragments will be looked upon as a sign of poor writing skills rather than an indicator of creative style!

The fragment is a major problem for many student writers. In the writer's mind, a thought may be clear; however, on paper the idea may turn out to be incomplete, missing a subject or a verb. In this chapter, you will improve your ability to spot incomplete sentences (fragments), and you will learn how to correct them. This practice will prepare you to avoid such fragments in your own writing.

Remember the definition of a sentence:

> **DEFINITION**
>
> A **complete sentence** has a subject and a verb and expresses a complete thought.
> **Example:** The cat drank.

Notice that it is not necessary to know *what* the cat drank in order for the sentence to be grammatically complete.

A Typical Casual Conversation

The following conversation is one that a couple of students might have at the start of their English class.

JOHN: Early again. *Missing subject*
LESIA: Want to get a front-row seat.
JOHN: Your homework done?
LESIA: Nearly.
JOHN: Think he'll give a quiz today?
LESIA: Hope not.
JOHN: Looks like rain.
LESIA: Better not. Haven't got a bag for these new books.
JOHN: Going to the game Saturday?
LESIA: Probably.

Remember, when you write in complete sentences, this writing is likely going to be quite different from the way you would express the same idea in everyday conversation with a friend. In the conversation above, not one sentence is complete. There is at least one fragment on every line. If this dialogue were to appear in a novel, punctuated correctly with quotation marks, it would be perfectly acceptable. But using fragments in texts that call for standard English form is, quite simply, an example of poor writing skills.

What Is a Fragment?

DEFINITION

A **fragment** is a piece of a sentence.

Examples: Which is not what the teacher wanted to hear.

Because the bus was late.

Whereas she was better at math.

Fragments often begin with the relative pronoun *which* or the subordinating conjunctions *because* and *whereas*.

A group of words is a fragment, not a sentence, if any one of the following is true:

a. The subject is missing.

> delivered the plans to my office

b. The verb is missing.

> the architect to my office

c. Both the subject and verb are missing.

> to my office

d. The group of words is a dependent clause. In other words, a subject and a verb are present, but the words do not express a complete thought.

> when the architect delivered the plans
> which the architect identified as her favourite design
> because the bus was late
> the reason being the bus was late

Sometimes a fragment might look like a complete sentence because it is fairly long, starts with a capital letter, and ends with a period. Obviously, these criteria are not enough to identify a complete sentence.

Practice 1 Understanding Fragments

Each of the groups of words on the next page is a fragment. In the blank to the right of each fragment, write *a, b, c,* or *d* to identify what change would make the fragment into a sentence. An example has been done for you. Check your answers against those in the Answer Key on page 455.

> a. Add a subject.
> b. Add a verb.
> c. Add a subject and a verb.
> d. Add or delete words to express a complete thought. (A subject and a verb are present, but the group of words is a dependent clause.)

Fragment	Change Needed
the red fox	b. Add a verb.
1. returned to the river	_____
2. a bird on the oak branch	_____
3. between the island and the mainland	_____
4. the hawk in a soaring motion	_____
5. the fishing boats on the lake	_____
6. dropped like a stone into the water	_____
7. because the fisherman put the net away	_____

How Do You Correct a Fragment?

You can eliminate fragments in two ways:

1. Add the missing part or parts to develop the fragment into a complete sentence:

> *Fragment:* along the coastal road
> *Add:* subject and verb
> *Sentence:* He drove along the coastal road.

2. Join the fragment to another sentence. In order to do this, you may need to make use of the comma, the colon, or the dash, or you may not need to use punctuation. For example:

   a. Using the comma

   > *Fragment:* including a stop at the shoe store
   > *Other sentence:* He has to make a number of purchases.
   > *Fragment eliminated:* He has to make a number of purchases, including a stop at the shoe store.

   b. Using the colon

   > *Fragment:* action, science fiction, and comedy
   > *Other sentence:* I like three types of movies.
   > *Fragment eliminated:* I like three types of movies: action, science fiction, and comedy.

   c. Using the dash

   > *Fragment:* more often than she should
   > *Other sentence:* She goes to the casino every day.
   > *Fragment eliminated:* She goes to the casino every day—more often than she should.

[handwritten notes: — making comments / — after parties]

d. Using no punctuation

Fragment: on top of the mountain
Other sentence: We planned to plant the flag.
Fragment eliminated: We planned to plant the flag on top of the mountain.

 Practice 2 Turning Fragments into Sentences

Change the fragments of Practice 1 into complete sentences by adding the missing part or parts that you identified. Check your answers against those in the Answer Key on page 455. (The Answer Key will give you sample answers, but there are many ways of correcting these fragments.)

1. returned to the river

_____

2. a bird on the oak branch

_____

3. between the island and the mainland

_____

4. the hawk, in a soaring motion

_____

5. the fishing boats on the lake

_____

6. dropped like a stone into the water

_____

7. because the fisherman put the net away

_____

Practice 3 Turning Fragments into Sentences

The following groups of words may or may not be fragments. If the group of words forms a complete sentence, write "complete." Otherwise, rewrite it, adding whatever is necessary to correct the fragment. Check your answers against those in the Answer Key on page 455. (The Answer Key will give you sample answers, but there are many ways of correcting these fragments.)

1. As long as it's a windy day.

_____

2. Into the forest, armed with a machine gun.

_____

3. It's great.

_____

4. Along a deserted and dusty road.

_____

5. Where the deer and the antelope play.

_____

6. The groundhog run over by three different cars.

_____

7. A jeep has parked.

_____

 Exercise Turning Fragments into Sentences

Each of the following passages contains one or more fragments. First read each passage. Then locate the fragments in it. Correct the fragments by joining them to other sentences using a comma, a colon, a dash, or no punctuation. There can be more than one correct answer for each passage.

1. Fishing is one of the oldest sports in the world. And can be one of the most relaxing. Someone with a simple wooden pole and line can have as much fun as a professional angler. With expensive equipment. For busy executives, overworked teachers, and even presidents of nations. Fishing can be a good way to escape from the stress of demanding jobs.

2. The first electric car was built in 1887. Six years later, it was sold commercially. At the turn of the century, people had great faith in new technology. In fact, 300 electric taxicabs were operating in New York City by 1900. However, electric cars soon lost their popularity. The new gasoline engine became more widely used. With our concern about pollution. Perhaps electric cars will become desirable once again.

3. Most sports evolve over many years. But not basketball. A Canadian-born teacher invented basketball in December 1891. Working at a YMCA training school in Massachusetts. The coach needed an indoor game to keep his students fit over the winter. Dr. James Naismith created goals. By nailing two peach baskets to the gym balcony.

Don't Confuse Phrases with Sentences

Fragments are usually made up of phrases. These phrases are often mistaken for sentences because they are groups of words. However, they do not fit the definition of a sentence.

What Is a Phrase?

> **DEFINITION**
>
> A **phrase** is a group of words that go together but lack one or more of the elements necessary to be classified as a sentence.
>
> **Example:** In the barn at the back of the house

In the example above, two prepositional phrases have been put together (see #3, below). It is another example of a fragment.

How Many Kinds of Phrases Are There?

In English, there are a number of types of phrases that you should learn to recognize. Some of them you have already studied in the previous chapter. Remember, a phrase is not a complete sentence; it is a sentence fragment, and as such must be either joined to another sentence or made into a complete sentence.

1. **Noun phrase:** a group of words that functions as a noun

   Noun phrase: large square bricks
   Complete sentence: The garage is built out of large square bricks.

2. **Gerund phrase:** a type of noun phrase; a group of words beginning with a gerund (an *-ing* word that looks like a verb, but functions as a noun)
   Gerund phrase: jogging every morning at 6:00
   Complete sentence: Jogging every morning at 6:00 is something
   I cannot miss.

3. **Prepositional phrase:** a group of words beginning with a preposition (For a list of common prepositions, see page 8.)

   Prepositional phrase: on the porch
   Complete sentence: Many of our neighbours are sitting on the porch.

4. **Verb phrase:** a group of words that functions as a verb

   Verb phrase: is walking
   Complete sentence: My best friend is walking to my house.

5. **Infinitive phrase:** a group of words beginning with an infinitive

   Infinitive phrase: to have a good job
   Complete sentence: I think it's important to have a good job.

Practice 1 Identifying Phrases

Identify each of the underlined phrases in the following sentences. Check your answers against those in the Answer Key on page 455.

1. <u>To visit Montreal</u> is a thrill for most Canadians.
2. Many people love <u>to see the French culture</u>.

3. Museums, restaurants, shopping, and the varied night life offer endless possibilities <u>for the tourist</u>.
4. <u>On the subways</u>, tourists experience one of the cleanest underground transit systems in North America.
5. <u>My brother Don</u> rode the subway under the St. Lawrence River.
6. <u>A landowner from the country</u>, he enjoyed the continental atmosphere of Quebec's largest city.
7. Montreal's continual fascination is its rich mix <u>of cultures and lifestyles</u> from all over the world.

 Practice 2 Identifying Phrases

In the following sentences, identify what kind of phrase each numbered group of underlined words is. Check your answers against those in the Answer Key on page 456.

<u>In Canada</u>,① crime seems <u>to be increasing</u>② <u>at an alarming rate</u>.③ Stories about <u>many major crimes</u>④ <u>can be seen</u>⑤ almost daily <u>in the newspapers</u>.⑥ <u>To avoid</u>⑦ the issue will not solve the problem. Citizens <u>should be concerned</u>⑧ and try <u>to make their views known</u>⑨ <u>to their elected officials</u>.⑩

1. _____
2. _____
3. _____
4. _____
5. _____
6. _____
7. _____
8. _____
9. _____
10. _____

Making a Complete Sentence from a Fragment That Contains a Verbal

> **DEFINITION**
>
> **Verbals** are words that look like verbs, but that function as nouns, adjectives, or adverbs. There are three types of verbals: **infinitives, participles,** and **gerunds.** All three of these types of verbals appear in phrases. These phrases by themselves are not complete sentences. They are fragments.

Infinitive phrases: to kill a mockingbird
to tour the West

Complete sentences: It is a sad thing to kill a mockingbird.
He began to tour the West.

Participial phrases: beaten to a pulp
running like the wind

Complete sentence: I was afraid I would be beaten to a pulp.
Running like the wind, he's never looked more afraid in his life.

Gerund phrases:	working on the car
	sitting on the bench
Complete sentence:	Working on the car can wait until she's finished her supper.
	All players hate sitting on the bench.

Participial phrases function as adjectives. Gerund phrases can look like (present) participial phrases (because both end in *-ing*), but when they appear in complete sentences, gerund phrases function as nouns.

> **TIP**
>
> Watch out for *-ing* words. No word ending in *-ing* can be the complete verb of a sentence.
> **Fragment:** The reason being the bus was late.
> **Complete sentence:** The reason is the bus was late.

You can form a sentence from a fragment that contains a participle in any of the following ways.

Fragment: he talking in his sleep

1. Add a helping verb to the participle:

   He *is talking* in his sleep.

2. Change the participle to a different form of the verb:

   He *talks* in his sleep.

3. Use the participle as an adjective, being sure to provide a subject and verb for the sentence:

   Talking in his sleep, he muttered something about his boss.

4. Use a gerund phrase (which has the same form as the present participle) as a subject:

   Talking in his sleep got him into trouble.

Practice 1 Correcting a Fragment That Contains a Participle

Make four complete sentences from each of the following fragments. An example has been done for you. Check your answers against those in the Answer Key on page 456. (The Answer Key will give you sample answers, but there are many ways of correcting these fragments.)

Fragment: using the back stairway

a. He *is using* the back stairway.
b. He *uses* the back stairway.
c. *Using the back stairway,* he got away without being seen.
d. *Using the back stairway* is not a good idea.

1. climbing in the Rockies

    a. _____

    b. _____

    c. _____

    d. _____

2. playing video games

    a. _____

    b. _____

    c. _____

    d. _____

3. going clubbing on Tuesdays

    a. _____

    b. _____

    c. _____

    d. _____

 Practice 2 Recognizing Fragments

The paragraph below contains fragments. Read the paragraph. Then write *complete* after each example that is a complete sentence. Write *fragment* after each example that is a phrase or piece of a sentence. Keep in mind that a sentence must have a subject and verb as well as express a complete thought. Check your answers against those in the Answer Key on page 456.

> That summer, she cycled through the backcountry of southern France. Discovering early that her bike was ideal. The perfect mode of transportation. Because they are cycling fanatics. The French almost always treated her with respect and kindness. In spite of her halting attempts at the language. They would shout encouragement. As she puffed up a hill. The waitress in a café where she stopped to rest. Urged her to eat more, slipping an extra portion onto her plate.

1. That summer, she cycled through the backcountry of southern France.   _____

2. Discovering early that her bike was ideal.   _____

3. The perfect mode of transportation.   _____

4. Because they are cycling fanatics.   _____

5. The French almost always treated her with respect and kindness.   _____

6. In spite of her halting attempts at the language.

_____

7. They would shout encouragement.

_____

8. As she puffed up a hill.

_____

9. The waitress in a café where she stopped to rest.

_____

10. Urged her to eat more, slipping an extra portion onto her plate.

_____

Practice 3 Editing for Fragments

The paragraph below may contain fragments. Rewrite the paragraph, correcting any fragments that appear. You may use any method you have learned to make the corrections, but change the content as little as possible. Circle any changes you have made. Check your answer against the Answer Key on page 456. (The Answer Key will give you one possible answer, but there are many ways to revise this paragraph.)

Soccer's World Cup in 2006 was won by Italy for the first time in 24 years, but it is a public disgrace for which the game will be remembered by the world. By halftime, the final game between Italy and France was tied 1–1. After 120 minutes, the game was still tied. The final victory depended on the penalty shootout. Which took the game to 5–3 for Italy. But 10 minutes before the end of extra time. France's illustrious captain, Zinedine Zidane, was expelled. For head-butting Marco Materazzi. Apparently, Marco had called him a terrorist. And had insulted both his mother and his sister. Was this a deliberate, desperate, and cheap attempt to achieve final victory in what had become a gruelling final game? Celebrations by Italians around the world were unstoppable. Partying with abandon. But soccer scandal continues to loom over the Italian team. Zinedine Zidane exited from his last World Cup under an umbrella of shame. Because he didn't take the moral high road. While millions of fans watched his every move.

Exercise Correcting a Fragment That Contains a Participle

The following passage includes four fragments containing participles. Circle the fragments and correct them in one of the four ways shown in Practice 1. There can be more than one correct answer.

At last taking the driving test. I felt very nervous. My mother was sitting in the back seat. All my papers sitting on the front seat. The inspector got into the car and sat on my insurance form. He looked rather sour and barely spoke to me. Trying not to hit the curb. I parallel parked surprisingly well. I managed to get through all the manoeuvres. Now tensely waiting for the results.

Chapter Review Exercises

 Exercise 1 Correcting the Fragment

Rewrite each fragment so that it is a complete sentence. There can be more than one correct answer.

1. early morning a time of peace in my neighbourhood

   _____

2. the grey mist covering up all but the faint outlines of nearby houses

   _____

3. the shapes of cars in the streets and driveways

   _____

4. to sit and look out the window

   _____

5. holding a steaming cup of coffee

   _____

6. the only sound the rumbling of a truck

   _____

7. passing on the highway a kilometre away

   _____

Exercise 2 Correcting the Fragment

Revisit the paragraph in the exercise "Correcting a Fragment That Contains a Participle" on page 85. Rewrite the paragraph, correcting each of the fragments you identified in one of the following ways:

- Join the phrase to the sentence preceding it.
- Join the phrase to the sentence that follows it.
- Add a subject, a verb, or both so that the sentence is complete.

There can be more than one correct answer.

Exercise 3 Correcting a Fragment

Each of the following passages contains a fragment. Underline the fragment, and on the lines beneath each passage, rewrite the passage so that it is composed of complete sentences. There can be more than one correct answer.

1. The moon rose high in the sky. All of us worked quickly to pitch the tent. Then making a fire.

   Revised passage: _____

   _____

   _____

2. Raising the drinking age to 21 improves the safety of all drivers. The drinkers and nondrinkers. Every province should raise the drinking age to 21.

   Revised passage: _____

   _____

   _____

3. Companies do a great deal of research before they name a new product. Based on the results of a market research team. The company makes its final selection.

   Revised passage: _____

   _____

   _____

4. The day of my eighteenth birthday, the reservations made at a fine restaurant. My father came home early from work.

   Revised passage: _____

   _____

   _____

5. In 1930, Clint Benedict of the Montreal Maroons donned professional hockey's first face mask. It was a crude leather device intended to protect his broken nose. During the game, an opponent jammed the mask into Benedict's face. Causing further injury. Benedict tore off the mask and quit the game forever.

   Revised passage: _____

   _____

   _____

Working Together: Editing Ad Copy

Read the Pure Michigan (destination brand of the U.S. state of Michigan) advertisement illustrated below. Notice that this advertisement contains several fragments. The writing we must produce for academic or professional purposes is often very different from the kind of writing we find in advertisements and other kinds of popular writing. Why do you think the advertiser would choose to include fragments? Rewrite the entire advertisement using only complete sentences. In your small group, choose a representative to read the two versions out loud. Discuss with people in your group which one is more effective. Why?

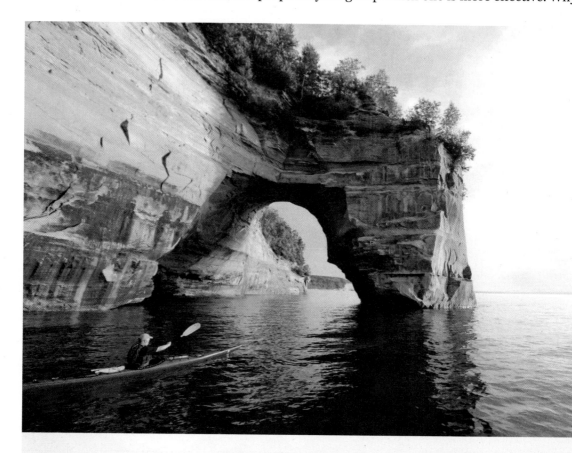

We go this way to school.
That way to work. One way home.
And before we know it, we get stuck in a routine.

So let's take a left instead of a right.
Instead of the direct route, let's take the scenic route.

To a place where something new and exciting
is waiting for us just around the corner.

Right this way to Pure Michigan.

PURE *M*ICHIGAN®
Your trip begins at michigan.org

Chapter 7 **Correcting Run-Ons**

Quick Quiz Test yourself on your knowledge of run-ons. Some of the examples below are complete sentences; some are run-ons (two or more independent clauses inadequately separated). Write *C* if the example is correct. Write *R* if the example is a run-on. Answers are upside down beside the quiz.

_____ 1. Strong competition exists among computer companies, each carefully guards its new software designs.

_____ 2. Last year, newspapers carried the story of the great video game design robbery, in fact, it sounded like a spy movie.

_____ 3. A young worker for a California company wanted money to buy a sports car, so he tried to sell the secret company designs to an Asian competitor.

_____ 4. The worker thought the designs were safely hidden on a disk in an airport locker, however, the police caught him and recovered the disk.

_____ 5. The company pressed charges, the worker was given a suspended sentence.

Answers:
1. R
2. R
3. C
4. R
5. R

Run-Ons Are Not "Long Sentences"

Many people think that a run-on is simply a sentence that "runs on and on and on." This is not the definition of a run-on. The question of whether a sentence is a run-on or not does not depend on length. The following is a run-on sentence even though it is quite short: *I did, he didn't.* A run-on is simply two or more independent clauses without adequate separation. There are many ways to provide this separation. It is important that you be able to recognize runs-ons in your writing and separate the clauses properly to solve the problem.

> **DEFINITION**
>
> A **run-on** is two or more complete thoughts without adequate separation. (A comma alone is NEVER adequate separation between independent clauses.)
> **Examples:** Everyone watched silently as the bus pulled into the school parking lot, then each person stepped onto the bus in a very orderly fashion.
> I came to school, however, I was late.

Both examples in the definition box above are run-ons. In the first sentence, the word *then* is used incorrectly as if it were a coordinating conjunction. It is not. It is not one of the "FANBOYS" (see page 55 in Chapter 5: "Coordination and Subordination"). In the second sentence, the adverbial conjunction *however* separates two complete thoughts. It, therefore, requires a semicolon before it, not just a comma.

What Kinds of Run-Ons Are There?

> **The Different Kinds of Run-On Sentences**
>
> 1. The *fused run-on:* two or more independent clauses that run together without any punctuation
>
>   **I met Diana again we were happy to see each other.**
>
> 2. The *comma splice:* two or more independent clauses that run together with only a comma
>
>   **I met Diana again, we were happy to see each other.**
>
>   (The comma splice is the most common type of run-on sentence.)
>
> 3. The *"and" run-on:* two or more independent clauses that run together with a coordinating conjunction but no punctuation
>
>   **I met Diana again and we were happy to see each other and we talked for hours.**

Note: A long sentence is not necessarily a run-on. The following sentence might be considered long, but it is not a run-on:

> I met Diana again, and despite the fact that we hadn't seen each other in years, we both felt as if we hadn't parted at all, as strange as that may seem to everyone.

How Do You Make a Complete Sentence from a Run-On?

Guide for Correcting Run-Ons

There are three different ways to correct a run-on.

1. Make two simple sentences with end punctuation:

    I met Diana again. We were happy to see each other.

2. Make a compound sentence using one of the three methods of coordination:

    I met Diana again, and we were happy to see each other.
    I met Diana again; furthermore, we were happy to see each other.
    I met Diana again; we were happy to see each other.

    (For more on using the semicolon correctly—either with adverbial conjunctions or alone—see pages 57–62 in Chapter 5: "Coordination and Subordination.")

3. Make a complex sentence using subordination:

    When I met Diana again, we were happy to see each other.
    We were happy to see each other when I met Diana again.

Exercise   Recognizing and Correcting Run-Ons

The following story is written as one sentence. Rewrite the story, breaking it up so there are no run-ons. Put a period at the end of each complete thought. You may have to omit some of the words that loosely connect different ideas, or you may want to use coordination and subordination (see Chapter 5). Remember to start each new sentence with a capital letter. More than one correct answer is possible.

> My best friend is accident-prone if you knew her you'd know that she's always limping, having to write with her left hand, or wearing a bandage on her head or ankle last week for example, she was walking down the street minding her own business when a shingle from someone's roof hit her on the head and she had to go to the emergency ward for stitches then this week one of her fingers is purple because someone slammed the car door on her hand, in fact, sometimes I think it might be better if I didn't spend too much time with her you know her bad luck might be catching!

Practice 1   Correcting Run-Ons

Each of the following examples is a run-on. Supply four possible ways to correct each one. Check your answers against those in the Answer Key on page 456. Refer to the guide above if you need help.

1. Five-year-old Davie asked Grandpa for an iPod for his birthday, he started crying because Grandpa didn't know what that was.

Two simple sentences (sentences with a single subject, a verb, and one complete thought):

a. _____

_____

Two kinds of compound sentence (two simple sentences connected with either a comma and a coordinating conjunction, a semicolon and an adverbial conjunction, or just a semicolon):

b. _____

_____

c. _____

_____

Complex sentence (an independent clause and a dependent clause connected using subordination):

d. _____

_____

2. Many people are opposed to gambling in all its forms, therefore, they will not even buy a lottery ticket.

Two simple sentences:

a. _____

_____

Two kinds of compound sentence:

b. _____

_____

c. _____

_____

Complex sentence:

d. _____

_____

3. Hockey may be Canada's national sport, the game can be quite brutal.

Two simple sentences:

a. _____

_____

Two kinds of compound sentence:

b. _____

_____

c. _____

_____

Complex sentence:

d. _____

_____

4. Many young people manage to travel, they find ways to do it cheaply.

Two simple sentences:

a. _____

_____

Two kinds of compound sentence:

b. _____

_____

c. _____

_____

Complex sentence:

d. _____

_____

5. The need for a proper diet is important in any health program, however, all the junk food on the grocery shelves makes it hard to be consistent.

Two simple sentences:

a. _____

_____

Two kinds of compound sentence:

b. _____

_____

c. _____

_____

Complex sentence:

d. _____

_____

 Practice 2 Correcting Run-Ons

Each of the following examples is a run-on. Supply four possible ways to revise each one. Check your answers against those in the Answer Key on page 457. Refer to the guide on page 91 if you need help.

1. The airline has begun its new route to the islands everyone is looking forward to flying there.

   Two simple sentences:

   a. _____

   _____

   Two kinds of compound sentence:

   b. _____

   _____

   c. _____

   _____

   Complex sentence:

   d. _____

   _____

2. The movie begins at nine o'clock, therefore, let's have dinner before the show. Two simple sentences:

   a. _____

   _____

   Two kinds of compound sentence:

   b. _____

   _____

   c. _____

   _____

Complex sentence:

d. _____

_____

3. The studio audience screamed at the contestant, after all, they wanted her to try for the big prize.

Two simple sentences:

a. _____

_____

Two kinds of compound sentence:

b. _____

_____

c. _____

_____

Complex sentence:

d. _____

_____

4. Maya needs new shoes, she is running in the marathon.

Two simple sentences:

a. _____

_____

Two kinds of compound sentence:

b. _____

_____

c. _____

_____

Complex sentence:

d. _____

_____

5. My actor friend grabbed my arm, she wanted to tell me about her new part in the movie.

Two simple sentences:

a. _____

_____

Two kinds of compound sentence:

b. _____

_____

c. _____

_____

Complex sentence:

d. _____

_____

Practice 3 Editing for Run-Ons

Rewrite the following paragraph, correcting the run-on sentences using any of the methods you have learned. Check your answers against those in the Answer Key on page 457. (The Answer Key will give you one possible answer, but there are many ways of revising this passage.)

Mythology is the study of myths and myths are known as the oldest form of literature and the oldest myths are creation myths. Cultures from around the world have their own creation myths all of them are amazingly similar despite the vast geographical distances between these cultures and the fact that there are no known ways in which communication could have taken place between certain ones. Details of these myths change from one culture to the next, however, various themes of the myths remain the same. For example, although characters (most of the time, but not all of the time) take on new names from one culture to another, every culture refers to the existence of a creator, also the number of gods differs from one mythology to another, nevertheless, every mythology has at least one god or one heroic figure in it. All in all, myths are incredible stories that, in many cases, have lasted thousands of years no matter where they come from and what they are about, they bear striking similarities from one culture to another, and they all share a wisdom about something that never changes: our human nature.

Practice 4 Editing for Run-Ons

Rewrite the following paragraph, correcting the run-on sentences using any of the methods you have learned. Check your answers against those in the Answer

Key on page 457. (The Answer Key will give you one possible answer, but there are many ways of revising this passage.)

Sigmund Freud and Carl G. Jung were both psychiatrists, they have had a great deal of influence on the study of psychology to this day, for example, each was famous for his own model of the human psyche. In Freud's model, there are three main parts, they are the ego, the id, and the superego. In Jung's model, there are also three main parts, they are the conscious, the personal unconscious, and the collective unconscious. Freud (Jung's teacher and subsequent collaborator until they parted due to a major disagreement in 1912) and Jung both believed that dreams come from the unconscious part of our psyche (for Freud, this meant the id and superego), nevertheless, they disagreed a great deal in the area of dream interpretation.

Chapter Review Exercises

Exercise 1 Editing for Run-Ons

Rewrite the following paragraph, correcting all run-on sentences. There is more than one correct answer.

Commercial farming in Atlantic Canada is concentrated in the dairy, poultry, and horticultural sectors, the most important crop in the region, particularly in New Brunswick and Prince Edward Island, is potatoes. In Ontario and Quebec, farming is highly diversified and includes specialty crops such as soybeans, tobacco, fruit, and vegetables. In the Prairie region, most of the country's wheat, oats, barley, rye, flaxseed, canola, mustard, and sunflowers are grown livestock raising is also very important in Canada with the majority of ranches being located in the three prairie provinces.

Exercise 2 Editing for Run-Ons

Rewrite the following paragraph, correcting all run-on sentences. There is more than one correct answer.

Although the metric system was legalized in Canada in 1871, the British Imperial system of units, based on yards, pounds, gallons, etc., continued to be used until the 1960s, with rapidly expanding technology and worldwide trade, the need for an international measurement system became apparent. Britain decided to convert to the system the United States was studying a similar move. A number of Canadian businesses favoured the metric system in January 1970 the government passed legislation stating that a single, coherent measurement system based on metric units should be used for measurement purposes in this country.

Exercise 3 **Editing for Run-Ons**

Rewrite each of the following run-ons in two different ways using the different methods you have learned. There is more than one possible answer for each example.

1. I had to buy a new DVD, I gave my only copy to my brother.
2. I'm taking guitar lessons, four of us want to start a band.
3. It was hot outside, I wanted to get some exercise.
4. The storm came on suddenly, we were lost.
5. There were no right answers to the questions, we tried to answer them.
6. He is a politician, he serves his community well.
7. Where is Kanata, I think it's near Ottawa.
8. When did Canada last win the World Junior Hockey Championships, I think it was a long time ago.
9. Our tour was interesting, four of us became lost in Edmonton.
10. We tried our hardest, the exam was too difficult.

 Exercise 4 **Editing for Run-Ons**

Rewrite any run-ons below in at least two ways using any of the different methods you have learned. If a sentence is already correct, write C beside it.

1. The right answer was not at the end of the chapter, it was at the beginning of the next one.
2. I was late for school, however, the teacher wasn't in class today.
3. The pizza was cold, then again, it was still good.
4. At the edge of the table, the marble slowed down and began to roll the other way.
5. The time was right, it was now or never.
6. Listening to the radio at dawn, I found myself singing the words to every song.
7. My teacher is dedicated to her profession, furthermore, she's the best teacher I've ever had.

 Working Together: Operation "Plot without Run-Ons"

Choose a movie or book you have seen or read recently, and retell the plot. In about twenty minutes, write as much of the story as you can remember. (Be careful to write only on every other line, separating words clearly, and write neatly so your classmates can read what you have written.) Exchange papers and read the paper you receive in order to check for run-ons. If you find what you believe to be a run-on, put a mark beside that sentence, and be ready to read the sentence, or put it on the board for class discussion.

Chapter 8 **Parallel Structure**

Quick Quiz Test yourself on your knowledge of parallel structure. In each of the sentences below, the underlined portion is not parallel with the rest of the sentence. Revise these underlined groups of words as needed to make the sentences parallel. Answers are upside down in the margin.

1. While the men go out in their boats, the women and children stay in camp, cook meals, and <u>to take care of the dog teams.</u>

2. The weather on the East Coast is often wet, windy, and <u>the temperatures are low.</u>

3. His office is without windows, on the fourth floor, and <u>you have to go down a dark hallway to get there.</u>

4. Carmelita does her work quickly, accurately, and <u>with cheerfulness.</u>

5. The mayor promised lower taxes, less crime, and <u>the number of jobs would be higher.</u>

Answers:
1. take care of the dog teams
2. cold
3. down a dark hallway
4. cheerfully
5. more jobs

What Is Parallel Structure?

> **DEFINITION**
>
> **Parallel structure** is balance in a sentence that contains a list. The list might consist of words, phrases, or clauses. Balance occurs when all the items in the list are in the same grammatical form: all nouns, all adjectives, and so on.
> **Example: Parallel:** She went out with him because of the twinkle in his eye, the swagger in his step, and his love for movies.
> **Unparallel:** She went out with him because of the twinkle in his eye, swaggering, and he loves movies.

In the first sentence above, at the heart of each of the three items in the list is a noun: *twinkle*, *swagger*, and *love*. They are all nouns (with modifiers), so the sentence is parallel.

In the second sentence, the first item is still a noun, the *twinkle* in his eye; the second item is a verbal (a gerund), *swaggering*; and the third item is an independent clause starting with the pronoun *he* (which refers back to the man being talked about rather than the qualities he possesses). These grammatical forms are all different. This sentence, therefore, is not parallel.

Which of the following sentences is better balanced?

> Her favourite pastimes are reading novels, listening to jazz, and to go to films.

> Her favourite pastimes are reading novels, listening to jazz, and going to films.

If you selected the second sentence, you made the right choice. The second sentence uses parallel structure (all three items in the list begin with *-ing* words (gerunds): *reading, listening,* and *going*). By giving each first word of the items in the list the same *-ing* structure, you make the sentence easier to understand and more pleasant to read. Any list of words, phrases, and even clauses should be parallel.

RULE 1

Words in a list should be the same part of speech.

> ***Incorrect:*** The town was small, quiet, and the atmosphere was peaceful.

(The list is composed of two adjectives and one clause.)

> ***Correct:*** The town was small, quiet, and peaceful.
> (*Small, quiet,* and *peaceful* are all adjectives.)

RULE 2

Phrases in a list should be the same kind of phrase (infinitive phrases, prepositional phrases, verb phrases, noun phrases, participial phrases).

> ***Incorrect:*** Her lost assignment is in her closet, on the floor, and the clothes are hiding it.

(two prepositional phrases and one clause)

> ***Correct:*** Her lost assignment is in her closet, on the floor, and under a pile of clothes.

(three prepositional phrases beginning with *in, on,* and *under*)

RULE 3

Clauses in a list should be parallel.

> ***Incorrect:*** One clerk polished the antique spoons; they were placed into the display case by the other clerk.

> ***Correct:*** One clerk polished the antique spoons; the other clerk placed them in the display case.

Practice 1 Making Sentences Parallel

Each of the following sentences has an underlined word, phrase, or clause that is not parallel. Make the underlined section parallel. There may be more than one correct answer for each sentence. Check your answers against those in the Answer Key on page 458.

1. My favourite armchair is lumpy, worn out, and <u>has dirt spots everywhere.</u>

   _____

   _____

2. She enjoys reading novels, studying the flute, and also <u>sews her own clothes.</u>

   _____

   _____

3. He admires teachers who make the classroom an exciting place and <u>willingly explaining material more than once.</u>

   _____

   _____

Practice 2 Making Sentences Parallel

The following sentences all lack parallel structure. In each one, underline the word, phrase, or clause that is not parallel with the other items in the pair or series and revise it so that the sentence is balanced. An example has been done for you. There may be more than one correct answer for each sentence. Check your answers against those in the Answer Key on page 458.

Incorrect: The best leather comes from Italy, from Spain, and is imported from Brazil.

Correct: The best leather comes from Italy, from Spain, and from Brazil.

or: The best leather comes from Italy, Spain, and Brazil.

1. Winter in Edmonton is very windy and has many bitterly cold days.

   _____

   _____

2. I would prefer to fix an old car than watching television.

   _____

   _____

3. Alex is a talented athlete, a top student, and even generous to her friends.

   _____

   _____

4. The apartment is crowded and without light.

   _____

   _____

5. The dancer is slender and moves gracefully.

   _____

   _____

6. The trees were tall and had a lot of leaves.

   _____

   _____

7. My friend loves to play chess, to read science fiction, and working out at the gym.

   _____

   _____

 Practice 3 Making Sentences Parallel

Each of the following sentences lacks parallel structure. Underline the word, phrase, or clause that is not parallel, and revise it so that its structure balances with the other items in the pair or series. There may be more than one correct answer for each sentence. Check your answers against those in the Answer Key on page 458.

1. The dog had to choose between jumping over the fence, or he could have dug a hole underneath it.

   _____

   _____

2. She was great at swimming, canoeing, and as a rock climber.

   _____

   _____

3. As I looked down the city street, I could see the soft lights from restaurant windows, I could hear the mellow sounds of a nightclub band, and carefree moods of people walking by.

   _____

   _____

4. The singers have been on several road tours, have recorded for two record companies, and they would also like to make a movie someday.

   _____

   _____

5. They would rather order a pizza than eating homemade cooking.

_____

_____

6. I explained to the teacher that my car had broken down, my books had been stolen, and I left my assignment pad at home.

_____

_____

7. That night the prisoner was sick, discouraged, and filled with loneliness.

_____

_____

To help you with the chapter review exercises, here is a reminder of all the rules for parallel structure. (For further explanation of these rules, refer back to page 100.)

RULE 1

Words in a list should be the same part of speech.

RULE 2

Phrases in a list should be the same kind of phrase (infinitive phrases, prepositional phrases, verb phrases, noun phrases, participial phrases).

RULE 3

Clauses in a list should be parallel.

Chapter Review Exercises

Exercise 1 Making Sentences Parallel

Each of the following sentences has a part that does not work with the rest of the sentence; therefore, the sentences lack parallel structure. Find the errors and correct them. There may be more than one correct answer for each sentence.

1. Now that he was retired, he started tending to his garden, drank his latte at his favourite café every day, and a new book project was something he was eager to launch.

_____

_____

2. The dancer was used to eating her banana, stretching for an hour, and then rehearsal for the next performance kept her busy for the rest of the day.

_____

_____

3. The car wasn't in the garage, nobody could find it on the street, and we found out the police hadn't towed it.

_____

_____

4. After volunteering at a senior's residence, doing his chores for his parents, and once his homework was finished, he had no time left for his girlfriend.

_____

_____

5. He had to put salt on the ice, food in the dog's dish, and he had to make sure that the driveway was shovelled.

_____

_____

 Exercise 2   Making Sentences Parallel

Revise each sentence below to make it parallel. There may be more than one correct answer for each sentence.

1. Most of the neighbours are friendly, considerate, and they give help.

_____

_____

2. She is charming and has beauty.

_____

_____

3. I enjoy reading, writing, and to conduct laboratory experiments.

_____

_____

4. Either going for a ride or to lie in the sun is my idea of a good time.

_____

_____

5. She got a new job with a higher salary, increased benefits, and she also works fewer hours than before.

_____

_____

Working Together: Practise Making Sentences Parallel

Read the following paragraph. Look for places that lack parallel structure, then write a corrected version of the paragraph. When you're finished, check your answers with another student in the group or class, preferably someone with whom you would not normally sit.

I've had several great summer jobs. They include desk clerk for a student residence, cashier for a busy convenience store, and I even worked as an assistant janitor in an elementary school where my boss and I had some of the best conversations I've ever had. The best summer job, however, was organizing the Miss Glace Bay Pageant. The titillation factor associated with a beauty competition was certainly one reason. Other reasons for enjoying the job included auditioning talent for the entertainment component, I wrote the script for the emcee, and meeting a young woman among the contestants whom I'd already met six months earlier. First, because I love music, having a say as to who performed on the big evening was exciting beyond description. Second, I've always enjoyed writing. And writing what the emcee would say that evening gave me experience with a kind of writing I'd never tried before. But most important, when I saw Sherry with her long golden hair among the contestants on the first day of rehearsals, I knew this second meeting was no coincidence. And about a week later when she sat down next to me, laid her head on my shoulder, and "Hello, there," was whispered into my ear, I knew we'd be dating before too long. She didn't win the pageant, but she definitely won my heart. I'd had some great summer jobs, but organizing the pageant was the one that etched that summer onto the wall of my memory storehouse forever.

Chapter 9 Pronouns

Quick Quiz Test yourself on your knowledge of pronouns. In each of the following sentences, choose the correct pronouns. Answers are upside down beside the quiz.

1. Between you and (me, I), the reason I can't go is that I lost my ticket.

2. The girl I'm dating is taller than (I, me).

3. (We, Us) students are going to Cancun for the spring break.

4. Would you spare some change for my son and (I, me)?

5. (Him, He) and (me, I) spent lots of money on the weekend.

Answers:
1. me
2. I
3. We
4. me
5. He, I

A discussion of pronouns never fails to be interesting because of the potential controversy surrounding usage. Even well-educated people disagree sometimes on what is acceptable. Those who tend to support a particular usage, even if it's not grammatically correct will argue that it's acceptable because that's what they hear everyone else saying. But what everyone seems to be saying is not always correct, and what is not correct, is still unacceptable in most situations. In the final analysis, the more correct grammar you know, the safer you'll be.

Most people acquainted with a basic knowledge of English grammar know, for example, that it is improper to say, "Me and him are going downtown." But not everyone knows that it is also improper to say, "Between you and I . . ." (the correct usage is "Between you and me . . ."). Some English instructors accept "Everyone has their own way of doing things," while fewer instructors accept "To who should I give this book?" In any event, this text is still partial to the correct way. If there is widespread movement toward acceptance of certain pronoun usage that was once and might still be considered incorrect, you might simply have to make a personal decision. But don't do this before considering the rules of grammar.

DEFINITION

A **pronoun** is a word that replaces a noun (person, place, or thing).

Examples: The boy came across his lucky charm quite unexpectedly.

He came across *it* quite unexpectedly.

Note: *He* replaces *the boy*, and *it* replaces *his lucky charm*.

DEFINITION

A **personal pronoun** is a pronoun that refers to the person speaking (*I, me, we, us*), the person spoken to (*you*), or the person(s) spoken about (*he, she, it, they, him, her, them*).

Pronouns and Case

RULE

The case of a personal pronoun is determined by the function it serves in a sentence. Pronouns can function as subjects, as objects, or as indicators of ownership (possessive case).

Guide to Pronoun Case

Pronouns Used as Subjects (Subjective Case)	Pronouns Used as Objects (Objective Case)	Pronouns Used as Possessives (Possessives Case)	Possessive Adjectives
I	me	mine	my
you (sing.)	you (sing.)	yours	your
he	him	his	his
she	her	hers	her
it	it	its	its
who	whom	whose	whose
whoever	whomever	whosever	
we	us	ours	our
you (pl.)	you (pl.)	yours	your
they	them	theirs	their

Use the guide to choose the correct answers in the following examples:

1. (She, Her) is singing at the concert tonight.
2. He bought those tickets for Jan and (I, me).

TIP

When you have a compound subject or object (one with two nouns), it is easier to pick the correct pronoun if you read the sentence leaving out one of the subjects.

Example: He bought those tickets for (I, me).

(The correct answer to sentence 2 above is more obvious now: *me*.)

3. He sold (us, we) the best seats in the house.
4. To (who, whom) should I address the letter?
5. Her voice is much stronger than (he, him, his).

TIP

In a comparison, it is easier to pick the correct pronoun if you complete the comparison.

Example: Her voice is much stronger than (he, him, his) voice is.

(The correct answer to sentence 5 above is more obvious now: *his*.**)**

6. (Who, Whom, Whose) music was left on the piano?
7. She is dating a man who is shorter than (she, her) is.

DEFINITION

Possessive adjectives, technically speaking, are not pronouns; they do not replace nouns. They are adjectives because they modify nouns. But both the possessive adjective and the noun it modifies can be replaced by a possessive pronoun.

Example: He returned *my* book.

He returned *mine*.

The word *my* is a possessive adjective. The word *mine* in the second sentence is a possessive pronoun (see the chart "Guide to Pronoun Case" on page 107).

Who vs. Whom

Who is the subjective form; *whom* is the objective form. Use *who* whenever *he, she, they, I*, or *we* could replace *who*. Likewise, use *whom* when *him, her, them, me*, or *us* could replace *whom*. (You might need to mentally rearrange the word order as shown in parentheses after the following examples):

1. To *whom* were you talking? (Were you talking to *him*?)

TIP

Keep in mind the rule that the subject of the sentence is not ever part of a prepositional phrase.

In sentence 1 above, *to* is a preposition (see pages 7–8). So the objective form of *who*, which is *whom*, must be used after it.

However, the following two examples show the exception to the rule.

2. I get angry when I have to listen to people who talk on cell phones in a movie theatre. (*People* talk on cell phones.)
3. The matter of *who* should pay was not decided. (*He or she* should pay.)

The rule that a subject never follows a preposition is broken in sentences 2 and 3 because the word *who*, on the one hand, is the object of a preposition, but is also a subject (the doer of an action). **Choose the *subjective* form of the relative pronoun (*who* or *whoever*) when it is both an object and a subject in a sentence.**

Exercise 1 Choosing Correct Pronoun Forms

Circle the correct pronoun in each of the sentences below.

1. Matthew and (she, her) presented the project today.
2. Between you and (I, me), I think it was outstanding.
3. Their visual materials will help (whoever, whomever) will study the project later.
4. He is usually a better speaker than (she, her).
5. (Whoever, Whomever) heard them agreed that it was an impressive presentation.

6. (Who, Whom) do you think made the best points?
7. I am not as deeply involved in my project as (they, them).
8. Their research was much more detailed than (us, our, ours).
9. The professor gave both Carolyn and (he, him) A's.
10. My partner and (I, me) will have to work harder to reach this standard.

 Exercise 2 Choosing Correct Pronoun Forms

Circle the correct pronouns to complete the following paragraph.

When my mother and (I, me) decided to care for my very ill father at home, some of our friends objected. My sister and (they, them) said we would be exhausted and unable to handle the stress. To (who, whom) could we go for help in the middle of the night? My father, (who, whom) we believed would be happier at home, had been our first consideration. Of course, we would have benefited if my mother or (I, me) had been a nurse. However, we did have a visiting nurse available at times. We were more confident than (they, them) that we could handle the situation.

Pronoun-Antecedent Agreement

> **RULE**
>
> **A pronoun must agree in number (singular or plural) and in gender (masculine, feminine, or neutral) with any other word to which it refers.**

> **DEFINITION**
>
> The word to which the pronoun refers is known as the **antecedent** of the pronoun. Most errors in pronoun number agreement occur when a plural pronoun is used to refer to a singular noun, and vice versa.
>
> **Incorrect:** The school has their own way of doing things.
>
> **Correct:** The *school* has *its* own way of doing things.

The *antecedent* in the sentence above is *school*. Because *school* is singular and neutral (neither masculine nor feminine), use *its* as the pronoun that refers back to it.

The following sentences contain pronoun-antecedent disagreement in **number**—in both cases, the pronoun is plural, while its antecedent is singular:

> The *company* changed *their* name last month.
> *Everyone* worked on *their* final draft.

In the first sentence, the antecedent *company* is singular in number and neutral in gender. Therefore, the pronoun (or possessive adjective) referring back to it must be singular and neutral as well. Here is the corrected version:

> The company changed its name last month.

(The possessive adjective *its* is both singular and neutral. Notice there is no apostrophe in a possessive adjective.)

The problem in the second sentence is that *everyone* is a singular word (even though it refers to many people—see the discussion of **indefinite pronouns** below), but *their* is a plural pronoun. You may often have heard people use the plural pronoun *their* to refer to a singular subject. In fact, the second sentence above may sound correct, especially when it is heard during casual conversation, but it is still a mistake in formal writing. Here are two approaches a writer might take to correct this sentence:

> Everyone worked on *his* final draft.

This approach is currently unpopular because it is widely considered a sexist construction.

> Everyone worked on *his* or *her* final draft.

This form is technically correct, but if it is used several times, it sounds awkward and repetitious.

The best solution for this kind of construction is often to revise it so that the antecedent is plural:

> All the students worked on *their* final drafts.

Everyone is an **indefinite** pronoun. It may look plural, but actually, it is singular. For more on indefinite pronouns, see pages 46–47 in Chapter 4 (pages 46–47): "Subject-Verb Agreement."

Many other indefinite pronouns are singular, too (any pronoun with *-one*, *-body*, or *-thing* in it).

Indefinite Pronouns That Are Singular				
-one	everyone	someone	anyone	no one
-body	everybody	somebody	anybody	nobody
-thing	everything	something	anything	nothing
	each	another	either	neither

Another problem with pronoun-antecedent agreement in number occurs when a **demonstrative** pronoun (*this, that, these, those*) is used with a noun (such as *kind* or *type*). A demonstrative used this way is technically an adjective, although some will still call it a pronoun when it is used alone in a sentences such as "*This* is what I am talking about." The demonstrative must agree with the noun it modifies.

Singular: this, that

> **Incorrect:** *These kind* of shoes hurt my feet.
> **Correct:** *This kind* of shoe hurts my feet.

Plural: these, those

> **Incorrect:** *Those type* of cars always need oil.
> **Correct:** *Those types* of cars always need oil.

Exercise 1   Pronoun-Antecedent Agreement in Number

Rewrite each of the following sentences so that the pronoun agrees with its antecedent in number.

1. Everybody should believe they have choices.

    _____

    _____

2. Each of the children brought their own toys.

    _____

    _____

3. There was no one who invited us to their homes.

    _____

    _____

4. If the bird-watchers hope to see anything, one must get up early.

    _____

    _____

5. The association sent a memo to all their members about the special meeting.

    _____

    _____

6. Please pass the tissues; those kind of movies make me cry.

    _____

    _____

7. These type of shoes are "so yesterday."

    _____

    _____

 RULE 2

Pronouns must also agree with their antecedents in person.

"Person" refers to the doer of the action—first person (*I*); second person (*you*); third person (for example, *he, she, it* in the singular; *they,* among others, in the plural). First-person pronouns highlight the writer and are suitable for personal writing. Second-person pronouns focus on the reader and are useful for giving instructions. Third-person pronouns emphasize the topic of the text and are useful in professional and academic writing.

The following **incorrect** sentence contains a pronoun-antecedent disagreement in **person:**

> When mountain climbing, *one* must maintain *your* concentration at all times.

The sentence could be correctly rewritten in a variety of ways, including the following:

> When mountain climbing, *one* must maintain *one's* concentration at all times.
>
> When mountain climbing, *you* must maintain *your* concentration at all times.
>
> When mountain climbing, *I* must maintain *my* concentration at all times.
>
> When mountain climbing, *we* must maintain *our* concentration at all times.

 Exercise 2 **Pronoun-Antecedent Agreement in Person**

Rewrite each of the following sentences so that the pronoun agrees with its antecedent in person.

1. I enjoy math exams because you can show what you know.

   _____

   _____

2. When people take geometry, you discover that frequent review of past assignments helps make the course seem easy.

   _____

   _____

3. People always need to practise your skills in order not to forget them.

   _____

   _____

4. When you study for exams, one should not watch television at the same time.

   _____

   _____

5. Math is a subject we often neglect in school, but later you use it all the time.

   _____

   _____

Missing, Ambiguous, or Repetitious Pronouns

RULE

The antecedent of a pronoun should not be missing, ambiguous, or repetitious.

The following is a sentence with a missing antecedent:

Missing antecedent: In British Columbia, *they* have many challenging hiking trails.

Possible revision: British Columbia has many challenging hiking trails.

In the first sentence, who is meant by *they*? If the context has not told us that *they* refers to government departments or to tourist companies, for instance, then the antecedent is missing. The sentence should be rewritten in order to avoid *they*.

In the next sentence, the antecedent is ambiguous.

Ambiguous antecedent: Margaret told Lin that *she* needed to earn $1000 during the summer.

Possible revision: Margaret said that Lin needed to earn $1 000 during the summer.

In the first example, *she* could refer to either Margaret or Lin. The sentence should be revised in a way that avoids this confusion.

The next example illustrates a repetitious antecedent.

Repetitious pronoun and antecedent: The newspaper article, *it* said that Earth Day, 1993, re-established humankind's commitment to the earth.

Possible revision: The newspaper article said that Earth Day, 1993, re-established humankind's commitment to the earth.

The subject should be either *article* or, if there is already an antecedent, *it*. Using both the noun and the pronoun results in needless repetition.

 Exercise Sentences with Proper Antecedents

Each of the following sentences features a missing, ambiguous, or repetitious antecedent. Revise the sentences as necessary to correct their use of pronouns. There may be more than one correct answer for each sentence.

1. The biologist asked the director to bring back his microscope.

   _____

   _____

2. In the report, it says that the number of science and engineering students seeking doctoral degrees has fallen considerably since the mid-sixties.

_____

_____

3. At the laboratory, they said the research had run into serious difficulties.

_____

_____

4. The testing equipment was accidentally dropped into the aquarium, and it was badly damaged.

_____

_____

5. You can't believe anything they say in that newspaper.

_____

_____

Chapter Review Exercises

Practice **Making Pronouns and Antecedents Agree**

Each of the following sentences contains an error in pronoun use. Revise each sentence so that all pronouns agree with their antecedents and there are no missing or ambiguous antecedents. There may be more than one correct answer for each sentence. Check your answers against those in the Answer Key on page 458.

1. His father mailed him his high school yearbook.

_____

_____

2. No one wants their income reduced.

_____

_____

3. When a company fails to update its equipment, they often pay a price in the long run.

_____

_____

4. The graduate today has many more options open to them than ever before.

_____

_____

5. Everybody knows their own strengths best.

_____

_____

6. Each of the soccer players put effort into their game.

_____

_____

7. If the campers want to eat quickly, each one should help themselves.

_____

_____

 Exercise   Making Pronouns and Antecedents Agree

Read the following sentences carefully, watching for errors with pronouns. Revise the sentences as necessary so that pronouns agree with their antecedents and there are no missing or ambiguous antecedents. There may be more than one correct answer for each sentence. If a sentence is correct, simply write *C*.

1. The manager told Karen she was responsible for the mix-up in orders.

_____

_____

2. The county submitted their proposal for the bridge repairs.

_____

_____

3. We all rushed away from all the trees to our cars because you had to wait for the thunderstorm to stop.

_____

_____

4. A young person does not receive enough advice on how they should choose their career.

_____

_____

5. These type of watches are very popular.

_____

_____

6. People were taken forcibly from our homes.

_____

_____

7. No one ate their lunch in the cafeteria.

_____

_____

Working Together: Practise with Pronouns

Pair up with someone else in the class, preferably someone with whom you do not normally sit. Together, come up with ten sentences, each with at least three pronouns in it (including possessive adjectives). Each of the three pronouns should be in a different case: subjective, objective, and possessive. Come up with at least one sentence that is of a type that often has incorrect pronoun-antecedent agreement, and at least one where there is potential for pronoun ambiguity. Between the two of you, make sure all pronouns are correct. If you disagree on any, give the other student an explanation as to why you think yours is correct. Here is an example of a sentence that complies:

Jacquie and **I** are faster than **they**, so **they** have to not only pay **our** way to the festival, but also give **us** spending money once **we**'re there.

I, they, they, we: subjective case

our: possessive adjective

us: objective case

Chapter 10 Modifiers: Misplaced and Dangling

Quick Quiz Test your knowledge of dangling and misplaced modifiers by selecting the correct sentence in each pair below. Answers are upside down in the margin.

1. a. Sweeping the dust in the attic, the dead bugs numbered in the thousands.
   b. Sweeping the dust in the attic, I noticed that the dead bugs numbered in the thousands.

2. a. Reduce speed when wet.
   b. Reduce speed when roads are wet.

3. a. While shaving in the bathroom, Grant accidentally cut his ear with his razor.
   b. While shaving in the bathroom, the razor cut Grant's ear.

4. a. To make a good impression on your employer, ensure you have a neat and clean appearance.
   b. To make a good impression on your employer, a neat and clean appearance is advisable.

5. a. Though old and shoddy, Uncle Jake made the room in the back of the house look new again.
   b. Though the room in the back of the house was old and shoddy, Uncle Jake made it look new again.

Answers:
1. b
2. b
3. a
4. a
5. b

What Are Modifiers?

> **DEFINITION**
>
> **Modifiers** are words or groups of words that function as adjectives or adverbs.
> **Example:** *Coming back from his vacation*, Tanya's father was eager to give his daughter the gift.
> The modifier *coming back from his vacation* describes Tanya's father.

Modifiers describe or modify other words in the sentence. If a modifier is put in the wrong place or in an ambiguous or awkward place in the sentence, the meaning will be unclear. If the modifier has no word at all to modify, the result might be confusing or even unintentionally humorous (as in #2a above).

> **RULE**
>
> **A modifier must be placed close to the word, phrase, or clause it modifies so that the reader can understand the intended meaning.**

This chapter shows how to solve two types of modifier problems—misplaced modifers and dangling modifiers—in order to make the intended meaning clear. Study the examples carefully. Once you are able to recognize these problems in the exercises that follow, you will begin to recognize them in your own writing as well.

What Are Misplaced Modifiers?

> **DEFINITION**
>
> **A misplaced modifier** is a modifier that is in a wrong, ambiguous, or awkward position in the sentence.
> **Examples:** *While eating his cat food*, Johnny stepped on his kitten's tail.
>   (Because of the location of the modifier [in italics], it looks like Johnny is eating cat food.)
>   *Scurrying around with long and hairy legs*, Sylvia tried to kill the spiders.
>   (Because of the location of the modifier [in italics], it looks like Sylvia is scurrying around with long and hairy legs.)

There are three types of misplaced modifiers.

1. The modifier in the wrong place

   Wrong: The salesperson sold the used car to the customer that needed extensive bodywork.

   Who or what needs bodywork—the car or the customer?

   Revised: The salesperson sold the customer the used car that needed extensive bodywork.

   The following was found in a personals ad:

   If you are tired of meeting the wrong people like me, please leave me a message.

Does this make sense? If the person who made up the ad is an example of "wrong people," why would anyone respond? Perhaps what the person meant was this:

> If you, like me, are tired of meeting the wrong people, please leave me a message.

Be especially careful to put each of the following words closest to the word, phrase, or clause it modifies.

Common Modifiers				
almost	exactly	just	nearly	scarcely
even	hardly	merely	only	simply

Notice how the meaning of each of the following sentences changes with the placement of the modifier *only*.

Only Charlene telephoned my brother yesterday.
Charlene *only* telephoned my brother yesterday.
Charlene telephoned *only* my brother yesterday.
Charlene telephoned my *only* brother yesterday.
Charlene telephoned my brother *only* yesterday.

2. The awkward modifier that interrupts the flow of the sentence

> **Awkward:** Cheryl planned to only call my sister.

The adverb *only* could be better placed so that it would not split the infinitive *to call*.

> **Revised:** Cheryl planned to call only my sister.

3. The "squinting modifier"—a modifier placed ambiguously so that it could describe a word or words on either side of it

> **Squinting:** Anyone who can write clearly should have a blog.

Is the meaning here that only people who write clearly should have blogs, or that anyone who can write at all should, clearly, have a blog?

> **Revised:** If you can write clearly, you should have a blog.

What Are Dangling Modifiers?

DEFINITION

A **dangling modifier** is a modifier in a sentence that has no word, phrase, or clause that the modifier can describe.
Example: Riding the bicycle, the countryside seemed different.

In the above example, it sounds like the countryside is riding the bicycle. *Riding the bicycle* is the dangling modifier. It has nothing in the sentence to modify.

> **Dangling:** Working on the engine of the car, the dog barked all afternoon.

Who worked on the engine? Was it the dog?

> *Revised:* Working on the engine of the car, I heard the dog barking all afternoon.
>
> or
>
> The dog barked all afternoon while I was working on the engine of the car.

Chapter Review Exercises

 Practice **Revising Misplaced or Dangling Modifiers**

Revise each sentence to correct a misplaced or dangling modifier. There can be more than one correct answer for each sentence. Check your answers against those in the Answer Key on page 459.

1. Victor fed the dog wearing his tuxedo.

    _____

    _____

2. Visiting the Vancouver Aquarium, the otters entertained us.

    _____

    _____

3. The toddler that ate her breakfast cheerily started singing.

    _____

    _____

4. A band was playing in the park that we had heard earlier.

    _____

    _____

5. After running over the hill, the farm was visible in the valley below.

    _____

    _____

6. The truck caused a traffic jam, which was broken down on the highway, for kilometres.

    _____

    _____

7. Hanging from the ceiling in my bedroom, I saw three spiders.

    _____

    _____

Exercise   Revising Misplaced or Dangling Modifiers

Revise each sentence so there is no misplaced or dangling modifier. There may be more than one correct answer for each sentence.

1. Leaping upstream, we fished most of the day for salmon.

   _____

   _____

2. At the age of ten, my family took a trip to Fredericton.

   _____

   _____

3. Skimming every chapter, my biology textbook suddenly made more sense.

   _____

   _____

4. Waiting at the airport, every minute seemed endless.

   _____

   _____

5. Working extra hours last week, my salary increased dramatically.

   _____

   _____

6. We watched a movie in the theatre for which we had paid five dollars.

   _____

   _____

7. Dressed as Tinkerbell, he thought she looked charming.

   _____

   _____

 Working Together: Modifiers Making the Difference

Form groups of four or five. Look back at the list of common modifiers in the box on page 119. As a group, pick one modifier and create a sentence that includes it. Then move the modifier to as many different positions as possible while making sure the sentence still make sense. (See the example of five sentences using the modifier *only* below the box on page 119.) Then, figure out exactly what each sentence means based on the location of the modifier. Discuss what these changes in meaning suggest about the importance of word placement.

Chapter 11 **Punctuation**

Quick Quiz Test yourself on your knowledge of commas. In each of the following sentences, place commas wherever they should go. Answers are upside down beside the quiz.

1. White-collar criminals dishonest company executives are being exposed in growing numbers.

2. White-collar criminals are found in industrial plants government offices and banks.

3. For example manufacturers have been caught cheating the government and well-known banks have been caught laundering money.

4. In the past white-collar criminals have not been prosecuted very vigorously by the law.

5. However some executives are now being given jail sentences for their white-collar crimes.

Answers:
1. criminals, executives,
2. plants, offices, [second comma is optional]
3. example, government,
4. past,
5. However,

Correct Punctuation: A Strong Indicator of a Writer's Competence

Many people put commas in "where it feels right." Sometimes their feelings are absolutely correct, but sometimes they're not. Others use the dash when they are not quite sure what other punctuation mark to use instead. Like most aspects of writing, correct punctuation is a strong indicator of a writer's competence. Periods, commas, colons, semicolons, dashes, hyphens, quotation marks— all these tiny marks have incredible power over the meaning and ultimate effectiveness of the words and messages they accompany.

The Eight Basic Rules of the Comma

Many students feel very uncertain about when to use the comma. The starting point is to concentrate on a few basic rules. These rules will cover most of your needs.

The tendency now in English is to use fewer commas than in the past. There is no one perfect set of rules on which everyone agrees. However, if you learn the eight basic rules explained in this chapter, your common sense will help you figure out what to do in other cases. Remember that a comma usually signifies a pause in a sentence. As you read a sentence out loud, listen to where you pause. This is often your clue that a comma is needed. Notice that in each of the examples for the following eight rules, you can pause where the comma is placed.

RULE 1

Use a comma to separate parallel words, phrases, and clauses in a list.

> The sky was cloudy, grey, and ominous.
> I was dreaming of running in the race, finishing among the top ten, and collapsing happily on the ground.

With respect to Rule 1, note the following points:

- A list means more than two items.
- Some writers omit the comma before the *and* that introduces the last item.

> The sky was cloudy, grey and ominous.

- When an address or date occurs in a sentence, each part is treated as a separate item in a list. A comma follows each item even if there are only two items (as in the second example below):

> I lived at 14 Tartan Avenue, Halifax, Nova Scotia, for many years.
> He was born on August 17, 1980, on the same street where his father was born.

- A comma does not follow the last item in a list unless that last item is part of an address or a date.
- A group of adjectives may not be regarded as a list if some of the words "go together." You can test this by putting *and* between the items. If it doesn't work, then don't use commas.

> I carried my *torn, dusty* coat.
> In the yard was a *battered old maple* tree.
> I rode in his *new red sports* car.

Practice 1   Insert Necessary Commas

In each of the following sentences, insert commas wherever they are needed. Check your answers against those in the Answer Key on page 459.

1. Problems with the water supply of Canada the United States Europe and other parts of the world are growing.
2. Water is colourless tasteless odourless and free of calories.
3. You will use on an average day 90 L of water for flushing 120 L for bathing and washing clothes and 95 L for other uses.
4. It took 450 L of water to create the eggs you ate for breakfast 13 250 L to obtain the steak you might eat for dinner and over 200 000 L to produce the steel used to make your car.
5. The English-Wabigoon river system runs through Grand Narrows Ontario and had become polluted with mercury.

RULE 2

Use a comma before a coordinating conjunction that joins two independent clauses (complete thoughts). (See Chapter 5: "Coordination and Subordination.")

The house was on fire, but I was determined not to leave my place of safety.

The bees are dying, and one theory is that microwaves from cell phones are killing them.

With respect to Rule 2, note the following points:

- Be careful to use the comma before the conjunction only when you are combining independent clauses. If you are combining only words or phrases, no comma is used.

    The weather was hot and dry.
    He grabbed the ball and sent it flying.
    Larry was neither at third base nor at home plate.

- When clauses joined by a coordinating conjunction are short and closely connected, the comma is often omitted.

    Let's sit down and I'll dish out the food.

Practice 2 Insert Necessary Commas

In each of the following sentences, insert commas wherever they are needed. Check your answers against those in the Answer Key on page 459.

1. The most overused bodies of water are our rivers but they continue to serve us daily.
2. Canadian cities often developed next to rivers and industries followed soon after in the same locations.
3. The people of the industrial age can try to clean the water they use or they can watch pollution take over.
4. The Great Lakes are showing signs of renewal yet the struggle against pollution in them must continue.
5. Most people have not been educated about the dangerous state of our water supply nor are all our members of Parliament fully aware of the problem.

Use a comma to follow introductory material—words, expressions, phrases, or clauses that come before independent clauses (complete thoughts).

The following are examples of introductory material:

A. Introductory words (such as *yes, no, oh, well*)

> Oh, I never thought he would do it.

B. Introductory expressions (transitions such as *as a matter of fact, finally, secondly, furthermore, consequently*). A list of common transitions appears on the inside back cover of this book.

> Therefore, I will give you a second chance.

C. Introductory phrases. The comma signals the end of the introductory group of words and the beginning of the sentence proper.

> **Long prepositional phrase:** At the beginning of the course, I thought I would never be able to do the work.

> **Short prepositional phrases** don't generally need to be followed by a comma. However, a comma is often used if the phrase ends with a date.

> At night I like to watch the stars.
> In 2001, a moderate earthquake hit the West Coast.

> **Participial phrase:** Walking on tiptoe, the young mother quietly peeked into the nursery.

> **Verbal phrase:** By walking daily, I lost weight. (Gerund)
> Confident of her skills, she entered the contest. (Participle)
> To be honest, I don't like it. (Infinitive)

D. Introductory dependent clauses beginning with a subordinating conjunction (See Chapter 5: "Coordination and Subordination.")

> When the food arrived, we all grabbed for it.

Practice 3 **Insert Necessary Commas**

In each of the following sentences, insert commas wherever they are needed. Check your answers against those in the Answer Key on page 459.

1. A total solar eclipse when the moon's shadow blots out the sun completely is an outstanding cosmic event.
2. Once you see your first solar eclipse you start looking forward to the next one.
3. However witnessing this spectacle takes planning and the ability to travel to the best viewing spots.
4. In eastern Turkey on August 11 1999 a crowd of astronomers and "eclipse chasers" watched the last total eclipse of the millennium.
5. At the moment of totality people cheered clapped and even cried.

Note the following examples of Rule 4:

A. Interrupting word

> We will, however, take an X-ray.

B. Interrupting phrase

> **Prepositional phrase:** I wanted, of course, to stay.
> **Appositive phrase:** Ann, the girl with the red hair, has a wonderful sense of humour.

C. Interrupting clause

> He won't, I think, try that again.

Words, phrases, or clauses that interrupt the main idea of a sentence can be *restrictive* or *nonrestrictive*.

A **restrictive** word, phrase, or clause is essential to the meaning of the sentence and is not set off by commas from the rest of the sentence.

> The man with the red hat is my father.

The phrase *with the red hat* is essential in order to specifically identify the man with the red hat; otherwise, any number of unidentified men could be the father.

> Author Timothy Findley said it takes failure to become a great writer.

Likewise, the name *Timothy Findley* is essential to the meaning of the sentence above.

A **nonrestrictive** word, phrase, or clause is not essential to the meaning of the sentence, and is set off by commas from the rest of the sentence. (See more on nonrestrictive and restrictive clauses on pages 68–69 in Chapter 5: "Coordination and Subordination.")

> Ann, who has red hair, has a wonderful sense of humour.

> She came to the dance; however, she didn't stay long.

In the last sentence, *however* is used to combine independent clauses and therefore requires a semicolon before it.

> She did, however, have a good time.

In this sentence, *however* interrupts the main idea and therefore requires a comma before it and a comma after it (comma rule #4).

> **TIP**
> Some clauses can be used in different ways.

Ann, who has red hair, has a wonderful sense of humour.

In this sentence, *who has red hair* interrupts the main idea of the sentence. It is a **nonrestrictive clause**, so commas are used. The nonrestrictive clause is not essential to the meaning of the sentence.

The girl who has red hair is my sister Ann.

The clause *who has red hair* is used to identify "the girl." This **restrictive** clause does not interrupt the main idea but is necessary to and part of the main idea. Therefore, no commas are used.

Practice 4 Insert Necessary Commas

In each of the following sentences, insert commas wherever they are needed. Check your answers against those in the Answer Key on page 459.

1. Natural disasters I believe have not been historically significant.
2. They have however significantly affected the lives of many Canadians.
3. Canada's worst coal-mine disaster at Hillcrest, Alberta occurred on June 19 1914.
4. In Springhill, Nova Scotia furthermore 424 persons were killed in the mines between 1881 and 1969.
5. Avalanches, storms, and floods which are natural disasters have also made their marks on the face of our country.

> **RULE 5**
> Use commas to surround a noun in direct address.

Ali, can you help me with this problem?
I wonder, Michaela, if you really know what you're doing.

Practice 5 Insert Necessary Commas

In each of the following sentences, insert commas wherever they are needed. Check your answers against those in the Answer Key on page 459.

1. Honey I hope you're not planning to wear that hat.
2. I wonder Samir if the game has been cancelled.
3. Dad could I borrow five dollars?
4. Can you help me Doctor?
5. Ayesha is that you?

RULE 6

Use a comma in numbers of 1,000 or larger in some styles.

> 1,999
> 1,999,999,999

Note that in the metric system of measurement, spaces are used instead of commas, and numbers of four digits need not be separated. This practice is becoming more widespread in Canada.

> 4000 or 4 000
> 38 622

RULE 7

Use a comma to set off exact words spoken in dialogue.

> "The pen," she said, "is mightier than the sword."

The comma, as well as the period, is always placed **inside** the second quotation mark, as shown in the sentence above.

Practice 6   Insert Necessary Commas

In each of the following sentences, insert commas wherever they are necessary. Check your answers against those in the Answer Key on page 460.

1. "I'm innocent" he cried "of all charges against me."
2. He mumbled "I won't incriminate myself."
3. "I was told" the defendant explained "to answer every question."
4. "This court" the judge announced "will be adjourned."
5. "The jury" said Al Tarvin of *The Star* "was handpicked."

RULE 8

Use a comma where it is necessary to prevent a misunderstanding.

> Before eating, the cat prowled through the barn.

Practice 7   Insert Necessary Commas

In each of the following sentences, insert commas wherever they are needed. Check your answers against those in the Answer Key on page 460.

1. Kicking the child was carried off to bed.
2. To Maria Suzuki was the boss from hell.
3. When you can come and visit us.
4. Whoever that is is going to be surprised.
5. Skin cancer seldom kills doctors say.

Review this summary of the rules for comma usage. Then try the exercises that follow.

The Eight Basic Rules of the Comma
RULE 1: Use a comma to separate parallel words, phrases, and clauses in a list.
RULE 2: Use a comma before a coordinating conjunction that joins two independent clauses (complete thoughts). (See Chapter 5: "Coordination and Subordination.")
RULE 3: Use a comma to follow introductory words, expressions, phrases, or clauses that come before independent clauses (complete thoughts).
RULE 4: Use commas to surround words, phrases, or clauses whenever they interrupt the main idea.
RULE 5: Use commas to surround nouns in direct address.
RULE 6: Use a comma in numbers of 1,000 or larger in some styles (this practice is decreasing in Canada).
RULE 7: Use a comma to set off exact words spoken in dialogue.
RULE 8: Use a comma where it is necessary to prevent a misunderstanding.

 Exercise 1 Insert Necessary Commas

In each of the following sentences, insert commas wherever they are needed.

1. Fog-water collection is a relatively simple way to supply water to certain areas where water is scarce or polluted.
2. The collectors with screens made of a fine polypropylene mesh look like big volleyball nets.
3. Tiny water droplets which are blown sideways by the wind hit the screen and run down into a trough.
4. In El Tofo Chile 88 fog collectors supply clean water to the fishing village of Chungungo.
5. The El Tofo system on a high coastal ridge is the largest project so far.
6. Amazingly these collectors channel 13 000 litres of water per day to the village.
7. Once almost a ghost town Chungungo now boasts homes with running water and lush gardens.

 Exercise 2 Insert Necessary Commas

In each of the following sentences, insert commas wherever they are needed.

1. The first games known as the British Empire Games attracted 400 competitors from eleven countries.
2. The Commonwealth Games were first held in Hamilton Ontario in 1930.
3. By 1978 during the Commonwealth Games in Edmonton nearly 1500 athletes from 41 countries competed.
4. Canada has been a leading supporter of these games which are held every four years.
5. Memorable performances feats by both Canadian and non-Canadian athletes have become a hallmark of the games.

6. In Edmonton Canadian athletes won 45 gold 31 silver and 33 bronze medals in 1978.

7. Next to the Olympics the Commonwealth Games are one of the world's best international competitions.

Other Marks of Punctuation

The Apostrophe

The apostrophe has three uses:

1. Possession
2. Contraction
3. Avoiding confusion

RULE 1

To form the possessive, add 's or just an apostrophe.

With respect to Rule 1, note the following points and examples.

A. Add 's to singular nouns:

> the pen of the teacher = the teacher's pen
> the strategy of the boss = the boss's strategy

Be careful to choose the right noun to make possessive. Always ask yourself *who* or *what* possesses something. In the phrases above, the teacher possesses the pen and the boss possesses the strategy.

TIP

As a rule, nouns that are inanimate things should not be in the possessive. Use a phrase with *of* instead.

Examples: the leg of the table (NOT the table's leg)
the smell of the sewer (NOT the sewer's smell)
the noise of the cars (NOT the cars' noise)

In common expressions that refer to time and measurements and in phrases suggesting personification, possessives are generally acceptable:

> a stone's throw
> two weeks' vacation
> New Year's resolution
> winter's final blast

Note these unusual possessives:

Hyphenated words: mother-in-law's advice
Joint possession: Rita and Ashley's television special
Individual possession: John's and Steve's ideas

B. Add *'s* to irregular plural nouns that do not end in *-s.*

> the hats of the children = the children's hats
> the harness for the oxen = the oxen's harness

C. Add *'s* to indefinite pronouns:

> everyone's responsibility
> somebody's wallet

Indefinite Pronouns			
anyone	everyone	no one	someone
anybody	everybody	nobody	somebody
anything	everything	nothing	something

TIP

Possessive pronouns in English (*his, hers, its, ours, yours, theirs, whose*) do *not* use an apostrophe.

> *Whose* phone is this?
> The phone is *his.*
> The car is *theirs.*

D. Add only an apostrophe to regular plural nouns ending in *-s.*

> the nests of the hornets = the hornets' nests
> the store of the brothers = the brothers' store

TIP

A few singular nouns ending in the *s* or *z* sound are awkward-sounding if another *s* sound is added. You may, in these cases, drop the final *s.* Let your ear help you make the decision, and be consistent with your choice.

> Mr. Jones' car   *or*   Mr. Jones's car

RULE 2

To show where letters have been omitted in contractions, use an apostrophe.

> cannot = can't
> should not = shouldn't
> will not = won't (the only contraction that changes its spelling)
> I am = I'm
> she will = she'll
> it is/it has = it's

Note: The possessive adjective *its* (meaning "belonging to it") does not take an apostrophe.

> The dog buried its bone.

RULE 3

To form certain plurals in order to prevent confusion, use 's.

Numbers:	100's
Letters:	a's and b's
Years:	1800's or 1800s
Abbreviations:	Ph.D.'s
Words referred to in text:	He uses too many and's in his writing.

Do *not* use the apostrophe to form plurals in any situations other than these.
Here is a reminder of the uses and rules of the apostrophe:

The Three Rules of the Apostrophe

RULE 1: To form the possessive, add 's or just an apostrophe.

RULE 2: To show where letters have been omitted in contractions, use an apostrophe.

RULE 3: To form certain plurals in order to prevent confusion, use 's.

 Practice 1 Using the Apostrophe

Fill in each of the blanks below using the rules you have just studied for uses of the apostrophe. Check your answers against those in the Answer Key on page 460.

1. shirts for boys   _____ shirts

2. the house of them   _____ house

3. the bakery of Grandpa Moses   _____ bakery

4. the house of Antony and Maria

   (joint possession)   _____ house

5. the idea of nobody   _____ idea

6. The book belongs to him.   The book is _____ .

7. in the century of 1700   in the _____

8. It is their choice.   _____ their choice.

9. the nightlife of Vancouver   _____ nightlife

10. the dress of Wendy   _____ dress

 Practice 2 Using the Apostrophe

Fill in each of the blanks below using the rules you have just studied for uses of the apostrophe. Check your answers against those in the Answer Key on page 460.

1. the voice of Don Cherry   _____ voice

2. the flight of the geese   the _____ flight

3. the jackets of Carol and Tess

   (individual possession)   _____ jackets

4. the CD of somebody   _____ CD

5. The drums belong to her.   The drums are _____ .

6. the terrible year of two   the terrible _____

7. We cannot leave yet.   We _____ leave yet.

"I can't believe I went out with an apostrophe.
He was so possessive."

www.CartoonStock.com

Exercise **Using the Apostrophe**

Fill in each of the blanks below using the rules you have just studied for uses of the apostrophe.

1. the ice cream of Ben and Jerry   _____ ice cream

2. the spirit of the class   the _____ spirit

3. the centre for women   the _____ centre

4. the wish of everybody   _____ wish

5. The ideas belong to them.   The ideas are _____ .

6. The student mixes up *b* and *d*.   The student mixes up his

                                               _____ .

7. I will not leave this house.   I _____ leave this house.

8. the revenue of the company   the _____ revenue

9. the paw of the doggie   the _____ paw

10. the policies of Ridge School and

     Orchard School (individual possession)   _____ policies

Quotation Marks

Use quotation marks as follows:

RULE 1

Use quotation marks for a direct quotation (a speaker's exact words).

> "Please," he begged, "don't go away."

Do not use quotation marks for an indirect quotation (one person's idea put into someone else's words):

> He begged her to stay.

RULE 2

Use quotation marks for material copied word for word from a source.

> According to Statistics Canada, "Families or individuals spending 58.5 percent or more of their pre-tax income on food, clothing, and shelter are in financial difficulty."

RULE 3

Use quotation marks for titles of shorter works, such as short stories, one-act plays, poems, articles in magazines and newspapers, songs, essays, and chapters of books.

> "A Modest Proposal," an essay by Jonathan Swift, is a masterpiece of satire.
> Mavis Gallant wrote the short story "In Youth Is Pleasure" in 1975.

TIP

Titles of longer works, such as novels, full-length plays, and names of magazines or newspapers, are underlined when handwritten. In word-processed or published texts, these titles appear in italics: *Maclean's* magazine, *Country Living*.

RULE 4

Use quotation marks for words used in a special way.

> "Duckie" is a term of affection used by the British, the way Canadians would use the word "honey."

Here is a summary of rules for quotation mark usage:

The Four Basic Rules of Quotation Marks
RULE 1: Use quotation marks for a direct quotation.
RULE 2: Use quotation marks for material copied word for word from a source.
RULE 3: Use quotation marks for titles of shorter works, such as short stories, one-act plays, poems, articles in magazines and newspapers, songs, essays, and chapters of books.
RULE 4: Use quotation marks for words used in a special way.

Practice 1 Insert Necessary Quotation Marks

In each of the following sentences, insert quotation marks wherever they are needed. Check your answers against those in the Answer Key on page 460.

1. The Hot House is one of the stories contained in Rosemary Sullivan's *More Stories by Canadian Women*.
2. Nellie McClung said I'll never believe I'm dead until I see it in the papers.
3. The prime minister told his caucus that they would have to settle the problem in the next few days.
4. To diss is a slang term meaning to show disrespect.
5. She read the article Whiz Kids in *The Review*.

If the above five sentences were handwritten, which words would have to be underlined?

The Semicolon

Use the semicolon as follows:

> **RULE 1**
>
> **Use a semicolon to join two independent clauses (or complete thoughts) whose ideas and sentence structures are related.**

He decided to consult the map; she decided to ask the next pedestrian she saw.

> **RULE 2**
>
> **Use a semicolon to combine two sentences using an adverbial conjunction.**

He decided to consult the map; however, she decided to ask the next pedestrian she saw.

> **RULE 3**
>
> **Use a semicolon to separate items in a list when the items themselves contain commas.**

I had lunch with Linda, my best friend; Mrs. Zhangi, my English teacher; and Jan, my sister-in-law.

Notice in the last example that if only commas had been used, the reader might think six people had gone to lunch.

Practice 2 Using Semicolons

In each of the following sentences, insert a semicolon wherever one is needed. Check your answers against those in the Answer Key on page 460.

1. One of the best ways to remember a vacation is to take numerous photos one of the best ways to recall the contents of a book is to take notes.
2. The problem of street crime must be solved, otherwise, the number of vigilantes will increase.

3. The meal was composed of bruschetta, an appetizer, roast duck, the house specialty, and lemon mousse, a tart dessert.
4. The bank president was very cordial, however, he would not approve the loan.
5. New methods of production are being used in the factories of Japan eventually they will be common in this country as well.

The Colon

Use the colon as follows:

RULE 1

Use a colon after a complete thought (or independent clause) when the material that follows is a list, an illustration, or an explanation.

A. A list

> Please order the following items: five dozen pencils, twenty rulers, and five rolls of tape.

Notice that no colon is used (such as after *are*) when there is not a complete sentence before the colon:

> The courses I am taking this semester are English Composition, Introduction to Psychology, Art Appreciation, and Survey of Canadian Literature.

B. An illustration or explanation

> She was an exceptional child: at 7 she was performing on the concert stage.

RULE 2

Use a colon following the salutation of a business letter.

> To whom it may concern:
> Dear Madam President:

RULE 3

Use a colon between the hours and the minutes when telling time.

> We will eat at 5:15.

RULE 4

Use a colon between the title and subtitle of a book, article, essay, etc.

> *Plain English, Please: A Rhetoric*
> "Hemingway: His Foreshadowed Suicide"

Practice 3 Using Colons

In each of the following sentences, insert colons wherever they are needed. Check your answers against those in the Answer Key on page 460.

1. Two Canadian-born comedians have achieved great success in the United States Jim Carrey and Mike Myers.
2. The official has one major flaw in his personality greed.
3. The restaurant has lovely homemade desserts such as German chocolate layer cake and baked Alaska.
4. The college offers four courses in English literature Romantic Poetry, Shakespeare's Plays, The British Short Story, and The Modern Novel.
5. Arriving at 615 in the morning, Marlene brought me a sausage-and-cheese pizza, some ginger ale, and a litre of ice cream.

The Hyphen

Use the hyphen as follows:

RULE 1
Use a hyphen with two or more words that go together before the noun to act as one adjective.

> I am a second-year student.
> She is a well-known actor.

TIP
If the group of words that describes the noun comes after the noun, do not use a hyphen.

> The actor is well known.

TIP
If the group of words contains an -*ly* adverb, do not hyphenate.

> The dimly lit diner closed every night at eleven.

RULE 2
Use a hyphen at the end of a line to divide a word between syllables.

Make sure you divide the word at the right place. Check a dictionary if you're not sure. Otherwise, avoid splitting words altogether. Never split a one-syllable word.

> When Farah saw her boyfriend kissing another wom-
> an, she walked away from him for good.

RULE 3
Hyphens are used in some compound words.

Other compound words are not hyphenated. There is no rule to determine which is which. Use a dictionary to make the right decision. Where there is disagreement between dictionaries, pick one spelling and be consistent in your own writing.

The following are word spellings upon which all dictionaries agree:

father-in-law   hairbrush
trade-in   stepmother

RULE 4

Use hyphens with two-word numbers from twenty-one to ninety-nine.

thirty-seven
seventy-three

RULE 5

Use hyphens in words that contain the prefixes *self*, *ex*, and *all*; prefixes that are followed by proper nouns; and the suffix *elect*.

self-respect, self-confidence
ex-husband, ex-police officer
all-Canadian cast
anti-Catholic
Premier-elect Dalton McGuinty

 Exercise Inserting Hyphens Where Necessary

In each of the following sentences, insert a hyphen wherever it is necessary.

1. The students in third year weren't in class today, but all the second year students were.
2. Kelly loved her baseball glove despite its war torn appearance.
3. The all American company of actors was scared to come to Canada because of SARS.
4. Her low self esteem caused her to stay with her husband despite the repeated beatings he inflicted on her.
5. The widely acclaimed impressionist painter received a standing ovation before he accepted his 32 thousand dollar cheque.
6. Julia's forty four year old ex boyfriend returned all thirty three compact discs she had borrowed when she was enrolled in her postgraduate university program.
7. Faisal bought the all purpose cleaner that his mother in law recommended when he and his wife were still a happily married couple.

The Dash and Parentheses

Like the comma, both the dash and parentheses can be used to show an interruption of the main idea. The particular form you choose depends on the degree of interruption.

RULE 1

Use the dash for a less formal and more emphatic interruption of the main idea.

He came—I thought—by car.

She arrived—and I know this for a fact—in a pink Cadillac.

I could see you this weekend—for example, Saturday.

RULE 2

Use a dash before such words as *all*, *these*, and *they* when these words summarize a preceding list of details.

Periods, commas, colons, semicolons, dashes, hyphens, and quotation marks—all these tiny marks among words have incredible power over their meaning and ultimate effectiveness.

RULE 3

Use parentheses to insert extra information that some readers might want to know, but that is not essential to the main idea. Information within parentheses is de-emphasized.

Timothy Findley (1930–2002) wrote *The Wars*.

Plea-bargaining (see page 28) was developed to expedite court verdicts.

Practice   Using Dashes or Parentheses

In each of the following sentences, insert dashes or parentheses wherever they are needed. Check your answers against those in the Answer Key on page 460.

1. Herbert Simon is and I don't think this is an exaggeration a genius.
2. George Eliot her real name was Mary Ann Evans wrote *Silas Marner*.
3. You should in fact I insist see a doctor.
4. Health Canada's website has suggestions to help smokers quit visit www .infotobacco.com.
5. Mass media television, radio, movies, magazines, and newspapers are able to transmit information over a wide range and to a large number of people.

Chapter Review Exercises

Practice 1   Punctuation Overview

Insert any necessary punctuation into the following sentences. Check your answers against those in the Answer Key on page 461.

1. To measure crime, sociologists have used three different techniques official statistics, victimization surveys, and self-report studies.
2. David is one of the best loved poems of Earle Birney.
3. That show uses one thing I hate a laugh track.
4. Farley Mowat has written numerous books for adults however, he also writes very popular books for children.
5. Tuberculosis also known as consumption has been nearly eliminated by medical science.
6. The Victorian period 1837–1901 saw a rapid expansion in industry.

Practice 2   Punctuation Overview

Insert any necessary punctuation into the following sentences. Check your answers against those in the Answer Key on page 461.

1. Many young people have two feelings about science and technology awe and fear.
2. Mr. Doyle the realtor Mrs. Tong the bank officer and Ivan Petroff the lawyer are the three people to help work out the real-estate transaction.
3. The book was entitled *English Literature The Victorian Age.*
4. My computer, she said, has been crashing all day.
5. She brought a bathing suit, a towel, sunglasses, and several books to the beach.
6. The meeting to discuss a pay increase I'll believe it when I see it has been rescheduled for Friday.
7. The complex lab experiment has these two major problems too many difficult calculations and too many variables.

Exercise 1   Editing for Correct Punctuation

Read the paragraph below, then insert the following punctuation marks into it wherever they are needed:

a. commas to separate items in a series
b. comma with a coordinating conjunction to combine two complete thoughts
c. comma after an introductory word, phrase, or clause
d. commas around words that interrupt the main idea
e. comma to set off spoken words
f. parentheses
g. quotation marks
h. line under the title of a full-length work of art
i. semicolon
j. apostrophe

Tom Thomson 1877–1917 is often remembered as the artist of Canada's North. He was born on August 4 1877 near Leith Ontario. During the twenties Thomson apprenticed as a machinist enrolled in business college then he spent a few years in Seattle working as an engraver. In 1906 he took art lessons and first used oil paint. His first important painting done in 1917 and titled A Northern Lake was sold for $250 a great deal of money in those days. Thomson led the vanguard of a new movement in Canadian art. One reviewer said Thomson paints a world of phenomena of colour and of form which will not be touched by another artist. Thomson drowned at Canoe Lake Algonquin Park July 8 1917. Among his many works are Ottawa by Moonlight Autumn's Garland and Jackpine.

Exercise 2 Editing for Correct Punctuation

Read the paragraph below, then insert the following punctuation marks into it if and when they are needed:

a. commas to separate items in a series
b. comma with a coordinating conjunction to combine two complete thoughts
c. comma after an introductory word, phrase, or clause
d. commas around words that interrupt the main idea
e. comma in a number of 1,000 or larger
f. parentheses
g. quotation marks
h. line under the title of a full-length work of art
i. semicolon
j. colon
k. apostrophe

Albert Schweitzer was a brilliant German philosopher physician musician clergyman missionary and writer on theology. Early in his career he based his philosophy on what he called reverence for life. He felt a deep sense of obligation to serve humanity. His accomplishments as a humanitarian were great consequently he was awarded the Nobel Peace Prize in 1952. Before Schweitzer was 30 he had won an international reputation as a writer on theology as an organist and authority on organ building as an interpreter of the works of Johann Sebastian Bach and as an authority on Bachs life. When he became inspired to become a medical missionary he studied medicine at the university in Strasbourg Germany. He began his work in French Equatorial Africa now called Gabon in 1913 where his first consulting room was a chicken coop. Over the years he built a large hospital where thousands of Africans were treated yearly. He used his $33 000 Nobel Prize money to expand the hospital then he set up a leper colony in fact he even designed all the buildings. One of Schweitzers many famous books which you might like to find in the library is entitled Out of My Life and Thought. His accomplishments were so many music medicine scholarship theology and service to humanity.

 Working Together: Designing Punctuation Tests

Work with a group of your classmates. Together, make up an exam to test the other students' knowledge of punctuation. From any book, choose a paragraph that uses a variety of punctuation. Have one person from the group carefully write out or type the paragraph without its punctuation. Then make enough copies so a group or the entire class can take the test. Is your test a fair one? Is it too easy or too hard? Does it cover the material studied in this chapter?

Chapter 12 **Capitalization**

Quick Quiz Test yourself on your knowledge of capitalization. Correct any errors of capitalization in the following sentences. Answers are upside down in the margin.

1. I am hoping to go to the University in British Columbia in the fall, but if I can't, I'll have more money to spend at christmas.

2. My Doctor's appointment this afternoon is with doctor Shari Mohammed.

3. The pacific ocean is beautiful at Sunset.

4. I told the umpire, "you don't know the rules of baseball any more than grandma does!"

5. Sam and i have travelled through the rockies by Train three times now, for they are absolutely breathtaking.

Many students are confused or careless about the use of capital letters. Sometimes they capitalize words without thinking, or they capitalize words they feel are "important" words without really understanding what makes a word important enough to deserve a capital letter. The question of when to capitalize words becomes easier to answer when you study the following rules and carefully apply them to your own writing.

Ten Basic Rules for Capitalization

RULE 1
Capitalize the first word of every sentence.

RULE 2
Capitalize the names of specific things and places.

Specific buildings

I went to the Jamestown Post Office.

but

I went to the post office.

Specific streets, cities, provinces, states, countries

She lives on Elam Avenue.

but

She lives on the same street as my mom and dad.

Specific organizations

He collected money for the Canadian Cancer Society.

but

Janice joined more than one club at the school.

Specific institutions

The loan is from the Royal Bank of Canada.

but

The loan is from one of the banks in town.

Specific bodies of water

My uncle fishes every summer on Lake Winnipeg.

but

My uncle spends every summer at the lake.

RULE 3

Capitalize days of the week, months of the year, and holidays. Do *not* capitalize the names of seasons.

The second Monday in October is Thanksgiving Day.

but

I cannot wait until spring.

RULE 4

Capitalize the names of all languages, nationalities, races, religions, deities, and sacred terms.

My friend who is Ethiopian speaks very little English.
The *Qur'an* is the sacred book of Islam.

RULE 5

In a title, capitalize the first word, the last word, and every other word *except* articles, prepositions, and coordinating conjunctions (*for, and, nor, but, or, yet,* and *so*—FANBOYS).

"Recognizing Subjects and Verbs" and "Revising and Editing" are chapters in the textbook *The Canadian Writer's Workplace*.

RULE 6

Capitalize the first word of a direct quotation.

The teacher said, "You have been chosen for the part."

but

"You have been chosen," she said, "for the part."

*Note: fo*r is not capitalized in the second sentence because it is not the beginning of the sentence being quoted.

RULE 7

Capitalize historical events, periods, and documents.

the Rebellion of 1837
the Great Depression
the *Canadian Charter of Rights and Freedoms*

RULE 8

Capitalize the words *north*, *south*, *east,* and *west* when they are used as places rather than as directions.

He comes from the East.

but

The farm is about 40 kilometres west of Weyburn.

RULE 9

Capitalize people's names.

Proper names

George Hendrickson

Professional titles when they immediately precede the person's proper name

Judge Samuelson	*but*	the judge
Professor Shapiro	*but*	the professor

- Do not capitalize a title if it follows the name:

George Shapiro, professor of English

Term for a relative (like *mother, sister, nephew, uncle*) when it is used in the place of the proper name

> I told Grandfather I would meet him later.

- Notice that terms for relatives are not capitalized if a pronoun, article, or adjective is used with the name.

> I told my grandfather I would meet him later.

RULE 10

Capitalize brand names.

> Band-Aid
> Kleenex

Band-Aid and *Kleenex* are product names and therefore are proper nouns.

Here is a summary of these rules:

The Ten Rules for Capitalization
RULE 1: Capitalize the first word of every sentence.
RULE 2: Capitalize the names of specific things and places.
RULE 3: Capitalize days of the week, months of the year, and holidays. Do not capitalize the names of seasons.
RULE 4: Capitalize the names of all languages, nationalities, races, religions, deities, and sacred terms.
RULE 5: In a title, capitalize the first word, the last word, and every other word except articles, prepositions, and coordinating conjunctions (FANBOYS).
RULE 6: Capitalize the first word of a direct quotation.
RULE 7: Capitalize historical events, periods, and documents.
RULE 8: Capitalize the words *north, south, east,* and *west* when they are used as places rather than as directions.
RULE 9: Capitalize people's names.
RULE 10: Capitalize brand names.

 Practice   Capitalization

In the following sentences, capitalize wherever it is necessary. Check your answers against those in the Answer Key on page 461.

1. The italian student got a job in the school cafeteria.
2. Our train ride through the canadian rockies was fabulous.
3. The author often made references in his writing to names from the bible.
4. A student at the university of alberta was chosen for the national award.
5. My uncle's children always have a party on hallowe'en.
6. I met the president of bell canada last friday at a convention in winnipeg, manitoba.
7. The cobalt-60 cancer therapy unit was invented by a canadian, dr. donald green.
8. My niece said, "why don't you consider moving farther south if you hate the winter so much?"

9. The canadian auto workers voted not to go on strike over the new contract.
10. The book *women of the klondike* tells the story of the late-1890s gold rush in the north.

 Exercise **Capitalization**

In the following sentences, capitalize wherever it is necessary and put into lower case any capital letters that are incorrect.

1. Some people think the Cabot trail on Cape Breton island is the most spectacular drive on the North American Continent.
2. I'm taking five courses right now, but math 101 is my favourite.
3. I love the Text called *Canadian Writer's workplace*; I've already read 20 of its 28 Chapters.
4. Morris C. Shumiatcher is a Lawyer and Civil Rights Spokesperson who graduated from the University Of Calgary.
5. George Orwell wrote the novel *nineteen eighty-four* about a Government that punishes its people for thinking certain thoughts.
6. Born in Bombay, India, Writer Rohinton Mistry was raised in that City's Parsi Community.
7. The black honda accord and the white ford escape have collided at the Intersection of Chapel street and Bakersville avenue.
8. "I feel your pain," wrote rabbi Wittstein of Temple Israel of london to the muslim community, "And offer you whatever understanding, sympathy, and anger I possess. . . ."
9. Roman Polanski won an oscar for best director in 2002, but was unable to receive the award in person because if he had entered the United States, he would have been arrested for statutory rape.
10. Socrates was a greek teacher who is considered one of the founders of western philosophy.

 Working Together: Designing Capitalization Tests

Work with a group of your classmates to make up an exam to test the other students' knowledge of capitalization. From any book, choose a paragraph that uses a variety of capitalization. Have one person from the group carefully write out or type the paragraph without any capitalization. Then make enough copies so a group or the entire class can take the test. Is your test a fair one? Is it too easy or too hard? Does it cover the material studied in this chapter?

Chapter 13 **Unit I Review: Using All You Have Learned**

In this chapter of review practices and exercises, you have the opportunity to test yourself on the material in Unit I. Revisit any point of grammar that you know you need to work on a little more. If, for example, you find that you haven't quite understood how to use a semicolon correctly, then it would be a good idea to revisit Chapter 5 ("Coordination and Subordination"), Chapter 7 ("Correcting Run-ons"), and Chapter 11 ("Punctuation"). If you can't find what you're looking for right away, consult the index at the back of the book.

Often we think that if we can already speak the language to the extent that most people seem to understand what we're saying, there is no need to learn to write perfectly. When we speak, especially on informal occasions (which is most of the time), we get away with making mistakes every day. We do not check the grammar of those to whom we speak, nor do they check ours. When someone says, "Lunch?" we know what he or she means, and we don't stop to think, "That wasn't a complete sentence." But when we write, especially in formal situations such as those we encounter in our professional lives, we can not so easily get away with making the same types of errors. The extent to which we communicate properly will in part determine how far we go in meeting our professional goals.

Mastering a language is an ongoing process. And this textbook certainly doesn't cover everything there is to know about English. Nevertheless, it covers a great deal; you might want to keep it on your shelf as a reference tool even after your course is finished. That way, if ever you forget when you're supposed to use *whom* instead of *who*, this book will be there to remind you.

Editing Sentences for Errors

In the following exercises, you will find all the types of grammatical and mechanical problems that you have studied so far:

Fragments	Unparallel structure	Incorrect capitalization
Run-ons	Incorrect punctuation	Misplaced and dangling
Incorrect pronouns	Subject-verb disagreement	modifiers

Practice 1   Identifying Parts of Speech

Read the following paragraphs taken from Rosemary Ellen Guiley's book *Dreamwork for the Soul*. Identify the part of speech (as specifically as you can) for each underlined word. Feel free to refer back to Chapter 1 ("Parts of Speech: Overview") for help. The index at the back of the textbook can help for easy reference. Check your answers against those in the Answer Key on page 461.

The first one has been done for you.

(Carl G.) Jung's <u>dreams</u> ① were a <u>constant</u> ② source <u>of</u> ③ creativity <u>and</u> ④ inspiration to <u>him</u> ⑤. Dreams <u>inspired</u> ⑥ his study of archaeology and mythology, and later alchemy. <u>Throughout</u> ⑦ his life, as he developed <u>his</u> ⑧ ideas, Jung <u>was</u> ⑨ aided and guided by dreams. <u>When</u> ⑩ he searched for answers to questions, dreams <u>often</u> ⑪ led him in <u>the</u> ⑫ <u>right</u> ⑬ direction. . . .

Three days before he died, Jung <u>had</u> ⑭ the last of his visionary dreams and a portent of his own <u>impending</u> ⑮ death. In the dream, he had <u>become</u> ⑯ whole. <u>A</u> ⑰ significant symbol was tree roots interlaced with gold, the alchemical <u>symbol</u> ⑱ of completion. . . .

The story of Jung's life can be <u>properly</u> ⑲ understood <u>only</u> ⑳ from his inner experiences. The experiences of the <u>outer</u> ㉑ world were pale and thin by comparison <u>for</u> ㉒ him. <u>He</u> ㉓ said he <u>could</u> ㉔ understand himself only in the light of his inner <u>happenings</u>. ㉕

Answer: 1. *dreams*: common noun

Practice 2   Editing Sentences for Errors

The following sentences contain various types of errors studied in Unit I. If you think a sentence is complete and correct, mark it with a *C*. If it has an error, correct it (you may need to add, delete, or change words, punctuation, and capitalization). There can be more than one correct answer for each sentence. Check your answers against those in the Answer Key on page 462. An example has been done for you.

> **Incorrect:** A group of Roma people who now live in Ireland.
> **Correct:** A group of Roma people now live in Ireland.
> *or*
> A group of Roma people, who now live in Ireland, make their living by repairing pots and pans.

1. Roma (also known as Gypsies or Romany Gypsies) now living in many countries of the world.

   _____

   _____

2. The international community of scientists agree that these Roma originally came from India thousands of years ago.

_____

_____

3. After the original Roma people left India they went to Persia there they divided into groups.

_____

_____

4. One branch of Roma went West to Europe the other group decided to go East.

_____

_____

5. In the middle ages (476–1453), some Roma people lived in a fertile area of Greece called little egypt.

_____

_____

6. Roma often found it hard to gain acceptance in many countries because of their wandering lifestyle.

_____

_____

7. Today Roma families may be found from Canada to Chile living much as his ancestors did thousands of years ago.

_____

_____

Practice 3 Editing Sentences for Errors

The following sentences contain sentence errors studied in Unit I. If you think a sentence is complete and correct, mark it with a C. If it has an error, correct it. There can be more than one correct answer for each sentence. An example has been done for you. Check your answers against those in the Answer Key on page 462.

Incorrect: Science fiction writers have imagined magic rays that can destroy entire cities, but in recent years a magic ray in the form of laser beams have become scientific fact.

Correct: Science fiction writers have imagined magic rays that can destroy entire cities, but in recent years a magic ray in the form of laser beams has become scientific fact.

1. The laser beam a miracle of modern science already has many practical uses in today's world.

   _____

   _____

2. Laser beams are narrow, highly concentrated beams of light that burns brighter than the light of the sun.

   _____

   _____

3. Scientists have found many possible military uses for the laser, but they are hoping it can be converted into constructive uses.

   _____

   _____

4. John Polanyi, Canadian winner of the 1986 Nobel Prize for chemistry, conducted early experiments on the use of lasers.

   _____

   _____

5. The possibility of making a laser was first described in 1958 and two years later in California the first laser beam was created.

   _____

   _____

6. Since they are so precise, laser beams are used in medicine to help make a specific diagnosis and to perform operations such as repairing delicate retinas and the removal of cancerous tumours.

   _____

   _____

7. The future uses of the laser seems endless, and it is up to us to decide whether we want to use this invention for war or for peaceful purposes.

   _____

   _____

Exercise 1 Editing Sentences for Errors

The following sentences contain sentence errors studied in Unit I. If a sentence has an error or errors, correct it. More than one correct answer is possible for each sentence. If you think a sentence is complete and correct, mark it with a C. An example has been done for you.

> *Incorrect:* Frostbite an injury to the skin and underlying tissues is a serious danger in very cold weather.
>
> *Correct:* Frostbite, an injury to the skin and underlying tissues, is a serious danger in very cold weather.
>
> (commas added around a phrase that interrupts the main idea)

1. A common threat to outdoor adventurers frostbite can strike anyone who is not adequately protected against the cold.

_____

_____

2. Risk factors are of three types exposure, faulty judgment, and underlying medical conditions.

_____

_____

3. Ice crystals in the skin possibly starting to form at −6°C.

_____

_____

4. Symptoms of frostbite includes: cold numbness and a feeling of clumsiness or heaviness in the affected part of the body.

_____

_____

5. The first thing to do is find a warm shelter and remove any wet clothing.

_____

_____

6. Prevention measures includes wearing proper clothing, educating yourself about weather conditions, and awareness of risk factors.

_____

_____

7. Frostbite injury which gets worse with time should be treated immediately.

_____

_____

 Exercise 2 Making Sentence Parts Work Together

In each of the following sentences, one part does not work with the rest of the sentence. Find the error and correct it. There may be more than one correct answer for each sentence.

1. Two Statistics Canada studies, which have been reported recently on the CBC television network, links stress and obesity now with health problems later in life.

_____

_____

2. Suffering from stress and obesity, the researchers found that Canadians will probably suffer major health problems as soon as six years later.

_____

_____

3. People who suffer from stress and obesity become a perfect candidate for health problems such as arthritis and rheumatism, chronic bronchitis or emphysema, and stomach or intestinal ulcers.

_____

_____

4. One study shows that for men, diseases also include heart disease, and for a woman, asthma and migraine.

_____

_____

5. According to one of the studies, stress in men appeared to be worse where economic issues are concerned: job loss, demotions and taking pay cuts, for example.

_____

_____

6. An obese adult's chance of suffering from arthritis is 60 percent higher than an adult who is not obese.

_____

_____

7. They say stress goes down with age and up in low-income people.

_____

_____

Editing Paragraphs for Errors

 Exercise 1 Making Sentence Parts Work Together

Read the following paragraph, looking for errors in agreement, for lack of parallel structure, and for misplaced or dangling modifiers. Rewrite a corrected version. More than one correct answer is possible.

Cowboys became important in the United States after the American Civil War who lived on large ranches in Texas, Montana, and other western states. Canada, too, had its cowboys working on ranches on the prairies. One of the traditional names for cowboys are "cowpokes" although they prefer to be called "cowhands." The equipment for cowboys came into use because of his many practical needs. The wide-brimmed cowboy hat served as a bucket to hold water, as a sort of whip to drive cattle, and waving to other cowboys a few hills away. Cowboys began to wear tight trousers because they did not want loose pants to catch in bushes as they chased cattle. The rope is a cowboy's most important tool since they use it to catch cattle, pull wagons, tie up equipment, and even killing snakes. The famous roundup, which takes place twice a year, are important because cattle are separated, classified, and selected for market. When cowboys get together for such a roundup, they often hold a rodeo as a celebration. Rodeos give cowboys opportunities to compete in riding bareback, wrestling steer, and to rope calves. The Calgary Stampede is the modern result of these rodeos.

Exercise 2 Editing Paragraphs for Errors

Correct all the punctuation and grammatical errors in the following paragraph. More than one correct answer is possible.

Once upon a time whenever I tried to make my writing interesting and imaginative with all sorts of similes and metaphors and colourful language I forgot about my grammar and spelling my essays were full of sentence fragments comma splices and run-ons moreover my syntax was always scrambled even I had trouble figuring out what I had intended to say originally although I could tell that I had started with brilliant ideas help has finally arrived however since I have done all the exercises in my grammar book I now have perfect command of English grammar whereas one time I bit my nails when I handed in an assignment I worry no more no longer do I need to worry about essays being handed back bleeding to death after being savaged by some mean English teacher wielding his or her red pen no longer will my sleep be curtailed by hours of tedious rewrites moreover from now on I'm expecting straight As all the way.

Exercise 3 Editing Paragraphs for Errors

Correct all the punctuation, capitalization, and grammatical errors in the following paragraphs. More than one correct answer is possible.

Sleep is one of those things you never think about. As long as you're getting your full 40 winks at night. As soon as a bout of insomnia hits though sleep is the only thing on your mind. The ancient greeks had a god of sleep called hypnos who could appear as a bird, child, or friendly warrior those images don't suggest sleep to modern people though we prefer fields of sheep and mr. sandman.

Since the greeks scientists have made much progress in unravelling the secrets of sleep but many mysteries remain. They can't explain for example exactly how we fall asleep. Or wake up. Or what dreams are. However they know a lot about insomnia and other sleep disorder. Such as narcolepsy, sudden attacks of deep sleep, sleep apnea (the sleeper stops breathing for several seconds at a time) and, sleepwalking. Which are more amusing to hear about than to experience.

Millions of people suffer from insomnia either chronically, or from time to time. They will try anything to break the curse and science and folklore offers them a carload of choices everything from warm milk and lavender sachets to sleeping pills and sleep clinics. Not that any of these things help the true insomniac of course. And, how maddening it must be for someone who hasnt slept in weeks to come across a bus passenger fast asleep sitting up. Surrounded by strangers. These innocents are like people who stay skinny without having to diet.

Working Together: Remembering 9/11

© Carmen Taylor/Associated Press

Work with a group of your classmates. If you remember 9/11, you may choose to write a paragraph describing what the day was like either for you or your family. If you cannot remember or you choose not to remember, pretend you are a tourist on a street in New York who sees the plane in the picture on this page; write a paragraph about what might be going through your mind. Double-space your paragraph, and take about ten minutes to compose it.

Once your paragraph is finished, trade papers with someone else. Check the other student's paragraph for fragments, run-ons, lack of parallel structure, misplaced and dangling modifiers, and errors with pronouns, subject-verb agreement, punctuation, capitalization, and so on. When you are finished, hand it back and discuss the grammar (and the content if you wish to do so).

Unit II **The Writing Process**

© Design Pics/Don Hammond/Jupiter Images

Chapter 14 — The Four Stages of Writing for a Paragraph or an Essay

Few people can go to a desk and write a perfect composition from scratch without giving any of it even a second look. Most people need to go about the writing process in stages. This chapter introduces the writing process (for a paragraph or an essay) in terms of four stages: (1) prewriting, (2) outlining, (3) the rough draft, and finally, (4) postwriting (revising, editing, and proofreading). The chapter begins with some prewriting techniques designed to generate writing ideas and ends with proofreading. Revising and editing (other parts of stage four) are covered in this chapter, but are also examined in more depth in Chapter 17 of this unit.

Stage One: Prewriting

How many times have you heard yourself say, "I don't know what else to write"? Well, what if you really do have plenty to write about and simply don't realize it? The following **prewriting techniques** are designed to retrieve your thoughts and ideas and make sense of feelings you might have so that you can start exploring them on paper. These techniques include brainstorming, freewriting, keeping a journal, and clustering. Use any, all, or none of them—whatever works for you.

Brainstorming

One of the best ways of collecting ideas is through **brainstorming**. Brainstorming is simple—all you need is some time. It is best accomplished in groups of four or more people, but the numbers aren't as important as the generation of ideas.

Here's how brainstorming works:

1. Compile a list of ideas, as many of them as you can.
2. Don't criticize any idea initially. Assessing the ideas will come later. First, just focus on generating several of them.

3. If any ideas generate objections, work on developing alternatives to the ideas rather than simply discarding them.
4. Use ideas to stimulate discussion and to generate other ideas.
5. Make sure that everyone in the group completely understands the ideas generated.
6. Put your list of ideas aside for a while in order to think about them at your leisure. This "back burner" process often generates other ideas.

> **TIP**
>
> When you brainstorm, allow your mind to roam freely around the topic, letting one idea lead to another, even if the ideas seem unrelated or irrelevant. Jot down every word and phrase that pops into your mind when you think about your topic.

Here is what a brainstorming process might look like.

First identify a topic:

> hockey

Then, what things come to mind when you think of this topic?

coaches	referees
Stanley Cup	new drafts
Maple Leafs	Vancouver Canucks

Now, you may want to pick out a couple of these ideas and combine them:

> Maple Leafs   and   Stanley Cup

Expand the idea by reflecting on what you know and/or what you believe.

> The Maple Leafs can't seem to win the Stanley Cup.

At this point, a question might arise:

> Why can't the Leafs win the Stanley Cup?

Use a possible answer to suggest a topic sentence for a paragraph or a thesis statement for an essay:

> If they want to win the Stanley Cup, the Maple Leafs should commit to a realistic long-term plan rather than continue to cater to the demands of their short-sighted fans.

Freewriting

In freewriting, you don't have to worry about spelling, grammar, focus, or organization. You just write. Write whatever comes to mind. Let a force beyond your control guide your pen, be it your unconscious, your heart, or the spirit world. The idea here is to generate ideas for writing a composition at a later stage. In the meantime, just have fun letting words explode onto your paper or screen.

Keeping a Journal

When handing in her journal at the end of a semester, a young female college student once said, "The journal was better than any man I'd ever known. It listened to absolutely everything I had to say!"

You may have kept some kind of diary in your childhood. Each entry might have started with "Dear Diary" and continued with comments such as "I experienced my first kiss today. It was awkward, but amazing. . . ." Most diaries are logs of what goes on in the daily lives of their writers. As students get older, their diaries may evolve into journals that have a similar format but content with more depth and other engaging qualities. For example, rather than mention everything you did yesterday in last night's diary entry, you might concentrate on one specific thing that struck you forcefully. It might have been a dream you had that preoccupied you all day, or perhaps something in a conversation you overheard between two other students in front of you in a bus on the way to school. Perhaps this event or thought, whatever it was, made you angry or sad or hopeful or, at the very least, contemplative, causing one of your friends in the cafeteria, or your professor in class, to tell you to snap out of a daze.

Let Your Emotions Serve as a Guide

Think of a teacher from your past whom you remember well. Chances are it was someone who caused you to feel a great deal of emotion, either positive or negative. It might have been a teacher who made you feel stupid—or it might have been one who encouraged you to follow a certain path because of a talent he or she detected in you that your parents never noticed or encouraged. Emotion is often associated with memory. The same can be said for people whom you've dated in the past. You may remember some girlfriends/boyfriends more than others; those with whom you experienced strong emotions are probably the ones you tend to remember the most, no matter how long ago you were with them. Thus, your emotions can be your guide when it comes to choosing the topic of your journal entries and, subsequently, your essays (if your professor gives you enough choice, that is). What moves you, after all, may cause you to want to write more and will give you more material to write about. You'll experience fewer writer's blocks—fewer occasions on which you're thinking, "I don't know what else to write."

You may be asked to write a response to a piece of writing, either fiction or nonfiction. Does the story you just read remind you of a personal experience? Do you strongly disagree with how the character or writer dealt with his or her own situation because you would have reacted very differently? What should the character or writer have done, and why? If you are asked to respond to a movie, think about what your emotional response to it was. Again, don't try to control the direction of your entry. Let your feelings take you on paper (or on your computer screen) to wherever they seem to want to take you. Regard it as an inner journey into the unknown—a journey into your unconscious or your psyche. (*Psyche*, by the way, is Greek for "soul.")

Buy a Journal That Doesn't Remind You of School

Are you a cat lover? Buy a journal with a hard cover on which there's a picture of a richly exotic Siamese cat! If it's cars you're into, find a journal with a picture of a sexy sports car on the cover. In any event, try to find something that you actually look forward to writing in. Write every day or every night before you go to bed, or take your journal with you in your knapsack so that you can record fresh ideas as they come to mind throughout the day. Between classes, rather than call someone on your cell phone, do some journal writing. Develop a relationship with your journal the same way you would with a good novel that you find hard to put down. Do not allow journal writing to turn into a regular assignment that you feel forced to do just for the marks. Then it turns into meaningless drudgery, like too many things in life already are. It should be, instead, a record of the journey of your mind!

If you prefer to type your entries on a computer screen rather than write them in a paper journal, that's fine, too. Do whatever makes you feel most comfortable and inspired. Do whatever is likely to help you cultivate that relationship, not just the one with your journal, but also the one with yourself that you'll find you are developing as you start to write on a regular basis. Writing regularly in your journal not only can help you get in touch with your feelings and solve your personal problems (for a personal journalling exercise, see Working Together activity #3 on page 166), but it can also help you start writing more quickly and fluently whenever you're asked to complete a task that requires any writing at all.

Clustering (also known as Diagramming or Mapping)

Many students are visual learners: they learn best by *seeing* something get done rather than by reading or even hearing about it (in a lecture, tapes, etc.). The same can be said for generating ideas. **Clustering** is a kind of brainstorming that makes use of a diagram (see Figure 14.1 for an example). To begin, identify a topic you either have to or want to write on. Label it "main topic" and circle it. This topic becomes the central idea of your clustering activity. Draw a line from that circle up to the left, then another up to the right, etc., and write out other ideas that are related in some way to the central topic. Don't allow yourself to think for too long a time about what you will add to the diagram next; write down whatever comes to mind first. (Writing something down does not bind you in any way to using it in your final text.) Continue to expand the diagram, building on it in several directions. Eventually, certain ideas will begin to "take hold"—to seem stronger than the others—depending on what is familiar and important to you at the time.

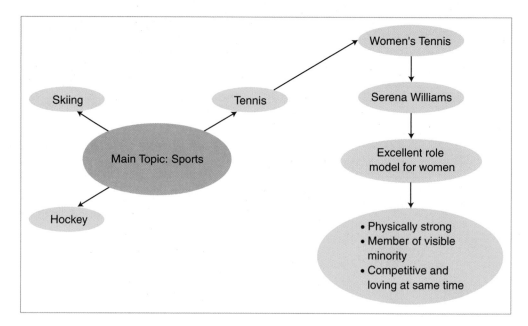

Figure 14.1: Clustering

Working from the cluster diagram, you could decide that you're interested in women's tennis, specifically in Serena Williams. If you feel strongly that Serena is an excellent role model for women, this feeling could provide a topic sentence for your paragraph.

Topic sentence: Serena Williams, a five-time World No. 1 women's singles
                        tennis player, is an excellent role model for women everywhere.

Then you might ask yourself the following question: Why is Serena an excellent role model for women?

The answer to this question might come in several parts, each of which can be used as a supporting point for your paragraph:

Supporting points:

1. She is physically strong.
2. She's a member of a visible minority, but this fact has not held her back.
3. She is living proof that she can be competitive and loving at the same time, as illustrated by her relationship with her sister.

Choosing the Topic and the Controlling Idea

Some people have no use for any of the above prewriting techniques. And that's fine. If you can come up with a topic and a controlling idea (your attitude toward the topic) right away, all the better. But remember, even if you can come up with a topic sentence for a paragraph (or a thesis statement for an essay) without prewriting techniques, using them can be helpful for other reasons, too, such as establishing a writing routine, dealing with personal upsets and difficulties, etc.

Jot down two or three different topics that appeal to you; for ideas, look through the lists of topics found throughout Unit III (look for the heading "Suggested Topics" under "Assignment" for the various writing strategies in each chapter). From one of these lists, select the topic you think would give you the best opportunity for writing. Which one do you feel most strongly about? Which one do you know the most about? Which one is most likely to interest your readers? Which one is best suited to being developed into a paragraph or an essay?

Unit IV in this text contains readings of nonfiction by Canadian writers. Immediately following every reading, there are four sets of questions. Read any piece in Unit IV that appeals to you; then practise your paragraph or essay writing by responding to one of the questions. Questions under the headings "Questions for Discussion" and "Writing Ideas" are particularly useful for this purpose. Choose the question you find most interesting.

Every Paragraph or Essay Must Be Persuasive

The word "essay" comes from the French verb *essayer*, which means "to try." What does a writer "try" to do in an essay? A writer tries to persuade the reader of a particular point of view. Even if the essay is considered more expository (writing that explains things) than argumentative, the writer still selects facts that he or she hopes will lead the reader to see things the way the writer does. Any essay—even a single paragraph—is an exercise in *persuasion*. (For more on persuasion, see Chapter 28: "Argumentation.")

Two of the most critical elements the writer must consider in order to maximize the persuasive power of a composition are its **audience** and its **purpose.**

Audience and Tone

Your primary audience is, no doubt, your professor. But whom do you have in mind when you're writing your composition? If you're writing a children's story, chances are you're neither going to be discussing the topic of venereal disease, nor will you be using five-syllable words. If you're writing a formal essay, you're not going to begin by saying, "I thought I'd spill a few thoughts down on some paper." The identity of your intended audience, aside from the professor who will be marking your assignment, determines not only what you write, but also how you write it.

Your intended audience, for example, determines the level of formality of your writing. If you're writing a formal research paper, use a formal tone. Don't, for example, use contractions (*he's, she'd*, etc.). Stay in the third person (don't use *I* or *you*).

Purpose

The main reason for writing a composition at this stage in your life is probably to get a passing grade so that you can move on to the next level of English course in order to eventually graduate in your program. The better your compositions are, the more likely you are to pass your English course. In the interest of producing a high-quality composition, be as mindful as you can of the specific reason for writing your particular piece.

This purpose should be crystal clear to you from the beginning. If it's not, it probably won't be clear to the reader either. First of all, is your purpose to inform, to persuade, or to entertain? Now that you've determined who your intended audience is, it's time you decided what you want that audience to think, do, and/or feel. Are you trying to inspire your readers to do something specific? Or do you simply want them to understand your particular point of view toward a controversial topic? Regardless, the clearer you are on the purpose of your composition, the more effective the result will be.

Stage Two: Outlining (or Organizing)

Most texts on writing suggest elaborate outlines for paragraphs or essays, some of which seem to be as long as the paragraphs or essays themselves. Here, however, we suggest a very short outline, one that is clear and that saves you time. The pattern of the outline for a paragraph is very similar to that for an essay.

This outline consists of four complete sentences, each of which will appear exactly the same way within the final product.

Outline for a paragraph:

1. The topic sentence
2. The first major supporting sentence
3. The second major supporting sentence
4. The third major supporting sentence

Outline for an essay (of five paragraphs):

1. The thesis statement
2. The topic sentence of the second paragraph
3. The topic sentence of the third paragraph
4. The topic sentence of the fourth paragraph

Of course, by the time you've finished your composition, you may find that the wording of some or all of these sentences has changed because of improvements you've made along the way. The outline is meant to help you ensure that your writing contains persuasive power. If your outline doesn't seem logical, chances are, neither will your composition.

Stage Three: The Rough Draft

After you have applied a prewriting technique and organized the material into some kind of order, the time has come to write a rough draft.

A rough draft is a first attempt at a piece of writing. The first attempt is "rough" because it will undergo many changes before it is finished. Parts may be missing, some paragraphs will probably lack sufficient detail, and some parts may be repetitious or inappropriate. Some sentences will sound awkward, and you will need to rewrite them later. The experienced writer expects all this and does not worry. All that you should try to accomplish in the rough draft is to get down on paper all of your initial ideas according to whatever plan you established in stages one and two. These first ideas will provide the seeds that can be better developed later on.

You may work on a rough draft alone, with a group, with a peer tutor, or directly with your instructor. Below is a list of basic questions you should consider at this most important stage of your work. (If any terms in this list are new to you, see Chapter 15 for terms related to the paragraph, Chapter 16 for those related to the essay, and Chapters 21–28 for those related to writing strategies.)

1. Does the rough draft satisfy the conditions for paragraph or essay form? Does it have a topic sentence or thesis statement, adequate support, and a concluding sentence or paragraph? Are there at least five sentences in every paragraph that you've written, but not more than twelve?
2. Does your paragraph or essay contain the writing strategy of your choice, such as narration, cause and effect, or description? Or does your essay combine several strategies, a different one in each paragraph? Does your composition focus on a single event rather than on a general situation? Where does the action take place? Can the reader see it? What time of day, week, or year is it?
3. Have you put the details of the paragraph or essay in a logical order?
4. Does the paragraph or essay seem complete? When you read what you have written, do any questions come to mind that you think should be answered in the text? Is there any material that is irrelevant and should be omitted?
5. Except for what is required in openings and closings, are there sentences or paragraphs that are repetitious?
6. Are there any places where you can substitute better verbs or nouns than the ones you first chose? Can you add adjectives to give the reader better sensory images?
7. Can you think of a better way to begin or end your paragraph or essay?
8. Can you show your draft to at least two other readers and ask them for suggestions?

Once you have a first draft, you have something with which to work. No longer is there a blank paper staring you in the face. This accomplishment is a great relief to most writers, but remember, you are far from finished.

Stage Four: Postwriting (Revising, Editing, and Proofreading)

If you have worked hard at revising the rough draft, you will be delighted with the improvements as you write the second draft. For a detailed examination of this part of the writing process, see Chapter 17: "Revising and Editing."

Feedback is an important aid in each of the final stages of writing a paragraph or essay. A good way to help yourself see your own work more clearly is to put the writing aside for a little while, if you can. Then read aloud to someone else what you have written, or even just to yourself if no one else is available. You may be surprised at the number of places where you will hear the need for a change.

Revising and Editing the Rough Draft

If you have time, put aside your rough draft for a day or two. Then, when you reread it, you will look at it with a fresh mind. In this important revision stage, you should be concerned with how you have organized your ideas. At this point, do not yet worry about grammar, spelling, and punctuation.

Begin this important stage by asking these major questions:

1. Is the paragraph or essay unified? Do you stick to the topic you have announced? Go through the text and take out irrelevant material.

2. Do you repeat yourself? Look back over your paragraph or essay to determine whether you have given any information more than once. Even if you find you have used different words, you should delete the repeated ideas.

3. Does the paragraph or essay make sense? Can a reader follow your logic, your train of thought, and the course of events you describe? (Giving the rough draft to someone else to read will often answer this question for you.) If the paragraph or essay is confusing to the reader, you must find out where it goes wrong and why. Sometimes when you read your writing out loud, you will feel that a sentence has leaped to some point that doesn't follow from the sentence before.

4. For an essay, are the paragraphs roughly the same length? For example, if you see a one-sentence paragraph, you know something is wrong. You may need to develop that paragraph more thoroughly, or the sentence may really belong with the paragraph that comes before or after it. Aim to develop the point of each paragraph using at least five sentences. The first and last paragraphs are usually the shortest paragraphs in the essay, but they still require approximately five sentences each. Check through your essay. Is each paragraph long enough without being too long? Do you need to change the paragraphing?

5. Do you have all the components essential to a paragraph, or all the types of paragraphs essential to an essay? For an essay, do you have the introduction with its thesis, at least three well-developed body paragraphs with transitional devices used to connect ideas, and a concluding paragraph? For a paragraph, do you have a topic sentence that contains the topic of the paragraph and its controlling idea, several sentences providing strong supporting detail, and a concluding sentence?

6. Can you add more specific details? Most writing instructors agree that nearly every paper they read could be improved by adding more details, more descriptive verbs, and more sensory images to make the writing come alive. You should make sure there is sufficient detail throughout your paper. Remember, however, that in an essay, none of the supporting detail should appear in your introductory or concluding paragraphs.

7. Can you add dialogue or a quotation from someone? A quotation, for example, might make an excellent opening in the introductory paragraph of an essay. (See page 200 in Chapter 16: "The Essay.") It might also serve as an excellent piece of evidence within a supporting paragraph of an essay.

8. Can you make the introduction, conclusion, or title more creative? These elements of writing are often not taken seriously enough by student writers. These three items, in fact, are critical components of composition. The title and introduction, in particular, serve to grab a reader's attention. Have you ever tried to read something that hasn't caught your interest? It can be a distressing and agonizing experience. The more time and effort you put into these three elements, the more interesting and effective your writing is likely to be.

Proofreading

An important step still remains. You must check each sentence to see that it is correct, including grammar, spelling, and punctuation. In the rush to get a paper in on time, this step is often overlooked. If you review each sentence by itself starting with the last and going backwards to the beginning, you will more easily be able to consider the sentence structure and individual words apart from the other aspects of the essay. Taking the time to look over a paper this way usually results in spotting several sentence-level errors.

As a proofreading exercise, you might like to try correcting the errors of grammar, spelling, and punctuation in the rough draft of the student essay on pages 211–212 of Chapter 18.

Note: In many cases, professors will not accept handwritten work, and you will be expected to submit a paper produced on a computer. Do not forget to proofread your work after it has been printed out; even if you have your paper typed for you, you are still responsible for errors. If there are not too many errors, you can make corrections neatly in ink on your printed copy before handing it in.

Proofreading
Check your rough draft for
Misspellings
Fragments or run-ons
Incorrect punctuation
Consistency of voice and tense
Verb problems
Agreement
Parallel structure

A checklist for the final preparation of a paragraph or essay follows.

Checklist for the Final Copy

1. Use 8 1/2-by-11-inch paper (21.5 cm by 28 cm).
2. Type or write (whichever is required) on one side of the paper only , unless your instructor states otherwise.
3. Double-space.
4. Leave margins approximately 1 inch (2.5 cm) wide on all sides of the paper (left, right, top, and bottom).
5. Do not hyphenate words at ends of lines without consulting a dictionary for the correct division of words into syllables.
6. Centre the title at the top of the first page.
7. Put your name, the date, and the title of your paper on a separate title page, unless your professor says otherwise.
8. If you have more than one page, number each one and staple or clip them all together in the upper, left-hand corner so they will not be lost.

Working Together: Prewriting Activities

1. Imagine yourself in the following situation: you and your classmates are guidance counsellors in a high school. You have been asked to produce a brochure entitled "When a Young Person Quits School." This brochure is intended for students who are thinking of dropping out. You and the other counsellors meet to brainstorm on the topic.

   Divide into groups. Each group will brainstorm for fifteen minutes or so, then come together again as a class. Make a final grouping of the ideas for this topic on the board, then discuss them.

2. In groups or as a class, construct an outline for the essay to be called "When a Young Person Quits School." (You can use the information gathered in the brainstorming activity if you've done #1 above.) Feel free to follow the suggestion of a brief outline under "Outlining" on page 162 in this chapter.

3. (If you think the following suggestion is too personal, feel free to try #1 or #2, above, instead.) As a topic for a journal entry, think of a movie you've seen or a dream you've had that you have found yourself thinking about over and over again. It doesn't matter how long ago you saw the movie or dreamt the dream because your long-term memory can be quite selective and doesn't always work on the basis of time.

   Describe in writing that part of the movie or dream that you seem to be remembering over and over again. It's possible that this part you're remembering may be calling out to you to express it, to explore it, to somehow come to terms with it—and perhaps most importantly, to learn something from it, something important for you. After all, it's not the movie that's calling out to you. It's something in you that's doing the calling, perhaps something in your unconscious—the part programmed to tell the whole truth about who you are, what you should be doing, where you should be going, and perhaps whom you should be seeing!

After you write about the part of the movie or dream that you remember the most, adding as much detail as you can, start to discuss how you feel. Then try to explain where those feelings are coming from. Finally, explore what that same place in your unconscious is trying to tell you about what you're supposed to learn from your preoccupation with that part of the movie or dream. You may find yourself the wiser, and the preoccupation with that part of the movie or dream may actually stop.

Describe the results of your activity with someone else in the class, and allow your partner to ask you questions about it. Then listen and respond as your partner discusses his or her results with you.

Chapter 15 The Paragraph

What Is a Paragraph?

> **DEFINITION**
>
> A **paragraph** is a group of sentences that develops one main idea. A paragraph may stand by itself as a complete piece of writing, or it may be a section of a longer piece of writing, such as an essay.

No single rule will tell you how long a paragraph should be. An effective paragraph is always long enough to develop the main idea being presented. If a paragraph is too short, the reader will think basic information is missing; if it is too long, the reader will be bored or confused. This textbook suggests, as a rule, that a healthy paragraph should consist of at least five sentences and no more than twelve sentences. You have undoubtedly read paragraphs in newspapers that are only one sentence long, but in acadmic writing, this is considered unacceptable.

What Does a Paragraph Look Like?

Margins, new-paragraph indication, and complete sentences are essential parts of paragraph form. Study the following paragraph from Elizabeth Pollet's "A Cold-Water Flat" to observe the standard form.

> I got the job. I worked in the bank's city collection department. For weeks, I was like a mouse in a maze: my feet scurried. Every seventh day, I received thirteen dollars. It wasn't much. But, standing beside the pneumatic tube, unloading the bundles of mail that pelted down and distributing them according to their texture, size, and colour to my superiors at their desks, I felt humble and useful.

A margin of adequate width is used on each side of the text (for a manuscript page, this margin should be 2.5 cm, or 1 inch). If another paragraph is added, make sure there is proper indication of the new paragraph. If the first line of the first paragraph is indented (as in the example on the previous page), ensure the first line of the second paragraph is also indented. If you follow the full-block style (no indentation of the first line of a paragraph), then make sure you skip a line between paragraphs. If you're already double-spacing, skip two lines between paragraphs. If you neither indent the first line of your paragraph nor skip an extra line between paragraphs, the reader cannot be expected to know where one paragraph ends and the next one begins.

You will note that the layout of this book follows a different format than that suggested for your essays. The book industry has its own standards and norms relating to page layout.

Figure 15.1 illustrates the structure of the paragraph.

Note: Any space left over at the end of the last line of a paragraph does not, in itself, properly indicate the end of a paragraph. As mentioned, proper indication of a paragraph means either indenting the first line of each one or skipping a line (or two lines, if you're already double-spacing) between paragraphs.

What Is a Topic Sentence?

DEFINITION

A **topic sentence** states the main idea of the paragraph. It contains the topic of the paragraph and a controlling idea (the writer's attitude toward the topic). It is the most general sentence of the paragraph. All the other sentences of the paragraph serve to explain, describe, extend, or support the controlling idea in the topic sentence.

Most paragraphs you read will begin with a topic sentence. However, some topic sentences come in the middle of the paragraph and some come at the end. Occasionally, a paragraph has no stated topic sentence at all; in these cases, the main idea is implied. You are advised to use topic sentences in all your paragraphs in order to be certain that your writing stays focussed and develops a single idea at a time. Whether you are taking an essay exam in a history course, doing a research paper for a sociology course, or writing an essay in a composition course, thoughtful use of the topic sentence will always bring better results. Good topic sentences help both the writer and the reader to think clearly about the main points.

The paragraph that follows makes a point, which is stated in its topic sentence. Read the paragraph and notice how the topic sentence is the most general sentence; it presents the main idea of the paragraph. The other sentences explain, describe, extend, or support the topic sentence.

Two Paragraph Types

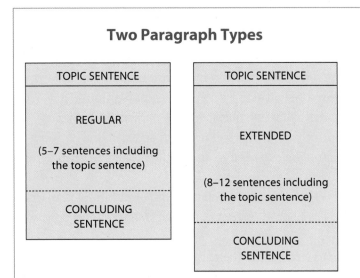

Regular and Extended Paragraphs

A **regular paragraph** has five to seven sentences. An **extended paragraph** is longer (eight to twelve sentences) because it has more supporting detail. The supporting detail of a paragraph is made up of sentences that directly support the topic sentence (see pp. 175–185). These sentences may be main supporting sentences, or they may be specific examples. Some instructors require a concluding sentence, especially when the paragraph stands alone. See "The Concluding Sentence" on pp. 185–186.

Sample Paragraph (Regular): The Value of Friends

One of the areas in which having choice can be extremely valuable is that of friends. Like leaving home to seek greater knowledge of yourself, picking your own friends from a greater number of people can aid in your journey to seek self-knowledge. After all, if you go out with the same group of small town friends all the time, not because you necessarily like them all that much but because they're the only ones available, this can prove quite limiting when it comes to your growth as an individual. The big city, on the other hand, offers an endless number of opportunities to meet people of like interests. You're much more likely to cultivate relationships with people who help you to grow.

Topic Sentence

A **topic sentence** includes two things: a *topic* and a *controlling idea*. The controlling idea is the attitude or position of the writer of the paragraph toward the topic identified in the topic sentence. The controlling idea gives direction to the paragraph. The topic sentence does not always appear first in a paragraph, but until you are well practised, place the topic sentence first. See "What Is a Topic Sentence?" on pp. 169–175.

Transitions

Transitional words or phrases are used to organize the paragraph better and to make the paragraph flow more smoothly.

Stands On Its Own

Any paragraph, even if it is part of a longer work such as an essay, should be able to stand on its own, just as each movie in a series should.

Paragraph Indication

There are only two ways **to indicate a new paragraph:**
   1. **Indent** the first line of the paragraph (see sample paragraph above), or
   2. **Skip a line** before starting the next paragraph. If you are already double-spacing your work, skip two lines, instead of one, before starting the next paragraph.

Figure 15.1: Structure of the Paragraph

The sample paragraph is from "City Life Beats the Small Town Blues" (see pages 294–295).

Model Paragraph: Let's Junk It!

We are the great "Let's junk it" society! Mountains of disposable diapers are thrown into garbage cans every day. Tonnes of yogurt containers, pop cans, and plastic items are discarded without so much as a stomp to flatten them out. If the old Chevy is not worth fixing, tow it off to sit with thousands of others on hectares of fenced-in junkyards. Radios, televisions, and toasters get the same treatment because it is easier and often less expensive to buy a new product than to fix the old one. Who wants a comfortable old sweater if a new one can be bought on sale? No thought is given to the fact that the new one will look like the old one after two or three washings. After all, what's bad for the environment is probably good for the economy!

All the examples in this paragraph support the topic sentence, which states that we are a "throwaway" society. Although the concluding sentence does not repeat the topic sentence in this case, it gives the paragraph a sense of closure. (For more on concluding sentences, see pages 185–86, later in this chapter.)

Practice **Finding the Topic Sentence of a Paragraph**

Each of the following paragraphs contains a topic sentence that states the main idea of the paragraph. Find this sentence and underline it. Check your answers against those in the Answer Key on page 462.

1. Love is a crazy, complicated affair, made trickier by the tangle of superstitions that go along with it. According to the book *Cross Your Fingers, Spit in Your Hat*, you must pull a hair from the head of the one you love to make him or her love you back. Or you can offer your loved one a glass of lemonade in which you have soaked your toenail clippings, or a bowl of soup to which you have added three drops of your blood. Once your sweetheart has devoured either of these concoctions, he or she will love you always.

2. The brain is one of the most remarkable organs, a part of the body that we have only begun to investigate. It will be years before we start to understand all its complex processes. When you remember something, your brain uses more than one method to store the information. You have short-term memory, which helps you recall recent events; you have long-term memory, which brings back items that are further in the past; and you have deep retrieval, which gives you access to long-buried information that is sometimes difficult to recall. Whether these processes are chemical or electrical, we do not yet know, and much research remains to be done before we can say which with any certainty.

How Do You Find the Topic in a Topic Sentence?

To find the topic in a topic sentence, ask yourself this question: What is the topic the writer is going to discuss? Below are two topic sentences. The first topic is underlined. Underline the topic in the second example.

> Backpacking in the mountains last year was an exciting experience.
> College registration can be stressful.

Practice **Finding the Topic in the Topic Sentence**

Find the topic in each of the following topic sentences. For each example, ask yourself this question: What is the topic the writer is going to discuss? Then underline the topic. Check your answers against those in the Answer Key on page 462.

1. Remodelling an old house can be frustrating.
2. College work demands more independence than high school work.
3. A well-made suit has three easily identified characteristics.
4. Growing up near a museum had a profound influence on my life.
5. My favourite room in the house would seem ugly to most people.
6. A student who goes to school full time and also works part time has to make careful use of every hour.
7. One of the disadvantages of skiing is the expense.
8. When we met for dinner that night, I was shocked at the change that had come over my friend.
9. According to the report, current tax laws greatly benefit those who own real estate.
10. Greek restaurants, to the delight of many Canadians, can be found in most of our cities.

What Is a Controlling Idea?

Every topic sentence contains not only the topic, but also a controlling idea.

> **DEFINITION**
>
> The **controlling idea** tells us the position the writer has taken on the topic. It gives the paragraph direction. It is the writer's attitude toward the topic.
> **Example:** Her trip to Kenya was *exciting*.

For example, in the topic sentence "Backpacking in the mountains last year was an exciting experience," the topic is "backpacking" and the controlling idea is that this backpacking trip was "exciting." Another person on the same trip might have had another attitude toward the trip. The person might have found the trip exhausting or boring. A single topic can therefore have any number of possibilities for development, since the writer can choose from a limitless number of controlling ideas, depending on his or her attitude.

How Do You Find the Controlling Idea of a Topic Sentence?

When you look for the controlling idea in a topic sentence, ask yourself this question: What is the writer's attitude toward the topic?

In each of the following examples, the topic is underlined and the controlling idea is circled.

Sealfon's Department Store is my (favourite) store in town.
Sealfon's Department Store is (too expensive) for my budget.

 Practice **Finding the Controlling Idea**

Below are seven topic sentences. For each sentence, underline the topic and circle the controlling idea. Check your answers against those in the Answer Key on page 462.

1. Vigorous exercise is a good way to reduce the effect of stress on the body.
2. St. John's and Corner Brook differ in four major ways.
3. Many so-called wonder foods are less than wonderful.
4. The number of athletic scholarships available to women is increasing.
5. Caffeine has several adverse effects on the body.
6. Madame Benoît, a famous gourmet cook, had an amusing personality.
7. Computers will make newspapers obsolete by 2020.

Choosing Your Own Controlling Idea

Professors often assign one general topic on which all students must write. Likewise, when writing contests are announced, the topic is sometimes the same for all contestants. But it is much less likely that all papers will have the same controlling idea. There could be as many controlling ideas as there are people to write them. The secret of writing a good topic sentence is to use a controlling idea that strongly and accurately expresses your attitude or feeling toward the topic.

Exercise   Choosing Controlling Ideas for Topic Sentences

Below are two topics. For each topic, think of three different possible controlling ideas, and then write a different topic sentence for each of these controlling ideas. An example is done for you.

Topic: My mother

Three possible controlling ideas:
1. Unusual childhood
2. Silent woman
3. Definite ideas about alcohol

Three different topic sentences:
1. My mother had a most unusual childhood.
2. My mother is a very silent woman.
3. My mother has definite ideas about alcohol.

1. **Topic:** My neighbourhood

Controlling Idea A: _____

Topic Sentence A: _____

_____

Controlling Idea B: _____

Topic Sentence B: _____

_____

Controlling Idea C: _____

Topic Sentence C: _____

_____

2. **Topic:** The Internet

Controlling Idea A: _____

Topic Sentence A: _____

_____

Controlling Idea B: _____

Topic Sentence B: _____

_____

Controlling Idea C: _____

Topic Sentence C: _____

_____

 Exercise Further Practice Writing the Topic Sentence

Develop each of the following topics into a topic sentence. In each case, the controlling idea is missing. First, decide on an attitude you might take toward the topic. Then use that attitude to write your topic sentence. When you are finished, underline your topic and circle your controlling idea. Make sure your topic sentence is a complete sentence and not a fragment. An example has been done for you.

Topic: My brother's car accident
Controlling idea: Tragic results
Topic sentence: <u>My brother's car accident</u> had (tragic results) for the entire family.

1. **Topic:** Sending e-mail

Controlling idea: _____

Topic sentence: _____

_____

2. **Topic:** Two years in the armed forces

Controlling idea: _____

Topic sentence: _____

_____

3. **Topic:** Making new friends

   Controlling idea: _____

   Topic sentence: _____

   _____

4. **Topic:** Working as a waiter or waitress

   Controlling idea: _____

   Topic sentence: _____

   _____

5. **Topic:** Going on a diet

   Controlling idea: _____

   Topic sentence: _____

   _____

What Is a Supporting Detail?

DEFINITION

A **supporting detail** is a piece of evidence used by the writer to make the controlling idea of the topic sentence convincing to the reader.

Once you have constructed your topic sentence with its topic and controlling idea, you are ready to move on to supporting your idea with details. These details will convince your readers that what you are claiming in the topic sentence is believable or reasonable.

The Structured Approach

Some instructors require a more structured approach than others when it comes to developing supporting details for a paragraph. This textbook recommends a structured approach. Once you become familiar with the structured approach, you are more likely to be able to take liberties without sacrificing necessary paragraph development.

Two Types

Supporting details can be broken down into two basic types, both of which should be present in every paragraph to make it effective:

1. Main supporting sentence
2. Example sentence (or extended example, which is, simply, a longer example—see page 179)

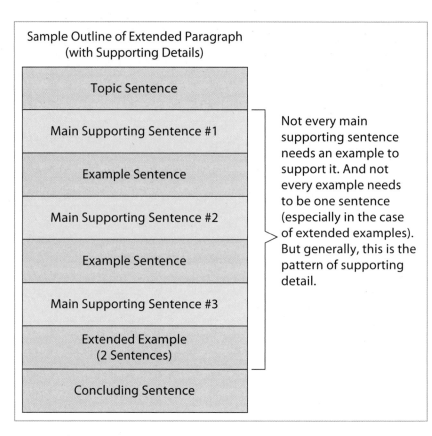

Figure 15.2: Sample Extended Paragraph Outline (with supporting details)

For a sample paragraph showing a breakdown of main supporting sentences and their examples, see the section "Examples (Example Sentences)" on pages 178–179.

Supporting Detail Type #1: Main Supporting Sentences

DEFINITION

A **main supporting sentence** contains a main point that directly supports the topic sentence of the paragraph. A paragraph may have only one main supporting sentence or it may have several.

The first type of supporting detail is the main supporting sentence. This type of detail usually follows the topic sentence immediately. The main supporting sentences contain the main points within the paragraph that support the topic sentence directly. They are often distinguished by the fact that they contain not only main points, but also appropriate **transitions;** these include (but are by no means limited to) *first, second, third,* and *finally.* (For a more extensive list of common transitions, see the inside of the back cover.) There is no definitive proper number of main supporting sentences for a paragraph, but instructors generally like the number three, corresponding to three main points per paragraph. A main supporting sentence is often followed by the second type of supporting detail: an **example** that directly supports the main supporting sentence.

The following extended paragraph is taken from page 280 (in Chapter 23: "Process") about what it takes to get a good night's sleep. It begins with a clear topic sentence, which is then followed by several strong supporting details.

The process of getting a good night's sleep depends on several factors. First, the conditions in your bedroom must be correct. Be sure the room temperature is around 18 degrees Celsius and the room is as quiet as possible. Next, pay attention to your bed and how it is furnished. For example, a firm mattress is best, and wool blankets are better than blankets made of synthetic material. Similarly, a firm pillow is best; after all, one that is too soft can cause a stiff neck and lead to a night of poor sleep. Also, keep in mind that what and how you eat are part of the process of preparing for bed. For example, do not go to bed hungry, but do not overeat, either. And avoid candy bars or cookies; the sugar they contain acts as a stimulant. Finally, do not go to bed until you are sleepy. Do something relaxing until you are tired. In conclusion, everything you do can have an effect on how well you sleep.

Notice that the topic sentence gives us the topic (a good night's sleep) and the writer's attitude toward the topic (that it depends on several factors). Each of the sentences that follow this topic sentence is a supporting detail that convinces us that the controlling idea is a reasonable attitude.

The following shows the breakdown of the topic sentence and the main supporting sentences that support it directly. Example sentences have been omitted for now.

Topic sentence:	The process of getting a good night's sleep depends on several factors.
First main supporting sentence:	First, the conditions in your bedroom must be correct.
Second main supporting sentence:	Next, pay attention to your bed and how it is furnished.
Third main supporting sentence:	Also, keep in mind that what and how you eat are part of the process of preparing for bed.
Fourth main supporting sentence:	Finally, do not go to bed until you are sleepy.

Note the transitions that begin each main supporting sentence: *first, next, also,* and *finally.*

 Exercise **Finding the Topic Sentence and Main Supporting Sentences**

Read the following paragraph. Write down the topic sentence, then list the main supporting sentences.

Loneliness comes at any time. It comes in times of sickness or when friends are absent. It comes during sleepless nights when the heart is heavy, during times of failure at work or in relationships. It comes when we lose trust in ourselves and in others. In old age, loneliness can rise up and threaten to overwhelm us. At such times, life can lose its meaning. Loneliness can feel like death.

Jean Vanier, "Heart of Loneliness"

Supporting Detail Type #2: Examples (Example Sentences)

> **DEFINITION**
>
> An **example** supports (and therefore normally follows) a main supporting sentence. It is a very specific illustration or piece of evidence—more specific than the main supporting sentence it supports. Examples make general ideas more concrete and therefore easier to comprehend and remember. An example may be part of a sentence, it may be an entire sentence on its own, or it may be more than one sentence long.

The same paragraph that was used to illustrate main supporting sentences can be used to demonstrate what examples can look like.

> The process of getting a good night's sleep depends on several factors. First, the conditions in your bedroom must be correct. Be sure the room temperature is around 18 degrees Celsius and the room is as quiet as possible. Next, pay attention to your bed and how it is furnished. For example, a firm mattress is best, and wool blankets are better than blankets made of synthetic material. Similarly, a firm pillow is best; after all, one that is too soft can cause a stiff neck and lead to a night of poor sleep. Also, keep in mind that what and how you eat are part of the process of preparing for bed. For example, do not go to bed hungry, but do not overeat, either. And avoid candy bars or cookies; the sugar they contain acts as a stimulant. Finally, do not go to bed until you are sleepy. Do something relaxing until you are tired. In conclusion, everything you do can have an effect on how well you sleep.

Here is the breakdown of the topic sentence and main supporting sentences again, but this time, the example sentences are also included. Notice how they come after each main supporting sentence, providing even more specific information.

Topic sentence:	The process of getting a good night's sleep depends on several factors.
First main supporting sentence:	First, the conditions in your bedroom must be correct.
Example sentence:	Be sure the room temperature is around 18 degrees Celsius and the room is as quiet as possible.
Second main supporting sentence:	Next, pay attention to your bed and how it is furnished.

Example sentences:	For example, a firm mattress is best, and wool blankets are better than blankets made of synthetic material. Similarly, a firm pillow is best; after all, one that is too soft can cause a stiff neck and lead to a poor night of sleep.

(Note that the above passage actually contains three examples made up of a total of two sentences.)

Third main supporting sentence:	Also, keep in mind that what and how you eat are part of the process of preparing for bed.
Example sentences:	For example, do not go to bed hungry, but do not overeat, either. And avoid candy bars or cookies; the sugar they contain act as a stimulant.

(Note that the third main supporting sentence above is followed by two sentences made up of three examples. The sentence, starting with *"For example, do not go to bed"*, is followed by another sentence that contains a more specific example than that of the first sentence.)

Fourth main supporting sentence:	Finally, do not go to bed until you are sleepy.
Example sentence:	Do something relaxing until you are tired.

Examples may be given in more than one way. They may appear as lists of specific items to illustrate a particular point, or they may be written as extended examples.

DEFINITION

Extended examples include lengthy descriptions or stories that are usually several sentences long (or even an entire paragraph long in an extended piece of writing such as an essay).

A good piece of writing is filled with both kinds of examples—specific items and extended examples—that fit together to create a well-developed, convincing whole. Read the following paragraph on the terminology used in weather forecasting. As you read, look for different examples that show how listening to the weather forecast can be a challenge.

Model Paragraph: The Shortcomings of Forecasting

Not only are weather forecasters often wrong with their forecasts, but they speak a language that only the most knowledgeable meteorologist can understand. For the average television viewer or radio listener, a dictionary is a necessity when listening to the weather forecast. "Watch out for the Alberta clipper, folks. It's coming this way!" seems to be part of the forecasters' lexicon in the winter. Or maybe it's the summer. In any case, what is an Alberta clipper? Are we supposed to hide under a table when it approaches? I've never understood the term, nor have I understood the significance of the dew point or a temperature inversion. How could I ever understand these terms when no one has ever defined them for me? Yet they roll off the tongues of weather forecasters as if everyone should know what is happening. The relative humidity mystifies me, as do troughs and ridges of pressure. I know one thing, however: if the forecast is for a sunny day, be sure to take an umbrella.

 Exercise 1 Finding Examples

Analyze the model paragraph "The Shortcomings of Forecasting," above. What kind(s) of examples can you find in the paragraph?

 Exercise 2 Finding Examples

Find a newspaper or magazine article on a subject that interests you. Examine the article for paragraphs containing lists of examples and paragraphs containing extended examples. How has the writer made the article interesting and memorable through the use of examples?

Qualities of Good Supporting Detail

What makes a good supporting detail? Whether it is a supporting sentence or an example, a supporting detail is stronger if it has these characteristics: it is based on fact, not opinion; it is specific; and it shows respect for other points of view. Your writing will be stronger if, while choosing details to include in your paragraph, you keep these qualities in mind. Each is discussed in more detail below.

State Facts

When you choose your supporting details, focus on facts rather than opinion. Readers do not necessarily have to agree with the point of view you present in your topic sentence or thesis statement, but your supporting details should be accurate and numerous enough to convince your readers to respect your position. You are likely not the only one who has knowledge of a particular subject, so be sure that you don't present vague assertions that leave you open to contradiction. For example, if you may have had many problems with a particular make of car and want to write a paragraph detailing its faults, remember to state exactly what happened; don't rely on further opinions to support your initial opinion.

Use Specific Examples

Remember that specific details tend to stay in readers' minds much longer than general ideas. The statement "over 34 600 males died of cancer in Canada in the year 2000" is much more effective and memorable than "cancer has killed many people." Specific details also make a piece of writing more interesting. When the reader has concrete objects, particular people, or recognizable places to hang on to, the contents of the writing become a pleasure to read.

The more precise your examples, the more clearly they will illustrate your points. For example, in the model paragraph "The Shortcomings of Forecasting" (on pages 179–180), the specific example "Watch out for the Alberta Clipper, folks!" backs up very clearly the statement in the preceding supporting sentence that "a dictionary is a necessity when listening to the weather forecast."

See also the section "How Do You Make Supporting Details Specific?" on pages 183–185, later in this chapter.

Respect Other Points of View

While you hope to convince your reader that what you are saying is true and worthy of belief, remember that no matter how good your supporting sentences and examples are, they might not convince some readers who may have education and experience that you lack. So don't "preach" to the reader or imply in your tone that your point of view is the only one that is valid.

Avoid Restating the Topic Sentence

One of your most important jobs as you write a paragraph is to recognize the difference between a genuine supporting detail (either a main supporting sentence or an example sentence) and a simple restatement of the topic sentence. The following is a poorly constructed paragraph; its sentences merely restate the topic sentence, which has been underlined:

Time Captured in a Picture (I)

<u>My grandmother's photograph dates from a period when she and her family came to live in St. Petersburg.</u> I like to look at the photograph and wonder about how life was in those days. From the clothes that my grandmother is wearing in the old photograph, it looks as if she is ready for a formal occasion. It is difficult to tell, though, because the photograph is old and faded. I don't think she enjoyed formal occasions.

The supporting sentences tell the reader very little about the period in which the photograph was taken. There is no description given of the clothing or why the writer might feel that it was a formal occasion. And even though the photograph is old and faded enough that details can't be seen, the writer assumes that his or her grandmother isn't having a good time.

By contrast, the following paragraph, from Michael Ignatieff's *The Russian Album*, has good supporting details:

Time Captured in a Picture (II)

In the family album there is a photograph of my grandmother, Natasha Ignatieff, that dates from the period when she and her family came to live in St. Petersburg in the dark and cluttered apartment two blocks from the Neva river. She is dressed for a formal winter evening, a fox fur draped over her shoulders. Brussels lace [decorates] the bodice of her velvet gown, her hair [is] swept back in a tight chignon, and a twelve-strand pearl choker [hugs] her stiffly upright neck. She is thin and pale, the cheekbones of her long angular face taking the light, the eyes deep-set and dark. Her expression is guarded, and she seems at odds with the occasion. She was a private soul: in the public glare, she shrank back. She hated Petersburg society: paying courtesy calls on the wives of Paul's superiors, making curtsies and small talk and all the while feeling she was up on a high wire one step from a fall.

Ignatieff's paragraph has vivid illustrations of life in Russia during his grandmother's time. In the first place, naming her gives a personal element to the paragraph. His descriptions of the apartment ("dark and cluttered"), her formal wear ("fox fur," "Brussels lace," "twelve-strand pearl choker"), and her appearance ("hair [is] swept back," "thin and pale," "cheekbones of her long angular face") all support the overall topic: the photograph mentioned in the first sentence. The author provides concrete evidence to back up his statement that she hated St. Petersburg society: her "guarded" expression, the fact that she was a "private soul," and her feeling of being "on a high wire one step from a fall." These details give a clarity and personality to the discussion of the old picture in this paragraph.

Practice **Avoid Restating the Topic Sentence**

Each of the topic sentences below is followed by four additional sentences. Three of these additional sentences contain acceptable supporting details, but one of the sentences is simply a restatement of the topic sentence. In the space provided, identify each sentence as either *SD* (if it supplies supporting detail) or *R* (if it is a restatement). Check your answers against those in the Answer Key on page 462.

1. I am surprised at myself when I think how neat I used to be before I started school full-time.

   _____ a. In my closet, I had my clothes arranged in matching outfits with shoes, hats, and even jewellery to go with them.

   _____ b. I always used to take great pride in having all my things in order.

_____ c. If I opened my desk drawer, compartments of paper clips, erasers, staples, pens, pencils, stamps, and rulers greeted me without one lost penny or safety pin thrown in out of place.

_____ d. On top of my chest of drawers sat a comb and brush, two oval frames with pictures of my best friends, and that was all.

2. Iceland has a very barren landscape.

_____ a. One-tenth of the island is covered with ice.

_____ b. Not one forest with magnificent trees is to be found.

_____ c. Nature has not been kind to the people of Iceland.

_____ d. Three-fourths of the island is uninhabitable.

 Exercise **Distinguishing a Supporting Detail from a Restatement of the Topic Sentence**

Each of the topic sentences below is followed by four additional sentences. Three of these additional sentences contain supporting details, but one of the sentences is simply a restatement of the topic sentence. In the space provided, identify each sentence as *SD* for supporting detail or *R* for restatement.

1. In the last thirty years, the number of people living alone in Canada has increased by 400 percent.

_____ a. People are living alone because the number of divorces has dramatically increased.

_____ b. Many young people are putting off marriage until they are financially more secure or emotionally ready.

_____ c. More and more Canadians are finding themselves living alone.

_____ d. An increasing segment of our population is in the over-65 age group, which includes many widows and widowers.

2. Writing as Sandra Field and Jocelyn Haley, romance author Jill MacLean makes love pay the bills.

_____ a. Her first book, To Trust My Love, was published by Harlequin.

_____ b. Jill received a royalty cheque of about $1800 for her first book.

_____ c. She is the author of thirty-six full-fledged romance novels.

_____ d. Jill MacLean writes love stories under two pen names.

How Do You Make Supporting Details Specific?

Students often write paragraphs that are made up of only general statements. When you read such paragraphs, you doubt the author's knowledge and you suspect that the point being made may have no basis in fact. Here is one such paragraph that never gets off the ground.

Don't Trust Doctors (I)

Doctors are terrible. They cause more problems than they solve. I don't believe most of their treatments are necessary. History is full of the mistakes doctors have made. We don't need all those operations. We should never ingest all those drugs doctors prescribe. We shouldn't allow them to give us all those unnecessary tests. I've heard plenty of stories that prove my point. Doctors' ideas can kill you.

Here is another paragraph on the same topic. This paragraph is much more interesting and convincing because the general statements have been changed throughout the essay to supporting details.

Don't Trust Doctors (II)

Evidence shows that "medical progress" has been the cause of tragic consequences and even death for thousands of people. X-ray therapy was thought to help patients with tonsillitis. Now many of these people are found to have developed cancer from these X-rays. Not so long ago, women were kept in bed for several weeks following childbirth. Unfortunately, this cost many women their lives, since they developed fatal blood clots from lying down day after day. One recent study estimates that 30 000 people each year die from the side effects of drugs that were prescribed by doctors. Recently, the Centers for Disease Control reported that 25 percent of the tests done by clinical laboratories were done poorly. All this is not to belittle the good done by the medical profession, but to impress on readers that it would be foolish to rely totally on the medical profession to solve all our health problems.

This second paragraph is much more likely to be of real interest to a reader. Even if someone disagreed with the author's point, it would be very hard to dismiss these supporting details, which are based on facts and information that can be researched. Because the author sounds reasonable, readers can respect him or her even if they have a different position on the topic.

In writing effectively, the ability to go beyond the general statement and get to accurate pieces of information is what counts. A writer who has a statistic, a quotation, an historical example, or a descriptive detail can use these items to clarify the theme. If the examples are well chosen, readers should go away wanting to share with everyone they meet the surprising information they have just learned.

Good writing is filled with supporting details that are specific, correct, and appropriate for the subject. Poor nonfictional writing is filled with generalizations, stereotypes, vagueness, untruths, and/or insults.

 Exercise 1 Creating Main Supporting Sentences

Below are five topic sentences. Supply three main support sentences for each one. Be sure each sentence is specific, not general or vague. Add appropriate transitions.

1. Jim's entire wardrobe should be burned.

    a. _____

    b. _____

    c. _____

2. The Internet is more valuable than television.

    a. _____

    b. _____

    c. _____

3. Dr. Kline is an easy instructor.

    a. _____

    b. _____

    c. _____

4. It is difficult to stop eating junk food.

    a. _____

    b. _____

    c. _____

5. Learning another language will make your life richer.

    a. _____

    b. _____

    c. _____

 Exercise 2 Creating Examples

After completing Exercise 1, in which you were asked to create main supporting sentences, add an example sentence for every main supporting sentence you wrote. Again, add appropriate transitions such as *for example* or *for instance*.

The Concluding Sentence

Some instructors will require that you add a concluding sentence to your paragraph, especially if you're writing a paragraph that stands on its own and not as part of a larger essay. The concluding sentence should give the paragraph a sense of closure. It should be logical and appropriate. It may or may not restate the topic sentence, but it must not introduce new evidence (supporting detail). It should be more general than the sentences that provide supporting detail. It also should be the last sentence in the paragraph. Look back over the two sample paragraphs entitled "Don't Trust Doctors" (I and II) in the previous section (page 184). Find the concluding sentence in each paragraph. Notice that in one case, the controlling idea of the concluding sentence seems a bit stronger than that of the topic sentence, and in the other case it seems a bit weaker. Either way, however, the concluding sentence reinforces the original controlling idea and does not contradict it.

Concluding Sentences
A concluding sentence • Does not contain new evidence • Is more general than any individual supporting detail • Should be the last sentence in the paragraph • Restates, or at least reinforces, the controlling idea established in the topic sentence (and, therefore, does not contradict the controlling idea of the paragraph) • Gives the paragraph closure • May offer a final commentary on the paragraph

Sample Outline Format

Now that you have learned what all the components of a good paragraph are, it is time to piece them all together. What follows is an outline format that can be used for an **extended paragraph.** How many main supporting sentences to include, how many examples to back up each one, and how many sentences it takes to present each example will depend on the content and on what evidence comes to mind when you are writing. So the following format is merely a suggested one to help you see how everything might fit together. Feel free to use it if it can help guide you as you're practising paragraph development.

For a reminder of the difference between main supporting sentences and examples, review the section "Two Types" earlier in this chapter (pages 175–180).

Topic sentence: _____

_____

Main supporting sentence #1: _____

_____

Example: (2 sentences) _____

_____

_____

_____

Main supporting sentence #2: _____

_____

Continued on next page...

Example: (2 sentences) _____

_____

_____

_____

Main supporting sentence #3: _____

_____

Example: (1 sentence) _____

_____

Concluding sentence: _____

_____

Total: 10 sentences (extended paragraph)

Working Together: Controlling Ideas and Supporting Details

1. While doing the various exercises in this chapter, you have written many topic sentences. Choose one of your best sentences and put it on the board. Read the sentences that other students write on the board; choose one, and underline the topics and circle the controlling ideas. If you think the sentence needs improvements, write your own version underneath the original so the class can compare and contrast them.

2. Every topic contains numerous possibilities for controlling ideas. Take, for example, the topic of education. Think for a moment and jot down one or two controlling ideas that come to your mind regarding this topic. Then, as a class, share your ideas (one student could list all the different controlling ideas on the blackboard). Finally, select one of the controlling ideas on the board (it doesn't have to be one you generated) and use it as the basis for a paragraph.

3. Divide into groups. As a group, select one of the topic sentences on page 185. Together, make a list of as many supporting details or examples as you can. Then, working individually, write a paragraph selecting details from the list prepared by your group.

   Share your paragraph with the other members of your group and read everyone else's. Be sure to give every member enough time to read through all the group's papers. Then discuss the various paragraphs that have been written. Even though each paragraph began with the same topic sentence and supporting details, did all of the paragraphs turn out differently? Why?

Chapter 16 The Essay

Writing Is a Skill

Very few writers can "dash off" a masterpiece. We sometimes think that a person is "a born dancer" or "a born writer," but the reality is that anyone with a high level of skill in an area such as these has worked long hours for many years to reach that point. Writing is no exception. Like playing the piano, cleaning a patient's teeth, or managing a restaurant, writing is a skill. It helps to have talent, but talent must still be developed, and skills must be mastered, even by talented people.

When you learned to write a well-developed paragraph in Chapter 15, you were creating something that could be a support paragraph for an essay. An essay is a longer piece of writing, usually five or more paragraphs, in which you develop a topic in much more depth than you can in a single paragraph. An essay may also be called a composition, thesis, or paper. In most schools, such writing is an important part of many courses, not only English composition.

Transferability

While writing essays is required in any number of areas of study—law enforcement, business studies, office administration, technology, social sciences, journalism, broadcasting, and more—its purpose goes beyond fulfilling the requirements of a postsecondary-level education. Writing essays also helps prepare students for careers by providing the skills necessary to write corporate reports, evaluations, summaries, research papers, letters, memos, and job applications. Although different jobs call for different kinds of written texts with somewhat different structures, the essay is the basic form at the heart of them all. Spelling, grammar, and logic, which are essential to the composition of an effective essay, remain paramount in all forms of writing, as does the ability to express yourself clearly. In short, the skills you develop when you learn how to write an essay are transferable in countless ways. Contrary to what some people

say—that the essay is an outdated exercise—the essay is timelessly practical because of this obvious transferability.

You learned in Chapter 15 that a paragraph, with its topic sentence and supporting details, must have an organization that is both unified and coherent. An essay must also have these characteristics. Furthermore, since an essay develops a topic more thoroughly, making all the parts work together becomes an added challenge. Figure 16.1 illustrates the structure of an essay.

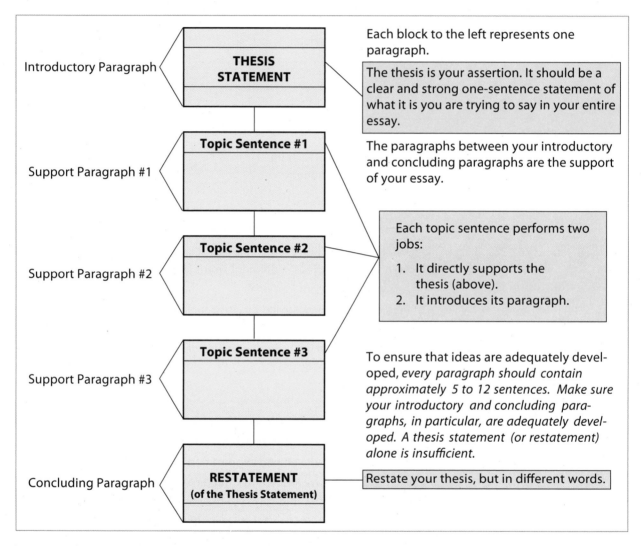

Figure 16.1: The Structure of an Essay

The Components of an Essay

Three types of paragraphs must always be present in an essay: an introductory paragraph, support paragraphs, and a concluding paragraph.

1. **The introductory paragraph is the first paragraph of the essay.**
   Its purpose is to be so inviting that the reader will want to continue reading. This introduction must contain a thesis statement.

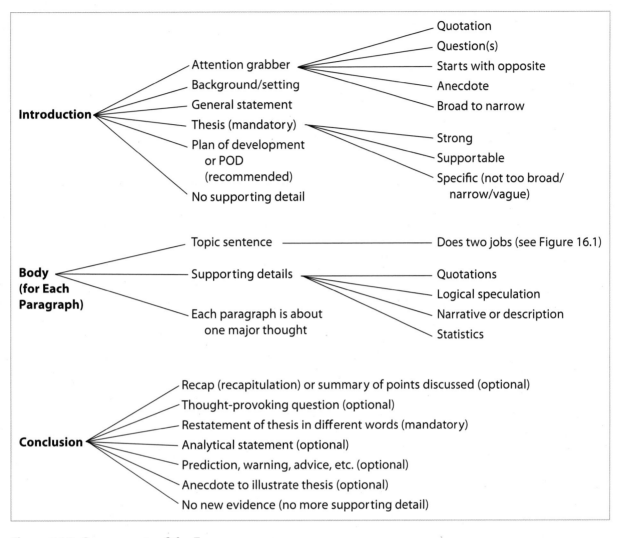

Figure 16.2: Components of the Essay

2. **Support paragraphs (sometimes called body paragraphs) provide the evidence that shows your thesis is valid.** An essay normally has at least three well-developed support paragraphs. (These are the kinds of paragraphs you have studied in Chapter 15.) For an essay, however, one paragraph must flow logically into the next. This flow is accomplished by the careful use of **transitional devices** (discussed later in this chapter).

3. **The concluding paragraph is the last paragraph of the essay.** Its purpose is to give the reader a sense of coming to a satisfying ending—a feeling that everything has been said that needed to be said.

Figure 16.2 illustrates these components of an essay.

Moving from the Paragraph to the Essay

The paragraph can be consdered a mini-essay of sorts. A well-written paragraph includes all the skeletal elements of a full-fledged essay. For it to be transformed, it needs to be expanded and fleshed out. Figure 16.3 shows the relationship between the two structures.

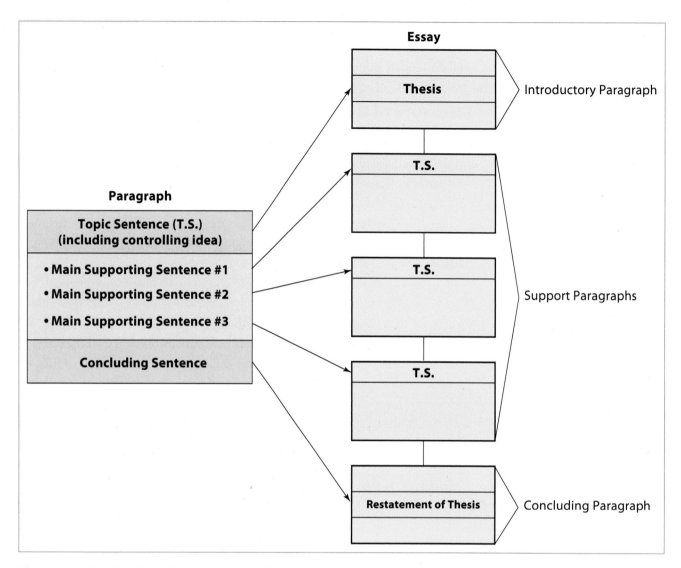

Figure 16.3: Moving from the Paragraph to the Essay

As the figure above shows, once the basic structure of a paragraph (left) has been transferred to the corresponding structure of an essay (right), it is just a matter of adding detail, especially in the area of examples, to make the essay complete. (For more about examples, see pages 178–180 in Chapter 15: "The Paragraph.") The most important work—the identification of the topic, of the controlling idea, and of the main points (in the form of main supporting sentences in the paragraph) has already been done. The main supporting sentences in the paragraph translate into topic sentences in the essay. In fact, the wording of a main supporting sentence in a paragraph and of the corresponding topic sentence in an essay can be exactly the same.

A Third Format: The Preliminary Essay

Although not nearly as traditional as either the paragraph or the essay, a third format, the preliminary essay, is used by some instructors to fill the gap between the two more traditional formats. Learning to write preliminary essays allows you

to progress from writing paragraphs to writing essays more gradually so the task does not become unmanageable. The resulting products are more likely to be well developed and effective.

Structure of the Preliminary Essay

Chapter 15 on the paragraph introduced two types of paragraphs: the regular-sized one and the extended one. This chapter introduces the standard essay as a five-paragraph composition starting with an introductory paragraph, continuing with three support paragraphs, and ending with a concluding paragraph. You might expect the structural size of the preliminary essay, logically, to be somewhere in between those of the paragraph and the essay. You would be correct.

This textbook recommends that a preliminary essay include a one-sentence thesis statement plus three support paragraphs. The support paragraphs should directly support, and be introduced by, the thesis statement.

In order to properly introduce the support paragraphs when composing a preliminary essay, one can write a three-point thesis statement (one point for each support paragraph). Some instructors might require this. But unless your instructor makes this a requirement, it is not necessary as long as the topic sentences that begin your support paragraphs are effectively written.

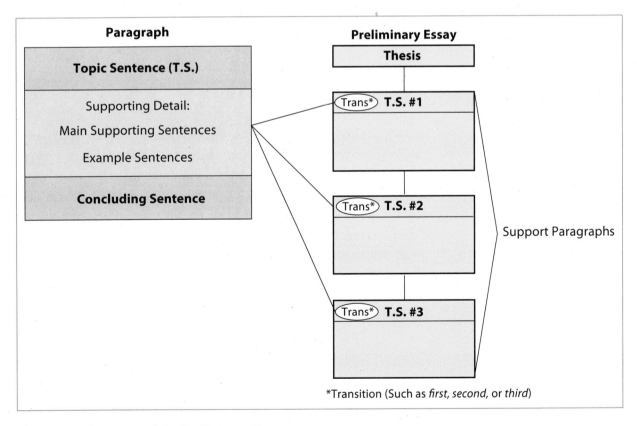

Figure 16.4: Structure of the Preliminary Essay

Exercise **Writing a Preliminary Essay**

Look at the picture of Prince William and Kate Middleton (now the Duke and Duchess of Cambridge) as they arrive on Parliament Hill in Ottawa in July 2011. Write a preliminary essay in response to one of the following topics:

1. What challenges does this couple face in their new life together?
2. Do you wish you were in William's or Kate's shoes? Why or why not?

THE CANADIAN PRESS/Sean Kilpatrick

Look at the photo below of Wayne Gretzky taking part in the opening ceremonies of the 2010 Vancouver Olympics. Write a preliminary essay in response to the following topic:

Was Wayne Gretzky a good choice to light the torch at the opening ceremonies of the Vancouver Games? Why or why not?

AP Photo/The Canadian Press, Adrian Wyld

Features of the Essay

Before you begin the process of writing your own essays, this chapter will prepare you to understand and work with these special essay features:

- Thesis statement
- Introductory paragraph
- Transitions between body paragraphs
- Concluding paragraph

What Is a Thesis Statement?

DEFINITION

The **thesis** of an essay is a statement of the main idea of that essay. It usually contains an element of opinion or argument. It is sometimes described as the claim that the evidence in the rest of the essay is expected to support.

The thesis states what you are going to explain, defend, or prove about your topic. It is usually placed in the middle or at the end of the introductory paragraph.

Plan of Development or POD

DEFINITION

A **plan of development,** or **POD,** is an introduction to the main points that are intended to support the thesis statement. The best place for this POD is in the introductory paragraph, immediately after the thesis statement.

Some books on writing say that a thesis statement itself should contain within it the three points that you will discuss throughout the supporting paragraphs of your essay. For purposes of this book, a three-point thesis is not necessary for either a preliminary essay or an essay. In fact, it is recommended here that in an essay you instead introduce these points after the thesis statement using a plan of development (POD) (see Figure 16.2, "Components of the Essay"). Separating the thesis from the points that will be used to support it allows you more freedom to write a forceful and effective thesis statement. That said, if you do come up with a thesis that introduces your three support points and is still clear, brief, and strong, feel free to go with it.

How to Recognize a Thesis Statement

1. **The thesis statement is a complete sentence.** Students sometimes confuse a thesis statement with an essay's title. Remember that titles are usually phrases rather than complete sentences.

   Title: The Advantages of All-Day Kindergarten
   Thesis: Schools should offer parents the option of an all-day kindergarten program for their children, not only for the benefit of mothers who work outside the home, but also for the sake of the children.

2. The thesis statement presents a viewpoint about the topic that will be defended or shown in the essay. It may be based on facts, but it is not itself a fact.

      Fact: Nearly all kindergartens in Canada offer a half-day of instruction.

    Thesis: Parents know there is more than one reason why most five-year-old children should be in school for only half a day.

Practice Recognizing the Thesis Statement

In the space provided, identify each of the following as (1) a title, (2) a thesis, or (3) a fact that could be used to support a thesis. Check your answers against those in the Answer Key on page 463.

_____3_____ 1. The personal interview is the most important step in the employment process.

_____1_____ 2. Looking for a job

_____3_____ 3. Sixty percent of all jobs are obtained through newspaper advertisements.

_____2_____ 4. The best time to begin learning a foreign language is in grade school.

_____1_____ 5. The importance of learning a foreign language

_____3_____ 6. By the year 2000, the number of students studying foreign languages was dramatically lower than what it had been a decade earlier.

_____2_____ 7. Most Canadians doing business with Japan do not know a word of Japanese.

Writing an Effective Thesis Statement

An effective thesis statement has two or three parts:

1. **It contains a topic that is not too broad.** Broad topics must be narrowed down in scope. You can do this by *limiting the topic* (changing the term to cover a smaller part of a broad topic) or *qualifying the topic* (adding phrases or words to the general term that will narrow down the topic).

      Broad topic: Swimming

   Limited topic: Learning to float (Floating is a kind of swimming, more specialized than the term *swimming*.)

  Qualified topic: Swimming for health two hours a week (The use of the phrase "for health two hours a week" narrows the topic down considerably. Now the time spent swimming and the reason for swimming are parts of the topic.)

There are a number of ways to narrow a topic in order to make it fit into a proper essay length, as well as make it fit your experience and knowledge.

2. **It contains a controlling idea that you can defend.** The controlling idea is what you want to show or prove about your topic; it is your attitude

about that topic. The controlling idea is often an adjective, such as *beneficial,* *difficult,* or *maddening.*

> Learning to float at the age of 20 was a *terrifying* experience. Swimming two hours a week brought about a *dramatic* change in my health.

3. **Optional: It indicates what strategy for development is to be used.** To indicate the strategy, you can use words such as description, steps, stages, comparison, contrast, causes, effects, reasons, advantages, disadvantages, definition, analysis, persuasion, classification.

Although not all writers include the strategy in the thesis statement, they must always have in mind what major strategy they plan to use to prove their thesis. Professional writers often use more than one strategy in a text. However, in this book, you are asked to develop your essays by using one major strategy at a time. By working in this way, you can concentrate on understanding and developing the skills needed for each specific strategy.

Study the following thesis statement:

> Although a date with the right person is marvellous, going out with a group can have many advantages.

Now look back and check the parts found within it.

General topic:	Going out
Qualified topic:	Going out in a group
Controlling idea:	To give the advantages
Strategy for development:	Contrast between the couple date and the group date

 Exercise   Writing the Thesis Statement

Below are three topics. For each one, develop a thesis statement by (1) limiting or qualifying the general topic, (2) choosing a controlling idea (what you want to explain or prove about the topic), and (3) selecting a strategy that you could use to develop that topic. (Possible strategies include narration, description, process, comparison or contrast, definition, classification, and cause and effect.) An example has been done for you.

General topic: Senior citizens

a. Limited or qualified topic:

Community services available to the senior citizens in my town

b. Controlling idea:

To show the great variety of programs

c. Strategy for development:

Classify the services into major groups.

Thesis statement: The senior citizens of New Glasgow, Nova Scotia, are fortunate to have programs available to help them deal with health, housing, and leisure time.

1. Winnipeg (or another city with which you are familiar)
   a. Limited or qualified topic:

   _____

   b. Controlling idea:

   _____

   c. Strategy for development:

   _____

   Thesis statement:

   _____

   _____

2. Shopping
   a. Limited or qualified topic:

   _____

   b. Controlling idea:

   _____

   c. Strategy for development:

   _____

   Thesis statement:

   _____

   _____

3. Canadians
   a. Limited or qualified topic:

   _____

   b. Controlling idea:

   _____

   c. Strategy for development:

   _____

   Thesis statement:

   _____

   _____

Answering a Question in the Form of a Thesis Statement

One of the most effective ways to begin an essay is to start with a thesis statement that directly answers a question. Your thesis statement should include the important parts of the question and should also give a clear indication of the approach you intend to take in your answer.

For example, suppose you were going to write an essay in response to the following question:

> Why did the Conservatives under Stephen Harper win a majority of seats in the federal election of 2011?

An effective way to begin would be to write the following thesis sentence:

> The Conservatives under Stephen Harper won a majority of seats in the federal election of 2011 for several reasons.

The reader would then know that this was the topic you had chosen and would also know how you intended to approach this topic.

Note: This is not a three-point thesis statement; it does not introduce all the supporting points that will be in the body paragraphs of the essay. But it is worded in such a way that the reader might expect a few reasons to be introduced immediately following the thesis in the form of a plan of development (POD).

 Exercise Writing Thesis Statements

Answer each of the following questions in the form of a thesis statement. Read each question carefully and underline the important words or phrases in it. Then formulate a thesis that is a one-sentence direct answer to the question. An example has been done for you.

Essay question: How does one <u>learn another language</u>?
Thesis statement: The process of learning another language is complicated, but usually follows four distinct stages.

1. Essay question: Should or should not the Canadian government support young artists?

    Thesis statement:

    _____

    _____

2. Essay question: What is the value of being able to speak two languages in Canada?

    Thesis statement:

    _____

    _____

3. Essay question: Is it harmful or beneficial to adopt a child from one culture and raise that child in another culture?

    Thesis statement:

    _____

    _____

4. Essay question: In what ways can the Canadian government discourage people from smoking?

Thesis statement:

_____

_____

5. Essay question: Are some forms of advertising harmful, and, if so, should harmful advertising be banned?

Thesis statement:

_____

_____

The Introductory Paragraph

DEFINITION

An **introduction** has a purpose that is two-fold: to grab your readers' attention so that they will keep reading and to establish the thesis or your main idea.

There is no one way to write an introduction. However, since many good introductions follow a few common patterns, you will find it helpful to look at a few examples of these patterns as you learn to write your own introductions. In the following examples, the thesis statement is usually at the end.

1. **Begin with a general subject that can be narrowed down to the specific topic of your essay.** Here is an introductory paragraph on astronomy, from *Universe* by W.J. Kaufmann:

   > Speculation about the nature of the universe is one of the most characteristic human endeavours. The study of the stars transcends all boundaries of culture, geography, and politics. The modern science of astronomy carries an ancient tradition of observation and speculation, using the newest tools of technology and mathematics. In the most literal sense, astronomy is a universal subject—its subject is, indeed, the universe.

2. **Begin with specifics (a brief anecdote, a specific example or fact) that will broaden into the more general topic of your essay.** Here is the introduction to Miriam Waddington's "The Hallowe'en Party," an essay about a family of Russian Jews settling on a prairie farm just outside of Winnipeg:

   > The year that I was twelve, my father came home one day and announced that he had bought a farm. My sister Helen and I could hardly wait to see the farm which, according to my father, consisted of 26 acres in St. Vital, just beyond the outskirts of Winnipeg. . . . My father had dreamed of such a farm all the years he was shut up in the dark greasy machine shop where he earned his living. Now as I look back, I can understand my father's deep hunger for land.

3. **Give a definition of the concept that will be discussed.** Here is the introduction to "Love Hurts," an essay by Jenny Yuen about the problem of love and sex addiction (see pages 302–304 in Chapter 25). The actual definition is in the last sentence.

> For love and sex addicts, Valentine's Day may not be simply roses and candy, but rather a traumatic reminder that love hurts. February 14 may bring back painful memories of past breakups, or trigger the need to go out and find a "special someone" who may not turn out to be all that special. Sexual and love addiction is the continuing pattern of unwanted compulsive romantic behaviour that has a negative impact on the addict's personal, social and /or economic standing.

4. **Include a plan of development** (a brief summary of points that will support your thesis) **after your thesis statement.**

> Are you a *Law and Order* junkie? Well, if you are, you'll know that the State of New York has the death penalty. And it seems that it gets applied every now and again, if the TV show is any indication. But in Canada, the death penalty was abolished, and it's time to bring it back. One reason to do so is the money that taxpayers will save when the state no longer has to maintain the lives of hardened criminals who will never be freed anyway. Secondly, there is no redemption for criminals who are sentenced to life in prison. And lastly, the punishment should fit the crime.

5. **Start with an idea or statement that is a widely held point of view.** Then surprise the reader by stating that this idea is false or that you hold a different point of view. Here is an example from "A Planet for the Taking," by David Suzuki:

> Canadians live under the remarkable illusion that we are a technologically advanced people. Everything around us denies that assumption. We are, in many ways, a Third World country, selling our natural resources in exchange for the high technology of the industrialized world. Try going through your home and looking at the country of origin of your clothes, electrical appliances, books, car. The rare technological product that does have Canada stamped on it is usually from a branch plant of a multinational company centred in another country.

6. **Include a familiar quotation or a paraphrase of something said by a famous person,** as Zack Goodman does in the following example from "City Life Beats the Small Town Blues." (For the whole essay, see pages 294–295 in Chapter 24.)

> Growing up in a small town has its perks. You might have fewer friends than you have in the big city, but you tend to keep them closer. The East Coast small town author Hugh MacLennan once said that writers who grow up in small towns have a greater knowledge of human intimacy even if their writing ideas stemming from this knowledge run dry before they

turn 40. Well, not everybody agrees with either of those points. In fact, city life can offer just as much knowledge of intimacy if not more than small town life can. Life is better in the big city, and it all comes down to one general reason: more choice.

7. **Give a number of descriptive images that will lead to the thesis of your essay.** The descriptive images can make up the plan of development, which, in the case of the following paragraph, comes *before* the thesis statement.

> The nuclear family is breaking up. Both parents are working and children are left on their own for long periods of time, or are sent to daycare centres. Youngsters are learning about life from television and from movies, although the life that they learn about is often far removed from the truth. The incidence of crime is increasing among children because they receive little guidance, and even less teaching, on the difference between right and wrong. Social, moral, and religious values are declining. These are among the reasons why the fabric of society is decaying.

What *Not* to Say in Your Introduction

1. Avoid telling your reader that you are beginning your essay:

   > In this essay I will discuss . . .
   > I will talk about . . .
   > I am going to prove . . .

2. Don't apologize:

   > Although I am not an expert . . .
   > In my humble opinion . . .

3. Do not refer to later parts of your essay:

   > By the end of this essay, you will agree . . .
   > In the next paragraph, you will see . . .

4. **Don't use trite expressions.** Since they have been so overused, they will lack interest. Using such expressions shows that you have not taken the time to come up with your own words to express your ideas. Some examples of trite expressions include the following:

   > He was busy as a bee.
   > You can't tell a book by its cover.
   > Haste makes waste.

Using Transitions to Move from One Idea to the Next

Successful essays help the reader follow the logic of the writer's thinking by using transitional expressions when needed. Transitions usually occur when the writer is moving from one point to the next. They are also useful whenever an idea is complicated. A writer may also use transitions when summarizing the points covered thus far, emphasizing a point already made, or repeating an important point. A transition may be a word, a phrase, a sentence, or even a paragraph.

In an essay, composition, or research paper, transitions link paragraphs and the ideas in them in the same way that they link ideas within a sentence or a paragraph. Here are some examples of transitional expressions you might use to help the reader make the right connections between paragraphs. For your convenience, refer to the **chart on the inside back cover of this book.**

1. To make your points stand out clearly:

the first reason	second, secondly	finally
first of all	another example	most important
in the first place	even more important	all in all
	also, next	in conclusion
	then	to summarize

2. To present an example of what has just been said:

> for example
> for instance

3. To present the consequence of what has just been said:

> therefore
> as a result
> then

4. To make a contrasting point clear:

> on the other hand
> but
> contrary to current thinking
> however

5. To admit a point:

> of course
> granted

6. To resume your argument after admitting a point that does not support it:

> nevertheless
> even so
> nonetheless
> still

7. To call the reader's attention to the organizational structure of the text:

> Before attempting to answer these questions, let me . . .
> In our discussion so far, we have seen that . . .
> At this point, it is necessary to . . .
> It is beyond the scope of this paper to . . .

A more subtle way to link one idea to another in an essay is to repeat a word or phrase from the preceding sentence.

> I have many memories of my childhood in the Yukon. These *memories* include the aunts, uncles, grandparents, and friends I left behind when I moved to Ontario.

Sometimes instead of the actual word, a pronoun will take the place of the word.

> Like many Northerners, I've had to learn to adapt to an urban way of life. *It* hasn't been easy, but today I almost think of myself as a Torontonian.

The Concluding Paragraph

A concluding paragraph has one main purpose: to give the reader the sense of reaching a satisfying ending to the topic discussed. Students often feel they have nothing to say at the end. A look at how professional writers frequently end their essays can ease your anxiety about writing an effective conclusion. You have more than one possibility; here are some of the most frequently used patterns for ending an essay.

1. **Come full circle—that is, return to the material in your introduction.** Finish in your conclusion what you started in your introduction. The material returned to might be "the grabber," as in the case of the following example. But remind the reader of the thesis, also. Whether you're only returning to the thesis, which is mandatory, or reminding the reader of the initial grabber, also, remember to remind the reader with different wording. To illustrate this, here are excerpts from the first and last paragraphs of the essay "The Cell Phone: Tomorrow's Medical Menace?" (see pages 242–251 in Chapter 20).

First paragraph:

> Cell phones are the latest craze—a modern addiction. For young people, the cell phone not only contributes to the look of "cool" in the way smoking once did and perhaps still does for some, but also offers them a degree of independence—a way to stay in touch with friends without having to check at home for messages. . . . Until it is known for certain whether people will develop serious diseases such as dementia or cancer directly due to cell phone use, it would be wise for cell phone users to err on the side of caution and take steps to minimize potential damage to the brain.

Last paragraph:

> Someone walking down the street with a cell phone at his or her ear, for many young people, still rates high on the meter of "cool." It makes some people feel important when it looks like they are "well connected." . . . For those who cannot quit using cell phones any more easily than it is for some to quit smoking, they might want to try the tips listed in this essay. . .

2. **Summarize by repeating the main points.** The following example of a concluding paragraph is from the essay "City Life Beats the Small Town Blues," by Zack Goodman, which appears in its entirety on pages 294–295.

> A small town has its advantages; that's true. The cost of living is lower. The streets are probably safer at night. And it might even be easier to meet someone special. But if you're an arts lover who enjoys the company of people from all over the world, and you're interested in cultivating friends who help you to grow spiritually and not just to get drunk on a Saturday night, city life is tough to beat.

3. **Show the significance of your thesis by making predictions, giving a warning, giving advice, offering a solution, suggesting an alternative, or telling the results.** This example is from David Suzuki's essay "A Planet for the Taking," whose introductory paragraph was discussed earlier in this chapter, on page 200.

> But Canadians do value the spiritual importance of nature and want to see it survive for future generations. We also believe in the power of science to sustain a high quality of life. And while the current understanding of science's power is, I believe, misplaced, in fact the leading edges of physics and ecology may provide the insights that can get us off the current track. We need a very profound perceptual shift and soon.

4. **End with an anecdote that illustrates your thesis.** This example is from an essay, again by David Suzuki, entitled "Hidden Lessons" on the danger of unintentionally giving children the idea that the environment is disgusting.

> It's not easy to avoid giving these hidden lessons. I have struggled to cover my dismay and queasiness when Severn and Sarika come running in with a large wolf spider or when we've emerged from a ditch covered with leeches or when they have been stung accidentally by yellow jackets feeding on our leftovers. But that's nature. I believe efforts to teach children to love and respect other life forms are priceless.*

What *Not* to Say in Your Conclusion

1. Do not introduce a new point:

> Something else of importance . . .
> Additional information has come to light . . .
> A new idea . . .

2. Do not apologize:

> Unfortunately, this essay cannot end on a more positive note . . .
> If there were more space . . .
> It is impossible to be sure of every point . . .

*David Suzuki, "Hidden Lessons." Reprinted by permission of the author.

3. Do not end with a statement that is "up in the air," leaving the reader feeling unsatisfied. This sometimes happens when the very last sentence is not strong enough:

> Maybe the problem will never be solved . . .
> There is no obvious solution . . .
> Hopefully, things will get better . . .

Titles

Be sure to follow the standard procedure for writing your title.

1. Try to think of a short and catchy phrase (approximately three to six words). Avoid complete sentences, even if they're short. Often writers wait until they have written a draft before working on a title. There may be a phrase from the essay that will be perfect. If you still cannot think of a clever title after you have written a draft, choose some key words from your thesis statement, especially that part of the thesis that suggests the point of view you have taken.
2. Capitalize the first letter of the first word and the last word; then capitalize the first letter of the other words except articles (*the, a, an*), prepositions (such as *in, of*, and *on*), and short conjunctions (such as *and, but*, and *so*).
3. Do not put quotation marks around the title when it is in the title position.
4. Centre the title at the top of the page, and remember to leave about 2.5 cm (1 inch) of space between the title and the beginning of the first paragraph.

Sample Outline Format

Now that you have learned the various components of an essay, it's time to put them all together. The following is a suggested format for an essay outline. It includes suggestions for length, but how long each element is depends on what your instructor's requirements are, what evidence comes to your mind when you are writing the essay, and so on. Next time you write an essay for practice, try using this sample format to help you structure your essay properly.

For a reminder of the difference between a supporting sentence and an example, see pages 175–180 in Chapter 15: "The Paragraph."

Essay title: _____
(see "Titles" on page 205)

First Paragraph (introduction):
Attention grabber: (1 sentence) _____
General statement: (2 sentences) _____

_____

Thesis: (one sentence) _____

Continued on next page...

Plan of development: (one sentence) _____

_____

Second Paragraph (first support paragraph):

Topic sentence: _____

Supporting detail #1: _____

Example: _____

Supporting detail #2: _____

_____

Example: _____

Third Paragraph (second support paragraph):

Topic sentence: _____

Supporting detail #1: _____

Example: (2 sentences) _____

_____

Supporting detail #2: _____

Example: (1 sentence) _____

Supporting detail #3: _____

Supporting detail #4: _____

Fourth Paragraph (third support paragraph):

Topic sentence: _____

Supporting detail #1: (2 sentences) _____

_____

Supporting detail #2: _____

Example: (2 sentences) _____

_____

Supporting detail #3: _____

Fifth Paragraph (conclusion):

Recap: (3 sentences) _____

_____

_____

Thesis restatement: _____

Question for further research: _____

Thought-provoking idea (prediction): _____

Working Together: Education Endangered?

1. The cartoon below uses the technique of a multiple-choice quiz to suggest reasons that education in North America is in trouble. As a class or in groups, discuss each of the four areas of concern raised by the cartoonist. Then write a five-paragraph essay on the subject (be sure it has an introductory paragraph, three supporting paragraphs, and a paragraph of conclusion). Use the information you have learned in this chapter to write a good introduction and conclusion. For your supporting paragraphs, choose three of the four areas of concern shown in the cartoon and make each one the main idea for one of the supporting paragraphs. Be sure to make use of the ideas generated during the class discussion.

TOLES © 1989 *The Washington Post*. Reprinted with permission of UNIVERSAL UCLICK. All rights reserved.

2. Join one of three groups in the class. In your group, study the introductory and concluding paragraphs in any essay in the "Readings" section of this book (Unit IV). Analyze each introduction and conclusion to decide if the author has chosen one of the patterns suggested in this chapter. Can you point to one sentence as the author's thesis statement?

Chapter 17　Revising and Editing

The Final Stage

Too many writers finish a first draft and then immediately start rereading to catch mistakes. Their idea is to get the editing process over with as soon as possible. If the writer misses a few little mistakes, who's going to notice? But revising and editing involve much more than a quick rereading, hoping any mistakes jump out. This stage involves a well-planned approach to making improvements, finding mistakes, and discovering better ways of writing.

Revising and editing are essential components of the writing process. Of course, you'll need to proofread your final copy for typos and other mistakes you may have made, but the revising and editing steps must come before proofreading.

What Is the Difference between Revising and Editing?

Revising and editing are often thought of as one and the same thing. They are not. Specifically, revising is rereading your first draft very carefully and making major improvements. You might replace an entire paragraph with a new one, for example. You might cut the length of a large anecdote in half and add a different, smaller one. Editing, on the other hand, usually means making smaller, but still important, changes. Revising often refers to changing the content, whereas editing often refers to improving the organization of the composition and the style of the writing. Too many people do not spend enough time on these parts of the writing process. However, it's better to make improvements yourself at this stage than to have your professor point out the need for them later.

Proofreading

After the revising and editing are finished, proofreading begins. Proofreading refers, mostly, to correcting mistakes at a more "micro" level, for example, grammar or spelling errors. Minor factual errors in content might also be caught at this stage.

The Right Conditions for the Tasks

When you've finished the first draft of your work, set it aside for a day or two if you can. Then read through the whole thing, making notes, corrections, or additions based on the checklists that start below, which are adapted from *The Reluctant Writer* by Roger Mann and John Roberts. Many instructors recommend that you read your essay out loud. Some say that writers can catch up to 70 percent of their own errors this way. At the final stage, it is important to print a hard copy of your final draft in order to proofread your work. You will have a better chance of spotting errors this way than if you do your final read-through onscreen, since the eyes read better with reflected light (off paper) than with emitted light (from a computer screen).

What you need first is a quiet place and a block of time that will allow you to complete the task in one sitting. When you have completed your own revising and editing, you might also ask someone else to read your material and offer a second opinion on the quality of your work and suggestions for improvement. Finally, keep in mind that your computer's spell check and grammar check programs are not infallible. As the writer, you are ultimately responsible for your own work; that includes the revising, the editing, and the proofreading.

Master Checklist for Revising and Editing

1. Check the macrocomposition: the content and the overall arrangement of ideas. (See Macrocomposition Checklist below.)
2. Check the microcomposition: the flow of thought, the sentence structure, and the wording, grammar, and usage. (See Microcomposition Checklist on the next page.)
3. Check the spelling.
4. Check the punctuation.
5. Check the manuscript form.

Macrocomposition Checklist

1. Have you provided enough background explanation at the outset for the reader to:
   a. recognize the context?
   b. understand what follows?
   c. want to read further?
2. Do the ideas introduced in the beginning connect logically to a continuous line of thought that moves sensibly from introduction to discussion and ends in a conclusion? Are appropriate connecting words used?
3. Are the thoughts packaged in small chunks of information that the audience is capable of following? Will the sequence of ideas convince and enlighten the reader?
4. Is the information sufficient to do the job it is intended to do? Are there any gaps? Is all of the discussion relevant to the subject and the purpose?
5. Is the point of view consistent throughout the text?
6. Are the time sequences logical and consistent? Are all the verbs in the correct tense and mood?
7. Is the wording concise, and are physical references precise and concrete? If you are dealing with ideas and concepts, are they adequately explained and illustrated? Is the wording geared to the presumed reading level of the reader?
8. Is the tone appropriate to the situation, the purpose, and the reader? Is it consistent throughout the text?
9. Does the conclusion fulfill the intended purpose? At the end, will the reader understand the message, agree with what you have said, and be motivated to act?

Microcomposition Checklist

Check your sentences for *grammar:*
1. Is every sentence grammatically complete, with no sentence fragments?
2. In sentences with two or more independent clauses, are the clauses grammatically parallel, and either connected by coordinating conjunctions or separated by semi-colons, with no run-ons?
3. Are subordinate clauses and verb phrases clearly related to the words they modify, with no dangling or misplaced modifiers?
4. Are the elements of each sentence consistent in grammar and in thought?
   - Do subjects agree with verbs?
   - Do pronouns agree with their antecedents and with each other in person and in number?
   - Is it clear which nouns the pronouns stand in for?
   - Are the verb tenses consistent?
   - If you have used lists, are the elements of each list grammatically parallel?
   - Is the word order appropriate and easy to follow?

Check your sentences for *style:*
1. Are the beginnings of your sentences varied—do some start with the subject, some with introductory phrases or clauses, and a select few with reversed word order?
2. Have you varied the clause structure of your sentences—some simple, some compound, and some complex?
3. Have you mixed your sentence lengths effectively—long sentences to convey information and establish a rhythm, short sentences to get important points across?

Check your *wording* and *usage:*
1. Have you used vocabulary suitable to the reader and the situation?
2. Are your nouns concrete, tangible, and specific?
3. Are your verbs active or passive as is appropriate to the context?
4. Have you used adjectives and adverbs selectively and sparingly? Can you replace any adjective-noun or adverb-verb combinations with carefully selected single nouns or verbs?
5. Could you explain the reason for your choice of every word and its placement in the sentence?
6. Have you used any words that you are not entirely sure about—the spelling, the meaning, or the way the words should be used?
7. Have you used any clichés? If so, can you justify using them? If not, can you think of original expressions to replace them?
8. Have you used any idiomatic expressions? If so, are you sure you have used them correctly and appropriately?
9. Have you used jargon, such as technical terms or acronyms? Are you sure the reader will understand these terms?

Check your *punctuation:*
1. Have you used periods at the ends of sentences and after abbreviations?
2. Do question marks indicate the ends of interrogative sentences?
3. Have you used exclamation marks to emphasize especially important points or statements? (Do not overuse this device!)
4. Have you used quotation marks properly—for all direct speech, direct quotations from sources, and titles of short works?
5. Have you used, but not overused, commas to pace the reader's understanding of the text, to separate internal parts of your sentences, and to clarify potentially ambiguous word combinations?
6. Have you used semicolons to separate parts of a sentence that are grammatically distinct, or to separate items in a complex list?
7. Have you used dashes and colons correctly?

Check your spelling, capitalization, and apostrophes:
1. Have you checked the words you traditionally have trouble with?
2. Have you checked *ie* combinations, spelling changes caused by suffixes, and consonants that must be doubled or not?

(continued)

(continued)

3. Have you used capital letters properly—for titles, names, places, months, countries, etc.?
4. Have you used apostrophes correctly—for possessive nouns and indefinite pronouns, or for contractions?

Check your manuscript form:

1. Has all your source material been suitably acknowledged and documented? (See Chapter 20: "Documentation.")
2. Have you used the proper format conventions for the form you are writing—memo, letter, report, essay?

Now that the theory behind this stage of the composition process has been discussed, it's time to apply it to an actual sample of a student essay. Of course, just as no two chefs, carpenters, or painters approach their work in quite the same way, no two writers work in exactly the same way. Yet most successful writers go through a surprisingly similar series of steps to reach a polished finished product.

Here is a summary of the steps in the final stage of the writing process.

Stage Four (Postwriting: Revising, Editing, and Proofreading)

1. Revise and edit the rough draft (some writers revise their work through many, many drafts before they are satisfied).
2. Write the second draft.
3. Proofread (check grammar, spelling, style, etc.).
4. Type or word-process the essay if necessary and print.
5. Check the final copy for errors (especially typos).

A Sample Student Essay in Its Fourth Stage

Some instructors have no problem with their students writing essays in the first person (using the word "I," for example). However, the following student essay is written in a more formal tone, using the third person (without the pronouns "I" or "you"). For model essays written in a formal tone, see Chapter 20: "Documentation"; Chapter 25: "Definition"; Chapter 26: "Classification"; and Chapter 28: "Argumentation."

Sample Student Essay: Revising and Editing the Rough Draft

What follows is a rough draft that a student has written. In the margin are comments that have been added by the student's writing instructor to aid in revision. At this stage, the student is focussing on organization and content rather than punctuation and grammar. The student may correct some of the grammatical errors—for example, upon rewriting, deleting, or adding material.

Day Care

A more creative title? One that does more to reflect the thesis?

Add an attention grabber: what is a parent's worst fear in dropping a child off at day care?

As any parent knows, not all day care centres are created equal, and as a result, parents need to spend a great deal of time and attention selecting the day care centre their child will attend. Few consumer decisions parents make can have a greater impact on their child's life than this one. Luckily, parents should be able to recognize a good day care centre by examining its facilities, programs, and staff.

A good day care centre will offer a variety of programs designed to stimulate a child's physical, social, and intellectual development. Children should be given the opportunity to learn and interact with groups as well as the opportunity to learn through individual activities. A good centre will offer a balance between structured and unstructured learning environments. In addition to these programs, a good centre will provide nutritious meals and snacks, as well as a quiet rest period after lunch. Parents should have the opportunity to meet with their child's caregiver regularly and should receive regular feedback on their child's behaviour and progress.

The facilities should be well maintained, safe, and attractive. On the outside, there should be a fenced and shaded play area with a locked gate so that strangers cannot wander into the playground. Equipment should be safe and stimulating, and in order to protect young knees and elbows, the playground should be surfaced with something other than cement. The play area should also offer a variety of play experiences. On the inside, the entire facility should be in good repair, organized and clean.

The most important component of a good day care centre is the people who work there. The centre should have performed background checks on all staff members to ensure that no one with a criminal record has contact with children. The staff should be professional; they should have degrees or training in child development and first aid. There should be enough staff to adequately supervise children, no more than a one-to-five ratio for infants and a one-to-ten ratio for older children. The attitude and personality of the staff are also important. Caregivers should be warm, friendly, and, above all, patient with children. Nothing is worse than a staff member who loses patience and yells at a child.

A good day care centre will help that child develop into a responsible and well-adjusted adult. Once parents find a good day care centre, they can rest a little easier knowing that their child is receiving day care as good, if not better, than they themselves would be able to provide.

Preparing the Final Copy

If you have worked hard in revising and editing the rough draft, you will feel proud of the improvements you've made as you write the final copy.

At this stage of the writing process, it is time to proofread and to use the "Checklist for the Final Copy," which can be found on page 166 in Chapter 14: "The Four Stages of Writing."

In the revised version of the essay that follows, the revisions made in response to the instructor's comments and suggestions—in the left-hand margin alongside the rough draft above—are underlined.

Switch this paragraph with the next one so that points are discussed in the order they are introduced—see last sentence of first paragraph. Add a transition.

Give an example of a program or programs.

Add a transition.

Add examples in support of this point.

Add transitions that help the reader to recognize the main supporting sentences.

Add a positive note to end this paragraph.

Restate the three points upon which basis a day care centre should be chosen.

The title has been changed to reflect the thesis; now, it's much more specific.

An attention grabber that discusses the fears of parents has been added.

A transition for the topic sentence has been added.

This paragraph has been switched with the following one in response to the instructor's suggestion.

Examples of "play experiences" and ways in which the facility could be organized have been provided. Adding concrete detail of this nature strengthens the paragraph.

A transition for the second topic sentence has been added.

The transitions "first," "second," "next," and "more important than training, however" have been added to begin the main supporting sentences in this paragraph for better organization of the supporting detail and better flow of the paragraph in general.

A Student Essay in Progress: The Revised Version

Choosing a Good Day Care Centre

Nothing is harder for working parents than dropping their child or children off at a day care centre before going to work or school. At worst, visions of all the horror stories they've heard on TV about abused, mistreated, or molested children swim through their heads as they drive away. At best, parents worry that their children are not getting adequate stimulation, attention, or affection. As any parent knows, not all day care centres are created equal, and as a result, parents need to spend a great deal of time and attention selecting the day care centre their child will attend. Few consumer decisions parents make can have a greater impact on their child's life than this one. Luckily, parents should be able to recognize a good day care centre by examining its facilities, programs, and staff.

To begin, the facilities, both exterior and interior, should be well maintained, safe, and attractive. On the outside, there should be a fenced and shaded play area with a locked gate so that strangers cannot wander into the playground. Equipment should be safe and stimulating, and in order to protect young knees and elbows, the playground should be surfaced with something other than cement. The play area should also offer a variety of play experiences. On the inside, the entire facility should be in good repair, organized and clean. There should be individual cubbies for each child's coat and backpack, cots or mats for naps, and child-sized tables, chairs, sinks, and toilets. Also, walls and bulletin boards should be decorated with colourful, stimulating displays, preferably of the children's artwork.

In addition to offering excellent facilities, a good day care centre will offer a variety of programs designed to stimulate a child's physical, social, and intellectual development. Programs such as art, music, and dance stimulate all three skills at once. Children should be given the opportunity to learn and interact with groups as well as the opportunity to learn through individual activities. A good centre will offer a balance between structured and unstructured learning environments. In addition to these programs, a good centre will provide nutritious meals and snacks, as well as a quiet rest period after lunch. Parents should have the opportunity to meet with their child's caregiver regularly and should receive regular feedback on their child's behaviour and progress.

The most important component of a good day care centre is the people who work there. First, the centre should have performed background checks on all staff members to ensure that no one with a criminal record has contact with children. Second, the staff should be professional; they should have degrees or training in child development and first aid. Next, there should be enough staff to adequately supervise children, no more than a one-to-five ratio for infants and a one-to-ten ratio for older children. More important than training, however, is the attitude and personality of the staff. Caregivers should be warm, friendly, and, above all, patient with children. Nothing is worse than a staff member who loses patience and yells at a child, and

A positive example of attitude has been added in response to the instructor's suggestion. It strongly suggests that a good day care facility is not just one with the absence of negative attitudes, but with the presence of positive ones.

A recap of the three main points in this essay has been added at the beginning of the concluding paragraph.

nothing could be better than a caregiver who greets each child with a warm smile and makes each feel valued and special.

Parents should choose the centre their child attends based not on cost or convenience but on the quality of the centre's facilities, programs, and staff. A good day care centre will provide a safe, supportive, and stimulating environment for a child and, and as a result, will help that child develop into a responsible and well-adjusted adult. Once parents find a good day care centre, they can rest a little easier knowing that their child is receiving day care as good, if not better than they themselves would be able to provide.

Exercise 1 Making Revisions

Read the following paragraph. Based on the instructional material in Chapter 15: "The Paragraph," add suggestions for improvements in the left-hand margin. Then proceed to carry out these suggestions by writing the paragraph in a revised form.

It's the last time I allow my younger sister to entertain without a chaperone of my choosing. My apartment was an absolute mess. I came home to find beer bottles everywhere. I found potato chips and peanuts under the sofa. Upon closer examination, I could see cake icing on the wall, hard to see at first because the icing was a very similar colour to that of the wall paint. The enamel of the bathroom sink had been cracked. The superintendent called the next day to inform me that the police had been called because of noise complaints from several neighbours and that this would go on my record since the lease was in my name. It wasn't until I got ready to take a shower that I discovered a male teenager still passed out in the bathtub.

Exercise 2 Making Revisions

Read both the first draft of the essay above and the final product. Taking into consideration the instructions in the left-hand margin of the draft essay and instructional material on supporting detail of the paragraph in Chapter 15 and the essay in general in Chapter 16, what different or further improvements could be made to the final essay? Rewrite a new version of the final essay underlining improvements that you have made.

Working Together: Revising and Editing Activity

Write two to three paragraphs in answering the following question:

Should volunteer work be a required component of a postsecondary (college or university) education?

Take twenty minutes to write a first draft. Then exchange it with someone else in class. Based on the content of this chapter, revise and edit the draft you've been given; then discuss what you have done with the student who wrote the draft. What have you learned from this revising and editing process?

Chapter 18 Summarizing and Paraphrasing

Many companies assign reading to their employees, much like instructors do to their students. At a Monday morning staff meeting, for example, each employee might be expected to summarize a booklet, manual, catalogue, or document for the benefit of everyone. If you are that employee, you might also be expected to produce a written summary for everyone who isn't at the meeting.

The ability to **summarize and paraphrase** well is perhaps one of the most useful skills you will learn. Summarizing and paraphrasing are techniques for rewriting something you have read; they require putting in your own words the main idea or ideas of the original text. They are especially useful techniques when studying for tests and exams and writing research essays because they develop and demonstrate your understanding of the material you have read. When writing a research assignment, the techniques of summarizing and paraphrasing are important in making a coherent document out of your various sources. Translating ideas and information into your own words also helps you remember them better because in order to summarize something you have read, you must have a complete understanding of it. The better you understand something, the less likely you are to forget it.

Summarizing

> **DEFINITION**
>
> A **summary** is written in your own words, but it is a condensed version of an original source.

We practise summarizing all the time in our day-to-day lives. When telling friends about a movie, you don't repeat the story or dialogue from beginning to end. Instead, you relate the main points in the plot, or things about the movie that captured your interest.

A summary states the main idea of a passage. The purpose of a summary is to shorten the original piece of writing, providing only important information and eliminating nonessential points. A summary allows the reader to understand the main facts and ideas in the original without reading the entire passage. A summary should be no more than one-third the length of the original passage. The words you use should be your own. To avoid charges of plagiarism, you should not use more than three words at a time from the original. (Plagiarism is discussed in more detail later in this chapter.)

Take a look at this example of a summary. The following passage is taken from a longer piece entitled "Canadian Internet Use Survey" from *The Daily*, published by Statistics Canada on August 15, 2006. Immediately following this excerpt is a summary about a third the length of the original.

> Two-thirds of adult Canadians surfed the Internet in 2005, and those living in larger cities were much more likely to have done so than those in rural areas and small towns, according to the Canadian Internet Use Survey (CIUS).
>
> An estimated 16.8 million adult Canadians, or 68%, used the Internet for personal non-business reasons during the twelve months prior to the survey.
>
> Only 58% of residents living in small towns or rural areas accessed the World Wide Web, well below the national average. In contrast, rates in Canada's largest census metropolitan areas ranged from 68% in Montreal to 77% in both Ottawa-Gatineau and Calgary.
>
> The survey also showed that the Internet has changed the way many Canadians do banking and access news. Roughly 6 of every 10 Internet users used it to read news or sports, or to conduct their banking online. Even so, three-quarters of Canadians expressed strong concerns about privacy and security.
>
> The new survey, which replaces the Household Internet Use Survey, was redesigned to focus on individual Internet use. The CIUS did show that in 2005, an estimated 7.9 million Canadian households (61%) were connected to the Internet, up slightly from the nearly 60% reported in 2004 by the Survey on Household Spending.*
>
> (206 words)

Acceptable Summary:

> A recent survey shows that two-thirds of adult Canadians (16.8 million) used the Internet in 2005. Usage in small towns averaged 58%, compared to 68% to 77% in Canada's large cities. Many people who accessed the Internet to do online banking also have strong privacy concerns. The survey also shows that the number of households connected to the Internet was up slightly in 2005 from 2004 (61% from 60%).
>
> (69 words)

Tips on Writing a Successful Summary

1. **Read the passage and identify the topic sentence and controlling idea.** Underline the sentence that you think best expresses the main point of the passage. Rewrite this sentence in your own words.

---

*From "Canadian Internet Use Survey, 2005," published in *The Daily*, Catalogue 11-001, August 15, 2006, URL: http://www.statcan.ca/Daily/English/060815b.htm.

2. **Identify and eliminate minor supporting ideas.** Specific facts or examples may be important in developing a main idea, but they are not to be included in a summary.

3. **Write out the major supporting details in full sentences in your own words.** Use as few words as possible, and remember not to use more than three words at a time from the original.

4. **Count the words.** Make sure the total is no more than one-third of the original.

5. **Reread your summary.** Make sure that the meaning of the passage is conveyed clearly and that your sentences work together.

6. **Edit for spelling and grammar.**

Exercise 1 Writing Summaries

Find single words to replace the following phrases. (There can be more than one correct answer in each case.)

1. perform an analysis of _____

2. create a reduction in _____

3. engage in the preparation of _____

4. give consideration to _____

5. is dependent on _____

Exercise 2 Summarizing a Paragraph

Summarize the following passage, reducing it to approximately one-third of its original length of 216 words.

Canadian society in the twenty-first century is very different from that of early Canadians, and not just because we have televisions and VCRs. Two hundred years ago, people lived half as long as they do today, and families had twice as many children. In general, all Canadians are living longer, which means not only is our working life extended, but we can expect to retire from work and live another 15 to 20 years to enjoy the fruits of our labours. Canadians born in 1700 had an average life expectancy of 30 to 35 years due to poor diet, disease, and accidents. By 1831, four generations had passed, and there had been a slight improvement in life expectancy, with males expecting to live to age 40 and females to 42. During the next four generations major medical breakthroughs and public health education eliminated a number of infectious diseases and reduced infant mortality, so that Canadians' life spans were almost double what they were a little more than a century previously. But while Canadians can expect a long and healthy life, with many living well into their seventies or eighties, the average life span will not increase indefinitely. While we can expect to live longer than the Canadians of the 1700s, we can't expect to live forever.

Exercise 3 Summarizing an Article

Peter Cheney wrote this 1075-word article. Write a summary of it that is one-third its length (approx. 350 words).

Angry Ontarians, Quebecers and Albertans Top Survey on Road Rage*

There is a good reason why cars are not available with missile launchers. If they were, I might have reduced the Canadian driving population by at least half a dozen, starting with the street-racer who almost killed me and my wife on the Queen Elizabeth Way last summer.

Then there was the Vespa rider who decided to keep me from passing, even though he was doing about 20 in a 50 zone. I spotted him a few hours later at a Dairy Queen, lounging on the very scooter he had blocked me with for a good five miles.

I walked over and bent one of his rear view mirrors in half. Not the right thing to do, but I was in my 20s then, and road rage had turned me into Mr. Hyde.

According to a new poll commissioned by Globe Drive, I'm far from alone. Harris-Decima interviewed a thousand Canadian drivers about road rage, and came up with a fascinating picture of what brings out the beast in us when we're behind the wheel.

Based on the survey, Ontario is the road rage capital of Canada, closely followed by Quebec and Alberta. If cut off by another driver, some 29 per cent of Ontario drivers said they would honk the horn, while 14 per cent would shout profanities or gesture.

But in the Atlantic provinces only seven per cent said they would shout or make gestures; which made sense to me. I spend a lot of time in Nova Scotia and New Brunswick, and if you're looking to get ticked off on the road, this isn't the right place—the traffic isn't thick enough to work up a decent rage, and the people are too laid back. Even if another driver does manage to get you enraged, the small population tends to act as a governing mechanism – no matter how badly a driver ticks you off, you hold back, since you might be seeing them later.

In national traffic hellholes like Calgary or Toronto, things are different. Here, you are lost in the crowd – when you deliver a digital salute on the 401 or the Deerfoot Trail, you can safely assume you'll never encounter the recipient again.

If you want to be road-rage free, you might consider moving to Manitoba or Saskatchewan. The Harris-Decima poll found that 74 per cent of drivers there would simply let it go if another driver cut them off. Again, this made sense. I spent a couple of weeks in Saskatoon on a story once, and it was one of the most soothing driving experiences of my life. My fellow drivers and I cruised beneath the giant blue dome of the prairie sky, and we always seemed to have more than enough room—like yachts sailing the infinity of the Pacific, we occasionally glimpsed each other, but that was all.

*Peter Cheney, "Angry Albertans, Ontarians Top Survey on Road Rage," *The Globe and Mail* (12 May 2010). © Globe and Mail. All rights reserved.

The Harris-Decima findings also seem to reflect our Canadianness. Although it seems to be changing in places like Toronto, we are still abidingly polite—like when we arrive at a four-way stop, and find ourselves immobilized, unwilling to go first in case we look pushy (I call this the Canadian Stand-Off). And the survey numbers seemed to bear out my stereotype of the polite Canadian—nationally, 62 per cent of drivers surveyed said they would let it go if another driver was rude to them. I wondered what the figure would be in, say, New York City. Zero?

There were also strong regional differences when it came to road rage provoked by talking or texting at the wheel. In Alberta, 76 per cent of the drivers surveyed cited talking or texting as a factor. In Ontario, the figure was only 56 per cent. The difference is easily explained—Ontario has banned hand-held phones, Alberta hasn't.

Other poll findings

- Drivers with highest incomes ($100 000-plus) are the least likely to let it go if someone cuts them off (57%) and the most likely to shout or make gestures (15%).
- Women (64%) are only slightly more likely than men (60%) to ignore it if someone cuts them off.
- Drivers using handheld devices are the biggest concern to 58% of respondents, far ahead of elderly drivers (10%), teenage drivers (8%) and cyclists (6%).
- Women are more likely than men to be bothered by other drivers talking on the phone or texting—62% vs. 54%.
- Men are much more likely (18%) than women (8%) to name bad traffic as the thing than aggravates them most when driving. Women's biggest bugbear (14%) is being cut off by another driver.

The survey came up with some findings that I could never have imagined—like the role of cab drivers in road rage. Although I wasn't surprised that cabbies were a factor, I was amazed at the way they're perceived by different age groups. Only four per cent of all Canadians said they feared cab drivers, but among young respondents (age 18–24) the number was more than three times higher—13 per cent.

The survey charts the strange contours of road rage. Although some of the findings seemed logical (like the higher incidence of road rage in the busiest provinces) others didn't (like the inexplicable, age-related differences in the way cab drivers were perceived). But that didn't really surprise me. Road rage is a function of human nature, and we all know how simple and easy to understand THAT is. In his excellent book on roads and driving (*Traffic: Why We Drive the Way We Do*), author Tom Vanderbilt calls traffic "a living laboratory of human interaction, a place thriving with subtle displays of implied power." The regional road-rage differences highlighted by the Harris-Decima survey reflect that when it comes to traffic, small town Nova Scotia is a different laboratory than Montreal.

But again, we come back to human nature. My run-in with the Vespa rider that I had so desperately longed to kill so many years ago occurred on the outskirts of Wolfville, N.S., the town where I was born, and one of the most peaceful and bucolic places on the face of the earth. Our showdown played out on a road that ran through a landscape straight out of a Wordsworth poem.

Road rage has no country. There are no rules. All you need is two people, and two vehicles. And as someone once said: "A man drives as he lives."

WHAT ARE YOU LIKELY TO DO IF ANOTHER DRIVER CUTS YOU OFF?

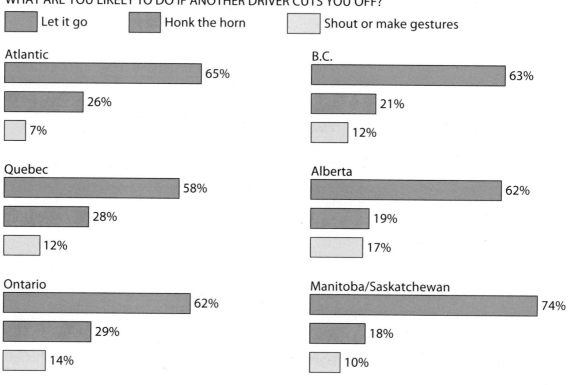

Let it go   Honk the horn   Shout or make gestures

Atlantic
65%
26%
7%

B.C.
63%
21%
12%

Quebec
58%
28%
12%

Alberta
62%
19%
17%

Ontario
62%
29%
14%

Manitoba/Saskatchewan
74%
18%
10%

Paraphrasing

DEFINITION

Paraphrasing is the process of putting another writer's work into your own words. A paraphrase can be as long as or even longer than the original.

An effective **paraphrase** follows not only the line of reasoning in the original source, but also the sequence of ideas or evidence. You paraphrase in an essay when it is important that every idea of the original work be conveyed to your reader. But like summarizing, paraphrasing should be done in your own words. Paraphrasing is typically done for shorter passages that are about a paragraph or two in length. Don't worry, your instructor won't ask you to paraphrase a whole book!

Now look at an example to see how a successful paraphrase differs from an unsuccessful one. The sample paragraph below is followed by examples of both unacceptable and acceptable paraphrases.

Original:

"Reality-based" TV programs, which have become very popular recently, appear to capture spontaneous events on film. However, most viewers are not aware that much of the action that transpires on these programs is staged. People who appear on these shows are often selected because producers think they will appeal to the audience, and directors often script important pieces of dialogue at critical moments during production. Therefore, relationships that develop between participants on these shows are often as contrived as those between characters on a TV sitcom or a soap opera.

Unacceptable Paraphrase:

"Reality-based" TV shows, which <u>have become popular recently</u>, seem to depict <u>spontaneous events on film</u>. Most people, however, do not know that a lot of the action that takes place <u>on these programs is staged</u>. The people on shows like these <u>are often selected because the producers</u> believe they will appeal to viewers, and directors frequently write <u>important pieces of dialogue at crucial moments</u> during the filming of the show. <u>Therefore, relationships that develop</u> are frequently as phony as those between personalities on TV sitcoms or soap operas.

This is an unsuccessful paraphrase because the overall structure and the phrasing of the underlined passages are almost identical to the original.

Acceptable Paraphrase:

The popularity of "reality-based" TV shows is founded on the belief that live events are being filmed, but many viewers do not know that much of what they see is made purposely dramatic. Producers of these shows often choose participants because they believe viewers will find them attractive, and the shows' directors often have them acting from scripts to heighten the drama. Thus, participants create relationships that are no more real than those we see on other TV shows, such as sitcoms or soap operas.

This passage is an example of good paraphrasing. The writer has taken the main idea of the original paragraph and restated it using his or her own words. All of the original details and examples appear, but they have been reworded and the sentences restructured.

Writing a Successful Paraphrase

1. **Read the passage and define all unfamiliar or technical terms.**
   Write all unfamiliar terms and their definitions on a separate sheet of paper.

2. **Reread the passage again, paying closer attention to the content and the order in which the ideas develop.** Make sure you have a clear understanding of the passage you are reading before you begin paraphrasing it.

3. **Begin converting the language of the passage into your own words, sentence by sentence.** Look for synonyms of words used in the passage. Alter sentence structure and vocabulary until you are conveying the original ideas in your own voice. If the original uses the first person (*I*), change it to the third person (*he* or *she*).

4. **Write out your paraphrase in full sentences of your own.** Remember not to use more than three words at a time from the original.

5. **Edit for spelling and grammar.**

Exercise Writing Paraphrases

Use your own words or phrases to express the following. A wide range of correct answers exists for each item.

1. utterly

   _____

2. Every cloud has a silver lining.

   _____

3. No pain, no gain.

   _____

4. He's like a wolf in sheep's clothing.

   _____

5. The apple doesn't fall far from the tree.

   _____

Acknowledging the Author (or Attribution)

When paraphrasing or summarizing, even if you are not required to document your sources, it is most often necessary to acknowledge the rightful author or source of the ideas you are expressing. (For times when you do have to document sources, see Chapter 20, "Documentation.") It's easy to do so right in the text. Here is an example acknowledging the authors of a reading in Unit IV entitled "No Great Sacrifice": *According to David Suzuki and Faisal Moola, Canadians should make more sacrifices than they do in their efforts to protect the environment.* This statement could be considered a one-sentence summary of the entire reading. But even though it's not in the words that the original authors have used, it's still their idea and should be attributed to them when discussed in someone else's writing.

Along with summarizing and paraphrasing properly, acknowledging other authors appropriately is yet another way to avoid being accused of plagiarism.

Plagiarism: A Serious Offence

Students who write unacceptable paraphrases can be accused of plagiarism. Plagiarism is a form of intellectual theft. It occurs when one person uses the ideas or words of another person *without giving credit to the original source or author*. You can avoid plagiarism by ensuring that credit for work other than your own is cited. (See Chapter 20: "Documentation.") When you paraphrase a passage, be sure to inform your reader about who the original author is and where the original work appeared.

Plagiarism in a school environment often results in a mark of zero on an assignment. If it is a major assignment, one case of plagiarism can result in the overall failure of a course. Plagiarism is not only contrary to school policy (because it is always a clear violation of academic honesty); it is also against the law. If you are not sure about how to avoid being accused of plagiarism, ask your professor for advice.

Avoid Unintentional Plagiarism

With so much information at our fingertips today, there may be a tendency and, perhaps, an irresistible temptation to use what is in front of us (such as a text on a website) for our papers without even realizing that we might be opening ourselves up to charges of plagiarism. Many instructors consider as few as three words together that are lifted from someone else's text to be plagiarism if these words are not in quotation marks and attributed to their original author. (For a discussion of how to quote properly, see pages 230–231 in Chapter 19: "The Research Paper.")

So if you are summarizing or paraphrasing and you want to avoid the plagiarism trap, here is a trick of the trade: Read the text closely enough that you understand it thoroughly. Then close the book, or the window on the computer (or reduce it so that you cannot see it for now). Write what you remember, or as much as you think you need for the purpose of your paper. Then go back to the original if necessary to check for accuracy. You also might want to check to make sure you haven't, by accident, ended up with phrases three words or longer that are in the original. If you have, change the wording of these phrases. If the original is relatively long, do this one paragraph at a time. Not only will you protect yourself, in this way, from accusations of intellectual thievery, but you will find yourself absorbing the reading material more efficiently. Developing this kind of good work habit can lead to all sorts of rewards when doing assignments that involve reading and writing.

And, of course, if you are writing a research paper, whether it be a review of literature, a report, or an academic essay, you will probably be expected to document your sources. The extent of the documentation required for a particular paper is something that will be determined by your instructor. (For more information, see Chapter 19: "The Research Paper" and Chapter 20: "Documentation.")

Exercise   Paraphrasing a Paragraph

The following passage was excerpted from an article entitled "A Dead End for Humanity," by Wade Davis. Write a paraphrase of this paragraph. The passage contains 79 words, so your paraphrase should be about the same length.

> Of the 6000 languages spoken today, fully half are not being taught to children. Effectively, these languages are already dead. By the end of the twenty-first century, linguistic diversity may be reduced to as few as 500 languages. A language, of course, is not simply vocabulary and grammar; it is a flash of the human spirit, the vehicle by which the soul of a culture comes into the material realm. Each language represents a unique intellectual and spiritual achievement.
>
> *The Globe and Mail* (December 28, 2000)

Analyzing and Critiquing

Summarizing and paraphrasing are useful skills, not just for their own sake but because they are a necessary part of more advanced responses to texts. Eventually, your professor will ask you not only to repeat what someone else has already written, but to agree or disagree and explain the reasons why.

In the Readings section of this book (Unit IV), each reading is followed by several questions, classified into four groups. The first group, "Comprehension Questions," require some summarizing and paraphrasing. To answer these questions, you will need to recall or look back at what you've read and then repeat, in one way or another, what the author has written.

The questions classified as "Questions for Discussion" and "Questions about Form," on the other hand, call for more thinking on your part. They require analysis and argumentation. To answer them, you will have to support or refute what the author has written. One skill you will develop in this area is usually referred to as *critical thinking*. It is often a requirement in courses across the curriculum at the postsecondary level; it is also a skill that can only help you in any workplace. For more on critical thinking and analysis, see Chapter 28: "Argumentation."

Working Together: Summarizing Opposing Points of View

Form groups of three or four. Look in your local newspaper for feature articles on controversial topics that are of concern to many Canadians, such as the effects of global warming or genetic engineering. Try to find one article that looks at the problem from one perspective, and another article that takes an opposing view. For instance, find an article that supports high-speed police chases and another where the author considers them to be too dangerous. Each group member then writes a summary of one of these articles, making sure that the opposing points of view are clearly indicated. You might use this information to discuss ways in which the media attempt to influence the attitudes of Canadians.

Chapter 19 **The Research Paper**

The Research Paper

With a research paper, you are given the opportunity to showcase your work. You finally have a chance to "sink your teeth" into something you've been curious about. You can devote more time to thinking about, reading for, and writing on a subject that interests you. Because a research paper generally requires a fair amount of independent reading, you should start it early—as soon as the project is assigned. You'll maximize your potential not only for a higher grade, but also for major insights. Indeed, a research paper enables you to go on a journey of intellectual discovery.

> **DEFINITION**
>
> A **research paper** is a paper that presents research in support of a thesis. All ideas that are not the writer's own are expected to be fully documented according to a specific academic style such as MLA or APA (see Chapter 20: "Documentation"). A good research paper should be well researched, well documented, and, most of all, insightful.

Standard Essay Structure

Often a research paper is assigned in a course other than an English course. If this is the case, it might be referred to by the instructor as a *report* or a *review,* rather than an essay. Your instructor might, therefore, require a number of specific subheadings and charts and/or graphs as part of the supporting detail in your paper. However, if the paper is required to be, specifically, a research *essay,* the question becomes, "What is the required format?"

Unless your instructor gives you specific direction in this regard, it can be assumed that the research essay generally should follow the structure and format of a standard essay. Usually, you will be given a word count requirement that is longer for a research essay than for a standard five-paragraph essay that might be scheduled to be written in class during, for instance, a two-hour period. A five-paragraph essay could be anywhere from 400 to 700 words, whereas a research essay might be 800 to 1200 words or longer if it's a paper for university.

Therefore, expect that a research essay will have more than five paragraphs. Keep in mind that no paragraph in academic writing, whether it be in the form of a standard essay or a research essay, should be more than twelve or fewer than five sentences long.

Often, even students who apply the rules of standard essay structure to in-class essay assignments in an English course will forget to apply the same rules to a take-home research essay—not just rules about paragraph length, but also those regarding other aspects of essay structure and format, such as including a one-sentence thesis in the first paragraph, writing topic sentences at the beginning of the support paragraphs, inserting specific examples in each support paragraph, etc. (For a reminder of these rules, review Chapter 16: "The Essay.")

Responsible Research

Once you have your topic and some idea of the direction you want to take, it's time to start your research. Don't worry about a thesis until after you've done some serious reading. And once you've decided what your thesis is and what points you want to make in support of it, make sure you can find at least two pieces of evidence for every point you want to make. If you're finding this difficult to do, change your point, or even your thesis, if necessary. When students report having trouble finding sources, it's often because they've set off in a certain direction (with a particular thesis in mind) far too early in their research process. As you do more reading on your subject, the direction your paper should take will become more and more clear. Knowing too quickly what you want to say and trying to force your research to support your ideas can cause you to waste a great deal of time, not to mention frustrate you very early in the process. Allow yourself to learn. Find what exists, not what you want to see.

Books, Periodicals, and the Internet

If your topic is current, such as the topic of the sample research essay in the next chapter (cell phones and their effects on our health), you may find that most of your sources will have to come from periodicals (materials published on a regular basis, such as newspapers, magazines, and academic journals) and the Internet. But if your topic is a well-established one, a good place to start is the library's catalogue for a search of relevant books. Ask the librarian for help. Every library is different. Until you are well acquainted with your library's resources, the librarian can give you some excellent advice to start you on your way.

The Literary Research Essay

Primary vs. Secondary Sources

If your instructor has assigned a research paper on literature, you may have to research both primary and secondary sources. **Primary sources** are the works of literature themselves. For example, if you are writing about Margaret Atwood, you might look up some of the novels she has written: *Cat's Eye*, *The Handmaid's Tale*, and so on. These are primary sources. But your instructor may want you to also include works by critics about her writing; these works are considered **secondary sources.**

The General Topic Research Essay

Primary vs. Secondary Research

For a general topic research paper, your instructor might require that you conduct primary as well as secondary research. The first can be more time consuming than the latter. **Secondary research** is done upon a trip to the library or by research on the Internet; **primary research,** however, might consist of an interview with an expert on the subject; an experiment that you have designed and conducted, including detailed observations; a survey that you have circulated among certain people who qualify, and so on. You can always control the amount of time you spend in a library. But when it comes to primary research, the process tends to get more unpredictable, and the plans you make don't always work out. Just setting up an interview, for example, can take more time than expected. Because the interview involves another human being, his or her schedule might not coincide with your own. The more time you give yourself to work on all of these things, the better.

Internet vs. Library Research

More and more students have computers at home nowadays with access to the Internet. As a result, whenever a research paper is assigned, the Internet is, for reasons of convenience, the first step in the research process. Whenever you do Internet research, it is important to determine the legitimacy of the online sources you consult (more on this later in the chapter, pages 229–230). Too often, unfortunately, students do not go beyond the Internet. Your instructor, however, may require you to do so. You may, for example, be instructed to go to a library to do the kinds of research that are not possible via the Internet. If so, ask a librarian for help.

Internet Research

If you already have a very specific topic in mind, start with search engines. Put in a string of keywords that are critical to your search and see what "hits" you get. The best way to determine which search engine is most appropriate is to try various ones yourself. The best one for you might depend on the project you are engaged in, as well as on your personal preferences. Here are some suggestions:

Search Engines

Google (www.google.com) is the most popular search engine on the Internet. The same company has also introduced "Google Scholar" (scholar.google.com), which is academically oriented, pointing the researcher toward technical reports, academic papers, books, and so on.

Other excellent search engines include the following:

- AllTheWeb.com (www.alltheweb.com)
- AltaVista™ (www.altavista.com)
- Lycos® (www.lycos.com)
- Ask Jeeves (www.ask.com)

Academic Directories

The majority of websites are commercial and therefore profit-oriented. Their domains end with .com, so domains that end differently are often more useful for academic purposes: *.ca, .org, .edu, .net, or .gov.* You can find these domains by doing an advanced search using Google: go to the box labelled "Search within a site or domain," then type in the desired suffix (such as *.org*).

General directories such as Yahoo! (www.dir.yahoo.com) aim to accommodate the general public. They do not meet the needs of academic research. Here is a list of academic directories designed to help researchers in specific areas:

- The Internet Public Library (www.ipl.org), organized by librarians, has links to thousands of articles, theses, magazines, newspapers, and books from around the world.
- The Librarians' Index to the Internet (lii.org) includes 14 000 sites assessed by librarians for their academic value.
- www.Virtual Library (www.vlib.org) is a multidisciplinary academic directory.
- www.infotrac-college.com (a free four-month membership comes with this book) provides articles from the *New York Times*.
- www.freefulltext.com includes over 7000 scholarly journals, but is browsable by title only.
- etext.Virginia.edu contains 70 000 texts in 13 languages, with links to research resources.

TIP

Be specific in the choice of words that define your topic.

If your subject search turns up too many hits to begin with, narrow your search by adding another term or by making the terms you've already entered more specific.

The use of quotation marks in your subject search can help you reduce the number of useless hits. It is particularly useful for names. For example, if you want to look up London, Ontario, but avoid all hits for London, England, type in "London Ontario."

By adding the word "AND" to your subject search you narrow your search by requiring that one subject be associated with the other in your hits.

By adding the word "OR" to your subject search, you broaden your search.

By adding "NOT" to your subject search, you can exclude a term you don't want to find, therefore narrowing your search.

 Exercise Using a Search Engine

Pick one of the following subjects and see what you can find using more than one search engine. List three sources dealing with the subject of your choice.

1. Effects of global warming

   _____

   _____

   _____

2. Stephen Harper's political career

   _____

   _____

   _____

3. Canadian soldiers in Afghanistan

   _____

   _____

   _____

4. Medicinal uses for marijuana

   _____

   _____

   _____

Analyzing the Legitimacy of Online Sources

A great deal of excellent material can be found on the Internet, much of it for free. But not everything online is legitimate. In fact, because the electronic medium is so difficult to regulate by governmental regulatory bodies, much illegitimate and even illegal material, such as hate literature, goes unchecked and its producers avoid prosecution. However, there are guidelines you can follow to make sure you are using only proper sources. (Much of the following advice can also be used to assess the legitimacy of regular print sources.)

1. Look for the name of the writer. If you find one, do an independent online search of the name to see what, if anything, anyone else says about this person, and what associations this person has. Are the associations with reputable organizations? If the source is not attributed to an actual name of a person, make sure that, at the very least, a reputable organization claims responsibility for the material. Do an independent online search of the organization. See what other organizations say about it, and, ultimately, based on the information you have gathered, use your common sense.

2. Is the writer of the source biased toward a particular point of view because of a connection to an organization with a specific agenda? Be aware of the one-sided approach of such writers. Does he or she give the other side fair

play in his or her writing? Is there a demonstrated respect for the other side of the argument? Try to discern between a point of view and an attack on an individual or identifiable group. (See the section "Common Fallacies" in Chapter 28: "Argumentation.") There are countless organizations, especially on the World Wide Web, whose only purpose, it seems, is to spew hatred at a particular group or groups of people. Avoid these attacks altogether. The writers who have the most credibility and develop the best arguments on a topic are, without question, those with no obvious agenda and no particular stake in the matter. Pieces written by such objective analysts, therefore, often make the best sources for your research paper.

3. Is the writing well edited and relatively free of errors? Is the site well designed and professionally presented? Has the site been revised recently, or does it seem to have been abandoned after being established a long time ago? In other words, how well is the site being maintained?

4. Are there links on the website? If so, where do they lead? Do they lead to other academic materials? Or to commercial or entertainment sites?

The answers to any of these questions may not provide you with conclusive evidence of anything. But with more information at your disposal, you'll be better equipped to assess the legitimacy of the sources you have found.

 Exercise **Evaluating Online Sources**

Revisit the three sources that you found as a result of doing the previous exercise on using search engines (pages 228–229). Assess the legitimacy of these sources using the above criteria.

Using Quotations

By the word *quotation*, this textbook means the exact words used by an author or speaker. Therefore, the most important thing when it comes to quotations is that you must be careful to use the precise word-for-word text of the author (or the person who was quoted within the source you are using). Some quoting is good because it breaks up text and generally makes an essay more interesting to read. However, try to keep your quoting to a minimum. Quote only those things that you cannot say better yourself. And remember, whenever you include a quotation, you are expected to explain to the reader why the quotation appears in your essay and how it connects to your thesis. You might also be expected to interpret the quotation if its meaning is not straightforward enough already.

How you incorporate a quotation into your essay depends on how long the quotation is. Short quotations are embedded within your regular paragraphs. Longer quotations are indented and set apart from your regular paragraphs.

Short (Integrated) Quotation

> **RULE**
>
> For a short quotation, four lines or under (some say forty words or under), place quotation marks around the quotation and integrate the quotation within the regular paragraph. Such a short quotation might be a sentence or two, or even a spot quotation, meaning a partial quoted sentence integrated within a sentence of your own.

Example of a short quotation:

Notice the introduction (without quotation marks) of the quotation followed by a comma.

Notice the absence of the word *that* between the word *says* and the quotation. The word *that* is reserved for paraphrases (see Chapter 18: "Summarizing and Paraphrasing").

The professor said *that* Campbell was a great mythologist.
The professor said, "Campbell was an accomplished mythologist." (no *that* between the introduction of the quotation and the quotation itself)

Notice that there is no indentation of the quotation.

A common theme in the study of mythology is that of the hero and the hero's journey. In his most famous book, *The Hero with a Thousand Faces,* Joseph Campbell says, "The battlefield is symbolic of the field of life, where every creature lives on the death of another."

Notice how the final period goes inside the quotation mark. If this is a documented paper, however, there would be no period inside the quotation mark. Instead, a set of parentheses (for the internal documentation) would follow the last quotation mark, and a final period would follow the parentheses. (For examples of internal documentation, see Chapter 20: "Documentation" (pages 235–238 for APA style and pages 238–241 for MLA style.)

Longer (Block) Quotation

> **RULE**
>
> If your quotation is longer than four lines (or forty words), you must set it apart from your regular paragraph. When you do this, indent (by a few spaces) the part that is quoted. Do not use quotation marks around or within this quotation at all unless there are quotation marks already within the original quotation.

Example of a block quotation:

The first two lines of the quotation are Campbell's words, so there are no quotation marks yet. But in the third line, there is a set of quotation marks around the words "after long, long years." These words are words that Campbell, himself, has taken from another source (the story by the Grimm Brothers).

In his most famous book, *The Hero with a Thousand Faces*, Joseph Campbell begins to tell the story of "Sleeping Beauty":

Indent the entire quotation

> Little Briar-rose (Sleeping Beauty) was put to sleep by a jealous hag (an unconscious evil-mother image). And not only the child, her entire world went off to sleep; but at last, "after long, long years," there came a prince to wake her. "The king and queen (the conscious good-parent images), who had just come home and were entering the hall, began to fall asleep, and with them the whole estate...."

Note the four periods at the end of the quotation before the final quotation mark. These four periods at the end of a quoted sentence indicate that the original quotation continues, but for the purposes of the quotation by Campbell, this is all that is necessary to support whatever point he is making.

Working Together: Finding Appropriate Sources

Read the sample research paper entitled "The Cell Phone: Tomorrow's Medical Menace?" on pages 242–251 of Chapter 20: "Documentation." Find *five* sources on the Internet that seem to oppose the point of view taken in the paper. Then answer the questions below and discuss your answers with others in your group or class.

1. How do you know if the sources you have located are legitimate?
2. What were the subject headings (or search terms) you used?
3. Did you use any other tips or information from the chapter to help you find appropriate sources?
4. Answer the following questions based on the information in this chapter and your reading of the full text of some of the sources that you've found:
   a. What observations have you made about these sources?
   b. What observations have you made about the overall issue of the possible health effects of cell phone usage?

Chapter 20 **Documentation**

Documentation

When your instructor assigns a research paper, ask what kind of documentation is required. Is a particular academic style (such as APA or MLA) required? Are internal and end references expected? How accurate must the punctuation for references be before marks are deducted? This part of the research paper is considered unimportant by many and is, therefore, often neglected. Instructors frequently complain, in fact, that students end up losing more marks in this area than they should. So be sure to ask what is required of you before you submit your final paper.

DEFINITION

Documentation is the formal acknowledgment of sources in a research paper. Correct documentation makes sure credit is given for others' work and protects a writer against charges of plagiarism (theft of ideas). It involves a combination of citations (internal documentation) and a listing of sources (end documentation). The citations are inserted within the text of the research paper, while the listing of sources is always at the end, on a separate page (or pages). A particular academic style, such as MLA or APA, must be applied consistently to both the citations and the list of sources.

For more on plagiarism, see page 223 in Chapter 18: "Summarizing and Paraphrasing."

Two Academic Styles of Documentation: APA and MLA

Although there are several academic styles of documentation, APA and MLA are the two most common. APA stands for American Psychological Association. MLA stands for Modern Language Association. These are universal styles in that they are known and used in research throughout the world. Which one is used depends on the subject matter. Generally speaking, APA is commonly used for the physical and social sciences: physics, medicine, psychology, sociology, and so on. MLA, on the other hand, is used for subjects in the humanities, such as literature, philosophy, religion, and the arts. In business, no one style is dominant. If the program in which you are enrolled requires that you use one of these two styles in your research, it would be wise to continue to apply the same style to English papers as long as your English professor does not object. If it does not matter to your instructors which style you choose, you might want to briefly examine the differences between the two styles outlined below and choose the one that you think most suits your needs. Regardless of which one you end up choosing, you must apply it correctly and consistently to both the internal and the end documentation of a research paper.

Two Mandatory Parts of Documentation: Internal and End

Both of the major academic styles involve two kinds of documentation in a research paper:

- Internal documentation (sets of parentheses incorporated throughout the essay)
- End documentation (a list of sources at the end)

Connection between Internal and End Documentation

Often, students do not see the reason that both forms of documentation must be provided in a research paper. They do not understand that the two are interdependent: each one needs the other to be valid. A citation in the form of parentheses surrounding information (usually author and page number) is used to show exactly where an author's idea has been used in your paper, either in the form of a direct quotation or a paraphrased or summarized idea. (See Chapter 18: "Summarizing and Paraphrasing.") Using the limited information between the parentheses, the reader can then go to the list of sources at the end of the paper and find out exactly what publication or website the idea was taken from. He or she could then locate the source if necessary for fact checking, further research, and so on.

Citations Not Just after Direct Quotations

Many students believe that citations are required only after direct quotations. They believe that if they put someone else's idea into their own words, then documentation is not required. This is not true. If an idea from another author has been paraphrased or summarized and is not considered common knowledge, its source must also be acknowledged in the form of both a citation and its listing at the end of the paper. If you are not sure whether or not the idea you're thinking of paraphrasing is common knowledge, check with your professor. It's better, after all, to be safe than sorry.

American Psychological Association (APA)

APA Format

Follow these guidelines for formatting your APA paper.

- **Title Page:** On a separate page, include the title (double-spaced if more than one line), your name, the course code, the professor's name, and the date of submission. Double-space everything on the title page, and centre everything, left to right and top to bottom. Do not italicize, underline, or place quotation marks around your title. Capitalize key words (see Rule 5 on page 144 in Chapter 12: "Capitalization"). See the title page of the sample essay at the end of this chapter (page 243).

- **Running Head:** On every page, place a shortened version of the title, in all capital letters, at the top left margin. Put the page number at the top right margin. You can do this using the "Header" option, found under the "View" or "Insert" menu in most word-processing programs.

- **Abstract (if your instructor requires it):** On a separate page following the title page, include an abstract, which is a block-paragraph (no indentation) summary of your paper. The title (Abstract) should appear centred, 2.5 cm (one inch) from the top of the page. Start your abstract one double line space after the title. The length of your abstract should be between 75 and 150 words.

Internal Documentation: Print Sources (APA)

Internal documentation in APA is referred to as **reference citations.** These citations must appear throughout the body of your research paper (approximately three to four per page). What they include (between parentheses) depends on what is already included in your text leading up to the citation. A typical reference citation immediately following a quotation includes the author's name, the year of publication, and the page number. See the following example.

When you do not name the author in your text:

> "The battlefield is symbolic of the field of life, where every creature lives on the death of another" (Campbell, 1973, p. 238).

See how the above reference citation corresponds to the APA bibliographic entry starting with Campbell on page 238, under "Entry (from a References list)."

On the other hand, if the author is already named in your text, it is common practice to put the year in parentheses immediately after the author's name when it is mentioned. After the quotation, the only citation necessary is that of the page number. See the example below.

When you do name the author in your text:

> In *The Hero with a Thousand Faces*, Joseph Campbell (1973) wrote, "The battlefield is symbolic of the field of life, where every creature lives on the death of another" (p. 238).

When you paraphrase or summarize:

When developing citations for paraphrased or summarized ideas rather than quotations, there is no need for the page numbers; see the following example.

> War is like life, in which some people have to die so that others can live (Campbell, 1973).

Or

> Campbell (1973) says that war is like life, in which some people have to die so that others can live.

Or if two or more books by Campbell have been used in the research:

> Campbell (1973) says that war is like life, in which some people have to die so that others can live (*The Hero*).

(*The Hero* is short for the full book title *The Hero with a Thousand Faces*.)

Internal Documentation: Electronic Sources (APA)

Electronic sources include the same information as other sources, though most of the time, for an electronic source, there will be no page number. In this case, if there is a paragraph number, use this number after the abbreviation "para." instead of "p." If there is no paragraph number, the author's last name and year of publication will suffice:

> (Jones, 2002)

If there is no author, use part of the title:

> ("Cell Phone Links," 2004).

TIP

Remember to put article titles (or parts of article titles) in quotation marks, but to italicize titles of major works such as books, journals, and newspapers.

End Documentation: Print Sources (APA)

The list of sources in APA style at the end of your essay is referred to as **References**. This is the word that should appear as the title of this list. The list of entries under this title must be alphabetized according to the first word (usually the author's last name) of each entry. If two entries begin with the same name, go to the year after the name and put the entry with the most recent year first, and so on.

Entry (from a References list):

The first name of the author is abbreviated with the initial(s) only.

The year of publication comes in parentheses immediately after the author's name. The period immediately follows the parentheses.

The book title is in italics. For titles of books and articles, only the first letter of the first word of the title is capitalized in this list. However, don't forget to use the capitalization rule for titles (see page 205) when using these titles in the text of your essay.

Campbell, J. (1973). *The hero with a thousand faces.* New York: Princeton University Press.

The second line (and any subsequent ones) of a References list in APA style must be indented. If there were a third line, it would align with the second line.

End Documentation: Electronic Sources (APA)

The general principle with electronic sources is that you should include as much information as you can so that someone else can find your source. Make sure the URL (website address) is copied with complete accuracy. The slightest incorrect detail (a hyphen, for example) can invalidate the entire URL. Include URLs without hyperlinks. To eliminate a hyperlink, right-click on the hyperlink, select "Remove Hyperlink" from the box of choices that appears, and left-click on this.

The following model is commonly used for citing electronic sources in APA style.

Article in a periodical:

The author's last name is followed by only an initial, not the full first name.

Because the source is a newspaper, the date includes the day and month as well as the year.

The title of the periodical is in italics. Because it is a major publication title, the regular capitalization rules for titles apply (see page 144).

McLean, C. (2006, July 27). Wireless overtakes local service. *Globe and Mail Update.* Retrieved July 30, 2006, from http://www .theglobeandmail.com/ . . .

The second date in the entry is the date when you last accessed the item on the Web.

If you consult an online academic journal, you may find that the articles each have a digital object identifier (DOI). This is a code designed to help researchers identify and locate the article on the web, even if they are moved to a different part of a website. For example, the article found at http://jama.ama-assn.org/ content/305/8/808 has the DOI 10.1001/jama.2011.186. If an item you used in your research has a DOI, provide the DOI in your reference list instead of the URL. (Again, be sure to copy it accurately.) You do not need to give a date of retrieval with a DOI.

Use the sources you have found as a result of the search engine exercise toward the end of the last chapter (pages 228–229). Formulate their entries for a References list (end documentation) according to APA style. Remember to list them alphabetically according to the first word of the entry.

Modern Language Association (MLA)

MLA   MLA Format

Follow these guidelines for formatting a paper using the MLA style of documentation.

- **Title Page:** For MLA style, a separate title page is not required unless your instructor requires one. If none is required, type the following information flush left and double-spaced, starting 2.5 cm (one inch) from the top of your first page: your name, your professor's name, your course code, and the date the paper is submitted:

  - Johann Hilton
  - Professor Einstein
  - COMM 301
  - 23 April 2011

- If your instructor does require a separate title page, centre your title (which should be not underlined, not in quotation marks, and not in italics). Apply capitalization rules for titles (see page 205 in Chapter 16: "The Essay"). Centre the information listed above underneath the title. Double-space this information here, also.

- **Headers:** Create a header with your last name and the page number (for example, Hilton 1) for the top right corner of all pages beginning with the first page of your paper (whether this is a separate title page or not). You will find the "Header" option under the "View" or "Insert" menu in most word-processing programs. This header also appears on the page containing the Works Cited list (see "End Documentation: Print Sources (MLA)" at the bottom of the next page).

Internal Documentation: Print Sources (MLA)

Internal documentation in MLA style is referred to as **parenthetical references** or **parenthetical citations.** As in any citation style, a parenthetical reference must appear after you refer to a source within your essay whether this reference is a direct quotation or paraphrased idea.

The parenthetical reference usually consists of parentheses containing the author's last name and the page number from which you have taken the quotation or idea.

When you do not include the author's name in your text:

> "The battlefield is symbolic of the field of life, where every creature lives on the death of another" (Campbell 238).

Notice that there is no period before the end quotation mark. The period that ends the sentence comes after the reference in parentheses. Also notice that there is no comma between the author's last name and the page number inside the parenthetical reference.

When you include the author's name in the body of your text leading up to the quotation or paraphrased idea, there is no need to include the name of the author within the parenthetical reference. The page number is enough.

When you include the author's name in your text:

> Campbell states, "The battlefield is symbolic of the field of life, where every creature lives on the death of another" (238).

Notice there is still no period before the second (end) quotation mark. The period still comes after the parentheses.

When the source has two authors:

> "Perhaps the Canadian experience can serve as a paradigm, since Canadian writers also searched for a voice through much of the twentieth century" (Sullivan and Levene 9).

When the same author has written at least two sources in your Works Cited list:

> "The battlefield is symbolic of the field of life, where every creature lives on the death of another" (Campbell, *The Hero* 238).

Notice that you need to mention the title in the parenthetical reference if the author is responsible for two different sources in your paper, so readers can tell which work is being referred to. But the title of the book need not be complete (*The Hero with a Thousand Faces*), as long as an important part of the title is present. Any title (or part title) of a book must be italicized (or underlined); the parenthetical reference is no exception.

Internal Documentation: Electronic Sources (MLA)

Electronic sources don't always provide page numbers. If you are citing one that does not, use the paragraph number preceded by the abbreviation "par." If neither a page number nor a paragraph number is provided, use the author's last name only. This is sufficient to link the citation to more information in the Works Cited list at the end of your paper.

> (Statistics Canada, par. 28)
> (Rogers)

End Documentation: Print Sources (MLA)

As already discussed, documentation would not be complete without a **Works Cited list** in which all your sources are listed. This list starts on a new page.

When a reader sees a parenthetical reference such as (Campbell 238), he or she may look right away at the Works Cited list to see more information on the book to which you have referred. In the Works Cited list, the first thing the reader looks for is the name Campbell, since it is the first thing in the parenthetical reference. The reader might find a Works Cited entry like the one below.

Works Cited entry:

The last name of the author comes first. If there are two authors, the second author's name is given first name first and last name last.

The title of the book is in italics. Capitalization adheres to the rule for titles (see page 144). All titles of major publications should be in italics (or underlined), including books, magazines, newspapers, CDs, and so on.

The city in which the book was published goes here (usually followed by the province or state; see below). Notice the colon that comes after the city. This is standard practice in both MLA and APA styles.

Campbell, Joseph. *The Hero with a Thousand Faces.* New York: Princeton UP, 1973. Print.

The second line is indented. If there were a third line, it would be indented also to line up with the indented second line.

After the colon comes the publisher's name, followed by a comma and, finally, the year of publication.

Every entry receives a marker that identifies the medium of publication. Most entries will say *Print* or *Web*, but other possibilities include *Performance*, *DVD*, and *TV*.

Notice that this city is not followed by the name of the state (which is also New York, of course) because New York is a famous enough city that its state or country is not necessary. But if the city were Moose Jaw, it would be followed by "SK" to help people locate it in Saskatchewan.

> **TIP**
>
> MLA requires that provinces and states be abbreviated using postal abbreviations (e.g., SK, ON, CA)

End Documentation: Electronic Sources (MLA)

The general rule for electronic sources in the Works Cited list is to include as much information as you can find. The URL (uniform resource locator) alone is never acceptable. You must give your readers enough information that they can find on the Internet exactly what you have found.

Citation for a web page with an author given:

> Author's full name (if provided), last name first, then the first name, followed by a period.

> Title and subtitle (if provided) of web page or article in quotation marks with a period typed inside the end quotation mark.

Birchard, Karen. "New Government Could Change Canada's Course on Higher Education." *The Chronicle of Higher Education* 52 (3 Feb. 2006). *Infotrac-College Edition.* n. pag. Web. 17 July 2011.

> Title of print source of information, if one is provided, with volume number (if any), followed by date of print source (the date when the web page was either established or last revised).

> Date of your access to this site (followed by a period).

> Title of website followed by a period.

- Both the title of a print source and the title of a website are italicized.
- When no publisher's name appears on the website, write *n.p.* for "no publisher." When there is no date of publication, write *n.d.* for "no date." For online journals that appear only online, add *(no print version)*. And on databases that do not provide pagination, write *n. page* for "no pagination."
- City (if provided) and publisher, followed by a period.
- If editor(s) of the print source are provided, add *Ed.* and then the name(s) (names not inverted, followed by a period) after the title of the journal.

Article in a periodical (with author's name):

> McLean, Catherine. "Wireless Overtakes Local Service." *Globe and Mail Update* 27 July 2006. Web. 30 July 2006.

Article in a periodical (without author's name):

> "Cellphone Radiation." *CBC News Online* 3 June 2004. Web. 29 July 2006.

Article from a database:

> "Long Mobile Phone Use Raises Brain Tumor Risk: Study." *Information Week* 3 April 2006. *Infotrac College Edition from Gale Group and Thomson Learning.* n.pag. Web. 28 July 2006.

 Exercise   Formatting MLA Entries for a Works Cited List

Use the sources you have found as a result of the exercise on search engines on pages 228–229. Formulate their entries for a Works Cited page according to MLA style. Remember to list them alphabetically according to the first word of the entry.

Sample Research Paper

An example of a formal research paper is presented below. The paper uses the APA style of documentation. At the end, one paragraph from it and the end documentation is repeated using the MLA style. The topic is cell phones and their possible effects on the human brain. (You may also wish to read the related text "Gadget-Savvy but Socially Inept?" starting on page 388 in Unit IV.)

APA **Sample Essay Using APA Style Documentation**

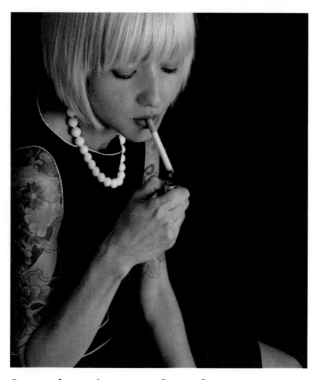

It was always important for a tobacco company to portray someone who smoked as "cool."

© Eva Serrabassa/iStockphoto

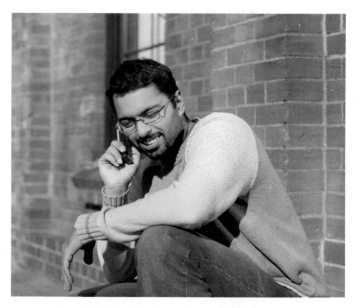

Some scientists say cell phone usage is the modern version of smoking. It might seem "cool" to some, but like smoking, it might prove to be addictive and dangerous. In the sample research essay that follows, the striking similarities between these two addictions are further discussed.

© absolut/Shutterstock

The Cell Phone: Tomorrow's Medical Menace?

By Leila Sayeed

ENG 101

Professor P. Muldoon

March 17, 2008

Cell phones are the latest craze—a modern addiction. For young people, the cell phone not only contributes to the look of "cool" in the way smoking once did and perhaps still does for some, but also offers them a degree of independence—a way to stay in touch with friends without having to check at home for messages. Like smoking, however, not everything about the cell phone is positive. The cell phone, for example, is being blamed for an increasing number of car accidents. And some claim that the cell phone, like the computer and the television, is just another piece of technology that people use—unconsciously, perhaps—to avoid real intimacy. But what might be the worst consequence of all is the one that users seem to be ignoring the most. Startling evidence from scientists around the world has shown that the cell phone does, in fact, interfere with DNA and the human brain. The trouble is no one is absolutely sure of the long-term effects because the technology is simply not old enough. Until it is known for certain whether people will develop serious diseases such as dementia or cancer directly due to cell phone use, it would be wise for cell phone users to err on the side of caution and take steps to minimize potential damage to the brain.

The cell phone is a microwave transmitter. It uses electromagnetic energy to transmit signals from fixed base stations. The growth rate of cell phone technology has been massive and rapid. The number of cell phone users reached 2 billion around the world at the end of 2005 (Reuters, 2005). In Canada, the number of cell phone users increased by 13 percent in 2005 to 17 million (McLean, 2006). Despite the enormity of the industry's expansion, the technology (the cell phone in its present form) has only been around since the 1980s. And those researchers who believe cell phones will cause cancer also say cancer takes decades to develop. It may be years if not decades, therefore, before we start to hear about cases of direct linkage between cell phones and brain cancer, making it easy for cell phone companies to insist in the meantime that their product is safe. This is ominously reminiscent of the decades during which tobacco companies had insisted smoking could not be linked to lung cancer.

Several studies of cancer and its possible link to cell phone use have been conducted in the United States and Europe between 1993 and the present day. One such study was sparked by a lawsuit that a Florida man filed in 1993. He claimed his wife's brain tumour had been caused by her cell phone. In response to this lawsuit, the Cellular Telecommunications Industry Association (CTIA) formed Wireless Technology Research (WTR) and granted it more than $25 million to study possible health risks of cell phone use. After six years, George Carlo, public health scientist and WTR's chairman, announced an alarming conclusion:

We found evidence of genetic damage in human blood. We have suggestions of excessive mortality from brain cancers among wireless phone users, and we have very clear evidence of a statistically significant higher risk of neuroepithelial tumors. We now have more data suggesting problems with wireless phones than the FDA (U.S. Food and Drug Administration) had when it banned silicone breast implants. (Bass, 1999, p. 62)

The CTIA, which funded the study, is, in turn, funded by huge companies that produce mobile phones and communications infrastructure. It is not surprising, therefore, that these results were not widely publicized. Cell phone companies, like tobacco companies before them, are in the habit of reporting that research has shown that their products pose "no known health risk" (Bass, 1999, p. 62).

In the book *Cell Phones: Invisible Hazards in the Wireless Age,* Dr. Carlo and syndicated columnist Martin Schram (2001) write how Carlo, after running the cell phone industry's research program for six years, quit due to a conscience he could no longer ignore. He could not say what the industry wanted him to—that all was well. "The big picture is becoming disturbingly clear: There is a definite risk that the radiation plume that emanates from a cell phone antenna can cause cancer and other health problems" (p. 248).

Links between microwave radiation and DNA damage in rat brains have been established by several scientists in the U.S. alone. U.S. neurosurgeons Henry Lai and N.P. Singh of the University of Washington in Seattle in 1997 reported damage to the brain cells of rats exposed to microwave radiation, according to U.S. magazine *Business Insurance.* The two neurosurgeons claim a "hot spot may develop in the brain, causing cell damage which could lead to neurodegenerative diseases [such as Alzheimer's] and cancer" (Aldred, 1997, p. 25). Although human brains are not rat brains, "we have similar physiology, and our brain cells work basically in similar ways to theirs," says Sheila Rogers (2003), founder and director of the international nonprofit organization Association for Comprehensive NeuroTherapy. Ross Adey is a professor of biochemistry at the University of California at Riverside. He found a link between low-intensity microwaves and DNA damage in rat brain cells. Even if cell phone microwaves do not damage human DNA, their interference alone may impede the ability of DNA to repair itself when damaged by other causes (Bass, 1999, p. 62).

In Europe, one of the most alarming major research studies was conducted in Sweden in 2006. Researchers at the Swedish National Institute for Working Life looked at 2200 cancer patients and compared them with an equal number of healthy control cases. Of the cancer patients, 905 had a malignant brain tumour, and a tenth of these were heavy users of cell phones (usage of at least one hour a day for at least 10 years). There was also a high incidence of the tumour appearing on the side of the head that the phone was generally used. Researchers in this study concluded that long-term mobile phone use raises the risk of brain tumours, especially in people who start using by the age of 20 (Reuters, 2005). And if anyone thinks cordless phones are safer, they should think again. Cordless phones (marked 900 megahertz or 2.4 gigahertz) give off the same microwave radiation as cell phones do (Worthington, 1998).

Not all of the research has resulted in negative findings. The National Cancer Institute (U.S.) supported an earlier study of approximately 1600 people in the year 2000. It found that cell phone users are "no more likely than anyone else to develop benign tumors or malignant brain cancers" (Kolata, 2000). The American Health Foundation, a private, nonprofit research organization in Valhalla, New York, conducted a smaller study in the same year. It found similar results after examining 1000 people. The latter study was funded by the U.S. government and the cell phone industry (Kolata, 2000).

It is extremely unlikely that an essay like this will convince anyone to get rid of his or her cell phone. But at the very least, there are some tips gathered from CBC News Online and CTV.ca that aim to minimize the damage to one's brain:

- Use a headset whenever possible, especially in a location where the signal to the phone is weak, such as in a basement. Headsets and cell phones with speakerphone capability are highly recommended. Both allow the phone to be positioned safely away from the user's brain.
- Try to use the cell phone only for emergency purposes, not for long conversations. When and where possible, use a landline or phone booth instead. The British government currently advises cell phone users to keep their calls short.
- Using the cell in a moving car is particularly dangerous, so minimize this usage as much as possible. Not only can it cause accidents, but a cell phone works particularly hard to receive a signal when the car is moving, so the electromagnetic field is stronger, putting one's brain further at risk.
- If you are not using a headset, do not put the cell phone to your head until after the call is established. Until the signal is established, the phone is working harder to find the signal, therefore increasing the electromagnetic field.
- Try as much as possible to use the cell phone only when it is fully charged or when the signal it receives is at its strongest (check the signal bars). Again, the harder the cell phone has to work to receive a signal, the harder it is on your brain.

- A person under the age of 16 should only use a cell phone for essential calls, since his or her head and nervous system might still be developing. Children under the age of 10 should not use cell phones at all.

Someone walking down the street with a cell phone at his or her ear, for many young people, still rates high on the meter of "cool." It makes some people feel important when it looks like they are "well connected." It can appear to take the loneliness out of being alone. But today's craze might be tomorrow's tragedy. Smoking has already proven to be the medical menace of today. What seems like a new addiction (especially among youth) may prove to be the medical menace of tomorrow. For those who cannot quit using cell phones any more easily than some could quit smoking, they might want to try the tips listed in this essay. But if others are more serious about self-improvement, the best solution is obvious: they should go back to using a landline. They might be saving some money. They might also be saving their lives.

References

magazine article

Aldred, C. (1997, January 6). Cell phone dangers require further study. *Business Insurance*, 31(1), 25.

magazine article

Bass, G. (1999, December). Radar: Is your cell phone killing you? *PC/Computing*, 62.

book with two authors

Carlo, G., & Schram, M. (2001). *Cell phones: Invisible hazards in the wireless age.* New York: Carroll & Graf.

online newspaper article

Cell phones not linked to brain cancer: Study. (2005, August 31). *CTV News, Shows and Sports.* Retrieved July 18, 2006, from http://www.ctv.ca

online newspaper article

Cellphone radiation. (2004, June 3). *CBC News Online.* Retrieved July 29, 2006, from http://www.cbc.ca/news/background/cellphones/radiation.html

newspaper article

Kolata, G. (2000, December 20). Two studies report no links to cancer in cell phones' use. *New York Times*, p. A1.

online newspaper article

McLean, C. (2006, July 27). Wireless overtakes local service. *Globe and Mail Update.* Retrieved July 30, 2006, from http://www.theglobeandmail.com

online news service

Reuters (2005, January 18). Two billion cell phone users and counting. MSNBC.com. Retrieved July 30, 2006, from http://www.msnbc.msn.com.

posting to a web forum

Rogers, S. (2003, January 31). Electromagnetic radiation: New study on mobile phones and brain. Message posted to ACN Forums. Retrieved July 29, 2006, from http://www.latitudes.org/forums/index.php?act=Print&client=printer&f=10&t=90

online magazine article

Worthington, A. (1998). Cellphones, shrink, brain, cells. *Health, Wealth & Happiness.* Retrieved July 17, 2006, from http://www.relfe.com/ cellphones_brain_cancer.html

MLA Sample Essay Using MLA Documentation

A portion of the previous essay is being repeated here to demonstrate how the same text would look using MLA parenthetical references (citations). A full Works Cited list in MLA style (the equivalent of the APA References list) is also provided.

Links between microwave radiation and DNA damage in rat brains have been established by several scientists in the U.S. alone. U.S. neurosurgeons Henry Lai and N.P. Singh of the University of Washington in Seattle in 1997 reported damage to the brain cells of rats exposed to microwave radiation, according to U.S. magazine *Business Insurance*. The two neurosurgeons claim a "hot spot may develop in the brain, causing cell damage which could lead to Alzheimer's disease and cancer" (Aldred 25). Although human brains are not rat brains, "we have similar physiology, and our brain cells work basically in similar ways to theirs," says Sheila Rogers, founder and director of the international nonprofit organization Association for Comprehensive NeuroTherapy. Ross Adey is a professor of biochemistry at the University of California at Riverside. He found a link between low-intensity microwaves and DNA damage in rat brain cells. Even if cell phone microwaves do not damage human DNA, their interference alone may impede the ability of DNA to repair itself when damaged by natural causes (Bass 62).

Works Cited

magazine article	Aldred, Carolyn. "Cell Phone Dangers Require Further Study." *Business Insurance* 6 Jan. 1997: 25. Print.
magazine article	Bass, Gordon. "Radar: Is Your Cell Phone Killing You?" *PC/Computing* Dec. 1999: 62. Print.
book with two authors	Carlo, George, and Martin Schram. *Cell Phones: Invisible Hazards in the Wireless Age.* New York: Carroll & Graf, 2001. Print.
online newspaper article	"Cell Phones Not Linked to Brain Cancer: Study." *CTV News, Shows and Sports* 31 Aug. 2005. Web. 18 July 2006.
online newspaper article	"Cellphone Radiation." *CBC News Online* 3 June 2004. Web. 29 July 2006.
newspaper article—late edition	Kolata, Gina. "Two Studies Report No Links to Cancer in Cell Phones' Use." *New York Times* 20 Dec. 2000, late ed.: A1. Print.
online newspaper article	McLean, Catherine. "Wireless Overtakes Local Service." *Globe and Mail Update* 27 July 2006. Web. 30 July 2006.
online news service	Reuters. "Two Billion Cell Phone Users and Counting." MSNBC.com. 18 January 2005. Web. 30 July 2006.
posting to a web forum	Rogers, Sheila. "Electromagnetic Radiation: New Study on Mobile Phones and Brain." Online posting. 31 Jan. 2003. ACN Forums. Web. 29 July 2006.
online magazine article	Worthington, Amy. "Cellphones Shrink Brain Cells." *Health, Wealth & Happiness* 1998. Web. 17 July 2006.

Questions for Analysis

1. What, in your own words, in one sentence, is the thesis of this research essay?
2. Which sentence in particular is the author's thesis?
3. What is the evidence that supports the thesis?
4. Does the author provide evidence that contradicts her thesis? If so, what is it?
5. If you answered "yes" to question 4, do you think this evidence helps or hinders the author's argument?
6. Is the author's argument effective? Why or why not?
7. Who is the intended audience?
8. What does the author want her audience to think or do as a result of reading this essay?
9. Do the sources seem legitimate? Why or why not?
10. Consider the sentence toward the top of page four of the essay: "Researchers in this study concluded that long-term mobile phone use raises the risk of brain tumours, especially in people who start using by the age of 20." What do the last few words, "who start using . . ." suggest? Does this suggestion correspond to anything else in the essay? Discuss.

Working Together: Documenting Sources

For this activity, which is competition-based, the class will need to be equipped with computers, or everyone will need to have a laptop with Internet access. Form groups of at least three people. If you haven't already done so, read the sample research essay ("The Cell Phone: Tomorrow's Medical Menace?"). Pretend that your group is planning to do more research on the issue of the possible long-term health effects of cell phone usage. Find as many sources as possible, and create a list of sources of which half seem to support the point of view taken in the essay and the other half seem to refute it. Be sure your list follows either MLA or APA style correctly (you must use one or the other consistently for the whole list). After one hour, the group with the longest list of correctly documented end sources wins.

Unit III Writing Strategies for the Paragraph and Essay

© Design Pics/Dean Muz/Jupiter Images

Chapter 21 **Narration**

All of the chapters in this unit apply to both the paragraph and the essay. If you wish, you can move immediately to the essay portion of any chapter (found roughly in the middle of the chapter). Even if you do this, however, you might also want to scan the first half of the chapter to see if you can pick up anything that could be of value to your writing experience. After all, where writing strategies are concerned, a great deal of what applies to the paragraph applies to the essay as well. Most suggested topics for paragraphs, for example, can also be used for essays and vice versa.

What Is Narration?

DEFINITION

Narration is the oldest and best-known form of verbal communication. It is, quite simply, the telling of a story.

Every culture in the world, past and present, has used narration to provide both entertainment and information for the people of that culture. Since everyone likes a good story, various forms of narration, such as novels, short stories, soap operas, and full-length movies, are always popular.

Developing Paragraphs: Narration

The following narrative paragraph, taken from an essay by Al Purdy titled "The Iron Road," tells the story of Purdy's trip westward in 1937, at the height of the Great Depression, when he was looking for work. In this passage, Purdy has been caught illegally riding a freight train by the railway police, and he is imprisoned in a caboose.

Model Paragraph: Prison-on-Wheels

When returned to my prison-on-wheels, I felt panic-stricken. I was only seventeen, and this was the first time I'd ventured far away from home. I examined the caboose-prison closely, thinking: two years. Why, I'd be nineteen when I got out, an old man! And of course it was hopeless to think of escape. Other prisoners had tried without success, and windows were broken where they'd tried to wrench out the bars. And the door: it was wood, locked on the outside with a padlock, opening inward. It was a very springy door, though. I could squeeze my fingertips between sill and door, one hand at the top and the other a foot below. That gave me hope, blessed hope, for the first time. My six-foot-three body was suspended in air by my hands, doubled up like a coiled spring, and I pulled. The door bent inward until I could see a couple of daylight inches between door and sill. Then Snap! and screws fell out of the steel hasp outside. I fell flat on my back.*

Working with Narration: Using Narration to Make a Point

At one time or another, you have met a person who loves to talk on and on without making any real point. This person is likely to tell you everything that happened in one day, including every cough and sideways glance. Your reaction to the seemingly needless and endless supply of details is probably one of fatigue and hope for a quick getaway. This is not narration at its best! A good story is almost always told to make a point: it can make us laugh, it can make us understand, or it can change our attitudes.

When Al Purdy tells the story of his escape from the caboose, he is careful to use only those details that are relevant to his story. For example, the way the door is constructed is important. Had it not been wooden and springy, he might never have been able to get his fingertips in and force an opening. He might have had to spend two years in prison. Then Purdy would have had a different story to tell.

What is Purdy's point in this paragraph? The excerpt is part of an essay about Purdy's experiences during the Depression; this part is specifically about the dangers of travelling illegally by train during that time, which many thousands of people had to do, illegal and dangerous as it was. On its surface, then, the story is merely about a trip, although an unusual one. Being imprisoned in the caboose, however, can also be seen as a metaphor: the caboose in which Purdy was imprisoned might represent the life of hopeless despair caused by unemployment that he and thousands of others were trapped in, and Purdy's escape could be a symbol of the escape from despair toward the hope that a trip to the West could bring, with its opportunities for a better life.

*"The Iron Road," *Starting From Ameliasburgh: The Collected Prose* of Al Purdy, by Al Purdy, edited by Sam Solecki, 1995, Harbour Publishing, www.harbourpublishing.com

Exercise   Using Narration to Make a Point

Each of the following examples is the beginning of a topic sentence for a narrative paragraph. Complete each sentence by providing a controlling idea that could be the point for the story.

1. During my trip to the East Coast, I was surprised by _____

   _____

2. When I couldn't get a job, I realized _____

   _____

3. After going to the movies every Saturday for many years, I discovered _____

   _____

4. When I arrived at the room where my business class was to meet, I found ____

   _____

5. When my best friend got married, I began to see that _____

   _____

Coherence in Narration: Placing Details in Order of Time Sequence

Ordering details in a paragraph of narration usually follows a time sequence. That is, you tell what happened first, then next, then after that, until finally you get to the end of the story. An event could take place in a matter of minutes or over a period of many years.

In the following paragraph, the story takes place in a single day. The six events that made the day a disaster are given in the order in which they happened. Although some stories flash back to the past or forward to the future, most use the natural chronological order of the events.

Model Paragraph: A Day to Forget

My day was a disaster. First, it had snowed during the night, which meant I had to shovel before I could leave for work. I was mad that I hadn't gotten up earlier. Then I had trouble starting my car, and to make matters worse, my daughter wasn't feeling well and said she didn't think she should go to school. When I eventually did arrive at the school where I teach, I was twenty minutes late. Soon I found out the secretary had forgotten to type the exam I was supposed to give my class that day. I quickly had to make another plan. By three o'clock, I was looking forward to getting my paycheque. Foolish woman! When I went to pick it up, the woman in the office told me that something had gone wrong with the computers. I would not be able to get my cheque until Tuesday. Disappointed, I walked down the hill to the parking lot. There I met my final defeat. In my hurry to park the car in the morning, I had left my parking lights on. Now my battery was dead. Even an optimist like me had the right to be discouraged!

Practice   **Coherence: Placing Details in Order of Time Sequence**

Each of the topics below is followed by six supporting details. These supporting details are listed in random order. Order the events according to time sequence by placing the appropriate number in the space provided. The first one has been done for you. Check your answers against those in the Answer Key on page 463.

1. The driving test

_____2_____   She had her last lesson with Mr. Panakos on Saturday morning.

_____5_____   As she ate breakfast Monday morning, Daniela read the driver's manual one more time because she knew it was her last chance to review.

_____1_____   Daniela's driving test was scheduled for Monday morning.

_____3_____   On Sunday afternoon her father gave her some advice on what to be careful of when she took her road test.

_____6_____   As her mother drove her to the motor vehicle bureau, Daniela tried to relax and not think about the test.

_____4_____   The night before her test, Daniela had phone calls from two friends who wished her good luck.

2. Making up my mind

_____   By the time I saw the dean for final approval of the change, I knew I had made the right decision.

_____   When I registered for my new courses for the next semester, I knew that I was doing what I should have done all along.

_____   I spent the summer of my second year thinking about the career I really wanted to follow.

_____   I suppose the experience taught me that you should always make a change in your life after you have thought it through completely.

_____   When I finally did decide to change majors, my friends acted as though I had decided to change my citizenship.

_____   When I told my favourite professor about my change of mind, he was very supportive, even though I had begun my major with him.

Writing the Narrative Paragraph Step by Step

To learn a skill with some degree of ease, it is best to follow a step-by-step approach so that various steps can be worked on one at a time. This approach will ensure that you are not missing a crucial point or misunderstanding a part of the whole. There are other ways to go about writing an effective paragraph, but here is one logical method you can use to achieve results.

Steps for Writing the Narrative Paragraph

1. Study the given topic, and then plan your topic sentence with its controlling idea.
2. List the events that come to mind when you think about the topic you have chosen.
3. Choose the five or six most important events from your list.
4. Put your final list in order.
5. Write at least one complete sentence for each of the events you have chosen from your list.
6. Write a concluding statement that gives some point to the events of the story.
7. Finally, copy your sentences into standard paragraph form.

Step-by-Step Example of Writing a Narrative Paragraph

The following example starts with a suggested topic and then uses the seven steps above to work through the writing process.

Topic: At one time or another, most people have to buy a car. Often it's not the type of car purchased that leads to a story, but the process of buying it. Write a narrative paragraph about buying a car (or some other expensive item, such as a stereo).

1. Write a topic sentence.

> Because my classes were at different campuses, and because I lived quite a distance from the college, I decided to buy a car.

2. Make a list of events.
   a. Tired of waiting for the bus
   b. Budget—gas, insurance, licence, repairs, financing
   c. Car loan
   d. Discussed with Dad
   e. Newspaper ads—dealerships
   f. Classified ads
   g. Asked friends for advice
   h. Comparison shopping

3. Choose the five or six events you believe are the most important for the point of the story.

> a, b, c, e, h

4. Make sure the order of your final choices makes sense. Re-order if necessary.

> In this case, the original order (a, b, c, e, h) makes sense.

5. Using your final list, write at least one sentence for each event you have chosen.
   a. I was tired of waiting for the bus on cold and rainy days, and being late for class when the bus was late didn't impress my professors.

b. My budget didn't allow me to purchase a new car, especially when I calculated the price of gasoline, insurance, repairs, licensing, and finance charges.

c. My bank manager was very helpful when it came to arranging a car loan, but even though the payments were spread out over a long period of time, it was still an expensive proposition.

e. I looked in the newspaper for ads from car dealerships, trying to decide whether I'd be better off buying from a dealer, with at least a minimal warranty on the car, or from a private seller.

h. Comparison shopping was a long and tedious, but necessary, process.

6. Write a concluding statement.

I finally bought a car, although it wasn't what I really wanted because of my financial situation. At least I don't have to wait for the bus anymore.

7. Put your sentences into standard paragraph form on a separate piece of paper or in a word-processing file.

Because my classes were at different campuses, and because I lived quite a distance from the college, I decided to buy a car. I was tired of waiting for the bus on cold and rainy days, and being late for class when the bus was late didn't impress my professors. My budget didn't allow me to purchase a new car, especially when I calculated the price of gasoline, insurance, repairs, licensing, and finance charges. My bank manager was very helpful when it came to arranging a car loan, but even though the payments were spread out over a long period of time, it was still an expensive proposition. I looked in the newspaper for ads from car dealerships, trying to decide whether I'd be better off buying from a dealer, with at least a minimal warranty on the car, or from a private seller. Comparison shopping was a long and tedious, but necessary, process. I finally bought a car, although it wasn't really what I wanted. At least I don't have to wait for the bus anymore.

Exercise Writing the Narrative Paragraph Step by Step

The following exercise will guide you through the construction of a narrative paragraph. Start with the suggested topic. Use the seven steps (repeated below) and the example on pages 258–259 to help you work through each stage of the writing process. Refer to the section above for a completed sample.

Topic: Recount the plot of a book you have read recently or a movie you have seen within the last few weeks.

1. Write a topic sentence.
2. Make a list of events.
3. Choose the five or six events you believe are the most important for the point of the story.

4. Make sure the order of your final choices makes sense. Re-order if necessary.
5. Using your final list, write at least one sentence for each event you have chosen.
6. Write a concluding statement.
7. Put your sentences into standard paragraph form.

On Your Own: Writing Narrative Paragraphs from Model Paragraphs

Model Paragraph: Better Early Than Late

I hate to be late. So, when I began my new job, I was determined to be on time for my first day. I awoke early, had a leisurely breakfast, and gave myself lots of time to get through the traffic. I entered my new office building and sat down at my new desk a good fifteen minutes before starting time. My boss noticed me, smiled, and came over to my desk. "I'm glad you're early," she said. "In fact, you're a week early. You start *next* Monday."

Assignment Narrative Paragraph

Write a paragraph telling the story of a day or part of a day in which you faced an important challenge of some kind. It could be a challenge you faced in school, at home, or on the job. The paragraph above gives an example.

SUGGESTED TOPICS:

(For more suggested topics, see the list given for the essay Assignment on pages 262–263.)

1. The day I started a new job
2. Becoming a member of a sports team
3. The morning of my big job interview
4. Facing a large debt
5. Sharing the telephone
6. The day I started driving lessons
7. Losing

Writing the Narrative Essay

Like the narrative paragraph, the narrative essay also tells a story. The essay, however, gives you the opportunity to write a longer story with more detail. Although the narrative is the most informal type of essay, you still need to organize it. Make sure there is some logic to the paragraphing—there should be some sort of shift with each new paragraph. You might, for example, devote each support paragraph to a single event or to a different character in your story. Don't fall into the trap of starting a new paragraph simply because the old one is getting too long. The following narrative essay was written by a former Centennial College student in 2001. As you read, see how Akis follows a logical sequence of events while keeping the reader in suspense.

For a review of the essay form and its standard format (which applies to all the writing strategies in this unit), see Chapter 16: "The Essay." For a review of the writing process that can be applied to both the paragraph and the essay, see Chapter 14: "The Four Stages of Writing for a Paragraph or an Essay."

The following narrative essay was written by a former Centennial College student in 2001. As you read, see how Akis follows a logical sequence of events while keeping the reader in suspense.

Model Essay: Transparent Silhouette*

by Akis Stylianou

On many lonely nights when I am too far from home to remember where home is and too beat to care where I lay my head, I have often heard an echo or seen a reflection that reminded me of a woman I knew. A silhouette through the window reflects the image of a petite yet shapely figure with long strands of silken hair falling over her shoulders. The wind whistling through the trees calls her name, taking me to another place where I can delay my misery.

We met early in life as classmates in elementary school. She used to stand alone in the schoolyard, surrounding herself with the walls she had built. It was a few years later before I could find the strength to enter those walls and discover her world. She told me she came from a broken home with an alcoholic mother and an abusive father. Being the only child, she was often the target of their frustration and rage, though she constantly dreamt of escaping her parents. By the time we reached our teens, she was running out of ways to numb her pain, and, soon after, she left home to live on the streets. Caring as much as I did, it tore me apart knowing there was nothing I could do to help.

She met the wrong kind of people and got involved with their crowds. She did many things she would come to regret, but, if the price was fitting, she was willing to sacrifice herself. My role as her friend was never to judge the path she had chosen; thus, friendship was never compromised. Most people considered her character unethical and immoral. However, she could smile with relief because she had finally escaped from the chains that weighed her down in the past.

One night, she was working as a dancer in a sleazy downtown bar when one of her customers began boasting about his position as an adult film producer. He told her that she had the look he was interested in. Soon after, she started acting, and her status as an adult film star rocketed. Before her twenty-fifth birthday, she had a brand new sports car, a beautiful apartment in the heart of the city, and a bank account holding her six-figure salary. On one occasion, we met at a restaurant for dinner. As she entered the room, all eyes were on her, as if they were in a hypnotic state. The men wanted to be

*Akis Stylianou, "Transparent Silhouette." Reprinted by permission of the author.

with her, and the women were jealous of her graceful presence. Behind all her jewellery, fur coat and expensive clothing, I could still see the frightened, bruised little girl I cared about. She pretended it didn't bother her, but beneath her polished exterior, I could see inside she wanted to explode.

That was the last chance I had to see her before her body was found lying lifeless in an empty apartment. The police said it was a burglary that went wrong and resulted in a homicide. She taught me to accept the good with the bad. After the rain falls, I walk the streets where she once lived, and the dried-up puddles remind me of her permanent tears.

Questions for Analysis

1. What, in your own words, do you think is the writer's thesis?
2. What is the writer's tone?
3. What is the meaning of the essay's title?
4. How do you think the writer feels about his friend?
5. Did the writer foreshadow the ending of the essay? (In other words, are there several clues throughout the essay that enable the reader to predict the eventual death of the writer's friend?)
6. If your answer to question 5 was yes, why did the writer foreshadow the ending? If your answer was no, why not?
7. Identify the transitions in the writer's essay.
8. Speculate on what might have caused the writer's friend's demise, in spite of what the police reported.

A model paragraph that answers question 5 above can be found on pages 337–338 in Chapter 28: "Argumentation."

 Assignment Rewrite the Conclusion

Rewrite the last paragraph of the essay using your own ideas. Try to stay faithful to the rest of the narrative essay so that you don't end up contradicting anything that comes before.

Assignment Narrative Essay

Choose a topic from the list below (or, if you prefer, from the list given for the paragraph "Assignment" on page 260) and write a narrative essay of at least five paragraphs to develop that topic.

SUGGESTED TOPICS:

1. My worst classroom experience
2. A parent who would not listen
3. My first _____
4. When I tried to convince someone to hire me for a job
5. My experience with an aggressive salesperson

6. A day when nothing went right

7. A misunderstanding with a friend

8. Trouble at the workplace

9. A day that changed my life

10. A major disappointment

11. How my nervousness made matters worse

12. A perfect evening

13. The best summer of my life

14. An embarrassing experience

15. Learning something surprising about myself

While developing your essay, you may want to review Chapter 14: "The Four Stages of Writing for a Paragraph or an Essay," in particular the following sections:

"Brainstorming"

"Choosing the Topic and the Controlling Idea"

"Outlining"

"The Rough Draft"

"Revising and Editing the Rough Draft"

"Proofreading"

"Checklist for the Final Copy"

For help in connecting your sentences and paragraphs smoothly and clearly, you may wish to consult the list of transitional words and phrases, categorized by their function, found on the inside back cover of this book.

 Working Together: Spontaneous Creativity or Combustion?

1. As a class or in smaller groups, try the old but still-amusing parlour game of telling a story by creating it on the spot. One person begins with a sentence that sets the scene. Then the story is continued, sentence by sentence, as each person takes a turn. (Elect one student to put the sentences on the board.) Continue for perhaps twenty minutes; then discuss the outcome. In what ways is the narrative a success? What are its weaknesses?

2. In an "Assignment" (page 262) for this chapter, you were asked to write a narrative essay. Divide into groups and share your essay with the other members of your group. Attach a sheet of paper to each essay you read and use it to critique the essay by answering the following two questions:

   a. In your opinion, what is one aspect of the essay that you believe is very strong? Explain.

   b. In your opinion, what is one aspect of the essay that still needs improvement? Explain.

Chapter 22 Description

What Is Description?

> **DEFINITION**
>
> **Description** is the use of words to help the reader understand how people, places, or things are perceived. How a particular food tastes, looks, and smells, for example, might be the subject of a descriptive paragraph or essay.

Description is one of the basic building blocks of good writing. When you are able to write an effective description of a person, an object, a place, or even an idea, you are in control of your writing. Good description also makes you able to control what your reader sees and does not see.

The key to writing a good description is the choice of the **specific details** you will use. Specific details make your descriptions real and help your reader remember what you have written. A careful writer always pays special attention to specific details in any piece of writing.

A second important aspect of good description is the use of **sensory images**.

> **DEFINITION**
>
> **Sensory images** are details that relate to your sense of sight, smell, touch, taste, or hearing.
> **Example:** The deafening screams and relentless yelling of the children on the school bus drove the driver mad.

When you appeal to at least some of the five senses in your descriptive writing, your reader will be able to relate directly to what you are saying. Sensory images also help your reader remember what you have written.

A third important aspect of good description is the **order** in which you place the details you have chosen. The combination of specific details, sensory images, and a well-chosen order in which you present these details and impressions will help your reader form a **dominant impression** of what you are describing.

Some descriptive writing is more objective than subjective (for example, a police report). If your descriptive piece is more objective, give the readers enough facts to allow them to come up with their own dominant impressions. If your descriptive piece is subjective, instead, your dominant impression should be suggested from the outset, even if it's not completely obvious. Establishing a dominant impression is the job of the topic sentence of a paragraph or the thesis statement of an essay.

Developing Paragraphs: Description

The following example of a descriptive paragraph includes all of the elements of a good description. As you read this description of a typical neighbourhood delicatessen, note the specific details and the sensory images the writer uses. After you have read the description, ask yourself whether the writer has provided a dominant impression. If so, state that dominant impression in your own words. What is your evidence for this conclusion? Does the paragraph feature subjective or objective description?

Model Paragraph: Delicatessen Decor

The delicatessen was a wide store with high ceilings that were a dark brown colour from many years of not being painted. The rough wooden shelves on both sides of the store were filled from floor to ceiling with cans of fruits and vegetables, jars of pickles and olives, and special imported canned fish. A large refrigerator case against one wall was always humming loudly from the effort of keeping milk, cream, and several cases of pop and juice cool at all times. At the end of the store was the main counter with its gleaming white metal scale on top and its cold cuts and freshly made salads inside. Stacked on top of the counter beside the scale today were baskets of fresh rolls and breads that gave off an aroma that contained a mixture of onion, caraway seed, and pumpernickel. Behind the scale was the friendly face of Mr. Rubino, who was in his store seven days a week, fourteen hours or more each day. He was always ready with a smile or a friendly comment, or even a sample piece of cheese or smoked meat as a friendly gesture for his "growing customers," as he referred to us kids in the neighbourhood.

Working with Description: Selecting the Dominant Impression

When you use a number of specific sensory images as you write a description, you should do more than simply write a series of sentences on a particular topic. You should also create a dominant impression in your reader's mind. Each individual sentence that you write is part of a picture that becomes clear when the reader finishes the paragraph.

For example, when you describe a place, the dominant impression you create might be of a place that is warm, or friendly, or comfortable; or it could be a place that is formal, or elegant, or artistic. When you write a description of a person, your reader could receive the dominant impression of a positive, efficient person who is outgoing and creative, or of a person who appears to be cold, distant, or hostile. All the sentences should support the dominant impression you have chosen.

Here is a list of descriptive words for you to use as a guide as you work through this chapter. (Not surprisingly, all these words are adjectives, since adjectives are words that *describe* persons, places, and things.) Picking a dominant impression is essential in writing the descriptive college paragraph.

Selecting the Dominant Impression

Possible Dominant Impressions for Descriptions of Places

crowded	cozy	inviting	cheerful	dazzling
romantic	restful	dreary	drab	uncomfortable
cluttered	ugly	tasteless	unfriendly	gaudy
stuffy	eerie	depressing	spacious	sunny

Possible Dominant Impressions for Descriptions of People

creative	angry	independent	proud	withdrawn
tense	shy	aggressive	generous	sullen
silent	witty	pessimistic	responsible	efficient
snobbish	placid	bumbling	bitter	easygoing

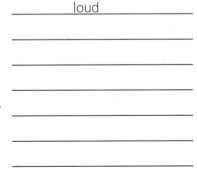 **Exercise Selecting the Dominant Impression**

Each of the following places could be the topic for a descriptive paragraph. First, the writer must decide on a dominant impression. Fill in each blank to the right of the topic with an appropriate dominant impression. Use the list above if you need help. The first one is done for you.

Topic   **Dominant Impression**

1. The college pub on pub night   _____loud_____

2. A park at dusk   _____

3. The room where you are now sitting _____

4. The variety store nearest you   _____

5. The college bookstore in September _____

6. An overcrowded waiting room   _____

7. The kitchen in the morning   _____

Revising Vague Dominant Impressions

Certain words in the English language have become so overused that they no longer have any specific meaning for a reader. Careful writers avoid these words because they are almost useless in descriptive writing. Here is a list of the most common overused words:

- good, bad
- nice, fine, okay

- normal, typical
- interesting
- beautiful

The following paragraph is an example of the kind of writing that results from the continued use of vague words:

Model Paragraph: A Day in the Life . . . (I)

I had a typical day. The weather was nice and my job was interesting. The food for lunch was okay; supper was really good. After supper, I saw my girlfriend, who is really beautiful. That's when my day really became fun.

Notice that all of the details in the paragraph are vague. The writer has told us what happened, but we cannot really see any of the details that are mentioned. This is because the writer has made the mistake of using words that have lost much of their meaning. Replacing the vague words in the paragraph will create an entirely different impression:

Model Paragraph: A Day in the Life . . . (II)

I had an event-filled day that was typical of the kind of day I've been enjoying lately. The weather on this summer day was perfect for late June, and the challenge of my job in the health-care field made me feel that this warm and sunny day was made just for me. I had a delicious lunch in a tiny Italian restaurant, and a supper to excite the taste buds at a cozy Greek restaurant that just oozed atmosphere. After supper, I met my girlfriend, who has a warm sense of humour and who is a partner in a major law firm down the street from where I work.

The following exercise will give you practice in recognizing and eliminating overused words.

 Exercise **Revising Vague Dominant Impressions**

In each of the spaces provided, change the underlined word to give a more specific dominant impression. An example has been done for you.

> ***Vague:*** The tablecloth was <u>beautiful.</u>
> ***Revised:*** The tablecloth was <u>of white linen with delicate blue embroidery</u>.

1. The sunset was <u>beautiful</u>.   _____
2. The water felt <u>nice</u>.   _____
3. Horseback riding was <u>fun</u>.   _____
4. The traffic was <u>bad</u>.   _____
5. The hotel lobby was <u>typical</u>.   _____
6. The main street is <u>interesting</u>.   _____
7. The dessert tasted <u>good</u>.   _____

Working with Description: Sensory Images

One of the basic ways all good writers communicate experiences to their readers is by using sensory impressions. We respond to writing that makes us see an object, hear a sound, touch a surface, smell an odour, or taste a flavour. When a writer uses one or more of these sensory images in a piece of writing, we tend to pay more attention to what he or she is saying, and we tend to remember the details of what we have read.

For example, if you come across the word *door* in a sentence, you may or may not pay attention to it. However, if the writer tells you it was a *brown wooden* door that was *rough to the touch* and *creaked loudly* when it opened, you would hardly be able to forget it. The door would stay in your mind because the writer used sensory images to make you aware of it.

The following sentences are taken from the description of Mr. Rubino's delicatessen on page 265. Notice how in each sentence the writer uses at least one sensory image to make the details of that sentence remain in our minds. The physical sense the writer is appealing to is indicated for each sentence.

1. A large refrigerator case against one wall was always humming loudly from the effort of keeping milk, cream, and several cases of pop and juice cool at all times.

    Physical sense: hearing

2. Stacked on top of the counter . . . were baskets of fresh rolls and breads that gave off an aroma that contained a mixture of onion, caraway seed, and pumpernickel.

    Physical sense: smell

3. He was always ready with . . . a sample piece of cheese or smoked meat as a friendly gesture. . . .

    Physical sense: taste

When you use sensory images in your own writing, you will stimulate your readers' interest and create images in their minds that they will remember.

Coherence in Description: Putting Details in Spatial Order

In descriptive paragraphs, the writer often chooses to arrange supporting details according to their location in space. With this method, you place yourself at the scene and then use a logical order such as moving from nearby to farther away, right to left, or top to bottom. Often you move in such a way that you save the most important detail until last in order to achieve the greatest effect.

In the paragraph about the delicatessen on page 265, the writer first describes the ceilings and walls of the store, then proceeds to the shelves and large refrigerator, and ends by describing the main counter of the deli with its owner, Mr. Rubino, standing behind it. The details are thus presented starting with the outer limits of the room and moving inward to the man who is central to the point of this paragraph. A description of a clothes closet might order the details differently—perhaps the writer would go from the ground up, beginning with the shoes standing on the floor and finishing with the hats and gloves arranged on the top shelf.

Here is a paragraph from Thierry Mallet's *Glimpses of the Barren Lands*, a description of his travels through the Canadian Arctic:

> Our camp had been pitched at the foot of a great, bleak, ragged hill, a few feet from the swirling waters of the Kazan River. The two small green tents, pegged down tight with heavy rocks, shivered and rippled under the faint touch of the northern breeze. A thin wisp of smoke rose from the embers of the fire.

Notice that the writer begins with a description of the landscape, then gives a description of the camp, and ends with a picture of the small fire. In spite of the shortness of the paragraph, we are able to follow the writer through the description because there is a logical plan. No matter what method of spatial order you choose to organize the details in a descriptive paragraph, be sure the results allow your reader to see the scene in a logical order.

Practice Coherence: Putting Details in Spatial Order

Each of the following topic sentences is followed by descriptive sentences that are out of order. Put these descriptive sentences in order by placing the appropriate number in the space provided. Check your answers against those in the Answer Key on page 463.

1. The young woman was a teen of the 21st century.
   (Order the material from top to bottom.)

   _____ She wore hip-hugging, low-rise faded jeans.

   _____ Her nose was pierced with a subtle gold stud.

   _____ She displayed a tasteful tattoo of a single red rose on her left shoulder blade above her tight-fitting tube top.

   _____ Her brown hair was cut unevenly and streaked with blond.

   _____ Her wedge sandals looked cute and comfortable at the same time.

2. The locker room was in chaos.
   (Order the material from near to far.)

   _____ Immediately to my right, I saw Pat and Chris slapping each other with towels.

   _____ Behind the pair, a row of locker doors banged open and shut.

_____ I squeezed past a noisy group crowding the doorway.

_____ At the back, the rest of the team was hugging and congratulating our hero in celebration of her winning goal.

Writing the Descriptive Paragraph Step by Step

To learn a skill with some degree of ease, it is best to follow a step-by-step approach so that you can work on the steps one at a time. This will ensure that you are not missing a crucial point or misunderstanding a part of the whole. There are other ways to go about writing an effective paragraph, but what follows is one logical method you can use to achieve results.

Steps for Writing the Descriptive Paragraph

1. Study the given topic, then plan your topic sentence, especially the dominant impression.
2. List at least ten details that come to mind when you think about the topic.
3. Choose the five or six most important details from your list. Be sure these details support the dominant impression.
4. Put your final list in a logical order.
5. Write at least one complete sentence for each of the details you have chosen from your list.
6. Write a concluding statement that offers some reason for describing this topic.
7. Finally, copy your sentences into standard paragraph form.

 Exercise   Writing the Descriptive Paragraph Step by Step

Starting with the suggested topic below, follow the seven steps outlined in the box above to work through the writing process for a process paragraph. (These steps are similar to those used for the narrative paragraph in Chapter 21; refer to pages 258–259 for a step-by-step example and a completed sample paragraph.)

Topic: A person you admire

On Your Own: Writing Descriptive Paragraphs from Model Paragraphs

Description of a Person

In the following model paragraph, from Alistair MacLeod's story "The Lost Salt Gift of Blood," the author describes his mother in Nova Scotia.

Model Paragraph: Mother Fortress

My mother ran her house as her brothers ran their boats. Everything was clean and spotless and in order. She was tall and dark and powerfully energetic. In later years, she reminded me of the women of Thomas Hardy, particularly Eustacia Vye, in a physical way. She fed and clothed a family of seven children, making all of the meals and most of the clothes. She grew miraculous gardens and magnificent flowers and raised broods of hens and ducks. She would walk miles on berry-picking expeditions and hoist her skirts to dig for clams when the tide was low. She was fourteen years younger than my father, whom she had married when she was 26, and had been a local beauty for a period of ten years. My mother was of the sea as were all of her people, and her horizons were the very literal ones she scanned with her dark and fearless eyes.

Assignment Descriptive Paragraph

Describe a person—preferably one you have observed more than once. If you have seen this person only once, indicate the details that made him or her stay in your mind. If you choose to describe a person with whom you are familiar, select the most outstanding details that will help give your reader a single, dominant impression.

SUGGESTED TOPICS:

(For more suggested topics, see the list given for the essay "Assignment" on page 274.)

1. A loyal friend
2. A local musician
3. A cab driver
4. A fashion model
5. A gossipy neighbour
6. A police officer
7. An aerobics instructor

Writing the Descriptive Essay

Like the topic sentence of a descriptive paragraph, the thesis of a descriptive essay identifies what is being described and includes the overall impression the author has of the topic. Each support paragraph might deal with one component of whatever is being described. The following is a brief outline of a descriptive essay:

Thesis:	The 100-year-old house was definitely haunted.
Topic sentence for paragraph #1:	First of all, every time people entered any room in the house, something seemed to be out of place, contrary to the owner's insistence that she never changes a thing.
Topic sentence for paragraph #2:	Secondly, visitors constantly scurry out of the house in a fright claiming later they've sighted at least one ghost.

Topic sentence for paragraph #3:

Scariest of all are the stories about visitors to the house constantly hearing what seems like moaning coming from all around, as if the walls are filled with sick people struggling to break free.

For a review of the essay form and its standard format (which applies to all the writing strategies in this unit), see Chapter 16: "The Essay." For a review of the writing process that can be applied to both the paragraph and the essay, see Chapter 14: "The Four Stages of Writing for a Paragraph or an Essay."

The following descriptive essay was a winning entry in Centennial College's Student Writing Contest. (Note that the paragraphs are shorter than the type of paragraph this book recommends; this is a more journalistic style.) What was Alexandra's inspiration for writing this piece? She was driving home from school one day and happened to notice a caravan in someone's backyard. What she didn't know yet was that Daphne, the subject of the piece, was not only a carpenter and artist, but also an English professor at Durham College.

Model Essay: A Profile of Daphne*

by Alexandra Savage-Ferr

The first time I saw her sitting amidst the Gypsy caravans, I knew this was a woman I had to meet. After all, we shared a love—a love of books, a love of secret, special places, and a love of the caravans we read and dreamt about in childhood. Daphne designs and builds unique living spaces based upon English Gypsy wagons at her home in the Durham Region of Ontario.

Using the frame and wheels of old farm wagons and the occasional antique CP [Canadian Pacific] baggage cart, she custom-builds wooden living spaces that writers and dreamers will truly appreciate. Each caravan is uniquely hand painted and decorated with themes from literature, such as Robin Hood's Sherwood Forest and Kenneth Grahame's *The Wind in the Willows*.

Today, surrounded by sun-drenched maples, this skilled craftswoman in sweater and jeans, ponytail a-flying, leads me from one work of art to the next, while a grey, shaggy dog—a rescued stray—prances about in circles of dappled sunlight. Several brightly coloured Gypsy caravans are dotted about the six-acre wooded estate located just north of Uxbridge.

Gypsies, also known as Roma or Romany Gypsies, have their origins in India over a thousand years ago. As they entered southeastern Europe at the end of the 13th century, it was thought that they were from Egypt. They were called 'Gyptians, which is how they became known as "Gypsies."

Learning woodworking as a child, using miniature tools alongside her father building boats, Daphne discovered more than just carpentry skills.

*Alexandra Savage-Ferr, "A Profile of Daphne." Reprinted by permission of the author.

Inside her rustic country home, the walls are lined floor-to-ceiling with row upon row of books, many of which belonged to her father. No fewer than six copies of *The Secret Garden*, and the entire set of Baum's Oz tales—first editions, of course—are friends. This literary multitude seems as much alive as the two cats that preen themselves before the fire. Fantasy abounds as I gaze over antique photographs, carousel horses, and a brimming bag of apples picked during an early morning snowfall. She serves me Russian Caravan Tea and cuts thick slabs of a sugary confection.

After building various theatre props over the years for the Scugog Choral Society and others, the old adage rang true: If you want one, build one. Conjuring magic for the stage, Daphne gazed into the crystal ball of her imagination and translated her visions into a real-life living space. Now she builds caravans for others with their own visions. "I'm interested in the ones who say, 'Wouldn't it be perfect for me?' because there's imagination there," she says. "They see it as their own spot."

These caravans are not intended for travelling, however. Rather, they are meant to be a dreaming, reading, and writing spot remote from the house, sequestered from interruptions and distractions. Since building her own personal retreat, she has crafted several more—the most recent one being commissioned as a unique guestroom for a Port Perry bed and breakfast.

Her own caravan roosts at the top of a hill overlooking the pond. "In the morning, the bulrushes are full of blackbirds," she relates. Indeed, the birds are singing now as our feet crunch through the hoarfrost-covered leaves. This earthy woman with carpenter's hands beckons me inside. I climb a small set of wooden steps and enter through the narrow Dutch door.

Inside, we are cozily sheltered from a sudden hailstorm pinging on the metal roof. Personal treasures, like sprites, peek from every nook and cranny. A crazy quilt travels the length of the platform bed beneath a window overlooking tangled briar. A hanging lantern, cherished books, photographs, and blessed gifts from her children hum with joyful verse. "This is my special place," she whispers.

I knew why I had to meet her, there by the gypsy caravans. I *knew* she had the secret. She'd had it all along.

Questions for Analysis

1. What part of speech enriches the descriptive value of this piece more than any other?

2. Give some examples from this piece of this particular part of speech.

3. What is the object of the description in this essay? Could it be argued there are two? Why or why not?

4. In paragraph 6, the writer uses both double quotation marks and single quotation marks. Explain their usage.

5. The last paragraph mentions "the secret." What "secret" did the writer know Daphne had all along?

 Assignment Descriptive Essay

Choose a topic from the list below (or, if you prefer, from the list given for the paragraph "Assignment" on page 271) and write a descriptive essay of at least five paragraphs to develop that topic.

SUGGESTED TOPICS:

1. The best job I ever had
2. The career of my dreams
3. My favourite aunt or uncle
4. My pet _____
5. My first car
6. The ideal mate
7. The most embarrassing date
8. The best dance club
9. My best friend
10. The best meal I ever had
11. The worst restaurant I've ever eaten in
12. My favourite music
13. My tattoos and/or piercings
14. The worst hospital I've ever been in
15. The best float in the _____ parade

While developing your essay, you may want to review Chapter 14: "The Four Stages of Writing for a Paragraph or an Essay," in particular the following sections:

"Brainstorming"

"Choosing the Topic and the Controlling Idea"

"Outlining"

"The Rough Draft"

"Revising and Editing the Rough Draft"

"Proofreading"

"Checklist for the Final Copy"

For help in connecting your sentences and paragraphs smoothly and clearly, you may wish to consult the list of transitional words and phrases, categorized by their function, found on the inside back cover of this book.

Working Together: The Hunt for a Roommate

The following personal advertisement appeared in a local newspaper:

> Young man seeks neat, responsible roommate to share off-campus apartment for next academic year. Person must be a nonsmoker and respect a vegetarian who cooks at home. Furniture not needed, but CD player would be welcome!

Finding the right roommate in a college or university residence, the right person with whom to share an apartment, or the right long-term companion can be difficult. People's personal habits have a way of causing friction in everyday life. Divide into groups for a brief discussion of the kinds of problems one finds in sharing the same space with another person.

1. Imagine that an agency that matches people up with roommates has asked you to write a paragraph or two in which you provide a character description of yourself. As you write, be sure you include information about your hobbies, habits, attitudes, and any other personal characteristics that could make a difference in the kind of person the agency will select for you.

2. Imagine that the agency has asked you to write a paragraph or two in which you provide a character sketch of the roommate you would like the agency to find for you.

Chapter 23 **Process**

What Is Process?

> **DEFINITION**
>
> **Process** is the explanation of how to do something or the demonstration of how something works. There are two kinds of process writing: **directional** and **informational.**

A **directional process** actually *shows* you, step by step, how to do something. For example, if you wanted to show someone how to brew a perfect cup of coffee, you would take the person through each step of the process, from selecting and grinding the coffee beans to pouring the finished product. Instructions on a test, directions for getting to a wedding reception, recipes for spaghetti sauce—these are a few examples of the kinds of process writing you see and use regularly. You can find examples of directional process writing everywhere you look: in newspapers, magazines, and books, as well as on the containers and packages of products you use every day.

An **informational process** *tells* you how something is (or was) done, for the purpose of informing you about it. For example, in a history course, it might be important to understand how Upper and Lower Canada were joined by the process of Confederation. Of course, you would not use this process yourself; its purpose would be to give you information.

Developing Paragraphs: Process

The following paragraph, from Mary Finlay's *Communication at Work*, is an example of directional process writing that describes some preliminary steps to follow when preparing an oral presentation.

Model Paragraph: Planning Your Presentation

Ascertain how long your presentation is expected to take. Normally, a speech is delivered at about 150 words a minute. Make sure that your material is adequate for the time allotted. Of course, this does not mean that a ten-minute oral report will be as dense as a 1500-word essay. Rehashing points you have already made in order to fill up your time is a sure-fire way to annoy and frustrate your listeners. Leave time for questions and feedback. If there is none, don't fill in the time by answering the questions nobody asked. This suggests that you are having second thoughts about the organization and planning of your report.

The following paragraph provides an example of informational process writing, giving an overview of the process leading up to Canadian Confederation:

Model Paragraph: Years in the Making

Confederation, the political union of British North America, didn't happen overnight. Starting as a topic of discussion among politicians before the 1860s, it began to take shape after 1864 with a conference in Charlottetown to discuss the possibility of a union, followed by a second conference at Quebec the same year. Details were hammered out at yet another conference in London, England, in 1866, leading to the passage of the *British North America Act* in March of 1867 and resulting in the formation of the Dominion of Canada on July 1, 1867.

Working with Process: Don't Overlook Any of the Steps

The writer of the process essay is almost always more of an authority on the subject than the person reading the essay. When giving directions or information on how something is (or was) done, it is possible to leave out a step that you think is so obvious that it is not worth mentioning. The reader, on the other hand, may not necessarily fill in the missing step as you did. An important part of process writing, therefore, is understanding your reader's level of ability. All of us have been given directions that, at first, seemed very clear, only to find that, when we actually tried to carry out the process, something went wrong. A step in the process was misunderstood or missing. The giver of the information either assumed we knew more than we did about certain parts of the process, or didn't stop to think through the process completely. To avoid causing this kind of difficulty for your reader, make sure the directions in your process writing are complete and accurate. Here is one further consideration: If special equipment is required in order to perform the process, be sure that the directions include a clear description of the necessary tools.

Exercise Is the Process Complete?

In the following process, try to determine what important step or steps have been omitted. Imagine yourself going through the process using only the information provided.

How to Prepare for an Essay Exam

1. Read the relevant chapters as they are assigned, well in advance of the test.
2. Take notes in class.

3. If the teacher has not described the test, ask him or her what format the test will take.
4. Get a good night's sleep the night before.
5. Bring any pens or pencils that you might need.
6. Arrive at the classroom a few minutes early in order to get yourself settled and to keep yourself calm.

Missing step or steps: _____

_____

_____

Coherence in Process: Order in Logical Sequence

When you are writing about a process, it is important to make sure not only that the steps in the process are complete, but also that they are given in the right sequence. For example, if you are describing the process of cleaning a mixer, it is important to point out that you must first unplug the appliance before you remove the blades. The importance of this step is clear when you realize that neglecting it could cost someone a finger. Improperly written instructions could cause serious injuries or even death.

Practice   Coherence: Order in Logical Sequence

The following steps describe the process of setting up an effective filing system. Number the steps in their proper sequence in the blanks to the left. Check your answers against those in the Answer Key on page 463.

_____ When your mind begins to blur, stop filing for that day.

_____ Now label a file folder and slip the piece of paper in.

_____ Gather together all materials to be filed so that they are all in one location.

_____ Alphabetize your file folders and put them away into your file drawer, and you are finished for that session.

_____ Add to these materials a recycling container, folders, labels, and a pen.

_____ Pick up the next piece of paper and go through the same procedure, but ask yourself whether this new piece of paper might fit into an existing file rather than one with a new heading.

_____ Pick up an item from the top of the pile and decide whether this item has value for you. If it does not, recycle it. If it does, go on to the next step.

_____ Finally, to maintain your file once it is established, riffle through each file folder you consult picking out and recycling the deadwood.

_____ If the piece of paper is worth saving, ask yourself the question "What is this paper about?"

Use transitional words and phrases to make a paragraph flow smoothly and coherently—see the section "Using Transitions to Move from One Idea to the Next" in Chapter 16 (pages 201–203), and the discussions of using time sequence and spatial order to order paragraphs in Chapters 21 (pages 256–57) and 22 (pages 268–70), respectively.

 Exercise Using Transitions to Go from a List to a Paragraph

Refer back to the process "How to Prepare for an Essay Exam" outlined in the first exercise in this chapter (pages 277–278). Using words listed under the heading "For Process" in the chart of common transitional words and phrases on the inside back cover of this text, change the list of steps from the exercise into a process paragraph that is coherent and flowing.

Writing the Process Paragraph Step by Step

To learn a skill with some degree of ease, it is best to follow a step-by-step approach so that you can work on the steps one at a time. This will ensure that you are not missing a crucial point or misunderstanding a part of the whole. There are other ways to go about writing an effective paragraph, but here is one logical method you can use to achieve results, which in itself is a process.

Steps for Writing the Process Paragraph

1. Write a topic sentence.
2. List as many steps or stages in the process as you can.
3. Eliminate any irrelevant points; add references to any equipment needed or special circumstances of the process.
4. Put your final list in order.
5. Write at least one complete sentence for each of the steps you have chosen from your list.
6. Write a concluding statement that says something about the results of completing the process.
7. Finally, copy your sentences into standard paragraph form.

Exercise Writing the Process Paragraph Step by Step

Starting with the suggested topic below, follow the seven steps outlined in the box above to work through the writing process for a process paragraph. (These steps are similar to those used for the narrative paragraph in Chapter 21; refer to pages 258–259 for a step-by-step example and a completed sample paragraph.)

Topic: How to burglar-proof your home

The incidence of break-and-enter crimes increases yearly, and many people are concerned about their homes when they are away on vacation. Give advice to a homeowner on how to protect a house against burglary.

On Your Own: Writing Process Paragraphs from Model Paragraphs

Directional Process: How to Care for Your Health

Concern for health and physical fitness is enjoying great popularity, bringing in big profits to health-related magazines, health clubs, health-food producers, and sports equipment manufacturers. The following paragraph tells us how to get a good night's sleep.

Model Paragraph: Road to Restfulness

The process of getting a good night's sleep depends on several factors. First, the conditions in your bedroom must be correct. Be sure the room temperature is around 18°C and the room is as quiet as possible. Next, pay attention to your bed and how it is furnished. For example, a firm mattress is best, and wool blankets are better than blankets made of synthetic material. Similarly, a firm pillow is best; after all, one that is too soft can cause a stiff neck and lead to a night of poor sleep. Also, keep in mind that what and how you eat are part of the process of preparing for bed. For example, do not go to bed hungry, but do not overeat, either. And avoid candy bars or cookies; the sugar they contain acts as a stimulant. Finally, do not go to bed until you are sleepy. Do something relaxing until you are tired. In conclusion, everything you do can have an effect on how well you sleep.

Assignment 1 Process Paragraph

Write a paragraph in which you give the major steps in some area of caring for your physical or mental health.

SUGGESTED TOPICS:

1. How to plan a daily exercise program
2. How to choose a sport that is suitable for you
3. How to live to be 100
4. How to pick a doctor
5. How to make exercise and dieting fun
6. How to stop smoking
7. How to deal with depression

Informational Process: How to Accomplish a Task

Note that the topics presented above are all examples of directional process writing. Read the following model paragraph for an example of informational process writing, describing how an insect builds a nest.

Model Paragraph: Waspy Ways

The insect known as the hunter wasp goes through a regular procedure when it builds a nest. First, it digs a small tunnel into the earth. Then it goes in search of a cicada, a large insect that resembles a cricket. After stinging and paralyzing the cicada, the hunter wasp brings it to the tunnel, lays an egg on the helpless insect, and seals the tunnel. The hunter wasp then leaves. When the egg hatches, the larva uses the cicada as a source of food.

Assignment 2 Process Paragraph

Write a paragraph in which you show how a task is accomplished. The task may be something that is frequently done by humans or that occurs in the world of nature.

SUGGESTED TOPICS:

(For more suggested topics, see the list given for the essay "Assignment" on page 284.)

1. How cheese is made
2. How to burn a CD
3. How people obtain a divorce
4. How to get a driver's licence
5. How yeast causes bread to rise
6. How a bill becomes a law
7. How planets are formed

Writing the Process Essay

Any process paragraph easily can be turned into a process essay by simply increasing the amount of detail in all of the steps. Follow the essay format and structure as described in Chapter 16: "The Essay," and devote each support paragraph to a single step in the process.

Exercise When Process Goes Wrong

It is your sister's birthday. You have bought her a gift that you must first put together. Carefully following the instructions, you try to assemble the item, but something is wrong. It does not work. Either you have not followed the instructions properly, or the instructions themselves are not clear. All of us have found ourselves in this situation at one time or another. It reminds us that it takes careful thought to write about a process, and that the writer should not assume the reader knows more than he or she is likely to.

Answer the following questions in further exploration of this topic.

1. Think of a time when you had to put something together but were not given adequate directions. What did you do?
2. When people write instructions or give directions, what do they usually neglect to keep in mind?

3. Recall a time when you had to explain a process to someone. Perhaps you were showing someone how to get somewhere or writing a detailed description of how to do a science experiment. What was the process? Was it hard to explain? Why or why not?

4. What was your worst experience with trying to follow a process? You could have been trying to work something out yourself or follow someone else's directions. How did you overcome your difficulty?

> For a review of the essay form and its standard format (which applies to all the writing strategies in this unit), see Chapter 16: "The Essay." For a review of the writing process that can be applied to both the paragraph and the essay, see Chapter 14: "The Four Stages of Writing for a Paragraph or an Essay."

Much of the instruction in this book is process writing. This very chapter, for instance, outlines the process of writing a process paragraph or essay. Some processes are familiar to most of us, such as assembling furniture from printed instructions. The sample essay below describes a process that everyone has heard about, but not everyone has actually done: changing a flat tire. Cara had never changed a flat tire until she accidentally came upon a brochure on how to do it. Until she read what the steps were, she assumed it was actually a difficult process. The power of words made her realize her fears were unfounded. So the next time her tire went flat, she proudly put her new skills to work. She hopes that her essay can serve the same purpose for others.

Model Essay: Replacing a Tire

by Cara Watters

What happens when you get a flat tire? Do you immediately call Roadside Assistance or the CAA (Canadian Automobile Association)? Or do you consider a flat tire the equivalent of your window washer fluid running out? If you wouldn't call the CAA to replace the fluid, why would you call someone to help you replace a tire, right? Well, that choice is yours. But if you haven't replaced a tire yet, and would like to know how to do it if you ever experience the need, read on. Maybe the sense of accomplishment in itself is worth forgoing the call for help. To replace a flat tire, you need to follow a few easy steps.

The first thing to do is ensure safety. As soon as you know your tire has "bitten the dust," drive the car, if you can, onto the shoulder of the road (where it is as level as possible) so that both you and the car are out of harm's way. Put the transmission into park and apply the parking brake. If you are driving a stick shift, place the shift into gear. Turn the engine off and turn on your hazard lights. With more and more drivers on their cell phones these days, you want to make sure you're as visible as possible. For this reason, it might also be a good idea to open your hood until you're ready to drive away.

Secondly, prepare the car for the tire change. You can start to pretend you're a doctor who's prepping for surgery. If you're not perfectly level, place a wheel chock (or large rock) either behind (if on an incline) or in front of (if on a decline) the wheel that is diagonally opposed to the one that needs changing. Get out the spare tire, a lug wrench (tire iron), and the car jack.

Thirdly, the actual changing of the tire, or surgery, so to speak, begins. Remove the hubcap, if necessary. Turning the lug wrench counterclockwise, loosen the lug nuts before jacking up the car. Loosen the lugs in star formation: this means first loosen one lug, then the one opposite, then another and so on until each lug has been loosened a few times. Carefully jack up the car. And never go under your car when only a jack is holding it up. Jack up the car a little higher than it is necessary to remove the old tire so that there is room to put the spare on. Remove the lug nuts all the way and put them in a place that is safe and where you know they will not roll away. Then remove the flat tire and put it aside. Put the spare on the threaded studs, making sure the air valve is facing out.

Now it's time to finish the job. Close up your patient by first replacing the lug nuts. Tighten them the same way you loosened them, by the star formation: tighten one a little, then tighten the one opposite a little. Go to the next lug, and so on. Every lug should be tightened a few times. Slowly lower the jack, and remove it. Give all the lug nuts a final tightening until you can't tighten any more. Replace the hubcap. Make sure everything you've put down is picked up, and you're ready to go.

Of course, once you've changed a tire the first time, it will automatically get easier the second time (if there is a second time). With these steps, the surgery promises to be quite painless. Before that first time, however, it's always a good idea to remember a few tips: for example, have a strong, hollow pipe (about two feet in length) in your car that can help you with leverage when you're using the lug wrench. Have some penetrating oil on hand that you can squirt on the lug nuts if they stick. (After you squirt some, wait a moment, and then try again.) Use gloves when removing a flat tire. If the tire is bald, after all, there may be steel strands sticking out that can cut you. And check your spare tire before any of this happens to make sure it is inflated properly. Apparently, many spare tires are flat because people don't check on this. Imagine going as far as taking your flat tire off only to find out your spare is flat too! You'd have to call for help after all.

Questions for Analysis

1. Is this process essay more directional or informational?
2. What method did the writer use for the introduction? (See pages 199–201.)
3. What method did the writer use for the conclusion? (See pages 203–204.)
4. How many main steps are there to the process as the writer described it?

5. Identify all the parts of the passage where the writer gives specific examples to make a step clear.

6. Identify some of the transitions used by the writer.

Assignment   Process Essay

Choose a topic from the list below (or, if you prefer, from the list given for the paragraph Assignment on page 281) and write a process essay of at least five paragraphs to develop that topic.

SUGGESTED TOPICS:

1. How to give a speech
2. How to do well in a job interview
3. How to plan a backpacking trip
4. How to buy a used computer
5. How to study for a test
6. How to choose the right college
7. How to redecorate a room
8. How to buy clothes on a limited budget
9. How to learn to sing
10. How to make new friends

Writing the Process Essay: How to . . .

Thousands of books and articles have been written that promise to help us accomplish some goal in life: how to start a business, how to cook, how to lose weight, how to install a shower, how to assemble a bicycle. In the essay you are about to write, you have the opportunity to describe how you once went through a process to achieve a goal of some kind.

While developing your essay, you may want to review Chapter 14: "The Four Stages of Writing for a Paragraph or an Essay," in particular the following sections:

"Brainstorming"

"Choosing the Topic and the Controlling Idea"

"Outlining"

"The Rough Draft"

"Revising and Editing the Rough Draft"

"Proofreading"

"Checklist for the Final Copy"

For help in connecting your sentences and paragraphs smoothly and clearly, you may wish to consult the list of transitional words and phrases, categorized by their function, found on the inside back cover of this book.

Working Together: Campus Woes

1. As a class, discuss and list some of the problems on your particular campus today. Then form groups of three or four. As a group, choose one of the problems from the list and discuss it for a few minutes, then draw up a list of steps that need to be taken in order to improve the situation.

2. Use the list to create sentences that will go into a letter to be sent to the appropriate college or university official suggesting the process that could be followed to solve the problem. Add an introductory paragraph that presents the problem and a conclusion that thanks the official for his or her attention. Write the finished letter.

3. Imagine you're an advice columnist who has received the letter shown here (to the right). Read the letter and answer the following questions: What would you tell this person to do? Explain the process she should follow in order to solve her problem.

> **DEAR ABBY,**
>
> I am doing my co-op placement at a cable television company as a computer operator. Lately, every morning when I sign in on my computer, I find suggestive messages from the man I relieve from the night shift.
>
> I am a single mother. I am also dating another man and have no interest in this co-worker. Should I report him to my supervisor? Someone in my office suggested that I file a sexual harassment charge.
>
> —Harassed

In a small group, consider the following questions:

a. Should the letter writer confront the man who is harassing her?

b. Should she go to her supervisor? Should she tell her co-workers about the problem?

c. Should she share her problem with the man she is dating?

d. Should she avoid the problem and quit her job?

e. How important is evidence for a person in this situation? How and when should she gather documentation for a possible formal action?

f. Does she need a lawyer? Does she need to consider the consequences of a formal action?

Chapter 24 **Comparison and/or Contrast**

What Are Comparison and Contrast?

Comparison and contrast are two related methods of explaining topics.

> **DEFINITION**
>
> **Comparison** emphasizes the similarities between two topics. **Contrast** emphasizes the differences. An essay or paragraph may deal with either similarities or differences, or with both.

We sometimes use the word *comparison* to refer to both similarities and differences between people or things, but it is more precise to use *comparison* for similarities and *contrast* for differences. For example, if you were to write about twin sisters you know, describing how close they are in appearance and personality, the similarities you noted would make up a comparison. On the other hand, if you wanted to emphasize some important differences between the two sisters, the result would be a contrast.

We use comparison and contrast in a variety of ways every day: we talk about what a boyfriend and girlfriend have in common; we put similar products side by side in the store before we decide to buy one of them; we listen to two politicians on television and think about the differences between their positions before we vote for one of them; and we read college and university catalogues and talk to our friends before we decide which school to attend.

Developing Paragraphs: Comparison and/or Contrast

Working with Comparison and/or Contrast: Choosing the Two-Part Topic

The most common problem most students face when it comes to writing a good comparison and/or contrast paragraph is finding an appropriate two-part topic. While you must be careful to choose subjects that have enough in common to make them comparable, you must avoid choosing two things that have so much in common that you cannot possibly handle all the comparable points in one paragraph or even in ten paragraphs. For example, a student trying to compare the French word *chaise* with the English word *chair* might be able to come up with only two sentences of material. With only a dictionary to consult, the student is unlikely to find enough material for several points of comparison. On the other hand, contrasting Canada with Europe would present such an endless supply of points to compare that the student would have room in a typical essay to give only general facts that most readers probably already know. When the subject is too broad, the writing is often too general. A better two-part topic might be to compare travelling by train in Europe with travelling by train in Canada.

A good comparison and/or contrast paragraph should devote an equal (or nearly equal) amount of space to each of the topic's two parts. If a writer is interested in only one of the topics, the paragraph may end up being very one-sided.

Formulating an Evaluative Topic Sentence

When writing a topic sentence for a comparison and/or contrast paragraph, keep in mind two things:

1. It should clearly identify the two items you've chosen to compare and/or contrast (the topic).
2. It should be **evaluative**—that is, it should tell the reader essentially what your feeling is with respect to the two things being compared and/or contrasted (the controlling idea). For example, it should indicate which one is better than the other (ideally using more specific language than the word *better*).

Here is an example of an evaluative topic sentence (the model paragraph that begins with this sentence can be found on page 289). The evaluative portion, in particular, is highlighted:

> Now, of course, I knew that it was going to be as difficult making an income as a freelance editor as it was as an editor on staff at the magazine, but the benefits of freelancing seemed to far outweigh the disadvantages.

There are several things one can assume about the rest of the paragraph based on this topic sentence:

1. There will be a contrast. There might be some comparison, but, for sure, the paragraph will not entirely be a comparison.
2. The two things being compared and/or contrasted are being a freelance editor and working as an editor on staff at the magazine.
3. In the end, after all the comparing and contrasting are finished, one will get the distinct impression that the writer prefers freelancing.

Now, with respect to the balance of content within the paragraph, here's an example of a one-sided contrast within a sentence:

While Canadian trains go to only a few towns, are infrequent, and are often shabby and uncomfortable, European trains are much nicer.

The following example is a more balanced contrast that gives more of an equal amount of attention to both topics:

While Canadian trains go to only a few large cities, run very infrequently, and are often shabby and uncomfortable, European trains go to virtually every small town, are always dependable, and are clean and attractive.

 Practice **Evaluating the Two-Part Topic**

Study the following topics and decide which are too broad for a paragraph and which are suitable as topics for a paragraph of comparison and/or contrast. Mark your choice in the appropriate space to the right of each topic. The first two have been done for you. Check your answers against those in the Answer Key on page 463.

Topic	Too Broad	Suitable
1. Australia and England	√	
2. Indian elephants and African elephants		√
3. Canadian wine and French wine		
4. Wooden furniture and plastic furniture		
5. Wood and plastic		
6. Photography and oil painting		

Two Methods: Point-by-Point and Block

The first method for ordering material in a paragraph or an essay of comparison and/or contrast is known as the **point-by-point method.**

DEFINITION

The **point-by-point method** is one way to order the material in a comparison and/or contrast paragraph or essay. In this method, you compare and/or contrast a particular point as it relates to one topic with the same point as it relates to the other topic before going onto the next point.

What follows is a paragraph in which the writer uses the point-by-point method to compare the difficulties of being a freelance editor with those of working as an editor on staff at a magazine.

Model Paragraph: The Freedom of Freelancing (I)

Now, of course, I knew that it was going to be as difficult making an income as a freelance editor as it was as an editor on staff at the magazine, if not more so, but the benefits of freelancing seemed to far outweigh the disadvantages. I would be at home hustling editing contracts via telephone, while everyone else spent their mornings at the office gabbing over endless cups of coffee. I sometimes resented having to work so hard to make a living, while my old colleagues on staff sat in meetings, went to conferences, and attended company luncheons. But I never envied them on their way to work on cold, dark winter mornings. And I wondered how many of them would have gladly switched places with me as I worked outside on my patio in the summer while they looked longingly out their office windows.

Notice how, after the opening topic sentence, the writer uses half of each sentence to describe a freelance editor's experience and the other half of the same sentence to describe the experience of an editor who works for a magazine. This technique is effective in such a paragraph, and it is most often used in longer pieces of writing that include many points of comparison. This method helps the reader keep the comparison and/or contrast carefully in mind at each point.

Looking at this paragraph in outline form will help you see the shape of its development.

Point-by-Point Method

Topic sentence: Now, of course, I knew that it was going to be as difficult making an income as a freelance editor as it was as an editor on staff at the magazine, if not more so, but the benefits of freelancing seemed to far outweigh the disadvantages.

Point one

>*First topic:* I would be at home hustling editing contracts via telephone . . .

>*Second topic:* . . . while everyone else spent their mornings at the office gabbing over endless cups of coffee.

Point two

>*First topic:* I sometimes resented having to work so hard to earn a living . . .

>*Second topic:* . . . while my old colleagues on staff sat in meetings, went to conferences, and attended company luncheons.

Point three

>*First topic:* But I never envied them on their way to work on cold, dark winter mornings.

>*Second topic:* And I wondered how many of them would have gladly switched places with me as I worked outside on my patio, while they looked longingly out their office windows.

What follows is another version of the same model paragraph, written using the **block method.**

Model Paragraph: The Freedom of Freelancing (II)

Now, of course, I knew that it was going to be as difficult making an income as a freelance editor as it was as an editor on staff at the magazine, if not more so, but the benefits of freelancing seemed to far outweigh the disadvantages. I spent my mornings hustling editing contracts on the telephone, and I sometimes resented having to work so hard to earn a living. On the other hand, I didn't envy my old colleagues on their way to work on cold, dark winter mornings. They could spend as much time as they wanted to gabbing over endless cups of coffee and going to meetings, conferences, and company luncheons; but I wonder how many of them would have gladly switched places with me as I worked outside on my patio in the summer.

In this version, the first half of the paragraph presents almost all of the details about being a freelance editor, while the second half presents all of the information about being an editor on staff. This method is often used in shorter pieces of writing, where it is possible for the reader to keep in mind a block of information on one topic while reading about the other.

Here is this version of the paragraph in outline form.

Block Method

Topic sentence: Now, of course, I knew that it was going to be as difficult making an income as a freelance editor as it was as an editor on staff at the magazine, if not more so, but the benefits of freelancing seemed to far outweigh the disadvantages.

First topic (points one, two, and three): I spent my mornings hustling editing contracts on the telephone, and I sometimes resented having to work so hard to earn a living. On the other hand, I didn't envy my old colleagues on their way to work on cold, dark, winter mornings.

Second topic (points one, two, and three): They could spend as much time as they wanted to gabbing over endless cups of coffee and going to meetings, conferences, and company luncheons; but I wonder how many of them would have gladly switched places with me as I worked outside on my patio in the summer.

You will want to choose one of these methods before you write a comparison and/or contrast assignment. The block method is most often used for writing shorter pieces such as paragraphs; however, you will have the opportunity to practise both the block method and the point-by-point method.

Practice Recognizing the Two Methods

Each of the following passages is an example of comparison and/or contrast. Read each paragraph carefully and decide whether the writer has used the point-by-point method or the block method. Indicate your choice in the spaces provided after each example. Also indicate whether the piece emphasizes similarities or differences. Check your answers against those in the Answer Key on page 463.

1. Female infants speak sooner, have larger vocabularies, and rarely demonstrate speech defects. (Stuttering, for instance, occurs almost exclusively in boys.) Girls exceed boys in language abilities, and this early linguistic bias often prevails throughout life. Girls read sooner, learn foreign languages more easily, and, as a result, are more likely to enter occupations involving language mastery. Boys, in contrast, show an early visual superiority. They are also clumsier, performing poorly at tasks such as arranging a row of beads, but excel at activities calling for total body coordination. Their attentional mechanisms are also different. A boy will react to an inanimate object as quickly as he will to a person. A male baby will often ignore the mother and babble at a blinking light, fixate on a geometric figure, and, at a later point, manipulate it and attempt to take it apart.

_____ Point-by-Point   _____ Block

_____ Similarities   _____ Differences

2. It is hard to decide who are the better inventors, Canadians or Martians. Canadians have invented wonderful devices that have made a significant contribution to their civilization, but then so have the Martians. Canadians invented the chainsaw, the paint roller, the power mower, and the zipper. But Martians are no slouches, having come up with the intergalactic spaceship, the long-range power blaster, and the moon-dust mobile home. Of course, not all Canadian inventions have been stellar successes; consider, for example, the cast-iron airship, the reverse cooking stove, and the patent medicine carrot cure-all. But neither have Martians hit a winner every time: who can forget the ill-fated interplanetary bicycle, the invisible mirror, or the boomerang rocket? In the ingenuity department, you'd have to say it's a tie.

_____ Point-by-Point   _____ Block

_____ Similarities   _____ Differences

Exercise Using the Point-by-Point and Block Methods

Choose one of the paragraphs from the above Practice and rewrite it using the opposite method for comparison and/or contrast. For instance, if a paragraph uses the point-by-point method, rewrite it using the block method.

Tips on Transitions: *Like* vs. *As*

Be careful to use transition words correctly when comparing and/or contrasting. In particular, watch out for *like* and *as*, which have different functions. Therefore, they cannot be used in place of each other.

TIP

Like is a preposition and is used within a prepositional phrase with a noun.

My sister is just *like* me.

TIP

As is a subordinate conjunction and is used in a clause below with a subject and a verb.

My sister sews every evening, *as* does her oldest daughter.

For additional common transitions, see the chart on the inside back cover of this book.

Writing the Comparison and/or Contrast Paragraph Step by Step

To learn a skill with some degree of ease, it is best to follow a step-by-step approach so that various skills can be worked on one at a time. This approach will ensure that you are not missing a crucial point or misunderstanding a part of the whole. There are other ways to go about writing an effective paragraph, but here is one logical method you can use to achieve results.

Steps for Writing the Comparison and/or Contrast Paragraph

1. Study the given topic, and then plan your topic sentence, especially the dominant impression.
2. List all your ideas for points that could be compared and/or contrasted.
3. Choose the three or four most important points from your list, and put them in order.
4. Decide whether you want to use the point-by-point method or the block method of organizing your paragraph.
5. Write at least one complete sentence for each of the points you have chosen from your list.
6. Write a concluding statement that summarizes the main points, makes a judgment, or emphasizes what you believe is the most important point.
7. Finally, copy your sentences into standard paragraph form.

Exercise   Writing the Comparison and/or Contrast Paragraph Step by Step

Starting with the suggested topic below, follow the seven steps outlined in the box above to work through the writing process for a comparison and/or contrast paragraph. (These steps are similar to those used for the narrative paragraph in Chapter 21; refer to pages 258–259 for a step-by-step example and a completed sample paragraph.)

> **Topic:** Compare and/or contrast going to work with going to college immediately after high school.

Assignment   Comparison and/or Contrast Paragraph

> Write a paragraph in which you compare and/or contrast two places you know, either from personal experience or from your reading.

SUGGESTED TOPICS:

(For more suggested topics, see the list given for the essay "Assignment" on page 295.)

1. Two neighbourhoods
2. Two towns or cities
3. Two vacation spots
4. Two provinces
5. Two countries
6. Two streets
7. Two colleges or universities

The Comparison and/or Contrast Essay

In a comparison and/or contrast essay, the thesis statement (like the topic sentence in a paragraph) identifies what is being compared and/or contrasted (the topic) and what the author's overall feeling toward the comparison and/or contrast is (the controlling idea). For example, here is a possible thesis statement for an essay on the contrast between two cars:

> The Honda Civic beats the Toyota Corolla in many respects.

If you're using the block method, the second paragraph of the essay might be used for everything you want to say about the Honda, and the third paragraph for everything you want to say about the Toyota (contrasting it with what you've said in the previous paragraph about the Honda). The fourth paragraph could then be a conclusion that contained a restatement of your thesis but in different words (for more on concluding paragraphs, see Chapter 16: "The Essay"). A four-paragraph essay would therefore be appropriate if you are using the block method for your comparison and/or contrast essay.

If, on the other hand, you're using the point-by-point method, the second paragraph of the essay would compare and/or contrast both the Honda and the Toyota based on the first point you have chosen. The third paragraph of the essay would deal with both cars in terms of your second point, and so on. Ideally, you will discuss your findings on the basis of three points, which would produce a standard five-paragraph essay: an introduction, three support paragraphs (one for each of your three points), and a conclusion.

For a review of the essay form and its standard format (which applies to all the writing strategies in this unit), see Chapter 16: "The Essay." For a review of the writing process that can be applied to both the paragraph and the essay, see Chapter 14: "The Four Stages of Writing for a Paragraph or Essay."

The sample essay below explores the differences between living in a small town and living in a big city. Although the opinion of its author, Zack Goodman, is pretty clear from the outset, someone else could just as easily argue for the opposite point of view. What's important in an essay is that the thesis is clear and that there is evidence supporting it. Determine if Zack achieves these goals.

Model Essay: City Life Beats the Small Town Blues

by Zack Goodman

Growing up in a small town has its perks. You might have fewer friends than you have in the big city, but you tend to keep them closer. The East Coast small town author Hugh MacLennan once said that writers who grow up in a small towns have a greater knowledge of human intimacy even if their writing ideas stemming from this knowledge dry up before they turn 40. Well, not everybody agrees with either of those points. In fact, city life can offer just as much knowledge of human intimacy if not more than small town life can. Life is better in the big city, and it all comes down to one general reason: more choice.

One of the areas in which having choice can be extremely valuable is that of friends. Like leaving home to seek greater knowledge of yourself, picking your own friends from a greater number of people can aid in your journey to seek self-knowledge. After all, if you go out with the same group of small-town friends all the time, not because you necessarily like them all that much, but because they're the only ones available, this can prove quite limiting when it comes to your growth as an individual. The big city, on the other hand, offers an endless number of opportunities to meet people of like interests. You're much more likely to cultivate relationships with people who help you to grow.

If you're the type of person who enjoys learning about other cultures and meeting people of many different ethnicities, you're much more likely to do both of these things in a big city. People from all over the world prefer the big city to which to emigrate because they might already have relatives there, or at least some sort of community similar to the one they've left in their country of origin. They might not have to learn English right away to get along because there are enough people with whom they can speak in their native tongue, and in general, the big city can afford more resources to make them more comfortable. In a small town, you might have to get used to a group of people of one origin, maybe even a community in which there is only one religion. If this is what you want, there's no problem. But if you consider yourself a citizen of the world, a one-ethnicity town might be pretty boring after a while.

And finally, if you're a person who enjoys the arts, the small town probably won't be able to hold a candle to the arts community of a big city. A small town might have one cinema that shows maybe three different movies at any one time. A big city can have more than 100 theatres showing at least a hundred different movies, and not all mainstream film, but independent film, B-movies, foreign film (do Canadian movies qualify as foreign films in Canada?) and second-run movies for those who missed them the first time around. But movies are only one form of entertainment in the big city on any given night. There's the Broadway musical, the independent stage theatre, ballet, modern dance, cabaret, poetry reading, cafés and nightclubs with live music including jazz, house, Latin, retro, hip-hop (you ask for it; the big city's got it), street festivals in the summer, outdoor skating and indoor tennis in the winter, and so on and so on. A small town may have some of this some of the time, but a big city is more likely to have most of it most of the time.

A small town has its advantages; that's true. The cost of living is lower. The streets are probably safer at night. And it might even be easier to meet someone special. But if you're an arts lover who enjoys the company of people from all over the world, and you're interested in cultivating friends who help you to grow spiritually and not just to get drunk on a Saturday night, city life is tough to beat.

Questions for Analysis

1. An essay of comparison points out the similarities between two subjects, while an essay of contrast examines the differences. With this in mind, is the essay you have just read an essay of comparison, of contrast, or of both? What is your evidence for your answer?

2. Does the writer use the point-by-point method or the block method in writing this essay?

3. Does the writer provide an equal number of details that relate to the small town and the big city?

4. Specifically, how does the writer demonstrate what he thinks is the superior nature of the big city?

Assignment Comparison and/or Contrast Essay

Choose a topic from the list below (or, if you prefer, from the list given for the paragraph "Assignment" on page 293) and write a comparison and/or contrast essay of at least five paragraphs to develop that topic.

SUGGESTED TOPICS:

Compare and/or contrast:

1. High school classes with college classes
2. Life in a city with life in a rural area
3. Two movies (the acting, the cinematography, the quality of the story)
4. A friend from your childhood with a present friend
5. Two similar items you have owned (e.g., cars, bicycles, radios)
6. Seeing a play with seeing a movie
7. Two vacation spots
8. Two apartments or houses where you have lived
9. Researching in a library with researching on the Internet
10. Cooking dinner at home with eating out

While developing your essay, you may want to review Chapter 14: "The Four Stages of Writing for a Paragraph or an Essay," in particular the following sections:

"Brainstorming"

"Choosing the Topic and the Controlling Idea"

"Outlining"

"The Rough Draft"

"Revising and Editing the Rough Draft"

"Proofreading"

"Checklist for the Final Copy"

For help in connecting your sentences and paragraphs smoothly and clearly, you may wish to consult the list of transitional words and phrases, categorized by their function, found on the inside back cover of this book.

 Working Together: Reaching Consensus

In a group of three to five students, decide among yourselves which two movies, fashion items, concerts, or advertisements you'd like to compare and/or contrast. Make sure that everyone in your group has seen both items. Then try to reach a consensus about your overall conclusion before you begin to compare and/or contrast the items on the basis of at least three points. Discuss your results with the rest of the class. Was it easy to reach consensus on everything? What did you learn by the process? Did most groups end up comparing, contrasting, or both?

Chapter 25 **Definition**

What Is Definition?

Definition is one of the most useful forms of writing. The ability to provide accurate definitions is crucial to ensuring your audience understands your words and ideas. Most of the essays you will write in college or university will require you to define terms.

Writing a definition means explaining what a word, phrase, or concept means. You will often need to define terms in your writing when they are likely to be unfamiliar to your reader. For example, the writer of a health-sciences report for the general public who uses the word *contusion* may want to explain that it is another word for a bruise. In fact, defining a term or concept is often an effective way to begin an essay. Thus, the writer of an essay on discrimination may first want to provide a definition of the term before describing examples of discrimination.

More Personal Meaning

There may also be situations where you want to give a more personal meaning to a common term. For instance, you may think that you have a clear idea of what the word *success* means. But if you talk with your classmates about their definitions of success, you will probably find that everyone has a different mental picture of what success looks like. For some, a successful person might be one who has a great deal of money. For others, success might mean achieving a personal goal, such as competing in the Olympics. Still others might think of success as having a happy family life. Personal definitions are useful in writing because they cast new light on ordinary terms and make us question our preconceptions about our day-to-day lives.

DEFINITION

A **definition** is an explanation of the meaning or significance of a term or concept. The starting point for a good definition is to group the term into a larger category or class. (See Chapter 26: "Classification.")

For example, a trout is a kind of fish, a doll is a kind of toy, and a shirt is an article of clothing. Here is a dictionary entry for the word *myth* (from the *Webster's New World Dictionary*, Second College Edition):

myth (mith) **n.** [LL. *mythos* < Gr. *mythos*, a word, speech, story, legend] **1.** a traditional story of unknown authorship, ostensibly with a historical basis, but serving usually to explain some phenomenon of nature, the origin of man, or the customs, institutions, religious rites, etc. of a people: myths usually involve the exploits of gods and heroes: cf. LEGEND **2.** such stories collectively; mythology **3.** any fictitious story, or unscientific account, theory, belief, etc. **4.** any imaginary person or thing spoken of as though existing.

To what larger category does the word *myth* belong? According to the first meaning above, it is a kind of story, or narrative.

DEFINITION

Once a word has been put into a larger class, its definition gives the **identifying characteristics** that make the word different from other members in the class.

Stating what class or category a word belongs to is typically the first step in defining it, but more is usually required. What makes a *trout* different from a *bass*, a *doll* different from a *puppet*, a *shirt* different from a *sweater*, a *myth* different from a *parable*? Once again, the dictionary can offer some assistance. From the first dictionary definition of *myth* above, we learn that a myth is a specific kind of story that offers an explanation of the behaviour of individual human beings or the religious practices of a people, often involving the adventures of gods and heroes.

When you write a paragraph or an essay that uses definition, the dictionary entry is only the beginning. It is not the function of a dictionary to go into great depth. It can provide only the basic meanings and synonyms. In order for your reader to understand a difficult term or idea, you will need to expand these basics into what is called **extended definition.**

DEFINITION

An **extended definition** seeks to analyze a concept in order to give the reader a more complete understanding.

For instance, you might include an historical perspective of a word or term. When or how did the concept begin? How did the term change or evolve over the years? How have different cultures understood the term? You will become involved in the connotations of the word (not just what it means, but what it implies). Extended definition uses more than one method to arrive at an understanding of a term.

Developing Paragraphs: Definition

Religion scholar Karen Armstrong is the author of *A Short History of Myth*. In the following passage from her book, the author's starting point resembles the first two meanings from the dictionary definition of "myth," but she goes on to shed light on the other two dictionary meanings as well. First, here is a reminder of the dictionary definition of the word:

> **myth** (mith) **n.** [LL. *mythos* < Gr. *mythos*, a word, speech, story, legend] **1.** a traditional story of unknown authorship, ostensibly with a historical basis, but serving usually to explain some phenomenon of nature, the origin of man, or the customs, institutions, religious rites, etc. of a people: myths usually involve the exploits of gods and heroes: cf. LEGEND **2.** such stories collectively; mythology **3.** any fictitious story, or unscientific account, theory, belief, etc. **4.** any imaginary person or thing spoken of as though existing.

Model Paragraph: The Meaning of Myth

By Karen Armstrong

Myths are universal and timeless stories that reflect and shape our lives—they mirror our desires, our fears, our longings, and provide narratives that attempt to help us make sense of the world. . . . Today the word "myth" is often used to describe something that is simply not true. . . . When we hear of gods walking the earth, of dead men striding out of tombs, or of seas miraculously parting to let a favoured people escape from their enemies, we dismiss these stories as incredible and demonstrably untrue. . . . A myth is essentially a guide; it tells us what we must do in order to live more richly. If we do not apply it to our own situation and make the myth a reality in our own lives, it will remain as incomprehensible and remote as the rules of a board game, which often seem confusing and boring until we start to play.

The author, like the dictionary, puts the term into a larger class: myths are stories. She also identifies the characteristics of these stories that are different from other stories: They are universal and timeless. They reflect and shape our lives. She also goes on to explain the relationship between one dictionary meaning and another that seems at first to be very different: a story that is about gods who walk the earth seems incredible and untrue; therefore, a myth comes to be known as a falsehood. She explains why the term *myth* seems to have lost its real meaning as a result of science. And she argues that it is important for humanity to reclaim the real meaning of the term "myth."

Exercise 1 Working with Definition: Class

Define each of the following terms by placing it in a larger class. Keep in mind that when you define something by class, you are placing it in a larger category so that the reader can see where it belongs. Use the dictionary if you need help. The first example has been done for you.

Chemistry is <u>one of the branches of science</u> that deals with a close study of the natural world.

1. A *motorcycle* is _____

2. *Poetry* is _____

3. *Democracy* is _____

4. *Sugar* is _____

5. A *viola* is _____

 Exercise 2 Working with Definition: Distinguishing Characteristics

Using the same terms as in Exercise 1, give one or two identifying characteristics that differentiate each term from other terms in the same class. An example has been done for you.

Chemistry is concerned with the structure, properties, and reactions of matter.

1. A motorcycle _____

_____

_____

2. Poetry _____

_____

_____

3. Democracy _____

_____

_____

4. Sugar _____

_____

_____

5. A viola _____

_____

_____

Writing the Definition Paragraph Step by Step

To learn a skill with some degree of ease, it is best to follow a step-by-step approach so that the various aspects of the skill can be worked on one step at a time. This approach will ensure that you are not missing a crucial point or misunderstanding a part of the whole. There are other ways to go about writing an effective paragraph, but the following is one logical method you can use to achieve results.

Steps for Writing the Definition Paragraph
1. Write a topic sentence that identifies what you are going to define.
2. List all the possible concepts for your extended definition.
3. Review the list and eliminate inappropriate concepts.
4. Put your final list in order.
5. Write at least one complete sentence for each of the concepts on your final list.
6. Write a concluding statement that summarizes the most important parts of your definition.
7. Finally, copy your sentences into standard paragraph form.

Exercise **Writing the Definition Paragraph Step by Step**

Starting with the suggested topic below, follow the seven steps outlined in the box above to work through the writing process for a definition paragraph. (These steps are similar to those used for the narrative paragraph in Chapter 21; refer to pages 258–259 for a step-by-step example and a completed sample paragraph.)

Topic: Intelligence

To help you get started on a topic sentence below, read the following:

We often equate intelligence with being "smart" or with having above-average ability in some area. Yet we likely all know some rather intelligent people who don't act very smart, or who are very absent-minded. We could also have a pet that is "intelligent." What is intelligence as you understand it?

Assignment **Paragraph of Definition**

Some of us are dreamers and some of us are realists; we all have distinguishing characteristics within the larger class of human being. Using one of the following suggested topics, write a paragraph of definition of who or what you are.

SUGGESTED TOPICS:

(For other suggested topics, see the list given for the essay "Assignment" on page 304.)

1. Happy-go-lucky
2. Creative
3. A friend to all
4. A comedian
5. Reserved

Developing an Essay of Definition

The thesis in this type of essay, of course, identifies what is being defined. It also should provide a good, but general, definition. Then each support paragraph explains a different component or aspect of what has been defined in the first paragraph.

For an example, see the essay on the next page by Jenny Yuen on sexual addiction, entitled "Love Hurts." The first support paragraph (the second paragraph of the essay) deals with the question of how common the addiction is. The third support paragraph (fourth essay paragraph) deals with a particular example. The fifth support paragraph (sixth essay paragraph) deals with the notion that attending twelve-step program meetings may not be enough to control this addiction. And so on.

No one support paragraph should deal with more than one component or aspect of whatever is being defined. But once the support paragraph has identified the component to be discussed in its first sentence (the topic sentence of that paragraph), the author, of course, can go ahead and add various supporting details (including examples) to support the topic sentence.

For a review of the essay form and its standard format (which applies to all the writing strategies in this unit), see Chapter 16: "The Essay." For a review of the writing process that can be applied to both the paragraph and the essay, see Chapter 14: "The Four Stages of Writing for a Paragraph or an Essay."

When Jenny wrote the following piece, she was a student in a journalism program. The piece was originally written for publication in a newspaper, which is why much of the writing seems journalistic in nature. The paragraphs are longer than typical newspaper paragraphs, however, because the story was adapted to suit a more academic style of essay for the purpose of this chapter.

Model Essay: Love Hurts*

by Jenny Yuen

For love and sex addicts, Valentine's Day may not be simply roses and candy, but rather a traumatic reminder that love hurts. February 14 may bring back painful memories of past breakups, or trigger the need to go out and find a "special someone" who may not turn out to be all that special. Sexual and love addiction is the continuing pattern of unwanted compulsive romantic behaviour that has a negative impact on the addict's personal, social and/or economic standing.

Sex and love addiction are more common than you might imagine, says Rob Hawkings, a psychotherapist at Bellwood Health Services in North York (part of Toronto), Ontario. These addictions are also very complex disorders in which the victims may not realize that their behaviour falls into the "addict" category. How can you tell whether you have "normal" relationship problems or that you're in love with love and sex? (See questionnaire at the end.) The answer is another question: Are you in control? But having self-control is much easier said than done. "We look for a pattern of out-of-control behaviour, whether that's with pornographic material or flirting or continually getting into romantic involvements in a serial kind of way or giving into simultaneous multiple [relationships],"

*Jenny Yuen, "Love Hurts." Reprinted by permission of Jenny Yuen.

says 51-year-old Hawkings, a recovering alcoholic and sex addict, himself, who has been working in the field for a decade.

Although the demographic of addicts varies, most of the people who attend the 12-step meetings are males in their late 20s to late 50s. Still, there are no definite statistics of how much of the Canadian population is affected by sexual and love addiction, although Hawkings says more patients would be checking into Bellwood for therapy if they realized it is a problem.

Judy, 37, tormented herself with obsessive sexual fantasies for four years. She had constant fantasies about extra-marital relationships, and suffered from sexual anorexia, trying to avoid her problems so she wouldn't have to deal with them. "I was in a marriage, and I started thinking about men outside my marriage so much that it was affecting my work life. I hate to use the word obsession, . . . but I found myself powerless over my thoughts."

While Bellwood is new at the sex addiction game, SLAA (or Sex and Love Addicts Anonymous), also known as The Augustine Fellowship, has been working worldwide with addicts for more than 20 years. SLAA champions the Alcoholics Anonymous 12-step program as an efficient treatment program for sufferers of sex and love addiction. Currently, SLAA has more than 1200 meeting locations throughout the world, open to all who believe they may have a problem. People who believe they may suffer from love and sexual addiction may come in anonymously and tell their stories and listen to others.

Although Bellwood avidly encourages its sex addiction patients to attend these meetings, Hawkings says 12-step programs are not enough. Bellwood's program includes life-skills coaching to help addicts deal with communication and feelings. In some special cases, Bellwood prescribes medication for sex addicts. "There are situations where there are some people who need a carefully prescribed anti-depressant," says Hawkings, who is careful not to recommend addictive medication such as Valium. "We sometimes get people coming in who have real psychiatric problems as well as addictions going on."

The question still remains: Can the love and sex addict be cured? "The classic stereotype is AA, where people are recovering for the rest of their lives, but for the rest of their lives need not forget they're alcoholics," Hawkings says. By and large, that is the case with sexual addiction. People are always going to be susceptible to using the sexual-addictive fix that they might have used in the past when they were under stress. "One thing we work very hard on in recovery is managing the stress in their lives."

Judy was fortunate enough to alter her sexual behaviours into healthier ones because of the SLAA program. "I felt freedom right away. I was really fortunate," Judy says. "You don't graduate from [a 12-step program]. They call it being 'restored to sanity,' but a better way to put it is we now have a choice over our decisions."

***

The following is a questionnaire to help determine if you are a sex and/or love addict. If you answer yes to most of these questions, you may be.

- Do you still see someone, even though you know the relationship has a destructive effect on you?
- Do you feel like you *have* to have sex?
- Do you have sex regardless of the consequences?
- Do you feel you lack dignity and wholeness?
- Is your life unmanageable because of your sexual or romantic behaviour?

Contact Information:

- SLAA Coxwell (Toronto) branch (416) 486-8201 or Toll-free 1-800-977-4325
- Bellwood Health Clinic (Toronto): Rob Hawkings, sex psychotherapist, (416) 495-0926, ext. 107 or toll-free 1-800-387-6198
- Dr. Patrick Carnes' Website: www.sexhelp.com
- Pia Mellody's Website: www.piamellody.com

Questions for Analysis

1. What is the central thing being defined in this essay?
2. In what ways is sexual addiction like alcoholism? In what ways is it different?
3. What surprises you the most in this piece by Jenny Yuen?
4. What do you think is the main purpose of this essay? Why?
5. Why do you think more men go to meetings for sex and love addiction than do women?
6. Do you think sex and/or love addiction can be as destructive as alcohol or substance abuse? Why or why not?

Assignment Essay of Definition

Choose one of the topics below, or come up with one of your own. Write an essay of definition to develop that topic. The essay should be at least five paragraphs long.

SUGGESTED TOPICS:

1. Definition of your favourite martial art
2. Definition of a particular disease or medical condition
3. Definition of love
4. Definition of a term in your particular field of study
5. Definition of "impressionism" or other kind of painting theory

While developing your essay, you may want to review Chapter 14: "The Four Stages of Writing for a Paragraph or an Essay," in particular the following sections:

"Brainstorming"

"Choosing the Topic and the Controlling Idea"

"Outlining"

"The Rough Draft"

"Revising and Editing the Rough Draft"

"Proofreading"

"Checklist for the Final Copy"

For help in connecting your sentences and paragraphs smoothly and clearly, you may wish to consult the list of transitional words and phrases, categorized by their function, found on the inside back cover of this book.

 Working Together: What Does the Cover Mean to You?

One could argue that to interpret a picture is to define it. Look at the cover of this book and come to a one-sentence conclusion as to what you think it means to you. Then use this one-sentence conclusion as the topic sentence or thesis statement for a paragraph or essay of definition. Look at the various components of the picture and pick the three that make the biggest impression on you. Write one or more sentences about each of these three parts as points that support your one-sentence interpretation.

Then exchange papers with someone else. Determine whether or not the three supporting points actually back up the topic sentence or thesis statement. Discuss your observations with a small group or as a class. Are there several interpretations of the book cover? Are there certain universal points that everybody has made? Do any or all of the interpretations relate to the study of writing?

Chapter 26 **Classification**

What Is Classification?

> **DEFINITION**
>
> **Classification** is the placing of items into separate categories for the purpose of helping us think about these items more clearly. This approach can be extremely useful and even necessary when large numbers of items are being considered.

In order to classify things properly, you must first establish a **basis for classification.** For example, if you are writing about computers, you could decide to classify them according to where they are made. Then put the items into **distinct categories,** making sure that each item belongs in only one category. For example, your categories might be Canadian-made computers, U.S.-made computers, and computers made overseas. However, if you made your categories imported computers, Canadian-made computers, and used computers, this would not be an effective use of classification; the category of used computers does not conform to the basis for classification you established (where the computers are made), and an imported computer or a Canadian-made computer could also be a used computer, so the categories are not distinct.

A classification should also be **complete.** For example, if you were to classify computers into the two categories of new and used, your classification would be complete because any item must be either new or used. But if you tried to classify computers into desktop computers and netbook computers, there would be many computers that would not fit either category (what about laptops that are larger than netbooks? tablet computers? large mainframes?).

Developing Paragraphs: Classification

In the following paragraph, the writer describes different classes of neighbours:

Model Paragraph: Nice and Neighbourly?

To me, there are only two kinds of neighbours: those who are friendly and those who are not. The friendly neighbours always greet me with a smile regardless of the situation. They are the ones whose names I usually know, and they are always either asking me to come over, or they're interested in talking about what's going on in their lives or asking me about mine. The unfriendly neighbours, on the other hand, could be mistaken for complete strangers no matter how long they've lived in the neighbourhood. I don't know their names. They pass me on the street as if they've never seen me before. It's those neighbours who make me think that if I dared to try and strike up a conversation with them, they'd scowl, or, in some way, they'd make me feel sorry for ever trying. I just hope that if one day my house is on fire, my friendly neighbours are at home so that I can run up to *them* for help.

In this paragraph, the writer presents two distinct types of neighbours: friendly ones and unfriendly ones. These are the only types that have any significance for the writer. The writer's classification is complete because it covers the entire range of neighbours—there are, in the writer's opinion, no kinds other than these two. Since most of us have neighbours, we might be able to identify with the writer to some extent even if we don't think the writer's classification system is complete enough.

Exercise 1 Working with Classification: Deciding on a Basis for a Classification

For each of the following topics, pick three different ways that topic could be classified. You may find the following example helpful.

Topic: Ways to choose a vacation spot

Basis for classification: by price, by its special attraction, by the accommodations

1. **Topic:** Cellular phones

   Basis for classification: _____

   _____

2. **Topic:** Relatives

   Basis for classification: _____

   _____

3. **Topic:** Snack foods

   Basis for classification: _____

   _____

4. **Topic:** News sources

   Basis for classification: _____

   _____

5. **Topic:** Medicines

Basis for classification: _____

_____

Making Distinct Categories

Once you have established your basis for classification, you're ready to come up with distinct categories. These are ways in which you have chosen to divide each basis for classification. In other words, they are examples of your basis for classification.

Topic	Basis for Classification	Distinct Categories
Ways to choose a vacation spot	price	first class
		medium price
		economy
	special attraction	the beach
		the mountains
		the desert
	accommodation	hotel
		motel
		cabin

Exercise 2   Working with Classification: Making Distinct Categories

First, pick a basis for classifying each of the following topics. Then use that basis to create distinct categories. You can list as many categories as you think the basis for classification requires—you don't have to stick with three.

Remember to choose your categories in a way that each item you classify will belong to only one category. For example, if you were to classify cars, you would not want to make sports cars and international cars two of your categories because several kinds of sports cars are also international cars. You may find the following example helpful.

Topic: Wine
Basis for classification: colour
Distinct categories: red, white, rosé
or
Basis for classification: national origin
Distinct categories: French, Australian, Italian, Canadian, Chilean, etc.

1. Clothing stores

Basis for classification: _____

Distinct categories: _____

_____

2. Television commercials

 Basis for classification: _____

 Distinct categories: _____

 _____

3. Olympic sports

 Basis for classification: _____

 Distinct categories: _____

 _____

4. Mail

 Basis for classification: _____

 Distinct categories: _____

 _____

5. Art forms

 Basis for classification: _____

 Distinct categories: _____

 _____

Writing the Classification Paragraph Step by Step

To learn a skill with some degree of ease, it is best to follow a step-by-step approach so that various aspects of the skill can be worked on one at a time. This approach will ensure that you are not missing a crucial point or misunderstanding a part of the whole. There are other ways to go about writing an effective paragraph, but here is one logical method you can use to achieve results.

Steps for Writing the Classification Paragraph
1. Write a topic sentence, stating the basis of the classification.
2. List all the possible distinct categories in your classification.
3. Review your list and eliminate any inappropriate distinct categories.
4. Put your final list in order.
5. Write at least one complete sentence for each of the distinct categories you have chosen from your list.
6. Write a concluding sentence that emphasizes the basis of the classification.
7. Finally, copy your sentences into standard paragraph form.

Exercise   Writing the Classification Paragraph Step by Step

Starting with the suggested topic below, follow the seven steps outlined in the box above to work through the writing process for a classification paragraph. (These steps are similar to those used for the narrative paragraph in Chapter 21; refer to pages 258–259 for a step-by-step example and a completed sample paragraph.)

Topic: Games

We play games as children. Some of these we continue to play as adults, and we play different types of games. We are even accused of "playing games"—mind games—from time to time. There are board games, mind games, and electronic games. How many other categories of games can you think of?

 Assignment   Classification Paragraph

Pick a topic from the list below, and write a paragraph in which you classify relationships.

SUGGESTED TOPICS:

(For more suggested topics, see the list given for the essay "Assignment" on page 313.)

1. Friends
2. Classmates or colleagues at work
3. Girlfriends/boyfriends
4. Pets
5. Teachers
6. Bosses
7. Casual acquaintances

Developing an Essay of Classification

The thesis statement of a classification essay, like the topic sentence of the classification paragraph, identifies what is being classified. In the essay, it's important to devote each support paragraph to a distinct category of the items you are discussing. For example, in the model essay below, Margo Fine classifies people into four groups according to what psychiatrist M. Scott Peck considers an evolution of spirituality. The first support paragraph (the second paragraph of the essay) deals only with the least spiritually evolved group (the first group); each subsequent support paragraph discusses one of the other groups. Because four groups are being classified, Margo found it appropriate to write a six-paragraph essay as opposed to the standard five that many professors insist upon, or at least strongly recommend, especially when students are required to complete the essay in a two-hour period or less.

> For a review of the essay form and its standard format (which applies to all the writing strategies in this unit), see Chapter 16: "The Essay." For a review of the writing process that can be applied to both the paragraph and the essay, see Chapter 14: "The Four Stages of Writing for a Paragraph or an Essay."

Model Essay: The Evolution of Spirituality

by Margo Fine

Psychiatrist and prolific author M. Scott Peck is probably most famous for his book *The Road Less Traveled*, which has appeared on the *New York Times* Best-Seller's List for more than 25 years. Peck entitled a sequel to this book *Further Along the Road Less Traveled*—a title that is appropriate if unoriginal. It is in this book, however, that Peck discusses a model of spiritual evolution into which, he says, every single person can be fit according to a particular classification system. Peck classifies people into four groups according to the extent to which they have spiritually evolved: the first group being the least evolved and the fourth being the most.

The first group is made up of people who are governed by their emotions. These are the quintessential charmers of the model. How nice they are, and therefore, how well they treat others, depends on whether they want something at that particular time. As soon as they get what they want, they're gone, or they're not so nice anymore: narcissism and greed are most apparent in this group. Their responses to people are generally unpredictable as these responses depend solely on these people's emotions. There is little or no self-examination or self-evaluation here.

The second group up from the bottom can quite aptly be called the "organizational clingers." These people are aware of the fact that left to their own devices, they would be completely governed by their own emotions like those in the first group. People in the second group inherently know this would prove disastrous. To avoid such a consequence, they opt to cling to an organization of some sort, one that promises to take care of them, one that offers a sense of protection and belonging, but also discipline by means of a strict code of conduct. This organization prevents them from depending on their emotions for answers to their important questions. Organized religion is often the structure to which people in this group cling. In fact, Peck would put most religious fundamentalists (of any religion) in this category.

The third group up from the bottom (and therefore, the second from the top) is the group that seems to react quite vehemently to the second group (especially to religious fundamentalists). These are the secularists. These people are often very well educated in the sciences or the arts, and they are often politically active or motivated. People in this group often pride themselves on being free thinkers, especially when they compare themselves to people in the second group. However, they, themselves, depend on a structure, however less rigid than those in the second group, for answers to their important questions. After all, the sciences, especially, are dependent upon laws and knowledge of the natural world—the world people can only perceive with any or all of their five senses, the part of existence that we can see and hear, etc. Despite their self-declaration of being the free thinkers of the world, it is often they who dismiss the idea that there is an order to the universe that is not explainable by science or that cannot be proven by anything empirical.

It is the fourth group that is most spiritually evolved, says Peck. These people, like their counterparts in the third group, are often very well educated. And although they probably call themselves secularists, they can probably be better described by the word "seekers," or perhaps "mystics." Like Albert Einstein, they may be highly regarded for their achievements in the secular world, but at the same time, they know there is more to life than that which we can see and hear or perceive with any of our five senses. People in the fourth group are very much aware of the importance of intuition, or an inner voice and the idea that something else is at work in the universe that cannot be explained by science that makes a great deal of sense whether we can understand it or not. They are not necessarily quick to call it God or Allah or a cosmic consciousness, but whatever it is, it is definitely in the realm of the supernatural. But unlike those in the second group, people in the fourth group are not satisfied with any one set of holy books or especially any one set of interpretations that a single religion can offer in its explanation of a higher power.

It's difficult to avoid value judgments (especially in the case of the first group) in this classification system of spiritual evolution, but Peck notes that the system is only a model. Most people are, most often, a combination of two or more of these groups, but he says every individual is usually more strongly associated with one group as opposed to any other. To which group does each of your friends/family belong? With which group do *you* identify? Life is constantly changing, and our spiritual evolution is no exception, says Peck. If you don't think you're in the fourth group, don't despair: self-awareness and self-examination are already indicators of upward movement.

Questions for Analysis

1. What are the topic, basis for classification, and distinct categories in this essay of classification?
2. Do you agree with Peck's classification system? Why or why not?
3. How do you think, based on the above essay, Peck would define "spirituality"?
4. Does the author of the above essay agree with Peck's classification system? What evidence is there to suggest the author does agree? Is there evidence to the contrary?
5. Do you know people that would clearly fit into one of these categories? Discuss.
6. Do you think it is possible to go backwards on this scale of evolution? Discuss.
7. If you agree with Peck, at least in principle, what do you think it usually takes for a person to progress (or regress?) from one category to another?
8. What role does education seem to play in Peck's classification? Could an educated person be found in the least spiritual group? Explain.

Assignment Essay of Classification

Choose a topic from the list below (or, if you prefer, from the list given for the paragraph Assignment on page 310) and write a classification essay of at least five paragraphs to develop that topic.

SUGGESTED TOPICS:

1. Different kinds of beer or wine
2. Different types of music
3. Different models of Honda (or any other make of car)
4. Different types of teachers/professors
5. Different types of fashion
6. Different kinds of first dates (blind, set-up, Internet, etc.)
7. Pick a typical classification system within your field of study

While developing your essay, you may want to review Chapter 14: "The Four Stages of Writing for a Paragraph or an Essay," in particular the following sections:

"Brainstorming"

"Choosing the Topic and the Controlling Idea"

"Outlining"

"The Rough Draft"

"Revising and Editing the Rough Draft"

"Proofreading"

"Checklist for the Final Copy"

For help in connecting your sentences and paragraphs smoothly and clearly, you may wish to consult the list of transitional words and phrases, categorized by their function, found on the inside back cover of this book.

 Working Together: Brainstorming for Classification

Brainstorming can be wonderfully helpful when several people put their heads together. As a class, select a classification topic. Divide into groups and brainstorm on one of the classification topics given below. After the members of each group have thought of everything they can, come together as a class and put your classifications on the board. Compare and contrast them. What makes one group's classification more successful than another? Can you use each other's material?

Suggested Topics for Brainstorming:

1. Fads
   What is a fad? Classify as many different types of fads as you can.
2. Friendship
   What is friendship? Classify as many different types of friendships as you can.

3. Causes of car accidents

   What are the causes of car accidents? Classify as many different types of causes as you can.

4. Sports events

   What are the different kinds of sports events? Classify as many different types of sports events as you can.

5. Alcoholic beverages

   What are the different kinds of alcoholic beverages? Classify as many different types of alcoholic beverages as you can.

Your professor might now ask you to write your own individual paragraph or essay using this material.

Chapter 27 **Cause and Effect**

What Is Cause and Effect?

People have always looked at the world and asked the questions "Why did this happen?" and "What are the likely results of that event?" Ancient societies created beautiful myths and legends to explain the origin of the universe and our place in it, while modern civilization has emphasized scientific methods of observation to find the cause of a disease or to determine why the planet Mars appears to be covered by canals. When we examine the spiritual or physical mysteries of our world, we are trying to discover the connections, or links, between events. In this chapter, we will refer to connections between events as **causal relationships.**

DEFINITION

Cause and effect is an examination of either the causes of a particular effect (why something happened) or the effects of a particular cause (what is likely to happen as a result of a particular event). In either case, the establishment of causal relationships must be based on a sense of logic.

Causal relationships are part of our daily lives and provide a way of understanding the cause, result, or consequence of a particular event. The search for a cause or effect is a bit like detective work. Probing an event is a way of searching for clues to discover what caused an event or what result it will have in the future.

For example, we might ask the question "Why did the car break down just after it came back from the garage?" as a way of searching for the cause of the car's new problem. Or we might ask, "What will be the side effects of a certain medicine?" in order to determine what effect a particular medicine will have on the body. This search for connections can be complex. Often the logical analysis of a problem reveals more than one possible explanation. Sometimes the best one can do is find *possible* causes or *probable* effects.

Two Types of Cause and Effect Paragraph or Essay

There are two types of cause and effect paragraph or essay. In the first type, the *cause* is identified in the topic sentence (for a paragraph) or thesis statement (for an essay), and the emphasis is placed on the effects; the supporting detail, therefore, is made up of several *effects*. In the second type, the *effect* is identified in the topic sentence or thesis statement, but the emphasis is placed on the causes; as a result, the supporting detail, this time, is made up of several *causes*.

> **TIP**
>
> Do not try to deal with *both* the causes *and* effects of an event in the supporting detail of a single cause and effect paragraph or essay.

Developing Paragraphs: Cause and Effect

The Topic Sentence of a Cause and Effect Paragraph

The **topic sentence** of a cause and effect paragraph should reveal whether the paragraph will focus on causes or effects. For example, the following topic sentence uses the word *factors* to indicate that causes are about to follow:

> Several factors contributed to my decision to lose weight.

Losing weight is the effect; the causes will be discussed in the remainder of the paragraph.

On the other hand, this next topic sentence begins with the cause and states that a number of *effects* are about to follow:

> Losing weight had a number of positive effects on my life.

Supporting Detail of a Cause and Effect Paragraph

Again, the supporting detail in this type of paragraph should contain *either* causes or effects, but not *both*.

Importance of Logic

In a good cause and effect paragraph, a cause must *lead to* an effect, not just come before it. That's why writing a cause and effect paragraph requires analysis to determine that a logical connection exists between events. For example, the fact that a person walked under a ladder just before he got hit by a car does not prove cause and effect. The walking under a ladder merely preceded the car accident. To suggest that walking under a ladder caused the accident is to use **faulty logic.** (See "Common Fallacies" on pages 335–337 in Chapter 28: "Argumentation.") It is the writer's responsibility to ensure that the relationship between a cause and its effects is clear.

Avoid These Common Errors in Logic
1. Do not confuse coincidence or chronological sequence with evidence.
2. Look for underlying causes beneath the obvious ones and for far-reaching effects beyond the ones that first come to mind. Often what appears to be a single cause or a single effect is a much more complex situation.

Here is an example of a possible error in logic:

> Every time I try to write an essay in the evening, I have trouble getting to sleep. Therefore, writing must prevent me from sleeping.

In this case, writing may indeed be a stimulant that makes it difficult to sleep. However, if the writer is serious about finding the cause of the insomnia, he or she must observe whether any other factors may be to blame. For instance, if the person is drinking several cups of coffee while writing each evening, caffeine is a more likely cause of the wakefulness.

The following is an example of a good cause and effect paragraph.

Model Paragraph: Recipe for Disaster

Notice how the topic sentence makes clear whether the emphasis in the paragraph will be on causes or effects.

A number of factors caused my car accident on Deerfoot Trail last week. First, the weather was horrible that night. It was dark, and the rain made it even harder to see where I was going. The rain also made the roads very slippery, which meant that controlling my car was more difficult than usual. There was another factor that made my car difficult to control that night. I was returning home with a very heavy concrete birdbath for our backyard. When I slammed on my brakes and turned the steering wheel to avoid getting hit, the weight in my trunk shifted and caused the back end of my small car to swing around. Perhaps the most important factor was negligence. The driver of a black sports car was speeding and driving erratically. Rather than slow down when I changed into his lane ahead of him, he sped up, swerved, and cut directly in front of me. I had to slam on my brakes and turn my steering wheel sharply to avoid hitting him. As a result, my car spun around in a complete circle in the middle of the highway. I wound up in a ditch on the side of the road, a little shaken, but realizing things could have ended much worse.

Practice 1 Looking for the Causal Relationship

Study each of the following situations. In each case, if the sequence of events is merely coincidental or chronological, put a *T* (for "time") in the space provided. If the relationship is most likely causal, write a *C*. Be prepared to explain your answers in class. Check your answers against those in the Answer Key on page 463.

_____ 1. Every time I carry my umbrella, it doesn't rain. I am carrying my umbrella today; therefore, it won't rain.

_____ 2. We put fertilizer on the grass. A week later, the grass grew five centimetres and turned a deeper green.

_____ 3. On Tuesday morning, I walked under a ladder. On Wednesday morning, I walked into my office and was told I had lost my job.

_____ 4. The child was born with a serious kidney condition. Seven days later, the child died.

_____ 5. Tar and nicotine from cigarettes damage the lungs. People who smoke cigarettes increase their chances of dying from lung cancer.

_____ 6. A political scandal was exposed in the city on Friday. On Saturday night, only twenty-four hours later, a power blackout occurred in the city.

_____ 7. Very few tourists came to the island last year. The economy of the island declined last year.

Practice 2   Separating the Cause from the Effect

In the following practice exercise, there is an action or event above a group of related sentences. Put a *C* next to sentences that describe causes and an *E* next to sentences that describe effects. Check your answers against those in the Answer Key on page 463.

1. I quit smoking.

_____ a. Smoking costs a lot of money.

_____ b. There are fewer public places that allow smoking now.

_____ c. My terrible cough is gone.

_____ d. I have gained 5 kg.

_____ e. It bothered my friends and family.

_____ f. I have found that my food tastes better.

2. I recently bought a new car.

_____ a. I got a great deal on financing.

_____ b. My old car was unreliable.

_____ c. I have less money every month because I have to pay more for insurance and gas.

_____ d. My popularity at school has increased.

_____ e. I was tired of having to take the train whenever I wanted to visit my family.

_____ f. I was embarrassed to drive my rusted old car.

Exercise **Separating the Cause from the Effect**

In each sentence, separate the cause, problem, or reason from the effect, solution, or result. Remember, the cause is not necessarily given first.

1. More than half of mothers with children under one year of age work outside the home, which has resulted in an unprecedented need for daycare in this country.

   Cause: _____

   _____

   Effect: _____

   _____

2. By 2000, two-thirds of all preschool children and four-fifths of school-age children had working mothers, facts that led to increased strain on our system of daycare.

   Cause: _____

   _____

   Effect: _____

   _____

3. In one national survey, over half the working mothers reported that they had either changed jobs or cut back on their hours in order to be more available to their children.

   Cause: _____

   _____

   Effect: _____

   _____

4. Many mothers who work do so only when their children are in school, while other mothers work only occasionally during the school year because they feel their children need the supervision of a parent.

   Cause: _____

   _____

   Effect: _____

   _____

5. Many mothers experience deep emotional crises as a result of their struggle to meet both the financial obligations of their home and their own emotional needs as parents.

   Cause: _____

   _____

   Effect: _____

   _____

Writing the Cause or Effect Paragraph Step by Step

To learn a skill that has so many different aspects, it is best to follow a step-by-step approach, so that one aspect can be worked on at a time. This approach will ensure that you are not missing a crucial point or misunderstanding a part of the whole. There are other ways to go about writing an effective paragraph, but here is one logical method you can use to achieve results.

Steps for Writing the Cause or Effect Paragraph

1. After you have chosen your topic, plan your topic sentence.
2. Brainstorm by jotting down all possible causes or effects. Ask others for their thoughts. Research if necessary. Consider long-range effects or underlying causes.
3. Cross out any points that are illogical, merely coincidental, or the result of only time sequence. Then choose the three or four best points from what remains on your list.
4. Decide on the best order for these points. (From least important to most important is one way to organize them.)
5. Write at least one complete sentence for each of the causes or effects you have chosen from your list.
6. Write a concluding statement.
7. Finally, put your sentences into standard paragraph form.

Exercise Writing the Effect Paragraph Step by Step

Starting with the suggested topic below, follow the seven steps outlined in the box above to work through the writing process for a cause or effect Paragraph. (These steps are similar to those used for the narrative paragraph in Chapter 21; refer to pages 258–259 for a step-by-step example and a completed sample paragraph.)

Topic: What are the effects when students have part-time jobs after classes?

On Your Own: Writing Cause and Effect Paragraphs from Model Paragraphs

The Causes of Disaster

The following model paragraph looks at the causes for the loss of life in the sinking of a supposedly unsinkable ship on its maiden voyage almost a century ago.

Model Paragraph: Titanic Blunders

One of the most tragic events of the twentieth century was the sinking of the British ship *Titanic* in the Atlantic Ocean on April 15, 1912, with the loss of over 1500 lives. The immediate cause of this terrible loss of life was a large iceberg that tore a ninety-metre gash in the side of the ship, flooding five of its watertight compartments. Some believe that the tragedy took place because the crew members did not see the iceberg in time, but others see a chain of different events that contributed to the tragedy. First was the fact that the ship was not carrying enough lifeboats for all of its passengers: it had enough boats for only about half of the people on board. Furthermore, the ship's crew showed a clear lack of concern for the third-class or "steerage" passengers, who were left in their cramped quarters below decks with little or no help as the ship went down. It has often been said that this social attitude of helping the wealthy and neglecting the poor was one of the real causes of the loss of life that night. Indeed, some of the lifeboats that were used were not filled to capacity when the rescue ships eventually found them. Finally, the tragedy of the *Titanic* was magnified by the fact that some ships nearby did not have a radio crew on duty and therefore missed the distress signals sent by the *Titanic*. Out of all this, the need to reform safety regulations on passenger ships became obvious.

Assignment   Cause and Effect Paragraph (Effects)

Select a community or area disaster that you have personally experienced or heard about. This could include a severe climatic condition or a manufactured disaster. Instead of writing a paragraph about the disaster's *causes* such as in the above paragraph, point out the *effects* it had on you or the people involved.

SUGGESTED TOPICS:

(For more suggested topics, see the list given for the essay "Assignment" on pages 323–324.)

1. The effects of an earthquake
2. The effects of a power blackout on a major city or town
3. The effects of a flood or other extensive water damage on a home or community
4. The effects of a chemical spill on land or offshore
5. The effects of a transit strike on a community
6. The effects of a major fire on a downtown block
7. The effects of the terrorist attacks on September 11, 2001 (see photo on page 154)

Developing the Cause and Effect Essay

Like the cause and effect paragraph, the essay of the same type should focus on either causes or effects, but not both. And it should be self-evident from the thesis statement of the essay which one will be discussed.

As in other kinds of essays, the thesis appears somewhere between the middle and the end of the first paragraph. Each support paragraph deals with one cause or one effect.

Bear in mind that all the causes or all the effects included in the essay should directly support your thesis, whatever it is. If not, you must make some adjustments: either change your thesis or change your support paragraphs. Which option you take is up to you. In some cases, only one support paragraph needs to be reworked. If you're writing the essay in class and have a rigid time limit, you may decide to make whatever changes require the least amount of time.

> For a review of the essay form and its standard format (which applies to all the writing strategies in this unit), see Chapter 16: "The Essay." For a review of the writing process that can be applied to both the paragraph and the essay, see Chapter 14: "The Four Stages of Writing for a Paragraph or an Essay."

Two model essays that demonstrate the strategy of cause and effect are found on the next few pages. The first, by Donald Pianissimo, is very informal and personal (notice the use of the word *I*). The second, which forms part of the exercise "Working Together: Identifying Causes" that concludes the chapter, is called "The Zen of Zzzzzz." Written by Antonia Zerbisias, it is much more formal and contains research that is used to support the author's claim.

Model Essay I: Whose Choice Is It, Anyway?

by Donald Pianissimo

It is so easy to think that the decisions you make are your own choices. But when you consider the events leading up to those decisions, it may not be so easy to claim the decisions as your own. My decision to go into journalism was, I thought, something I had chosen completely on my own without external influence. But when I think of three particular events in my life before leaving high school, I begin to think my say in the matter was minimal at best. I begin to think I was simply following a path that had already been laid out for me.

My mom used to be a nurse, and she confided in me long after I'd dropped chemistry in high school that she always wanted me to be a doctor. My dad, although a writer, never called himself a journalist; journalism was not the kind of writing he preferred to do. But perhaps I underestimated his influence on my choice to enter a writing career. In fact, it was he who encouraged me to publish an article in a local magazine when I was only nine years old. I still remember his editing my work. I also remember the thrill of my anticipation of seeing my name in print. It was the first taste of being published I would get, and it wouldn't be the last.

A second incident is as vivid in my memory as the first. In Grade 8, the first English teacher who would truly inspire me with his passion for teaching announced to the class one day that there were three essays he had marked that were worthy of recognition. He asked three students to read their essays out loud in front of the entire class, and I was one of them. He made me feel I had a gift, a gift worth sharing.

And finally, by the time I'd gotten to high school, a classmate and I were asked by a teacher to co-edit the school newspaper. I never thought I would have so much fun. Better still, the paper was a hit with the other students. Our high school hadn't seen so successful a student newspaper in years. I couldn't help but love the popularity that came with it, too.

I envied those students who knew they wanted to be doctors, or lawyers, or engineers since the time they could talk. I just figured I wasn't so blessed with such an ardent and focused career desire. By the time I'd graduated from high school, I chose to enter a field of study for my postsecondary education based on one of my most enjoyable pastimes: writing for an audience. Journalism seemed the logical choice. What didn't occur to me until much later was that my choice seemed the logical conclusion of a number of monumental events in my young life. Were they random events, or were they meant to lead me in a certain direction? Your guess is as good as mine.

Questions for Analysis

1. Of the two types of cause and effect essay discussed in this chapter, which type of essay is this?
2. Does the writer support the idea of free will, or the idea of fate?
3. What evidence in this essay suggests his support for one or the other?
4. How much does the author attribute his choices to the influence of parents and teachers?
5. What, in your own words, is the author's thesis? Which sentence states the actual thesis? Based on just this thesis, what would a reader think the support is going to be about? Why?
6. Is the thesis adequately supported? Explain.

Exploring the Topic

1. How did you decide to enter your current field of study? Was it free will or fate? Discuss.
2. Does reading this essay make you think twice about whether or not you made the choice to enter your field of study totally independently of outside influence? Explain.

Assignment   Cause and Effect Essay

Choose a topic from the list below (or, if you prefer, from the list given for the paragraph Assignment on page 321), or come up with one of your own. Write a cause and effect essay of at least five paragraphs to develop that topic.

SUGGESTED TOPICS:

1. The causes of war
2. The causes of failing a course
3. The causes of breaking up with a boyfriend/girlfriend
4. The causes of addiction (alcohol, drugs, sex, relationship, etc.)

5. The causes of lying
6. The effects of lying
7. The effects of parents who don't show their children affection
8. The effects of poverty in the home
9. The effects of fame
10. The effects of dating a real "hottie"

While developing your essay, you may want to review Chapter 14: "The Four Stages of Writing for a Paragraph or an Essay," in particular the following sections:

"Brainstorming"

"Choosing the Topic and the Controlling Idea"

"Outlining"

"The Rough Draft"

"Revising and Editing the Rough Draft"

"Proofreading"

"Checklist for the Final Copy"

For help in connecting your sentences and paragraphs smoothly and clearly, you may wish to consult the list of transitional words and phrases, categorized by their function, found on the inside back cover of this book. In particular, you may find the first section, "Transitions for Cause and Effect," useful for work in this chapter.

 Working Together: Identifying Causes

1. Read the following article by Antonia Zerbisias entitled "The Zen of Zzzzzz." Write either an extended paragraph or an essay in response to one of the following topics. Make sure the ideas you include are from the article by Zerbisias, and that you acknowledge the author in your composition. (For more on paraphrasing, summarizing, and acknowledging the author, see Chapter 18.)

   a. The causes of sleep deprivation
   b. The effects of sleep deprivation

Model Essay II: The Zen of Zzzzzz*

by Antonia Zerbisias

Sometime in my early 20s, in the early morning, something—a short circuit maybe—tripped Montreal's Cold War-era, the-Russians-are-coming air raid sirens.

While the entire city was ducking and covering under their beds, I remained blissfully unawake and unaware under the covers.

I am not joking when I say I could sleep through a nuclear war.

This is not to say I've haven't had my share of tossing and turning. An unfortunate encounter with bedbugs. Jet lag. The Sunday night blues. Noisy old hotels on busy European city streets. The now-gone monthly wakefulness that nature must have endowed women with so that we could be aware of predators following the scent of blood.

So I know what it is to stare at the clock, pound the pillows, kick out the sheets . . . But I have never experienced that yawning "hole in the night" that has plagued Patricia Morrisroe for just about every one of her 59 years.

She is not alone in the dark. Sleeplessness haunts one in seven Canadians over the age of 15, Statistics Canada reports, and some 40 million Americans.

Which is why the self-described "fourth generation insomniac" and former New York magazine contributor went on a quest to examine and understand sleep, one that resulted in her new book *Wide Awake: A Memoir of Insomnia.*

Part autobiography and part magical mattress tour, *Wide Awake* begins with her childhood in the "House of Punk Sleep" where her family tiptoed around her mother and, via drugstores, sleep labs, yoga, dream therapy, cognitive behavioural therapy, brain music therapy, and even an ice bed in Iceland, ends with illumination just two blocks away from her Manhattan home.

"Sleep seems to be a very, very hot topic these days; it's replaced depression," she says on the phone. "It's like people said, 'What more could be said about depression?' So we kind of needed to move on to sleep."

The New York Times recently introduced *All-Nighters*, a blog about insomnia, with musings from artists, scientists and opinionators.

Earlier this year, Arianna Huffington and *Glamour* magazine launched their joint "Feminist Sleep Challenge" because, although sleep deprivation is epidemic across the gender divide, working women are most affected.

"A nation of sleepy women is even less capable of greatness," wrote Huffington and *Glamour* editor-in-chief Cindi Leive in January.

*Antonia Zerbisias, "The Zen of Zzzzzz," *The Toronto Star* (1 May 2010). © 2010 Torstar Syndication Services.

Sleep, says Morrisroe, is a $24 billion business, if you factor in the herbal remedies, the hypnotherapy, the white noise machines, the ear plugs, the blackout drapes, the cushy new beds built so high a girl needs a step stool to climb in and all the desperate measures the sleep-disordered take in order to get some Zzzz.

How did we get to this?

"There are some people who just don't know when to turn off the computer and they just think that they can get by. Those are certain lifestyle choices. There are other people who just may not be able to sleep because they can't fall asleep; they have sleep maintenance insomnia when they wake up in the middle of the night; they may just have very fractured sleep; or they may not be getting enough deep sleep.

"I really knew nothing about sleep when I went into this. I just knew that I wasn't a great sleeper. And it was astounding to me the number of sleep disorders there are out there.

"There are people who will take their car, who will be sleep driving and not aware that they are doing that. There was somebody who went on ABC News and talked about trying to strangle and stab his wife repeatedly over a 30-year marriage, which is REM behaviour disorder. Another reason is sleep apnea which affects more men than women."

Except, of course, when affected men snore so loudly they keep their partners awake.

Morrisroe believes two factors in particular have made sleep "The New Depression"—aging Baby Boomers and Big Pharma.

"Sleep does fall off as you age. It's not as robust as it used to be," she says. "People need to accept that. But the Baby Boomer generation expect to be perfect in all things, that if they have problems with their knees, they'll just go get knee replacement surgery, hip replacement surgery."

Meanwhile, drug companies looking for conditions to medicalize and new markets to target have roused a dormant monster.

"Sleep used to be the backwaters of medicine," she explains, referring to when insomnia was seen as a symptom of something else: anxiety, depression, chronic pain, any one of a number of different problems. "I went back and looked at a lot of the articles and I could pinpoint exactly when we suddenly realized that we weren't sleeping.

"It was in the early 1990s, when Searle introduced Ambien," Morrisroe continues. "They got together with the National Sleep Foundation which is a non-profit organization—they do get a lot of money from drug companies—and started this 'Sleep in America' poll and, all of a sudden, it was how are we sleeping, how much are we sleeping. Not that pills, which include the much-advertised Lunesta, help much," insists Morrisroe: "When I started to look at the clinical trials, and when I really started to look at the amount of time of sleep you get on things like Lunesta and Ambien, it's really only 11.4 minutes over a placebo. It's very very small.

"And they can cause you to have a form of amnesia so that you don't remember how badly you have been sleeping. They can also leave you with some cognitive impairment the next day which can make you feel like you haven't slept."

It's no secret that staring at a computer or TV screen late into the night is not exactly restful. Teens texting late into the night stumble into class where teachers think they suffer from attention deficit disorders. The economy has been keeping millions awake. Some of the most sleep-deprived people anywhere are those with the longest commutes—and, as a study of 19 major cities published last month revealed, Torontonians have the worst commutes in North America, which might explain road rage.

And, if that doesn't keep you awake at night, how about this? Sleep deprivation messes with hormones — and could lead to overeating and obesity.

To counteract the effects of sleepiness, a whole new industry has sprung up.

"The new area is wake," notes Morrisroe. "A lot of students are taking modofinil and that's being used as a smart drug, to stay up.

"And then you have all those energy drinks, packed with caffeine. There's now caffeine-infused food, like caffeine-infused oatmeal. The idea that you have caffeine-infused food and even caffeine-infused drinks for children, that's not helping people sleep at all."

In fact, it's the stuff of nightmares.

But is insomnia a modern problem? Are we sleeping less than we used to? Did people in prehistoric and ancient times really crash with the sunset and sleep til the cocks crowed? Is the prescribed eight hours a construct to suit industrial times?

In his 2005 ground-breaking book *At Day's Close: Night in Times Past*, American historian Roger Ekirch documented how humans slept through the ages—but not necessarily through the night.

"He said that people slept in segmented sleep," says Morrisroe. "They'd fall asleep for a couple of hours. They'd get up. They might talk. They might have sex with their bedfellows as there were often multiple people in beds because they often had communal beds. They'd pray. They would analyze their dreams. Maybe some would go out and steal livestock. Then they would go back to sleep.

"So this concept of segmented sleep may be very natural to us."

And how is she sleeping since she completed her quest?

"I sleep much better—but right now I am sleeping much less because of all the press and this book coming out."

Jack Layton, the late leader of the national NDP, celebrates the party's historic results in the federal election of 2011.

REUTERS/Fred Greenslade

2. The class should divide into groups of three or four. Look at the picture above of Jack Layton, former national leader of the New Democratic Party of Canada, who in the spring of 2011 became the Leader of the Opposition in Parliament. Although he held the post for only a few months before succumbing to cancer in August 2011, Mr. Layton was the first NDP leader to have achieved this status in the history of this country. This photo shows him just after the election, raising his cane (which he needed as a result of hip surgery) in an expression of spiritual triumph. Collaboratively within your group, write a paragraph or essay on what you think are the causes behind the NDP's historic achievement in the federal election of 2011.

Chapter 28 **Argumentation**

What Is Argumentation?

So far, your purpose in many writing assignments in this text has been to describe, narrate, or explain by using various writing strategies for development. Still another purpose in writing is to argue.

> **DEFINITION**
>
> **Argumentation** is an attempt to change the reader's present viewpoint, or at least to convince her or him that your viewpoint is a valid one.

Every time you write a paper for a course, you are trying to persuade your professor that what you are presenting is a reasonable view of the subject matter. You might want to show, for example, that Canadian airlines are among the safest in the world, or that the crime novel is becoming Canada's favourite form of fiction. As you approach these types of assignments, you need to be aware of each part of the argumentative process so that you will be able to both analyze other people's arguments more effectively and write better ones of your own.

Argumentation vs. Persuasion

You could view most writing as persuasive, since one of the writer's main goals is to get the reader to see, think, and believe in a certain way. Although "persuasiveness" is a quality of *all* paragraph and essay writing strategies (narration, classification, etc.), formal **argumentation** is considered a separate writing strategy altogether, one that follows certain guidelines. If you have ever been a member of a debating team, you have spent a good deal of time studying this special form. How to use techniques of argument in your own writing is the main subject of this chapter.

Persuasive Appeals That Are Not Logical

Logic is always at the root of a good argument. However, effective persuasive techniques can also include appeal to emotion, aesthetic appeal (appeal to one's sense of beauty or appearance), and the restatement of a common point of view. These techniques are not necessarily wrong in themselves, but overuse or exclusive use of them can prove counterproductive.

- **Appeal to emotion:** Causing the reader to have a strong feeling can be an extremely effective persuasive technique. The writer makes the reader extremely sad, for example, by discussing the homelessness of a child. We can't help but to identify with the child in some way, perhaps because of his or her innocence.
- **Appeal to aesthetics:** Everyone has a sense of what is beautiful, even if this sense changes slightly from one individual to another. Advertisements on TV (and, it can be argued, most TV programs and films) use this type of appeal to sell products and services and to boost ratings.
- **Appeal to common points of view:** Writers sometimes take advantage of what they know are common beliefs, such as cultural values, to get their point across, even if these views are illogical. It's a safe bet that many readers will be on their side because of the popular appeal of the belief.

Other Argumentative Strategies

Some of the strategies you have already read about in this text also fall under the umbrella of argumentation. Cause and effect, for example, is argumentative most of the time, even where science is concerned. For example, the sample research essay on cell phones and their possible effects on our long-term health (pages 242–251 in Chapter 20) argues that there is a very good chance that cell phone usage and brain damage are connected. Despite the current sophistication of science, the results of this research are far from conclusive. So while this paper has its basis in science, it is, most definitely, argumentative. In fact, responsible scientists know that their findings are subject to further analysis.

Critical Thinking and Analysis

Students sometimes wrongly offer paraphrasing and summarizing (see Chapter 18) where argumentation is expected. Many instructors at the postsecondary level, in fact, agree that it is the original use of critical thinking and analysis that usually sets an "A" paper apart from others. Thinking critically and analyzing arguments are vital components in the argumentation process.

What Is Critical Thinking?

Critical Thinking in Everyday Life

Critical thinking is something you should practise every day, not just when forming an argument but also when considering the arguments of others. When you listen to a TV commercial, you should be asking, "Does this make sense?" Of course, an advertisement can still be effective even without a good argument; for example, it might carry with it an emotional or aesthetic appeal, as discussed earlier.

Most of the time, however, it is important that things do make sense. What you choose to eat, for instance, is probably not based only on what tastes good; you have to consider nutrition and other factors. How you vote in the next election likely does not just depend on how the candidates look on TV, but also on how much sense they make in their answers to questions. You are always making decisions, and much of the time, though surely not all of the time, you are making those decisions based on some aspect of critical thinking.

More Tools and Components of Argumentation

As mentioned earlier, the more familiar you become with the different parts of the argumentation process, the more likely you will be able to develop more effective arguments of your own.

Original analysis often is what sets apart a superior student paper from others, especially those that do not engage in analysis at all but merely quote, paraphrase, or summarize material from research conducted.

Claim	Capital punishment should be brought back to Canada.*	
+ Evidence	1. It costs too much to keep a murderer in jail.	
	2. A serial killer is not likely to be rehabilitated.	
	3. The punishment should fit the crime.	
Argument	The combination of both components (*claim* and *evidence*) above	

* Note that the words "I believe" are not used in the claim.

Figure 28.1: Components of an Argument

When you make a claim or write a topic sentence or thesis, there is no need to actually say "I believe" or "I think" because these words are, in fact, implied. It is generally agreed upon that the use of the word "I," in particular, makes the argument seem less effective. The word "I" is usually avoided when writing in a formal tone such as in a research paper.

Underlying Assumptions

When an argument is made, a claim and its supporting detail are often clearly expressed. What is often not apparent is an assumption underlying the argument. **An underlying assumption is a belief that someone holds about oneself, others or the world that he or she considers indisputably true.** An entire argument can fail if a faulty underlying assumption is detected, identified, and discredited.

> **Example:** Peter would be a great choice of a marriage partner. (claim)
>
> Peter is rich. (evidence)
>
> Anyone who is rich is a great choice of a marriage partner. (underlying assumption)

Why Are Underlying Assumptions Not Expressed?

There are two basic reasons that writers fail to express underlying assumptions: (1) they are unaware of their own assumptions, or (2) they don't want to draw attention to the underlying assumptions of the argument because, at some level, they know these assumptions are logically indefensible or, at the very least, unacceptable to many readers. Underlying assumptions may be the result of a writer's upbringing, religion, community values, etc. For example, racist sentiment or religious intolerance is an underlying assumption of many so-called arguments, even though you won't hear many people actually saying "people outside of my race or religion are inferior." Arguments built on top of such underlying assumptions must be constantly questioned and critically assessed.

Analyzing the Intention of Argument: The Importance of Virtue

Good writing should not only depend on effectiveness, but also on good intentions. Consider the actions of the characters in the movie *In the Company of Men* (dir. Neil Labute, 1997), in which two men decide to target a young, deaf woman who works at the same company they do. As part of a betting game, they both try to get her to fall in love with them, and one succeeds. In the end, she is emotionally crushed when she finds out that the man she has fallen in love with has no intention of being with her. The other man, who, in the meantime, does actually fall in love with her, asks the first man why he has hurt her so. The man replies, "Because I could."

Communication, like behaviour, cannot be independent of morality. More important than a writer's ability to convince ought to be his or her intention. For example, does the writer appear to be interested only in benefiting himself or herself, or his or her own? Or is there a more honourable attempt to achieve a greater good? Richard L. Epstein and Carolyn Kernberger, in their preface to their book *The Pocket Guide to Critical Thinking*, wrote, "Because your reasoning can be sharpened, you can understand more and you can avoid being duped. You can reason well with those you need to convince. . . . But whether you will do so depends not just on method, not just on the tools of reasoning, but on your goals, your ends. And those depend on virtue."

We Become What We Communicate

So whether you are formulating an argument of your own or responding to the argument of someone else, an analysis of the arguer's intention and underlying assumptions, which are often not obvious, is an essential part of critical thinking and our communication. Ultimately, the way we think and the way we communicate influence what we do and what we become. The method of arguing well is critical, but so is the reason behind the argument itself.

Argumentative Techniques

1. **State a clear topic sentence (for a paragraph) or thesis (for an essay).** Take an obvious stand or position. You might want to use words such as *must, ought*, and *should*, although they are, of course, not necessary (see the third thesis below). For example:

   > Canada's military should be better funded.
   > Canada must reform its prison system.
   > Romantic love and marriage are inevitably incompatible.
   > All information on the Internet should be free.

2. **Use examples.** Well-chosen examples are the heart of any paragraph or essay. Without them, the writing is flat, lifeless, and unconvincing. Providing a good example for each of your main points helps make a much stronger argument. Examples help your reader *see* what you are talking about.

3. **Use opinions from recognized authorities to support your points.** One of the oldest methods of supporting an argument is to cite one or more authorities that lend weight to your position. People usually believe what well-known experts claim. You should choose your experts carefully to help make your position on the topic more persuasive; be sure that your authority is someone who is respected in the area you are discussing. For example, if you are arguing that we must end the nuclear arms race, your argument will be stronger if you quote a respected scientist who can accurately predict the consequences of a nuclear war. Quoting a famous movie star saying the same thing might be more glamorous and get more attention, but would not be as convincing, as the star would not be as great an authority as the scientist.

4. **Answer your critics in advance.** When you point out beforehand what your opposition is likely to say in answer to your argument, you are writing from a position of strength. You are letting your reader know that you are aware that there is another side to the argument you are making. By pointing out this other side and then answering its objections in advance, you are strengthening your own position.

5. **Point out the results.** Help your reader see what will happen if your argument is (or is not) believed or acted upon as you think it should be. You should be specific and rational when you point out results, making sure that you avoid exaggeration of any kind. For example, if you argue against the possession of handguns, it would be an exaggeration to say that everyone is going to be murdered if the opposition's point of view is listened to instead of yours.

6. **Define certain terms that are central to the argument.** Often there seems to be disagreement where there should not be any, simply because the people who appear to be arguing have not defined their terms. For example, the term *religion* is potentially quite controversial in itself. Does it mean an organized system of beliefs that might be political as well as spiritual? Or does it refer to a narrower definition: the expression of a belief in the divine? Or perhaps its meaning refers to its Latin root, which translates literally as "to bind back." If it's the third definition that both parties agree upon, what does it mean to bind back to—old ways of living and traditions, or one's spiritual instead of material values? Or is religion one's way to bring about reconciliation with the paradoxes of human life? Clearly, before arguing what the benefits or harm of religion are, it is critical that a writer first define the term. The same is true, of course, of countless other terms and concepts.

7. **Avoid common fallacies** (errors) in your argument. And use critical skills in analyzing the fallacies of others. Several common fallacies are outlined in the next section.

Common Fallacies

Common fallacies help us identify bad arguments because they are based on faulty reasoning. It is impossible to present a definitive or complete list of all possible fallacies an argument might contain, but the following are some of the most common ones. Try to learn to recognize these fallacies whether you can name them or not—that way you can criticize them in someone else's bad argument and prevent employing them in your own.

1. ***Ad hominem* attack:** In this fallacy, the person making the argument expresses a personal attack against an opponent—literally, an attack "on the man"—rather than addressing the actual issue. Often, when someone resorts to the *ad hominem* attack it is in desperation, because he or she cannot find actual evidence to support a claim that makes someone else look bad.

    For example, Kim Campbell, the first and only female prime minister of Canada, ran for election against Jean Chrétien of the Liberal Party in 1993. The following was an argument made by the Liberals during the campaign, a campaign infamous for personal attacks made by both parties:

    > Kim Campbell is a divorcee. If Kim Campbell couldn't manage her marriage, how could she possibly manage the country?

    This is clearly an *ad hominem* attack on Kim Campbell. First of all, a divorce in itself is not necessarily the result of the inability to "manage a marriage." And secondly, it cannot automatically be argued that her divorce

Justin Trudeau has just finished giving the eulogy at the funeral of his father, Pierre Elliott Trudeau, former prime minister of Canada.

Paul Chiasson/Canadian Press

has anything to do with whether or not she is capable of serving as prime minister.

During the same campaign, the Conservatives were also guilty of an *ad hominem* attack. A photograph in which Chrétien's partial facial paralysis was prominent was used in a Conservative ad until it was pulled amid a huge public outcry.

Justin Trudeau, son of the late Pierre Trudeau, another former prime minister of Canada, gave a eulogy at his father's funeral in 2000. He said that as a child, with the aim of gaining his father's approval, he insulted a man whom he knew was his father's political rival. His father, with a stern look on his face, told Justin that it was fine to criticize someone's point of view, but that this ought to be done without attacking the individual on a personal level. Everyone, after all, deserves to live with dignity and respect. No one has the right to take those away. An *ad hominem* attack, unfortunately, aims to do just that.

2. **Practical (common) point of view or belief (also known as the democratic fallacy):** The person making an argument takes advantage of a common point of view to persuade the reader of another point of view. The danger here is the assumption that the will of the majority determines what is right and what is wrong. Mahatma Gandhi of India, on the other hand, once said that history will judge a country on the basis not of how it treats its majority, but of how it treats its minorities. This statement speaks volumes.

   Example: The teacher asks the students, "Is it okay to lie?" One student responds, "Lying is okay because most people do it."

   First of all, there is a dangerous assumption here. The student assumes that everyone lies. He or she may have evidence that his or her parents have lied on occasion. His or her friends might lie even more often. He or she sees evidence in the news of heads of state lying. And so the student's conclusion is that everyone lies. But these examples of evidence do not support the idea that everyone lies. Unless the student has evidence that actually shows all people lie (evidence that would be impossible to obtain), such a broad statement should never be made. Secondly, even if it could be proven that everyone does lie, does that make it fine for the student to lie? Is it not possible that everyone is doing something that is wrong?

3. **Straw man** ("Putting words into someone's mouth"): This fallacy consists of an attack on an argument that is similar to, but not exactly the same as, the one your opponent holds. For example, former U.S. president Bill Clinton vehemently told his country that he did not have sexual relations with former White House intern Monica Lewinsky. He meant what he said very technically, in that he did not have intercourse with her, when in fact he knew he was being accused of an improper relationship with her in general. He was guilty of employing a "straw man" to dispute a claim he knew to be true.

4. **False analogy:** This fallacy occurs when an argument involves an unfair comparison. When two things are so different they cannot be compared, but someone tries anyway, he or she is making a false analogy.

> ***Example:*** Guns don't kill people. People kill people. Guns are like cars. Therefore, it should be just as easy to get a gun as it is to get a car.

The fact is, guns are not like cars. A car is a vehicle. A gun is a weapon.

Writing the Argumentative Paragraph

In all of the previous chapters in this unit, more emphasis was placed on the development of the paragraph than on the essay. This chapter on the writing strategy of argumentation takes the opposite approach. The most effective arguments are those supported by several points that are treated thoroughly. For this reason, an argumentative essay is usually a more effective piece of writing than a single argumentative paragraph, so long as the points are thoughtful, well expressed, and directly supportive of the writer's overall assertion or claim. However, that is not to say that a good argumentative paragraph cannot be written. Of course it can. If you do attempt to write such a paragraph, just remember to establish your claim in the form of a topic sentence that is clear and strong, and to make sure your supporting details include the strongest evidence in support of your claim that you can find. (See Chapter 15: "The Paragraph.")

Developing Paragraphs: Argumentation

The following argumentative paragraph was written in response to one of the questions (#5 on page 262) that follows the narrative essay "Transparent Silhouette" (pages 261–262).

Question: Did the writer foreshadow the ending of the essay? (In other words, are there several clues throughout the essay that enable the reader to predict the eventual death of the writer's friend?)

Model Paragraph: Clues of an Unhappy Ending

Many clues exist in the story by Akis Stylianou that his friend will end up dead. First, there is the title of the essay itself: "Transparent Silhouette." It might conjure up the mental picture of the outline of a ghost. Second, there is the third line in the first paragraph of the story in which Stylianou mentions the words "the woman I knew"; "knew," after all, is in the past tense, not the present. Third, the last line in the first paragraph includes the words "where I can delay my misery." If Stylianou is miserable because of his friend, whatever has happened to her cannot be good. Fourth, the second paragraph describes her sad childhood, full of abuse and the loneliness that results. A traumatic childhood is often, though not always, an omen of bad things to follow in life. And finally, the events Stylianou describes throughout the story seem to get more and more dangerous, starting with getting mixed up with the "wrong" crowd, becoming an exotic dancer, and finally becoming a porn star. All in all, the abundance of clues throughout the story strongly suggests that the writer's friend will end up in a very bad state, as she does.

Questions for Analysis

1. How can you tell from the form of this text that it is one paragraph, and not two or three?
2. Is the paragraph a proper length, according to what Chapter 15 says about paragraph structure?
3. What is the topic sentence? Does it directly answer the question?
4. Are there transitions in the paragraph? What are some examples?
5. Is there sufficient support of the topic sentence? Discuss.
6. Is the difference between the main supporting details and specific examples or explanations that support them apparent?
7. Is there a concluding sentence in this paragraph? If so, what is it?
8. Is the transition "finally" used for the last supporting detail of the paragraph or for the concluding sentence?

Developing Essays: Argumentation

The following essay by Leanne C. Southall is about the relationship between attitudes and the oppression of women. As you read the essay, look for the major parts of an effective argument: strong thesis, carefully chosen examples, quotations from authorities, answers to the opposition, and predictions. Can you find any weaknesses or fallacies in the argument?

This piece was written in the form of a letter to the editor in response to an article published in the *Hamilton Spectator* on July 19, 2001. The article outlined the regulations proposed by the health minister of Turkey that would require female nursing students to undergo "virginity testing" in order to proceed with their training. These regulations were proposed "to ensure that nursing schools are not encouraging prostitution." The letter was sent on July 30, prior to the terrorist attacks of September 11, 2001. Because Leanne C. Southall's essay deals with a controversial topic, some people may offer counterarguments in response to the points she makes. However, the writer combines the results of several nations' experiences and those of Canada to persuade readers to change their attitudes where appropriate.

Model Essay I: Individuals Must Spur Change*

by Leanne C. Southall

Once again, attitudes toward females in a fundamentalist religious realm are perpetuating women's oppression. Regulations proposed by Turkey's health minister, Osman Durmus—stating that women training to be nurses

*Leanne C. Southall, "Individuals Must Spur Change." Reprinted by permission of the author.

must prove their virginity—are a discriminatory offence. He has suggested that nursing students who have ever been sexually active may lead schools to become places for prostitution. His statement implies that sexually active women are immoral. Since Durmus issued the directive, Turkish newspapers have reported that he has been told by government leaders to take a vacation.

But this situation is just one of many restrictions on women around the world. Essentially, being a woman anywhere may be reason enough for targeting. In countries such as India and Jordan, daughters can be viewed as property; "honour killings" are tolerated if a woman shames her family. Recently, in Iran, where girls are forced to cover their heads and bodies from age 9, ten prostitutes were murdered. A special investigation ensued, and the deputy governor-general for law enforcement explained, "They were little and unimportant." In Pakistan, where 80 per cent of women are subjected to domestic violence, there is emerging a pattern of husbands dumping kerosene on their wives, lighting a match, and claiming their death to be a stove accident. Acid attacks are now being seen in hospitals. Reasons for getting rid of wives may include a suspicion of other sexual partners, a dowry considered too small or a woman's failure to get pregnant. (Incidentally, a woman's testimony was once only half the weight of a man's in Pakistan.) Female genitalia mutilation is still a harmful custom in various countries around the world; some 4000 girls in Africa are to undergo this ritual in October.

In Afghanistan's past twenty years of war, women and girls have been beaten, raped, abducted and sold into prostitution. Since Taliban rule began in 1994, women are not permitted to work or attend school and must not make noise when they walk. They are not to leave their homes unless accompanied by a male relative, and certainly not without their restrictive burqua [a black veil that cloaks a woman's body from head to toe, leaving a small meshed window for her eyes to see through]. Their windows are painted black, ensuring that they cannot be seen from the street. In the United States, women are excluded from leading congregations because "Southern Baptists, by practice as well as conviction, believe leadership is male," as explained by Drafting Committee Chairman Reverend Adrian Rogers.

And what about Canada? Each of us should evaluate how our attitudes toward women affect lives. A mere 4 per cent of sexual assault charges result in convictions. The court process resembles a second violation, where [the victim's] medical records and previous charges can be subpoenaed and her credibility is put on trial. Women still earn less than men in the same jobs. The only exception may be fashion modelling, which demonstrates the emphatic value we place on a woman's beauty, versus intelligence or contribution.

Judged far too quickly are single moms supported by social programs. Provinces have tightened eligibility for social assistance and designed policies that lead single mothers into the labour market. However, with licensed day-care costs as high as $7000 per year and limited regulated spaces available, help is far beyond the means of many single moms. Consequently, 56 per cent of single-parent families headed by women are poor.

If violence toward women reflects societal attitudes, sexism is all too alive in Canada. Some 51 per cent of Canadian women report having experienced physical or sexual violence. In 1998, more than 90 000 women and children used emergency abuse shelters across Canada. While not every woman has experienced violence, there is virtually no one who has not feared it.

Globally, we must adopt a system that embraces gender equality within political, economic and social spheres. Working toward that day, as individuals, let us each be aware of our attitudes and the part we can play to improve the status of women around the world.

Questions for Analysis

1. In your own words, what is Southall's thesis statement? Which sentence, in particular, is *her* thesis statement?
2. What is her strongest supporting detail? Why? What is her weakest supporting detail? Why?
3. What does she want her readers to do?

Even more controversial, perhaps, is the following essay on euthanasia (mercy killing and physician-assisted suicide) in Canada. Try to keep an open mind as you read through it regardless of your views. Listen to Somerville's points. Which ones are strong? Which ones are weak? Is there anything you need to know more about before you can make an informed decision about where you stand?

The analysis and questions that follow the Somerville piece and accompanying sidebars are provided by the lead author of this textbook (not the author of the article) to foster an effective examination of the materials.

Model Essay II: The Case Against Euthanasia*

by Margaret Somerville

There is a trend in western democracies these days of increasing activism to legalize euthanasia and physician-assisted suicide.

Here in Canada we have seen a private member's bill (C-562) introduced in [June 2008, and another, Bill C-384, identical to C-562, in May 2009] by Bloc Québécois MP Francine Lalonde, which would amend the Criminal Code to allow a physician to "aid a person to die with dignity." So understanding the arguments both for and against these interventions is of crucial importance. But that's not necessarily easy to accomplish, if my own experience holds true more generally.

I teach a course, "Ethics, Law, Science and Society," to upper-year and graduate law students at McGill and, at the end of last semester, the topic was euthanasia.

I've researched euthanasia, physician-assisted suicide, the ethics and law of palliative care and pain relief treatment, decision-making at the end of life, and related topics, for nearly three decades and published a 433-page book, *Death Talk: The Case Against Euthanasia and Physician-Assisted Suicide*.

Yet, I came away from the class feeling that I had completely failed to communicate to most of my students what the problems with euthanasia were—that I was hitting a steel wall. This was not due to any ill-will on their part; rather, they seemed not to see euthanasia as raising major problems—at least any beyond preventing its abuse—a reaction I found very worrying.

The one student who tried to express a contrary view, although normally very articulate, ended up by saying, "Well, it's what I believe and I guess my background has something to do with that."

So, I e-mailed my students explaining I felt "that I had not done a good job in presenting the euthanasia debate . . . [and] decided to see if I could work out why not by writing about it." I attached an early draft of this article and asked for comments; I received several very thoughtful replies.

My concern went beyond failing to convince my students there was, at the least, a strong case to be made against euthanasia. It included the fear that their response was likely to be true also for the wider society.

The difficulty of communicating the case against euthanasia and the ease of communicating the case for it, is a serious danger, especially if, as seems likely, we are headed into another debate about whether we should legalize euthanasia in Canada. So why is the case against euthanasia so hard to establish?

When personal and societal values were consistent, widely shared and based on shared religion, the case against euthanasia was simple: God commanded "Thou shalt not kill."

---

*Margaret Somerville, "The Case Against Euthanasia," *The Ottawa Citizen* (27 June 2008). Reprinted by permission of the author.

Angus Reid Public Opinion: Most Canadians Generally Agree with Euthanasia[†]

Most people in Canada support the legalization of euthanasia, according to a poll by Angus Reid Public Opinion. Sixty-seven per cent of respondents share this point of view, down four points since August.

Yesterday, legislators in the Canadian province of Quebec began hearings on euthanasia. Members of the standing committee on health and social services are expected to hear from about 30 people on the subject, and will later use the findings to launch a public consultation on euthanasia in the province.

Dr. Yves Lamontagne, president of the Quebec College of Physicians, offered his views on legalizing euthanasia, saying, "That the person has a choice, I respect that. But what we do not want is the physician becoming the executor of someone else's choice."

Quebec lawmakers are not in a position to draft rules and regulations on euthanasia. Any legislation on the matter must be approved at the federal level.

The Netherlands, Belgium, Luxembourg, Switzerland, Albania and Thailand allow for some form of euthanasia, as well as the states of Oregon and Washington in the United States.

Polling Data

Generally speaking, do you support or oppose legalizing euthanasia in Canada?

	Feb. 2010	Aug. 2009
Support	67%	71%
Oppose	23%	21%
Not sure	10%	8%

[†]"Most Canadians Generally Agree with Euthanasia," *Angus Reid Monitor* (6 February 2010), http://www.angus-reid.com/polls/38352/most_canadians_generally_agree_with_euthanasia. Reprinted with permission.

Methodology: Online interviews with 1,003 Canada adults, conducted on Feb. 2 and Feb. 3, 2010. Margin of error is 3.1 per cent.

The Canadian Parliament over-whelmingly defeated today [April 21, 2010] the private members bill seeking to legalize euthanasia and assisted suicide.

The House of Commons rejected Bill C-384, proposed by Member of Parliament Francine Lalonde (La Pointe-de-l'Île, BQ), by a vote of 228 to 59, with two additional members noting immediately afterwards that they mistakenly voted for the bill when they had intended to vote against it.

In a point of order after the vote, Conservative Member and Parliamentary Secretary for Health, Stephen Fletcher, wished it to be recorded that he abstained from the vote. Fletcher urged that all possible support be given to patients in need, but also stressed that he believed "the individual is ultimately responsible" for his fate. Fletcher is a quadriplegic MP confined to a special motorized wheel chair.

Lalonde's campaign to legalize euthanasia and assisted suicide began in 2005 when she first intro-duced her bill into the House of Commons. Her first two attempts failed when her private members bills were shut down by the 2006 and 2008 federal elections.

This round, her third attempt, began when she introduced Bill C-384 into the House of Commons on May 13th, 2009. The bill received first reading with an hour of debate in October, but Lalonde has delayed a vote by trading back second reading three times. It was also delayed by the government's decision to prorogue Parliament late last year, which meant the bill had to undergo first reading again. The first hour of debate was March 16th and the second hour took place yesterday.

Alex Schadenberg, executive director of the Euthanasia Prevention Coalition, told LifeSiteNews that the defeat of Lalonde's bill means that Canada should now move on to finding better ways of offering true health care to Canada's vulnerable patients.

In a secular society based on intense individualism, the case for euthanasia is simple: Individuals have the right to choose the manner, time and place of their death.

In contrast, in such societies the case against euthanasia is complex. It requires arguing that harm to the community trumps individual rights or preferences.

One student explained that she thought I was giving far too much weight to concerns about how legalizing euthanasia would harm the community and our shared values, especially that of respect for life, and too little to individuals' rights to autonomy and self-determination, and to euthanasia as a way to relieve people's suffering.

She emphasized that individuals' rights have been given priority in contemporary society, and they should also prevail in relation to death. Moreover, legalizing euthanasia was consistent with other changes in society, such as respect for women and access to abortion, she said.

To respond to such arguments, we need to be able to embed euthanasia in a moral context without resorting to religion—that is, formulate a response that adequately communicates the case against euthanasia from a secular perspective.

That requires, first, countering the belief that individual rights should always prevail—a task I failed at in class.

We must show, as well, there are solid secular arguments against euthanasia, for example, that legalizing euthanasia would harm the very important shared societal value of respect for life, and change the basic norm that we must not kill one another. It would also harm the two main institutions—law and medicine—that paradoxically are more important in a secular society than in a religious one for upholding the value of respect for life. And, it would harm people's trust in medicine and make them fearful of seeking treatment.

So why now? There is nothing new about people becoming terminally ill, suffering, wanting to die, and our being able to kill them. So why now, after we have prohibited euthanasia for millennia, are we debating whether to legalize it?

Although the euthanasia debate usually centres on a dying, identified person, who wants euthanasia, I believe the answer to what has precipitated the debate lies in understanding a complex interaction of certain unprecedented changes in society. Identifying these factors can also help us to see what is needed to make the case against euthanasia clearer and stronger.

Dying alone or unloved seems to be a universal human fear. In democratic western societies many people have a sense of loss of family and community: relationships between intimates have been converted into relationships between strangers. That loss has had a major impact on the circumstances in which we die. Death has been professionalized, technologized, depersonalized and dehumanized. Facing those realities makes euthanasia seem an attractive option and easier to introduce. Euthanasia can be seen as a response to "intense pre-mortem loneliness."

We engage in "death talk" in order to accommodate the inevitable reality of death into the living of our lives. That talk helps us to live reasonably comfortably with that knowledge, which we must do if we are still to be able to find meaning in life.

"Death talk" (and other morals and values talk) used to take place in religion and its churches, synagogues, mosques and temples and was confined to an hour or so a week. Today, it has spilled out into our daily lives, especially through media. The euthanasia debate is one example of such "death talk."

Moreover, "secular cathedrals"—our parliaments and courts—have replaced our religious ones. That has resulted in the legalization of societal ethical and moral debates, including in relation to death. It is not surprising, therefore, that the euthanasia debate centres on its legalization.

Mass media and the mediatization of societal debates, including euthanasia, also have major impact. Media focus on individual cases: People, such as Sue Rodriguez—an ALS sufferer who took her fight to die to the Supreme Court of Canada—pleading for euthanasia, make dramatic, personally and emotionally gripping television.

The arguments against euthanasia, based on the harm that it would do to individuals and society in both the present and the future, are very much more difficult to present visually.

Moreover, the vast exposure to death that we are subjected to in both current-affairs and entertainment programs might have overwhelmed our sensitivity to the awesomeness of death and, likewise, of inflicting it.

But one of my students responded, "If anything, I think many of our reactions come not from an overexposure to death, but from an aversion to suffering, and an unwillingness or hesitancy to prolong pain."

Finding convincing responses to the relief-of-suffering argument used to justify euthanasia is difficult in secular societies. In the past, we used religion to give value and meaning to suffering. But, now, suffering is often seen as the greatest evil and of no value, which leads to euthanasia being seen as an appropriate response.

Some answers to the "suffering argument" might include that

- even apart from religious belief, it's wrong to kill another human;
- euthanasia would necessarily cause loss of respect for human life;
- it would open up an inevitable slippery slope and set a precedent that would present serious dangers to future generations. Just as our actions could destroy their physical environment, likewise, we could destroy their moral environment. Both environments must be held on trust for them;
- recognizing death as an acceptable way to relieve suffering could influence people contemplating suicide.

Might the strongest argument against euthanasia, however, relate not to death but to life? That is, the argument that normalizing it would destroy a sense of the unfathomable mystery of life and seriously damage our human spirit, especially our capacity to find meaning in life.

"Now that the bill's defeated, this gives us the chance in Canada to continue to improve care for the vulnerable, to examine issues around elder abuse and how to prevent elder abuse in Canada, to look at issues around suicide prevention, and . . . to ask Canadians to make sure that people with disabilities are offered true dignity and equality in Canada," he said. "This is the way Canada needs to be going, not to legalize euthanasia and assisted suicide."*

He did stress, however, that "there's always a need for vigilance on the euthanasia issue." "There will be another bill in the next Parliament," he predicted. "That's just what's going on. Our goal is to get ready for the next battle, which will be in a couple years after the next election."

*Patrick B. Craine, "Euthanasia Bill Defeated in Canada 228–59" (21 April 2010), http://www.lifesitenews.com/news/archive/ldn/2010/apr/10042118

Analysis

It's easy to see what Somerville's position is from the title of the article itself. Some people may not want to read any further, especially if they already know they have an opposing point of view. It takes courage on the part of a reader to challenge his or her own views, especially on such a controversial subject.

The fact that the article is written by an academic and not a doctor might cause a person to think, "What does she know? She doesn't deal with dying patients every day in the way a doctor might." But what if you were faced with two opposing points of view by two doctors, one who favoured euthanasia, and one who opposed it? Would it then seem more important to consider the arguments and not just the professions of the sources? It's a good idea to consider both the effectiveness of the argument and the source before drawing conclusions. The fact is that many doctors admit to not having enough in-depth ethical training, which is why they often rely on academics for ethical advice.

Although Somerville makes it clear from the beginning that she is opposed to euthanasia, she does not take the time to define it. It is important to note that the difference between the terms *active euthanasia* and *passive euthanasia* often determines the position a person takes on the issue in general. Active euthanasia is most often illegal, although acceptance of the practice is growing in some countries. It is still considered criminal homicide in Canada since it is the taking of life by a method of intervention, such as a lethal dose of a medication, in order, for example, to shorten someone's suffering due to a terminal illness. Passive euthanasia, on the other hand, is the suspension of medical intervention, which often allows the patient to die on his or her own, such as taking a patient off life support or making the decision to no longer feed a patient by means of a feeding tube.

The article announcing the Angus-Reid Poll results (see sidebar, page 341) lists the Netherlands among the countries that "allow for some form of euthanasia." Rachel Nowak, however, reported the following facts in "The Dutch Way of Death" in the book *Moral Philosophy for Modern Life* by Anthony Falikowski—facts that might cause people to question such medical practices in the Netherlands. For instance, at least a third of the 5000 or so Dutch patients who each year receive lethal doses of drugs from their doctors do not give their unequivocal consent. About 400 of those patients never even raise the issue of euthanasia with their doctors. Moreover, of those who willingly opt for euthanasia, only about 5 per cent do so because of unbearable pain. A much higher proportion, about a third, do so partly for fear of becoming dependent on others. Even if someone asks to be euthanized, how does one know if the person is of sound mind and able to make a free rational decision of such magnitude? The short answer is, one doesn't.

Questions for Discussion and Further Analysis

1. Did you support euthanasia before discovering these materials in *Canadian Writer's Workplace*?

2. Should people be allowed to die for the reason that they do not want to be a burden on society?

3. If euthanasia were legalized, would some doctors stop treating difficult cases and simply offer euthanasia as a viable "medical" option?

4. If respondents to the Angus-Reid Poll (see sidebar, page 341) were informed of the difference between active and passive euthanasia, and if they were aware of which one is legal in Canada and which one is not, might they have responded differently to the questions?

5. Why might it have been in Angus-Reid's interest to keep the questions vague?

6. Is active euthanasia in violation of the Hippocratic Oath (the fundamental oath all doctors take in which they swear they will never knowingly harm a patient)? Discuss.

7. Why do you think Parliament defeated the bill to legalize euthanasia in spite of the results of the Angus-Reid Poll?

8. Is Margaret Somerville likely to get as much respect for her opinion on the issue of euthanasia as a doctor who deals with dying patients every day? How much does the authority of a source influence the opinion of the reader? When should the effectiveness of the argument have more influence?

9. What is the main reason, according to Somerville, that so many people seem to support euthanasia nowadays? What might the relationship be between growing support for euthanasia and, for example, people's attitudes toward pain and suffering?

10. Examine the last paragraph in Somerville's essay. She says that "normalizing (euthanasia) would destroy a sense of the unfathomable mystery of life and seriously damage our human spirit, especially our capacity to find meaning in life." What does Somerville mean by "the mystery of life?" And why is our ability "to find meaning in life" endangered? Why is "meaning in life" important at all? Is there a relationship between "meaning in life" and pain (or suffering)?

Assignment Argumentative Paragraph or Essay

Choose a topic (see the suggestions below), and write either an extended paragraph or an essay of at least five paragraphs. Argue for or against the topic of your choice. Use the following argumentative techniques, discussed earlier in this chapter, as a guide for your writing.

1. Write a strong thesis statement.
2. Provide examples for each of your reasons.
3. Use at least one authority to support your thesis.
4. Admit that others have a different point of view.
5. Indicate the results or your predictions in the conclusion.
6. Define certain terms that are central to your argument.

SUGGESTED TOPICS:

1. Capital punishment
2. Censorship of books or movies
3. Same-sex marriages
4. Gun control
5. Prayer in public schools
6. Single-parent adoption
7. Control of pornography

Many, many more topics for argumentative paragraphs or essays can be found in Unit IV, under the heading "Writing Ideas" at the end of the questions immediately following each major reading. Some of the questions under the heading "Questions for Discussion" (also after each major reading) might also be deemed suitable argumentative writing topics.

While developing your paragraph or essay, you may want to review Chapter 14: "The Four Stages of Writing for a Paragraph or an Essay," in particular the following sections:

"Brainstorming"

"Choosing the Topic and the Controlling Idea"

"Outlining"

"The Rough Draft"

"Revising and Editing the Rough Draft"

"Proofreading"

"Checklist for the Final Copy"

For help in connecting your sentences and paragraphs smoothly and clearly, you may wish to consult the list of transitional words and phrases, categorized by their function, found on the inside back cover of this book.

 Working Together: Identifying Good and Bad Arguments

Form small groups of four or five. Look at several recent newspapers and choose an editorial about a subject of interest to everyone in the group. Read it and comment on the argument in terms of what you now know regarding good and bad arguments. Answer the questions below. You may want to assign a different question to each person in the group.

1. Are there any common fallacies in the writer's argument? Explain.
2. Does the writer employ the argumentative techniques listed in this chapter? Explain.
3. What is the writer's overall claim?
4. Is the evidence used to support the claim generally good or bad? Discuss.

Unit IV Readings

Many schools subscribe to the philosophy that reading and writing are inseparable components in the process of improving one's writing skills. The readings that follow include works of nonfiction, fiction, and poetry, all Canadian, and all written by seasoned writers. Many of these do not represent specific essay models as described earlier in this book, but as is often the case, a single essay written by a professional writer can contain a mixture of different modes and styles. These readings have been selected in the hope that they will inspire meaningful discussion and well-written student responses.

◆ ◆ ◆

Friend/Unfriend*

Peter Howell

Movie Critic for *The Toronto Star* Peter Howell was one of the first journalists in North America to establish a regular Internet column. His column was called "CyberPop," and it debuted in 1995. Before his role as a movie critic, Howell served as a pop music critic, also for *The Star*. In the following movie review of *The Social Network* (about the origin of Facebook) published in *The Toronto Star* on October 1, 2010, Howell discusses the irony of the notion that the website is all about friendship.

1   With so many interactions now reduced to status updates on Facebook or 140-character Twitter bursts, it may seem as though we have this messy human-to-human thing all figured out.

2   Except we don't. People in the 21st century are every bit as crude, brutal and self-serving as when cavemen were knocking each other over the head with clubs. The digital realm simply provides a new mask for base behaviour, even if that mask looks to be the smiley face of a friend.

Jessie Eisenberg (left) as Facebook founder Mark Zuckerberg and Justin Timberlake (right) as Sean Parker, co-inventer of Napster

*Peter Howell, "Social Network Possibly the Best Movie of Year," *The Toronto Star* (29 September 2010). © 2010 Torstar Syndication Services.

3   This is the eternal **verity** that director David Fincher and screenwriter Aaron Sorkin pursue so well and with such delicious **irony** in *The Social Network*, a drama about the creation of Facebook. It may be the year's best movie.

4   It stars Jesse Eisenberg as Mark Zuckerberg, the geeky Harvard student who in 2004 started Facebook in his dorm room, launching a social media revolution and making himself America's youngest billionaire. Zuckerberg's zeal also sparked two lawsuits from former friends and business associates, who claimed the baby-faced **boffin** used, conned and defrauded them.

5   You might well wonder why Hollywood big leaguers like Fincher (*Zodiac*, *Fight Club*) and Sorkin (TV's *The West Wing*) would be so fascinated in a **nebbishy** figure like Zuckerberg, the Peter Pan of the Internet.

6   Why not instead do a film about real characters like Steve Jobs, Bill Gates or the two guys who invented Google? Fincher and Sorkin realized, and the rest of us do upon seeing *The Social Network*, that Zuckerberg's transformation from carefree hacker into one of the world's most **avaricious** businessmen was a story of Biblical dimensions.

7   Here's a man who, as the story goes, gained 500 million Facebook "friends" and yet who sold out the one true pal who believed in him and supported him. Zuckerberg may be the epitome of modern falseness: an artificial friend for a virtual world.

8   He's essayed to perfection by Eisenberg, an actor of grace and skill who previously seemed fated to playing only well-meaning nerds in films like *Adventureland* and *Zombieland*. His Zuckerberg is a figure of **enigmatic malevolence**, deeper than he seems but also much darker, as drained of blood as a vampire's victim.

9   Eisenberg also brings a nice touch of black humour to the proceedings, expertly delivering the many zingers from Sorkin's wicked pen and personifying the subterranean rumble that is Trent Reznor's and Atticus Ross' soundtrack.

10   The film also boasts a peak performance by Justin Timberlake, whose real-life alter ego as a pop star more than equips him for the evil clown role of Sean Parker, the co-inventor of Napster. He arrives midway through the film seeming as little more than a party animal and fellow golden geek, but he's the catalyst for the film's most shocking act of betrayal.

11   The reputed treachery victim was Brazilian-born Eduardo Saverin, Zuckerberg's closest friend at Harvard and the co-founder of Facebook. A successful businessman even as a student, he staked Zuckerberg for an $18,000 line of credit and was Facebook's original business manager, before events took a twisted turn.

12   Played with understated brilliance by Andrew Garfield, who is about to become the new webslinger in a rebooted *Spider-Man* franchise, Saverin is everything that Zuckerberg isn't: a gentleman, a popular figure on campus and a ladies' man.

13   These qualities also describe twin rowing champs Cameron and Tyler Winklevoss (both played by the nimble Armie Hammer), who also allege Zuckerbergian **subterfuge**. They claim to have thought of Facebook first, along with their friend Divya Narendra (Max Minghella), and they conscripted Zuckerberg to help them create it.

14   Instead Zuckerberg reportedly went off on his own, misleading his friends and associates about his true intentions until it was too late and lawyers entered the picture. *The Social Network* **adroitly** slides between emotional confrontations and bone-dry courtroom procedures, at all times retaining its focus on the fascinating cipher that is Zuckerberg.

15   Sorkin's script is based on *The Accidental Billionaires*, a book by Ben Mezrich that ploughs much of the same turf; Zuckerberg naturally disputes both accounts.

16   The movie begins with a fictional, although emotionally truthful, barroom encounter between Zuckerberg and his frustrated girlfriend Erica (Rooney Mara), who first utters the "a—hole" condemnation that will be amplified and pondered throughout the film. She's the strongest female in a picture dominated by males and the most visible sign of humanity in the gladiator's pit of the Facebook wars.

17   Thirty-four years ago this fall, the buzz was about another media movie, one with just *Network* for a title. It featured a TV anchorman named Howard Beale, played by Peter Finch, who was "mad as hell" about the falseness of society and the loss of human values represented by a plugged-in populace.

18   Little did Beale realize that no matter how much he wailed, the future world illustrated by *The Social Network* would continue to make fake attachments while inventing diabolical new connections.

Glossary

verity: truth

irony: the expression of meaning using language that exresses the opposite

boffin: (*British slang*) expert in a technical field (e.g., computers)

nebbishy: (*Yiddish slang*) ineffectual; timid

avaricious: extremely greedy

enigmatic malevolence: unexplained will to do evil

subterfuge: lying to avoid blame

adroitly: cleverly

Comprehension Questions

1. The film is primarily based on true events, according to the author, but he points out that it begins with a fictional encounter between Zuckerberg

and his girlfriend Erica. What does the author argue is the purpose of this scene?

2. Specifically identify the former friends and business associates who alleged that Zuckerberg had conned and defrauded them. What were their relationships to Facebook?

3. What does Peter Howell say is ironic about the idea of "friendship" when it comes to Facebook, as explored in the movie?

4. What is the reason the author thinks the Hollywood creators of *The Social Network* were more interested in creating a movie about a character like Zuckerberg than Apple's Steve Jobs or Microsoft's Bill Gates?

Questions about Form

1. Paragraph 16 summarizes the first scene of the movie *The Social Network*. Why do you think the author waits this long to discuss the very first scene?

2. The last two paragraphs in the reading are about a movie with a similar title. Why does the author discuss this movie? And why do you think he ends the piece with this discussion?

Questions for Discussion

1. Howell states, "The digital realm simply provides a new mask for base behaviour, even if that mask looks to be the smiley face of a friend." What does this mean? Do you agree with the author? Why or why not?

2. Facebook has been criticized largely because of security issues. What do you think are the security concerns for anyone with a Facebook account?

3. What is your definition of "friendship"? Does Facebook's use of the word "friend" support your definition or not? Explain.

Writing Ideas

1. Write a paragraph or essay discussing the effects of social networks on the way students relate to each other.

2. People invite each other to become social network "friends." Write a paragraph or essay on the reasons why someone might refuse such an invitation, or choose not to be on social networks at all?

3. Write a paragraph or essay in which you outline the reasons in favour of using Facebook despite the growing criticism of it in some media.

♦ ♦ ♦

No Great Sacrifice*

David Suzuki with Faisal Moola

The world-famous scientist host of CBC's *The Nature of Things*, Dr. David Suzuki, was born in Vancouver in 1936. He's written more than 40 books, 15 of which explain nature to children. Dr. Suzuki is also known for his criticism of governments for their lack of action in protecting the environment. Dr. Faisal Moola is the program director of Terrestrial Conservation and Science at the David Suzuki Foundation, whose mission it is to protect the diversity of nature. Together, Suzuki and Moola write articles on the persecution of our planet; this piece first appeared in the weekly *Science Matters* column published in newspapers and magazines across Canada.

1   I recently read an article about a woman in Spokane, Washington, who doesn't like phosphate-free dishwashing detergents. Phosphate-containing detergents are banned in Spokane County because of their negative impact on the environment, so the woman drives 45 minutes to Idaho where phosphate detergents are still sold. The article also notes that the woman has a five-year-old daughter. I'm astounded.

2   People often argue that protecting the environment will require too many sacrifices. Is this what they mean? That they would risk their children's futures because they can't be bothered to rinse their dishes before putting them into the dishwasher?

3   Phosphates are added to cleaning products because they help cut grease and get rid of food particles on dishes. But they also have enormous negative impacts on rivers, streams, and lakes. By fertilizing the waters, phosphates can cause massive algae blooms that starve the water of oxygen and choke **aquatic ecosystems**, killing fish, amphibians, insects, and plants. Phosphates have been banned from laundry detergents in most places for a number of years now, but consumers have resisted moves to ban them from dishwashing detergents.

4   The article notes that the Spokane River is one of the most endangered in the U.S. and that phosphate pollution from the county's main wastewater treatment plant has been reduced by 14 per cent since the dishwasher-detergent law was passed in July. But apparently this woman doesn't care if the river is devoid of life when her daughter grows up—as long as her dishes are spot-free!

5   The woman claims to be "environmentally conscious." I guess she means that she cares about the environment only when it is convenient for her. This is a good example of the kind of challenges faced by people who really do care about the environment and the future. Part of the problem may be that some people can't really relate their own behaviour to the consequences. Think of parents with asthmatic children who continue to smoke in the house or drive

*David Suzuki with Faisal Moola, "It's No Great Sacrifice to Protect the Environment," May 4, 2009, http://www .davidsuzuki.org/blogs/science-matters/2009/05/its-no-great-sacrifice-to-protect-the-environment/. Reprinted with permission.

SUVs. Others are simply not willing to make even the smallest sacrifices when it comes to protecting the environment. Yet, for the most part, no real sacrifices are required.

6   At the David Suzuki Foundation, we hear almost daily from people who thought it would be difficult to get up a bit earlier and expend a bit more energy to cycle to work instead of drive, for example. But they soon found that the benefits of cycling—from getting in better shape to enjoying the outside world—far outweighed any of the negative consequences.

7   It's more about changing the way we think than about giving something up. If we take a broader, more long-range view of things, we see that we usually gain more than we lose when we make changes in our lives to protect our surroundings.

8   We see the same kind of resistance to things like a **carbon tax**. Never mind that market forces play a far greater role in fuel-price increases than a carbon tax ever will! People see that they might have to pay a few pennies more at the gas pump or for home-heating bills and they immediately cry that they will have to give up their cars and freeze in their homes during winter.

9   But we see immediate and long-term benefits from putting a price on carbon. People find ways to conserve energy, companies invest in technologies that use renewable energy, and we end up with less pollution and fewer **emissions** that contribute to global warming.

10   We live in consumer societies, especially here in North America. We've become convinced that we have to keep replacing our goods with newer and "better," often over-packaged, products. We dispose of things even before they have broken down. And the world suffers for it. People sometimes accuse me and other environmentalists of wanting to send us back to living in caves and **scrounging** for roots and berries. Nothing could be further from the truth.

11   We can lead lives that are even more fulfilling on a cleaner planet where more people have access to clean air, water, and food. All it takes is some imagination and some forward thinking. If we really cared about our world and about our children and grandchildren, we would be willing to make some sacrifices to make the world a better, healthier place. But in most cases, the sacrifices are as **illusory** as some of the benefits we think we are deriving from our **rampant consumerism**.

Glossary

aquatic: growing or living in or near water

ecosystems: communities of interacting organisms and the the physical environment in which they live

carbon tax: an environmental tax on the carbon content of fuel

emissions: discharges of exhaust, radiation, fuel, etc.

scrounging: searching to find something at no cost

illusory: seemingly existing but, in fact, not existing

rampant: spreading everywhere uncontrollably

consumerism: the preoccupation with, or promotion of, the buying of goods

Comprehension Questions

1. What are phosphates? What is the authors' argument with regard to phosphates in cleaning products?

2. According to the authors, what is the reason that people who claim to be environmentally conscious are still responsible for the decline of the environment? Explain.

3. Why, according to the authors, should people make sacrifices in order to preserve the environment? How do the authors compare the sacrifices people need to make to the benefits from consumerism they wish to derive?

4. Do Suzuki and Moola believe we should go "back to living in caves and scrounging for roots and berries" if we want to save the planet? Explain.

Questions about Form

1. Why do you think Suzuki and Moola started their article with an American example? Would it have been more effective if they used a Canadian one instead? Why or why not?

2. Even though the piece is written by two people, Suzuki with Moola, why is it that the word "I" is used in the first paragraph? Is this appropriate? Why or why not?

Questions for Discussion

1. After reading this article, do you think you will change your thinking toward conserving the environment? Why or why not?

2. What does it mean to be environmentally-conscious? How do Suzuki and Moola promote environmental consciousness in their article? Is their argument effective? Why or why not?

3. Is there a connection between environmental consciousness and environmental conservation? Explain.

4. Suzuki ends the first paragraph about the mother from Spokane, Washington, with the statement "I'm astounded!" Why does Suzuki seem so outraged? Is he justified in expressing such a strong sentiment? Why or why not? Do most parents seem to share this sentiment? Explain.

Writing Ideas

1. Write a paragraph or an essay on the ways in which you and your friends could change your lives on an everyday basis that would contribute to the preservation of the environment.

2. Write a paragraph or an essay outlining what challenges people face when they want to promote environmental protection.

◆ ◆ ◆

Satisfied Straggler*

Ashleigh VanHouten

Born in Halifax, Nova Scotia, VanHouten currently lives in Manhattan, New York. Working as a communications professional and freelance writer, she has published articles in magazines and newspapers in Canada, Bermuda, and the United States. One such magazine is the New York-based fashion and lifestyle magazine *New York Moves*. In the following piece published in Canada's national newspaper, *The Globe and Mail*, VanHouten tells her personal story of struggle and triumph as a marathon runner in her home province of Nova Scotia.

1   I am a bit of a **perfectionist**. I guess that's like you can be a bit pregnant, right? I want to do everything better than everyone else, and so I seek out the things in which I excel. Like most people, I've **cultivated** passions in areas where I am naturally **adept**, and the things I'm good at are the things I like to do. This, as most of us know, is a comfortable place to be.

2   My stepdad was the one who changed this for me. I was idly talking a few years ago about how I needed a New Year's resolution, and a good one this time— no swearing off chocolate or vowing to watch less TV. He looked at me with his usual mild expression and said: "Why don't we run a marathon?" I laughed,

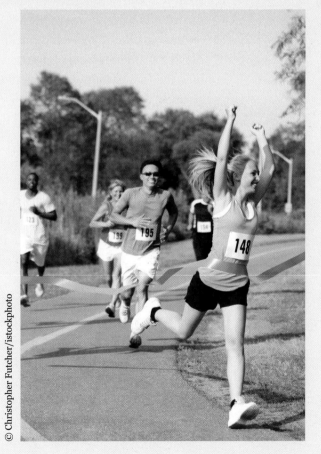

© Christopher Futcher/istockphoto

*Reprinted by permission of Ashleigh VanHouten.

then asked if maybe we shouldn't start off a bit slower, like a half-marathon. "If you're going to train for something like that, you might as well go the whole way," he said.

3   I liked his **rationale**, so I agreed. We had about nine months until October, prime marathon season, and I figured I could either get into running shape or come up with a good excuse not to by then. I started out running for 30 minutes at a time on a treadmill in my basement. No TV, no distractions, just me and an MP3 player. I was always in decent shape and liked to stay active, but I certainly wasn't a long-distance runner. I had never run more than five kilometres in my life, and slowly at that—I'm not built for speed or endurance.

4   Running was always a struggle, but the more I ran, the better I looked and felt, and the easier it became. By the time the weather warmed up, my stepdad and I were going for jogs outside, willing away the hours and miles in beautiful Shubie Park in Dartmouth, N.S. . . . Before I knew it, we were waking up at 8 A.M. on Sundays to run for four hours. We would park our car and start running down the Halifax waterfront, cross the Macdonald Bridge, go through the park and eventually end up back home.

5   These runs became something we looked forward to rather than dreaded. We became regulars on the trails and felt like real runners. Although I never got really good, and it never became really easy, every once in a while we had a great run, and nothing else compares with it. The best times were always as dusk turned into dark—it was cooler, less busy and the shadows seemed to soften the ground somehow. We would run around the lakes and amid the trees, and my breathing and legs would hit a **stride**, and I would glide. The whole runner's high they always talk about? It exists. It's like you retreat completely inside yourself, and your brain feels focused and sharp.

6   Still, running is not my thing. I don't mean I'm average. I mean I have to gasp and hobble and fight for every mile. Sure, I had a couple of great training runs, and I got to the point where I could eat eight pancakes for dinner because my metabolism was through the roof. But was I a good runner? Not even close. I finished my first marathon in 5 hours, 38 minutes, coming in 361st out of 402 finishers. The average finish time for a **novice** runner is between 4 and a half and 5 hours. I know people who could have walked a marathon faster than I ran it.

7   But even though I qualified as a **straggler** in the race, at 19, I was the youngest person to finish that year. People came to congratulate me on my hard work—people who had finished hours earlier. I felt grateful for their support and proud of myself, even though on paper I didn't do anything fantastic. I knew how hard I had worked to cross the finish line, and that was enough. The thing about this goal was that for the first time, I had to work hard to be average (let's be honest, worse than average). I had to be happy with just finishing something, instead of finishing first. I had to sleep at night knowing that I would never win a marathon; I'd never even be competitive at it.

8   It was the hardest thing I'd ever done, and despite having seen 60-year-olds breeze past me on mile 20 and not being able to walk properly for a week, I was

pleased as punch with my finish and my dedication. I felt that if I could run a marathon I could do pretty much anything, and it made me more willing to try things that seemed fun or exciting, not just things I knew I would be good at. Now 25, I've started over in several cities, and whenever I think something might be more trouble than it's worth, I remember the first race and how hard it was, how many times I wanted to stop and how good it felt when I finished.

9   My stepdad knew it all along, and it's a lesson many of us never learn: You have to do things that are truly hard if you want to learn and grow and get better. I would recommend everyone try it once in their lives: Do something you aren't good at. Do something to challenge yourself, and be a little bit uncomfortable for once. It's good for you, I promise.

Glossary

perfectionist: someone who engages in an uncompromising pursuit of faultlessness

cultivated: tried to acquire or develop

adept: highly gifted or skilled

rationale: the fundamental reason or logical basis of something

stride: a state of having reached a settled or steady rate of progress or level of performance

novice: beginner; an inexperienced person

straggler: someone who trails behind others in a race or march, etc.

Comprehension Questions

1. What does VanHouten mean by "a comfortable place to be"?

2. Explain how the idea of the marathon came about and why the author decided to run it.

3. How does the author define a "runner's high"?

4. Although the author finished the marathon at 361st, why was she, nevertheless, proud of herself?

Questions about Form

1. VanHouten clearly writes this piece in the first person. What purpose does this serve?

2. In your opinion, how effective is the title of the piece? Explain.

3. The author reminds the reader of her stepdad in the last paragraph. Why do you think she does this?

Questions for Discussion

1. Explain why the author changes her attitude, from "being a perfectionist" to being satisfied with just finishing something?

2. The author says, "You have to do things that are truly hard if you want to learn and grow and get better." What did she mean by this statement?

Writing Ideas

1. The author was not the best marathon runner. But she found the experience to be transformational (life changing). Write a paragraph or an essay about an activity that you were not good at but participated in anyway that changed your life.

2. Many people find it difficult to follow through with their New Year's resolutions. Write a paragraph or essay suggesting three things that people could do to boost their chances for success in this area.

◆ ◆ ◆

The $2-Million Comma*

Grant Robertson

Since Lynne Truss published the British bestseller *Eats, Shoots and Leaves* in 2003 about the importance of punctuation, some people have become more respectful of the proper mechanics of writing. But few people would believe that a mistake involving a comma could cost more than $2 million. Media reporter for *The Globe and Mail* Grant Robertson wrote the following piece, which was published on August 7, 2006.

1   It could be the most costly piece of punctuation in Canada.

2   A grammatical blunder may force Rogers Communications Inc. to pay an extra $2.13-million to use utility poles in the Maritimes after the placement of a comma in a contract permitted the deal's cancellation.

3   The controversial comma sent lawyers and telecommunications regulators scrambling for their English textbooks in a bitter 18-month dispute that serves as an expensive reminder of the importance of punctuation.

4   Rogers thought it had a five-year deal with Aliant Inc. to string Rogers' cable lines across thousands of utility poles in the Maritimes for an annual fee of $9.60 per pole. But early last year, Rogers was informed that the contract was being cancelled and the rates were going up. Impossible, Rogers thought, since its contract was **iron-clad** until the spring of 2007 and could potentially be renewed for another five years.

5   Armed with the rules of grammar and punctuation, Aliant disagreed. The construction of a single sentence in the 14-page contract allowed the entire deal to be scrapped with only one-year's notice, the company argued.

6   Language buffs take note—Page 7 of the contract states: The agreement "shall continue in force for a period of five years from the date it is made, and thereafter for successive five year terms, unless and until terminated by one year prior notice in writing by either party."

7   Rogers' intent in 2002 was to lock into a long-term deal of at least five years. But when regulators with the Canadian Radio-television and Telecommunications Commission (CRTC) **parsed** the wording, they reached another conclusion.

8   The validity of the contract and the millions of dollars at stake all came down to one point—the second comma in the sentence.

9   Had it not been there, the right to cancel wouldn't have applied to the first five years of the contract and Rogers would be protected from the higher rates it now faces.

10   "Based on the rules of punctuation," the comma in question "allows for the termination of the [contract] at any time, without cause, upon one-year's written notice," the regulator said.

11   Rogers was **dumbfounded**. The company said it never would have signed a contract to use roughly 91,000 utility poles that could be cancelled on such short notice. Its lawyers tried in vain to argue the intent of the deal **trumped** the significance of the comma. "This is clearly not what the parties intended," Rogers said in a letter to the CRTC.

12   But the CRTC disagreed. And the consequences are significant.

13   The contract would have shielded Rogers from rate increases that will see its costs jump as high as $28.05 per pole. Instead, the company will likely end up paying about $2.13-million more than expected, based on rough calculations.

14   Despite the victory, Aliant won't reap the bulk of the proceeds. The poles are mostly owned by Fredericton-based utility NB Power, which contracted out the administration of the business to Aliant at the time the contract was signed.

15   Neither Rogers nor Aliant could be reached for comment on the ruling. In one of several letters to the CRTC, Aliant called the matter "a basic rule of punctuation," taking a swipe at Rogers' assertion that the comma could be ignored.

16   "This is a classic case of where the placement of a comma has great importance." Aliant said.

The Comma Conflict

17   **The disputed sentence:** "This agreement shall be effective from the date it is made and shall continue in force for a period of five (5) years from the date it is made, and thereafter for successive five (5) year terms, unless and until terminated by one year prior notice in writing by either party."

18   **How Rogers reads it:** The contract is good for five years and is automatically renewed for successive five-year terms. The deal cannot be terminated within the first five-year term.

19   **How Aliant reads it:** The contract can be cancelled at any time provided one-year notice is given.

20   **What the experts say:** The presence of the second comma means the conditions of cancelling the contract apply to both the initial five-year term and subsequent five-year terms.

On August 21, 2007, *The National Post* reported that the CRTC had overturned its decision on appeal. In the appeal process, Rogers had argued that the French version of the contract contained commas that were in their proper positions. It was made clear in this version that Bell Aliant could not terminate the contract early.

Glossary

iron-clad: difficult to change or break

parsed: separated a sentence into its parts, explaining the part of speech, function, and relationship of one part to another

dumbfounded: made speechless; astonished

trumped: surpassed; outdid

Comprehension Questions

1. In one to two sentences and in your own words, what is the controversy in this article?

2. What is the actual sentence in which the comma in question is found?

3. Why won't Aliant Inc. reap all the benefits of the blunder?

Questions about Form

1. Why do you think this piece was included in this textbook?

2. Why are the paragraphs in this piece generally short?

3. Do you think there is a gap in the development of the argument that prevents a full understanding of it? Discuss.

Questions for Discussion

1. Why is it, specifically, that the second comma makes the difference that the CRTC said it does?

2. Do you think the original ruling by the CRTC was fair? Why or why not? Do you think the ruling in response to the appeal was fair? Why or why not?

3. What can companies learn from this situation with respect to contracts?

Writing Ideas

1. Write a paragraph or essay on the reasons it is important to have a better-than-average knowledge of grammar and punctuation.

2. Write a paragraph or essay discussing a situation in which you or someone you know either won or lost something as a result of bad communication. Feel free to refer, in your paper, to the article by Robertson in further support of your thesis.

◆ ◆ ◆

Canada, My Canada*

Tomson Highway

Celebrated novelist and award-winning playwright Tomson Highway is a Cree Native from Brochet, in northern Manitoba. He holds three honorary degrees and is a member of the Order of Canada. This piece by Highway, first published in 2000,

*Copyright © 2000 by Tomson Highway. First published by *Imperial Oil Review*, Spring 2000, Volume 84, No. 436. Reprinted by permission of Tomson Highway.

is quite flattering of our nation. How would you expect a member of an aboriginal group to view Canada today? When you finish reading the following piece by Highway, compare or contrast your answer to this question with your observation of Highway's article.

1 Three summers back, a friend and I were being hurtled by bus through the heart of Australia, the desert flashing pink and red before our disbelieving eyes. It seemed never to end, this desert, so flat, so dry. The landscape was very unlike ours—scrub growth with some exotic cacti, no lakes, no river, just sand and rock forever. Beautiful, haunting even—*what the surface of the moon must look like*, I thought as I sat in the dusk in that almost empty bus.

2 I turned to look out the front of the bus and was suddenly taken completely by surprise. Screaming out at me in great black lettering were the words CANADA NO. 1 COUNTRY IN THE WORLD. My eyes lit up, my heart gave a heave, and I felt a **pang** of homesickness so **acute** I actually almost hurt. It was all I could do to keep myself from leaping out of my seat and grabbing the newspaper from its owner.

3 As I learned within minutes (I did indeed beg to borrow the paper), this pronouncement was based on information collected by the United Nations from studies comparing standards of living for 174 nations of the world. Some people may have doubted the finding, but I didn't, not for an instant.

4 Where else in the world can you travel by bus, automobile or train (and the odd ferry) for ten, 12 or 14 days straight and see a landscape that changes so spectacularly: the Newfoundland coast with its white foam and roar; the red sand beaches of Prince Edward Island; the graceful curves and slopes of Cape Breton's Cabot Trail; the rolling dairy land of south-shore Quebec; the maple-bordered lakes of Ontario, the haunting north shore of Lake Superior; the wheat fields of Manitoba and Saskatchewan; the ranch land of Alberta; the mountain ranges and lush rain forests of the West Coast. The list could go on for pages and still cover only the southern section of the country, a sliver of land compared with the North, the immensity of which is almost unimaginable.

5 For six years in a row now the United Nations has designated Canada the No. 1 country in which to live.

© momentimages/Jupiter Images

6   We are so fortunate. We are water wealthy and forest rich. Minerals, fertile land, wild animals, plant life, the rhythm of four distinct, undeniable seasons—we have it all.

7   Of course, Canada has its problems. We'd like to lower the crime rate, but ours is a relatively safe country. We struggle with our health-care system, trying to find a balance between **universality** and affordability, but no person in this country is denied medical care for lack of money. Yes, we have our concerns, but in the global scheme of things we are well off.

8   Think of our history. For the greater part, the pain and violence, tragedy, horror and evil that have scarred forever the history of too many countries are largely absent from our past. There's no denying we've had our trials, but they pale by comparison with events that have shaped many other nations.

9   Our cities are gems. Take Toronto, where I have chosen to live. My adopted city never fails to thrill me with its racial, linguistic and cultural diversity. On any ordinary day on the city's streets and subway, in stores and restaurants, I can hear the muted ebb and flow of 20 different tongues. I can feast on food from different continents, from Greek souvlaki to Thai mango salad, from Italian **prosciutto** to Jamaican jerk chicken, from Indian lamb curry to Chinese lobster.

10   And do all these people get along? Well, they all enjoy a life of relative harmony, co-operation and peace. They certainly aren't terrorizing, torturing and massacring one another. They're not igniting pubs, cars and schools with explosives that blind, cripple and maim. And they're not killing children with machetes, cleavers and axes. Dislike—**rancour**, even—may exist here and there, but not, I believe, hatred of the blistering intensity we see elsewhere.

11   Is Canada a successful experiment in racial harmony and peaceful **coexistence**? Yes, I would say so—and proudly.

12   When I, as an aboriginal citizen of this country, find myself thinking about all the people we've received into this beautiful homeland of mine, when I think of the millions to whom we've given safe haven, following agony, terror, hunger and great sadness in their own home countries, well, my little Cree heart just puffs up with pride. And I walk the streets of Canada, the streets of my home, feeling tall as a maple.

Glossary

pang: sudden and brief pain, physical or emotional

acute: severe and sharp

universality: the quality of not being restricted to a privileged few

prosciutto: spicy Italian ham served in thin slices

rancour: continuing and bitter hatred

coexistence: living side by side

Comprehension Questions

1. What in the newspaper sparked Highway's interest? Upon what were the findings in the newspaper story based?

2. What does Highway say is the most important thing about Canada that makes it great?

3. What problems in Canada does Highway admit to, and how does he defend Canada in spite of them?

Questions about Form

1. In paragraph 1, Highway uses italics for the words "what the surface of the moon must look like." Why do you think he uses italics here? What is his tone? What effect is he looking for? Does he achieve this effect?

2. If this is a piece about Canada, why does Highway start out by talking about Australia?

Questions for Discussion

1. In paragraph 8, Highway refers to the history of Canada as being quite tame when compared to that of other countries. Compare or contrast this comment to the message Rita Joe is sending in her poem "I Lost My Talk," on pages 373–375. What do you make of the fact that both of these writers are Native Canadian?

2. Do you agree with Highway when he says Canada is a "successful experiment in racial harmony and peaceful coexistence"? Why or why not?

3. At any time throughout this piece, do you expect Highway to mention the fact that Canada has not always been kind to aboriginal peoples, or that the governments of the past have even committed genocide against his people? Why do you think he doesn't? Would it help to be told this piece appeared before in a journal called *The Imperial Oil Review*? Why or why not?

4. In paragraphs 9 and 10, Highway refers to the multicultural mix of Toronto in particular and of Canada in general. Compare or contrast his attitude to that of Neil Bissoondath in "Selling Illusions," which begins on page 392.

5. Paragraph 10 uses some rather harsh language. What countries do you think Highway might be referring to by the examples he uses?

6. Look up poems by the American poet Walt Whitman. Is there a poem whose title is similar to Highway's title of this piece? Account for the similarity.

Writing Ideas

1. In a paragraph or essay, compare or contrast Canada with any other one country in the world with which you are very familiar.

2. Is Canada one of the best places in the world to live? In a paragraph or essay, explain why or why not.

✦ ✦ ✦

My Body Is My Own Business*

Naheed Mustafa

Wearing the hijab, says Naheed Mustafa, is integral to her Muslim faith. And in this piece, first published in *The Globe and Mail* in 1993, she argues that wearing the hijab, contrary to popular belief, liberates her. Mustafa works as an editor in Toronto.

1   I often wonder whether people see me as a radical, fundamentalist Muslim terrorist packing an AK-47 assault rifle inside my jean jacket. Or maybe they see me as the poster girl for oppressed womanhood everywhere. I'm not sure which it is.

2   I get the whole gamut of strange looks, stares and covert glances. You see, I wear the *hijab*, a scarf that covers my head, neck and throat. I do this because I am a Muslim woman who believes her body is her own private concern.

3   Young Muslim women are reclaiming the *hijab*, reinterpreting it in light of its original purpose—to give back to women ultimate control of their own bodies.

4   The **Qur'an** teaches us that men and women are equal, that individuals should not be judged according to gender, beauty, wealth or privilege. The only thing that makes one person better than another is her or his character.

5   Nonetheless, people have a difficult time relating to me. After all, I'm young, Canadian born and raised, university-educated—why would I do this to myself, they ask.

6   Strangers speak to me in loud, slow English and often appear to be playing **charades**. They politely inquire how I like living in Canada and whether or not the cold bothers me. If I'm in the right mood, it can be very amusing.

7   But why would I, a woman with all the advantages of a North American upbringing, suddenly, at 21, want to cover myself so that with the *hijab* and the other clothes I choose to wear, only my face and hands show?

8   Because it gives me freedom.

9   Women are taught from early childhood that their worth is proportional to their attractiveness. We feel compelled to pursue **abstract** notions of beauty, half realizing that such a pursuit is futile

*Naheed Mustafa, "My Body is My Own Business." Reprinted by permission of Naheed Mustafa.

10   When women reject this form of oppression, they face ridicule and contempt. Whether it's women who refuse to wear makeup or to shave their legs or to expose their bodies, society, both men and women, have trouble dealing with them.

11   In the Western world, the *hijab* has come to symbolize either forced silence or radical, **unconscionable** militancy. Actually, it's neither. It is simply a woman's assertion that judgment of her physical person is to play no role whatsoever in social interaction.

12   Wearing the *hijab* has given me freedom from constant attention to my physical self. Because my appearance is not subjected to public scrutiny, my beauty, or perhaps lack of it, has been removed from the realm of what can legitimately be discussed.

13   No one knows whether my hair looks as if I just stepped out of a salon, whether or not I can pinch an inch, or even if I have unsightly stretch marks. And because no one knows, no one cares.

14   Feeling that one has to meet the impossible male standards of beauty is tiring and often humiliating. I should know, I spent my entire teenage years trying to do it. I was a borderline bulimic and spent a lot of money I didn't have on potions and lotions in hopes of becoming the next Cindy Crawford.

15   The definition of beauty is ever-changing; **waifish** is good, waifish is bad, athletic is good—sorry, athletic is bad. Narrow hips? Great. Narrow hips? Too bad.

16   Women are not going to achieve equality with the right to bare their breasts in public, as some people would like to have you believe. That would only make us party to our own **objectification**. True equality will be had only when women don't need to display themselves to get attention and won't need to defend their decision to keep their bodies to themselves.

Glossary

Qur'an: Holy book of Muslims.

charades: game in which somebody acts out a word or phrase and other players guess its meaning

abstract: not concrete; conceptual; hard to put into words

unconscionable: extremely unethical; morally wrong

waifish: skinny

objectification: act of treating like an object or "piece of meat"

Comprehension Questions

1. According to Mustafa, what does the Qur'an teach about equality?

2. How does the issue of attractiveness make it difficult to achieve equality between the sexes?

3. According to the author, what in the Western world has the hijab come to represent? What does it represent in reality, instead, according to Mustafa?

Questions about Form

1. Why does Mustafa begin her piece by referring to herself?

2. Most of Mustafa's paragraphs in this piece are extremely short, unlike those of a typical academic essay. Does the fact that this piece was written for *The Globe and Mail* (1993) offer a clue as to why it was written this way? Explain.

Questions for Discussion

1. If a woman is not a practising Muslim, but sympathizes with Mustafa's reasons for wearing a hijab, what could she do instead of wearing a hijab?

2. In the last paragraph, Mustafa says baring their breasts will only make women "party to our own objectification." What does this mean? Do you agree? Why or why not?

3. Many people would argue that sexual attraction is an intrinsic part of falling in love with someone. If this is true, how does one fall in love if another doesn't reveal his or her (especially her) sexuality by wearing revealing clothes?

4. Mustafa refers to the "tiring" and "humiliating" male standards of beauty in paragraph 14. What are women's standards of attractiveness in men? Are they just as tiring and humiliating? Discuss.

5. Look at the very last line of the article. Mustafa ponders a time when true equality between the sexes will be had. Has that time arrived? Cite evidence from life in Canada that supports your answer.

Writing Ideas

1. Write a paragraph or essay of cause and effect focusing on the causes of inequality between the sexes in North American culture. When you have finished your rough draft, decide whether you've assigned more blame to women or to men, or if you have placed it equally on both.

2. Is attention the same as respect? If a woman gets attention because of the way she is dressed, does that mean she's going to win respect, too? Write a paragraph or essay answering the above question and supporting your answer. Feel free to refer to Mustafa's piece for further support of your topic sentence or thesis statement regardless of your point of view.

♦ ♦ ♦

Leaving the Cave*

John Artibello

Plato's classic work *The Republic* is an account of a conversation in which the philosopher Socrates and a few of his friends are trying to lay out a plan for a perfect society. It seems we cannot understand what makes society work well without understanding what it means to be human and, especially, what makes

*John Artibello, "Leaving the Cave." Reprinted by permission of John Artibello.

people happy. According to Socrates, who is the main speaker in the book, human happiness depends on becoming enlightened, as illustrated by the famous myth called "The Allegory of the Cave." John Artibello, a philosophy professor and self-declared seeker, interprets this myth in the article that follows, written in 2003.

1   So, what's the secret? What makes us happy? Is it money, success, self-confidence, relationships, God? As long as we are human, we face the questions: How can I get it all together? How can I find what I need?

2   As we all know, the answers to these questions do not come easily. In fact, some people claim that if you are really taking these questions seriously, you are probably thinking too much. As the words of the song say, "We're here for a good time, not a long time . . ."

3   None of us can be blamed for suspecting that the really big questions are probably unanswerable. So, if that is the case, why not take the road of least resistance? Relax, chill. If anybody asks the tough questions (say on a first date, or in an English class), just smile and say, "Ignorance is **bliss**!"

4   The philosopher Socrates would never have agreed with the idea that ignorance is bliss. In fact, he would have insisted that ignorance or what he called "unenlightenment" is actually the cause of personal unhappiness, depression, social breakdown and even war. As Socrates puts it, *The unexamined life is not worth living*." That is, if you are not thinking about your life, it might be impossible to *really live*.

John Artibello *Leaving the Cave*

5   Fancy that! A person who claims *you are what you think*! But "thinking" for Socrates is not like going into the library to do your homework. It is more like a process of waking up, and it begins when you start to question all of the conventional, generally accepted ideas and values of the society in which we live.

6   People often say that human growth is a painful process. According to Socrates, the source of the pain is our tendency to prefer "comfortable **illusions**" to the hard realities and challenges that we all must face to become fully human. The central theme of the "**Allegory** of the Cave" is disillusion, and there is a great reward for the pain of moving away from the half-truths of common sense. As you move closer and closer to the real world, you draw closer and closer to your real Self.

7   In Socrates' story of the Cave, we are introduced to a series of powerful but troubling images. According to the philosopher, people who are unenlightened have very little self-knowledge and they are like people who live their whole lives in a darkened cave without ever discovering what is outside the cave. In fact, they don't even know that there is an "outside." Their dark cave and the shadows on the wall of the cave are their "reality." Their lives are, therefore, lives of complete illusion. This is the beginning of Socrates' ancient parable:

8   Here is a myth to illustrate the extent to which our nature may be enlightened or unenlightened. Imagine the condition of people living in a sort of cavernous chamber, with an entrance open to the light and a long passage all down the cave. Here they have been since childhood, chained by the leg and also by the neck, so that they cannot move and can only see what is in front of them because the chains will not let them turn their heads. At some distance higher up is the light of a fire burning behind them; between the prisoners and the fire is a track with a parapet built along it, like the screen at a puppet show, which hides the performers while they show their puppets over the top.

9   Now, behind this parapet, imagine people carrying artificial objects, including figures of men and animals in wood or stone or other materials, which project above the parapet. Naturally, some of these persons will be talking, others silent.

10   . . . Of course, if the prisoners were talking, their words would refer only to those passing shadows which they saw and not to the real objects which are the causes of the shadows.

11   Although this imagery is over two thousand years old, it resonates when we think, for example, of people "chained" to their televisions, watching an endless parade of chaotic, but amusing images. Of course, the deeper question is, what does it all mean?

12   At this stage of the story, Socrates is describing the lives of people who try to find happiness in material things. If you are a "material girl" or a "material boy," chances are you live pretty much on the surface of life ("the shadows"). Happiness consists of looking good, having a nice car, nice clothes, and a life based on the images and truths of popular magazines and television "reality" shows. This kind of life is for Socrates equivalent to a kind of slavery. Life is at bottom unsatisfying because it is based on a lie: the message of the advertisers,

which is "Don't accept yourself as you are; there is something wrong with you. You need more stuff to be happy. You need more illusion to be real."

13   Of course, the person who begins to see through the superficial messages of materialism is beginning a process of enlightenment, of coming out of the cave. This is what happens in the next part of the story.

14   Now consider what would happen if their release from the chains and the healing of their ignorance should come about in this way. Suppose one of the prisoners was set free and forced suddenly to stand up, turn his head, and walk toward the light and the objects before the fire.

15   . . . What do you think he would say if someone told him that what he had formerly seen was meaningless illusion, but now being somewhat closer to reality and turned towards more real objects, he was getting a truer view? . . . Would he not be perplexed and believe the objects now shown him to be not so real as what he formerly saw?

16   . . . And if he were to look at the fire itself, would not his eyes ache, so that he would try to escape and turn back to the more comfortable shadows? . . .

17   . . . And suppose someone were to drag him forcibly up the steep and rugged ascent and not let him go until he hauled him up into the sunlight, would he not suffer pain and vexation at such treatment, and, when he had come into

Courtesy of Jock MacRae

the light find his eyes so full of radiance that he could not see a single one of the things that he was now told were real?

18   . . . Now imagine what would happen if he went down again to take his former seat in the cave. Coming suddenly out of the sunlight, his eyes would be filled with darkness. He might be required once more to deliver his opinion on those shadows, in competition with the prisoners who had never been released, while his eyesight was still dim and unsteady; and it might take some time to get used to the darkness. They would laugh at him and say that he had gone up only to come back with his sight ruined.

19   The story shows the transition from looking at the "shadows" on the wall to looking at the "fire" to being hauled up into the "sunlight." These are very important symbols. The shadows represent the material world, the fire represents knowledge, and the sunlight represents goodness or morality. The ascent to the things in the "upper world," where the sunlight dwells, represents the upward journey of the mind to the world of spiritual meaning behind the physical things we see everyday. This is a metaphor for the learning process. Socrates further notes that, in the world of knowledge, the last thing to be perceived and only with great difficulty is the essential nature of Goodness (the sun). This means that our knowledge of reality is ultimately moral: when we look past the outward and obvious aspect of things, we will learn to distinguish the good from what "appears" to be good. All of our material things are thought to be essential to the good life, but after studying things more closely, we may need to change our minds.

20   So getting out of the cave involves a kind of learning that transforms us. Once we develop a deep knowledge of the world, we develop a deeper connection to it, and this is ultimately what makes us fully alive. The contrast between watching "shadows on the wall" and seeing the sun and the objects of nature (outside the cave) is meant to awaken our interest in connecting to the *real world* and to saying no to the crass commercialized world of our everyday experience. When our knowledge has called into question how we live, we are living what Socrates calls the "examined life," a life really worth living. An examined life and a passionate engagement with ideas are much more interesting than a life of working like a slave to pay for a superficial materialism and the accompanying depression that seems to be **epidemic** these days in North America.

21   Perhaps "living in the cave" is **symbolic** of a modern situation like this: think of a person riding a subway on the way to school. She does not usually read on the subway because books are pretty boring. She is attracted by an ad for a new pair of jeans. She sees herself in the shapely model wearing the clothes. The come-on is "if you don't have these jeans, you won't be happy." If you buy into the message of the ad, you are buying into a whole philosophy of life, which is that "life is about *having*, rather than *being*." And, "if you want to be beautiful, *buy, buy, buy*."

22   Of course, at this stage of your life, you don't know much about what is behind the images and the material objects you enjoy so much. You don't care, for example, that the people who make your jeans and sweaters are working for three or four dollars a day somewhere in the Third World. Your ideas of morality are pretty basic as well. Really bad people are terrorists and suicide bombers, but they live mostly in other countries. Living in the shadows is a metaphor for our tendency to immerse ourselves in superficial things as a way to avoid deeper and potentially threatening ideas and issues.

23   Some people, however, can't help asking tough questions. Why, for example, as our society becomes technologically more powerful, do individuals feel more and more powerless? Are all of the goods and gadgets that we work so hard to get making our lives more meaningful? To answer these questions, we need to get past "the shadows"; we need to break the chains and turn towards the light. This process of enlightenment, of moving into the light, is impossible apart from the search for truth, which in terms of the story, results in our understanding not just *how* things work (technology), but *why* things and people behave as they do (philosophy).

24   Consider a modern example of what the cave might represent: someone who is "in the cave" is like a person who owns a car without knowing what effect it has on the environment. If asked what makes the car work, this person says, "Just turn on the ignition, put her in gear, and off you go." If the car breaks down, the owner has no idea how to fix it. But someone who decides to take a course in auto mechanics or engineering is "breaking the chains" of **ignorance** and attempting to look at the "real objects" involved in the working of the car: things like the engine, the transmission, the spark plugs, alternator, and the burning of the fossil fuel without which there would be no cars, no highways, no drive-in movies and probably no wars in the Middle East! When your study has taken you "outside the cave," or to "the real world," you see the political, environmental and moral aspects of cars. A person who "sees the sun" (outside the cave) can put it all together. The person sees the bigger picture. The car that you love to drive is connected to a larger, more complex reality involving the politics of oil and the destruction of the environment, and as we all know, that can't be good!

25   In the story of the cave, Socrates is saying that humans are confronted with a fundamental option: reality or illusion. He suggests that the journey to your true self begins by going deeper and deeper into the world to find its true beauty and meaning. The philosophers will tell you that learning is the key, especially when you *explore* what really interests you. When you love to learn, it is because you are finding yourself in your study. The journey is endless, as are the rewards. As T.S. Eliot says,

26   We shall not cease from exploration
      And the end of all our exploring
      Will be to arrive where we started
      And know the place for the first time.

Glossary

bliss: great joy or happiness

illusions: mistaken perceptions

allegory: story in which people, things, and happenings have a hidden or symbolic meaning

epidemic: prevalent and spreading among many individuals in a community at the same time (said especially of a human contagious disease)

symbolic: of something that stands for or represents another thing

ignorance: lack of knowledge or education; unawareness (of)

Comprehension Questions

1. What do most people, according to Artibello, think happiness consists of?

2. What takes place in the cave (in Plato's myth) that relates to the material world?

3. What does Artibello cite as a modern example of what the cave symbolizes?

4. What is the difference, according to Artibello, between an ignorant person who owns a car, and an enlightened person who has a deeper knowledge of cars? How does morality relate to this contrast?

Questions about Form

1. What effect or effects do the illustrations that accompany this article have on you?

2. Some of the "Allegory of the Cave" is taken directly from a translation of Plato's *Republic*. Would it have made any difference if Artibello had simply paraphrased these parts?

3. The "Socratic approach" is one of asking deep, thought-provoking questions. In paragraph 23, for example, Artibello asks two questions that he does not proceed to answer directly. Do you think there is a reason for this? If so, what?

Questions for Discussion

1. Artibello is interpreting Plato to mean that, to be fully alive, we need to prefer the world of ideas to the world of "material things" such as cars, clothes, etc. Is it possible that the "material girl or boy" cannot be whole or happy? Discuss the role of ideas in the good life.

2. In the conclusion of the article, the concept of a "fundamental" or life option is introduced. Discuss the role of fundamental options and turning points in life. In what sense do these options involve a movement from illusion to reality?

3. Plato is known as an idealist philosopher. That is, he was critical of the physical world because it passes away while the deeper things such as the ideals of truth, virtue, and beauty are eternal. What images in the story of the cave reinforce this position? Do you agree with this idea? Explain.

4. If you were to lead an examined life, what would you need to do? Would you have to make changes to your lifestyle or in what you are studying? Discuss.

Writing Ideas

1. Write a paragraph or essay on what you think it means for people in general to lead examined lives. How would their lives have to change?

2. Now that you've read and perhaps discussed the article, write a paragraph or essay of definition explaining what "leaving the cave" means to you. What are some of your own examples of what "leaving the cave" represents?

Further Reading and Research

1. In a book entitled *Plato not Prozac*! Lou Marinoff explores the relationship between what we think and how we feel. He is exploring an ancient idea that being passionate about thinking, especially about deep and interesting issues (such as the meaning of life), is what keeps us sane.

2. Great philosophical ideas are often conveyed in stories, poems, and myths. Read T. S. Eliot's "The Waste Land," and compare the imagery of the poem to the imagery of the cave.

3. Iris Murdoch is one of the world's great interpreters of Plato. Her novel *The Philosopher's Pupil* is a fictional account of a philosopher's journey to "the dark side."

4. One source of beautiful poems about the journey to the light is Mary Oliver's *New and Selected Poems* (Beacon Press, 1992). See especially "The Journey" and "Wild Geese."

◆ ◆ ◆

I Lost My Talk*

Rita Joe

The writings of Rita Joe, a Micmac Native, are about aboriginal people. She was born on a reservation in Wycocomagh on Cape Breton Island in Nova Scotia. At the age of 12, after both her parents had died, she placed herself in an Indian residential school in Shubenacadie, Nova Scotia. An acclaimed poet, Rita Joe published several collections, including *Lnu and Indians We're Called* (1991). She became a member of the Order of Canada in 1990, and was active in Native issues before her death in 2007.

1   I lost my talk
       The talk you took away.
       When I was a little girl
       At **Shubenacadie** school.

*Rita Joe, "I Lost My Talk." From SONG OF ESKASONI. Reprinted with permission.

2   You snatched it away:
    I speak like you
    I think like you
    I create like you
    The scrambled **ballad**, about my word.

3   Two ways I talk
    Both ways I say,
    Your way is more powerful.

4   So gently I offer my hand and ask,
    Let me find my talk
    So I can teach you about me.

Glossary

Shubenacadie: a town in Nova Scotia

ballad: a popular song, generally of a personal or political nature

Comprehension Questions

1. What do you think Rita Joe is saying in the first stanza of her poem?

2. What does "scrambled ballad" mean? Might it have more than one meaning?

3. What does the author mean by the word *word* at the end of the second stanza (verse)?

Questions about Form

1. What is the difference in tone between the first line of the poem and the very last line? How might this contribute to an interpretation of the poem's theme?

2. What do you think might be the reason for the repetition in the second stanza?

3. How would you describe the type of language being used here? Does it contribute to an overall deliberate effect? Why or why not?

Questions for Discussion

1. What do you know of Canadian history that relates to this poem? What might have been the reasons the school authorities did what they did?

2. Does the knowledge that Rita Joe placed herself in the school at Shubenacadie affect your interpretation of her poem? Why or why not?

Writing Ideas

1. Do some research on what Canadian school authorities did to assimilate Native Canadians, and take a position either for or against this action in a paragraph or essay.

2. In a cause and effect paragraph or essay, discuss the repercussions of one's voice being denied. You may want to talk more specifically of a child whose voice is not taken seriously, or of women whose voice is silenced in certain cultures, or of North American Blacks who have been marginalized and/or discriminated against ever since the days of slavery, and so on.

3. Besides the obvious difference between this work by Rita Joe and the piece by Tomson Highway that begins on page 360, which is that they are two different genres, are there any other differences? In a paragraph or essay, compare or contrast the two works.

◆ ◆ ◆

Rats*

W. Frank Epling

Once named Outstanding Teacher of the Year in Psychology at the University of Alberta, Frank Epling taught behaviour analysis before he died in 1998 at the age of 54. He was known as a creative researcher whose ideas continue to permeate the scientific community. In this piece, first published in 1989, Epling takes a unique approach to the controversial subject of animal rights. Some essays do not include a clear thesis statement in the first paragraph, and this essay is an example of that type. Try to figure out Epling's thesis as you read. Although it can be argued his essay is dated, it can also be said that Epling's message is as applicable today as it was when he wrote it.

1   I am an animal researcher, and I work with rats. Now, for most people, the rat is an animal that does not **elicit** great sympathy. In fact, most people would hit a rat with a shovel if it dared to run across their basement floor. Of course, in Alberta, rats do not run across basement floors because the province is "rat free" and proud of it. This is not, however, exactly correct because some rats manage to sneak in from British Columbia and Saskatchewan, and I have some in my laboratory.

*W. Frank Epling, "Rats." Reprinted with permission of the author's estate.

© Memo Angeles/Shutterstock

Nonetheless, the Alberta Rat Patrol does an excellent job, and only very sneaky rats survive the border crossing. Since most of these are new arrivals and don't have a home, the Alberta winter usually gets what the Rat Patrol misses.

2　　　There are good rats and there are bad rats. I know this sounds absurd but stick with me and I will explain. Some time ago I was preparing a twelve-page written document that was an **ethics** justification for some proposed research with rats. I had to make certain that my rats got the very best food, shelter, and medical care. I also had to convince the local committees that I had the overall welfare of my rats foremost in my mind. This proposal took several days to write. The reason for all this is that I have good rats. Good rats live in laboratory cages.

3　　　Following the second day of work on my ethics proposal, I went home, opened a beer, put up my feet and flipped on the tube. *Fifth Estate* or *W5* was on, I don't remember which. Also, I can't recall the first news item, but I certainly can the second—it was about the Alberta Rat Patrol. On this show, the dedicated people of the Rat Patrol were keeping the cities, fields, and houses of Alberta rat free. This was not a fun time for those creatures who tried to invade the province. The documentary focused on the Alberta/Saskatchewan border. There are lots of rats in Saskatchewan. Well, let me tell you, the members of the Rat Patrol were shooting, hitting, and poisoning rats; these were bad rats. Bad rats do not live in laboratory cages.

4　　　There are other ways to be a bad rat. Rats that escape from their cages are not protected by ethics proposals. As soon as their feet hit the laboratory floor they become pests and are subject to traps, poison, and so on. Shotguns are not used because of damage to walls, noise, and the possibility of shooting a student or researcher. Believe me though, these rats are not held in high esteem. This is particularly true in Alberta because they could get out of the building and infest our rat-free province.

5   Another way that rats lose their good status is to be food. There are animals, like some very large snakes, that will not eat unless their prey items are alive. In order to keep these animals, they must be fed. Food is not protected by ethics committees.

6   All of this makes me wonder why I am spending a significant amount of time writing ethics proposals for rats, rather than doing research with them. Don't misunderstand me. I happen to like rats and I do not advocate mistreating them. I am against the use of these animals for testing cosmetics and for repeating research where the findings are well established and rats are made to suffer. I am, however, convinced that research with rats (and other animals) can lead to findings that promote human welfare, and I am in favour of doing that research. In order to understand why I am spending a fair amount of time writing ethics proposals for my rat research, it is necessary to consider the animal rights movement.

7   Over the past fifteen years, this movement has steadily grown in number of members, and it has received increasing attention from the press. So-called "animal activists" belong to a variety of organizations and they range from moderate to extreme in their views. I think it is fair to say, though, that all animal activists think that cute furry animals are nice animals—even when they are pests or food. Rats have two strikes against them, bad press and a long hairless tail. Also, the black plague did not help their cause. This prejudice for some animals and against others is curious. Not very many people are concerned about the live lobsters found at supermarkets. I think this is because the lobster is very tasty and looks vaguely like a large underwater insect. On the other hand, baby seals look cute, warm, cuddly, and helpless. Thus, the seal, but not the lobster gets sympathy. Returning to my point, the animal rights movement has created a public concern for the welfare of animals, and some of this has reached hysterical and absurd proportions.

8   A few of the more extreme views include stopping all medical research with animals, replacing animal subjects with humans, including animals in the United States Bill of Rights, recognizing **specism** as a prejudice similar to racism and so on. I don't know about you, but I can't imagine a rat, a lobster, or even a seal with the rights of free speech, assembly, and the pursuit of happiness. How would they know they had these rights? Also what happens when one animal, say a lion, **infringes** on a deer's right to life? All in all, these views seem a bit "wacky" to me, but they are taken seriously by some people.

9   One tactic of the more extreme animal activists has been overt violence and intimidation. Some individuals have joined paramilitary animal rights movements. This is an odd development since it is the only revolutionary movement I know of where none of the members are the creatures whose rights are being fought for. Nonetheless, these people are serious, and they have bombed the houses of animal researchers, released laboratory animals,

vandalized labs, threatened to inject meat products with poison, organized and promoted letter writing campaigns to stop legitimate research, and harassed reputable scientists with threatening letters and phone calls.

10   I don't know how many of my fellow citizens are members of, or in sympathy with, the animal rights movement, but I suspect not very many. This speculation is based on the number of steaks on display at my local grocery and the notable lack of concern for pit bull dogs in Edmonton. So, why all the fuss?

11   A few years ago, the *Edmonton Sun* called and wanted to interview me and several other animal researchers. We were encouraged to participate in this interview in order to "promote the benefits of animal research." Anyway, we had one of the best run and closely supervised facilities in Canada. The reporter and a photographer showed up and asked questions about my projects, photographed my rats, thanked me for giving them time, and left. I looked forward to local fame.

12   A week or so later, the *Sunday Sun* carried the article. I was not famous. They had so garbled my name that you could not tell whose research they were talking about. This was very fortunate (or perhaps intentional to prevent a civil suit). The first page of the Sunday supplement had a full-page picture of a monkey sitting in a restraining chair looking like it had just had a tooth pulled by a student dentist. None of the people interviewed by the Sun worked with monkeys and I recognized the picture. The photograph was a famous one that has appeared in antivivisectionist magazines and advertising campaigns for "save the animals." I don't know why the same picture is used over and over, but it is.

13   Articles like this portray animal researchers as modern day versions of **Dr. Mengele**. It would seem that we can't wait to torture animals in order to arrive at conclusions everybody knows already. We have not received "good press." I could present a case for doing animal research, but I would digress from the point I am trying to make. Writing ethics proposals that defend research with animals that are **arbitrarily** defined as good is bizarre.

14   As I have said, there are good and bad rats. At least in Alberta, it appears there are going to be bad rats for some time to come. Being a bad rat seems to depend on "the luck of the draw." Since bad rats are not considered worthy of ethics protection, I could use them in my research. There is, however, a problem. I could ask for bad rats, but they would automatically become good when they were placed in cages in my laboratory. To appreciate this, it is necessary to understand a few things about universities and public relations.

15   The people who run universities tend to place great value on "positive press": "negative press" is very much discouraged. This makes sense; the public supports universities, and if they don't like what is going on they may withdraw their support. Animal activists would like to stop all animal experiments, and they search for an opportunity to provide unfavorable press. Forcing scientists to justify the ethics of their animal research helps protect the university from this publicity. There are, however, unfortunate side effects. Large sums of money are spent on animal care staff who police laboratories. Time is wasted on writing ethics proposals, sitting on ethics committees, and waiting for ethics approval. This and more for an animal most citizens would stomp on if given the chance.

16   I am probably more concerned about the welfare of rats than most people. I have known many rats over the years and I have liked more than a few. I am in favor of kind treatment for rats and other animals that are used in scientific research. I do think, however, that a consideration of good and bad rats and lobsters and seals points to a confusion of ethics. So what can I do? Not much, write a commentary like this and then put in another two days writing another ethics proposal. Rats!

Glossary

elicit: draw out; evoke (an admission, response, etc.).

ethics: science of morals in human conduct.

specism: assumption of human superiority over animals.

infringes: trespasses; affects something so as to limit or restrict it.

Dr. Mengele: a ruthless Nazi doctor who performed experiments, mostly on Jewish inmates of death camps, during the Holocaust in World War II; many of these experiments resulted in the victims' sterility or death

arbitrarily: based on the unrestricted will of a person

Comprehension Questions

1. What does Epling mean when he says, "Good rats live in laboratory cages" at the end of paragraph 2?

2. How does Epling feel the press handled the story for which he was interviewed, and why?

Questions about Form

1. Why does Epling begin his article by identifying what he does for a living?

2. Although an "Alberta rat control program" does exist, there is no group of people in Alberta known officially as the "Rat Patrol." Why do you think Epling places such emphasis on this made-up label?

3. Why do you think Epling does not articulate a clear thesis in the first paragraph? Does the lack of a clear thesis weaken his essay? Discuss.

4. Why does Epling call his article "Rats"? Are there at least two meanings here?

Questions for Discussion

1. In paragraph 12, Epling says he doesn't know why the picture of the monkey keeps getting used over and over. Based on the rest of his article, what reasons might he give on further speculation?

2. What do you think, in your own words, is Epling's thesis? What is the sentence in the piece that comes closest to your answer? Do you agree with this thesis? Why or why not?

3. Read "No Great Sacrifice" by David Suzuki with Faisal Moola on pages 352–354. Is the notion of convenience common to both readings? Explain.

Writing Ideas

1. Do you favour the testing of rats for medical research purposes? Write a paragraph or essay supporting your stand. Refer to Epling's article in further support of your argument.

2. Does your attitude toward specism determine whether you favour animal research or not? Where does this attitude come from? Discuss your answers in a paragraph or essay.

◆ ◆ ◆

The Other Family*

Himani Bannerji

Himani Bannerji teaches in the Department of Sociology at York University in Toronto. She has an active teaching connection with India, especially West Bengal, through the School of Women's Studies, Jadavpur University, Kolkata. She has taught and published extensively in the areas of Marxist theory, anti-racist feminism, and nationalism. In the following story about a little girl and her mother, Bannerji gives us a glimpse into the home of an immigrant family caught between the desire to fit into a new community and the fear of losing its identity.

© Photos India/Photolibrary

*Himani Bannerji, "The Other Family." Reprinted by permission of Himani Bannerji.

1   When the little girl came home it was already getting dark. The winter twilight had transformed the sheer blue sky of the day into the colour of steel, on which were etched a few stars, the bare winter trees and the dark wedges of the housetops. A few lit windows cast a faint glow on the snow outside. The mother stood at her window and watched the little hooded figure walking toward the house. The child looked like a shadow, her blue coat blended into the shadows of the evening. This child, her own, how small and **insubstantial** she seemed, and how alone, walking home through a pavement covered with ice and snow! It felt unreal. So different was this childhood from her own, so far away from the sun, the trees and the peopled streets of her own country! What did I do, she thought, I took her away from her own people and her own language, and now here she comes walking alone, through an alien street in a country named Canada.

2   As she **contemplated** the solitary, moving figure, her own solitude rushed over her like a tide. She had drifted away from a world that she had lived in and understood, and now she stood here at the same distance from her home as from the homes which she glimpsed while walking past the sparkling clean windows of the sandblasted houses. And now the doorbell rang, and here was her daughter scraping the snow off her boots on the doormat.

3   Dinner time was a good time. A time of warmth, of putting hot, steaming food onto the table. A time to chat about the important things of the day, a time to show each other what they had acquired. Sometimes, however, her mother would be absentminded, worried perhaps about work, unsettled perhaps by letters that had arrived from home, scraping her feelings into a state of rawness. This was such an evening. She had served herself and her child, started a conversation about their two cats and fallen into a silence after a few minutes.

4   "You aren't listening to me, Mother."

5   The complaining voice got through to her, and she looked at the indignant face demanding attention from the other side of the table. She gathered herself together.

6   "So what did he do, when you gave him dried food?"

7   "Oh, I don't quite remember, I think he scratched the ground near his bowl and left."

8   The child laughed.

9   "That was smart of him! So why don't we buy tinned food for them?"

10   "Maybe we should," she said, and tried to change the topic.

11   "So what did you do in your school today?"

12   "Oh, we drew pictures like we do every day. We never study anything—not like you said you did in your school. We drew a family—our family. Want to see it?"

13   "Sure, and let's go to the living room, OK? This is messy." Scraping of chairs and the lighting of the lamps in the other room. They both made a rush for the most comfortable chair, both reached it at the same time and made a compromise.

14   "How about you sit in my lap? No? OK, sit next to me then and we will squeeze in somehow."

15   There was a remarkable resemblance between the two faces, except that the face of the child had a greater intensity, given by the wide open eyes. She was fine boned, and had black hair framing her face. Right now she was struggling with the contents of her satchel, apparently trying to feel her way to the paintings.

16   "Here it is," she said, producing a piece of paper. "Here's the family!"

17   The mother looked at the picture for a long time. She was very still. Her face had set into an expression of anger and sadness. She was trying very hard not to cry. She didn't want to frighten the child, and yet what she saw made her feel distant from her daughter, as though she was looking at her through the reverse end of a telescope. She couldn't speak at all. The little girl too sat very still, a little recoiled from the body of her mother, as though expecting a blow. Her hands were clenched into fists, but finally it was she who broke the silence.

18   "What happened?" she said. "Don't you like it?"

19   "Listen," said the mother, "this is not your family. I, you and your father are dark-skinned, dark-haired. I don't have a blond wig hidden in my closet, my eyes are black, not blue, and your father's beard is black, not red, and you, do you have a white skin, a button nose with freckles, blue eyes and blond hair tied into a ponytail? You said you drew our family. This is not it, is it?"

20   The child was now feeling distinctly cornered. At first she was startled and frightened by her mother's response, but now she was prepared to be defiant. She had the greatest authority behind her, and she now summoned it to her help.

21   "I drew it from a book," she said, "all our books have this same picture of the family. You can go and see it for yourself. And everyone else drew it too. You can ask our teacher tomorrow. She liked it, so there!"

22   The little girl was clutching at her last straw.

23   "But you? Where are you in this picture?" demanded her mother, by now thoroughly aroused. "Where are we? Is this the family you would like to have? Don't you want us anymore? You want to be a *mem-sahib*, a white girl?"

24   But even as she lashed out these questions, the mother regretted them. She could see that she made no sense to the child. She could feel the unfairness of it all. She was sorry that she was putting such a heavy burden on such young shoulders.

25   "First I bring her here," she thought, "and then I try to make her feel guilty for wanting to be the same as the others." But something had taken hold of her this evening. Panic at the thought of losing her child, despair and guilt galvanized her into speech she regretted, and she looked with anger at her only child, who it seemed wanted to be white, who had rejected her dark mother. Someday this child would be ashamed of her, she thought; someday she would move out into the world of those others. Someday they would be enemies. Confusing thoughts ran through her head like images on an uncontrollable television screen, in the chaos of which she heard her **ultimate** justification flung at her by her daughter—they wanted me to draw the family, didn't they? "They" wanted "her" to draw "the family." The way her daughter pronounced the words "they" or "the family" indicated that she knew what she was talking about. The simple pronoun "they" definitely stood for authority, for that uncontrollable yet organized

world immediately outside, of which the school was the ultimate expression. It surrounded their own private space. "They" had power, "they" could crush little people like her anytime "they" wanted to, and in "their" world that was the picture of the family. Whether her mother liked it or not, whether she looked like the little girl in it or not, made not one jot of difference. That was, yes, that was the right picture. As these thoughts passed through her mind, her anger ebbed away. Abandoning her fury and distance, the mother bowed her head at the image of this family and burst into sobs.

26   "What will happen to you?" she said. "What did I do to you?"

27   She cried a great deal and said many **incoherent** things. The little girl was patient, quietly absorbing her mother's change of mood. She had a thoughtful look on her face, and bit her nails from time to time. She did not protest any more, but nor did she cry. After a while her mother took her to bed and tucked her in, and sat in the kitchen with the fearful vision of her daughter always outside of the window of the blond family, never the centre of her own life, always rejecting herself, and her life transformed into a gigantic peep show. She wept very bitterly because she had caused this destruction, and because she had hated her child in her own fear of rejection, and because she had sowed guilt into her mind.

28   When her mother went to bed and closed the door, the child, who had been waiting for long, left the bed. She crossed the corridor on her tiptoes, past the row of shoes, the silent gathering of the overcoats and the mirror with the wavy surface, and went into the washroom. Behind the door was another mirror, of full length, and clear. Deliberately and slowly the child took off the top of her pajamas and surveyed herself with grave scrutiny. She saw the brownness of her skin, the wide, staring, dark eyes, the black hair now tousled from the pillows, the scar on her nose and the brownish pink of her mouth. She stood a while lost in this act of contemplation, until the sound of soft padded feet neared the door, and a whiskered face peeped in. She stooped and picked up the cat and walked back to her own room.

[. . .]

29   It was snowing again, and little elves with bright coloured coats and snow in their boots had reappeared in the classroom. When finally the coats were hung under pegs with names and boots neatly stowed away, the little girl approached her teacher. She had her painting from the day before in her hand.

30   "I have brought it back," she said.

31   "Why?" asked her teacher, "don't you like it any more?"

32   The little girl was looking around very intently.

33   "It's not finished yet," she said. "The books I looked at didn't have something. Can I finish it now?"

34   "Go ahead," said the teacher, moving on to get the colours from the cupboard.

35   The little girl was looking at the classroom. It was full of children of all colours, of all kinds of shapes of noses and of different colours of hair. She sat on the floor, placed the incomplete picture on a big piece of newspaper and started

to paint. She worked long at it—and with great concentration. Finally it was finished. She went back to her teacher.

36   "It's finished now," she said, "I drew the rest."

37   The teacher reached out for the picture and spread it neatly on a desk. There they were, the blond family arranged in a semicircle with a dip in the middle, but next to them, arranged alike, stood another group—a man, a woman, and a child, but they were dark-skinned, dark-haired, the woman wore clothes from her own country, and the little girl in the middle had a scar on her nose.

38   "Do you like it?"

39   "Who are they?" asked the teacher, though she should have known. But the little girl didn't mind answering this question one bit.

40   "It's the other family," she said.

Glossary

insubstantial: not large in size or amount; weak

contemplated: looked at or considered in a calm, reflective manner

ultimate: last, final

incoherent: unintelligible; not able to be understood

Comprehension Questions

1. Is there mutual respect between mother and daughter? Cite the evidence.

2. What was the immediate thing that upset the little girl's mother when she saw the first picture her daughter had drawn?

3. Of what is the mother afraid? Where is the evidence of this fear?

4. How did the little girl resolve the issue?

Questions about Form

1. Is this an essay or a story? Explain.

2. Although this piece is told in third-person narration, is the narrator more knowledgeable about a particular character? Explain.

3. Does the author make effective use of transitions in this piece? Give three examples of transitions.

4. What are the effects of the extensive use of dialogue?

Questions for Discussion

1. Because this piece is fictional, the author's thesis is not explicit. What do you think, in your own words, is the author's message? What evidence would you cite from the piece in support of your answer?

2. How do the mother's fears relate to the idea of young people dating people of other races and religions? How do problems in this area tend to get resolved?

Writing Ideas

1. How important are pictures and words when it comes to helping people develop strong self-esteem? Write a paragraph or essay supporting your answer, and refer, in your writing, to evidence from Bannerji's piece.

2. This piece is about the conflict between the desire to fit in and the fear of losing one's identity. Write a paragraph or essay in which you discuss a personal experience that relates to these themes, and explain how your own situation was resolved.

❖ ❖ ❖

Don Juan/Doña Juana*

Rosemary Sullivan

A professor of English at the University of Toronto, Rosemary Sullivan is also a novelist and writer of nonfiction. The following piece is taken from her book *Labyrinth of Desire*, published in 2001, which offers a collection of perspectives on different aspects of love and sex. The term *Don Juan* (from the mythological story of a man who is a lover of thousands of women) is often considered a good thing. Sullivan, however, reveals what lies beneath the term and in the depths of the psyche of the person "honoured" with the title. She also shows that the term should by no means be restricted to men.

1   In the age-old cliché, a man will fight over a woman as if she were the prize trophy. But a woman will compete against another woman for the prize in a ruthless, predatory way.

© archives/istockphoto

2   Anyone who has been involved in a triangular affair knows how this works. Neither our own motives nor our man's are examined. The other woman is the enemy. She must be defeated.

3   What kind of man precipitates such **acrimony**? Traditionally, the man who indulges in multiple lovers is a Don Juan **archetype**, a **narcissist**. And what characterizes a narcissist is that the only real relationship he is capable of is one with himself.

4   The novelist Leon Whiteson once remarked that most men who play this role do so to cover their fear of intimacy. "SIN for men," he explained, "is Safety In Numbers." Having many women is a guarantee against having to deal intimately with one individual woman. It's a perfect device for protecting the bottom line: *I need no one.* As soon as such a man allows himself to acknowledge need, he opens himself to betrayal. How can he trust that he will not be abandoned?

5   The bad luck for women is that we often find men who fit the Don Juan archetype to be so attractive. They fall impulsively into erotic relationships, and we women immediately get ourselves busy searching out the heart within these transparently sensitive men. We do not recognize that their whole strategy is to keep us unsettled: now you know him, now you don't. This kind of man can't deal with women candidly because to do so would compromise his power. And for us, the not-knowing, the continual shift in his affections, leaves us in a state of constant anxiety and self-doubt.

6   These affairs can only degenerate into very unpleasant **Tantalus** games. The dynamic is thoroughly destructive, a push/pull dance of misinterpretation. Nights of hysteria without sleep. Days plotting what to say. Then the accusatory barbs. A woman will find herself trivialized, undermined. She turns into the very thing she hates most: the **supplicating** female.

7   So much of obsessive love takes place in the head. We spend our time desperately trying to understand the other's perspective. It's as if we have failed a test we had no idea we were taking. We want to justify ourselves, to have our interpretation heard. We are left with lingering feelings of failure and guilt. We haven't the least clue what's going on.

8   I have been speaking as if there were no female equivalent to Don Juan, but of course there is a Doña Juana, though she hasn't been so named. She is variously called the *femme fatale*, the seductress, the siren, the vamp, *la Belle Dame Sans Merci*.

9   One of her most fascinating **incarnations** is as Scarlett O'Hara in the 1939 film *Gone With the Wind*. Scarlett is petulant, childish, totally limited in her feelings, and seemingly irresistible to men. She collects men as trophies for her beauty, using them for her own ends. She admits to having no real feeling for them and complains about the need to pretend she does. As a type, her power is incomprehensible to women. She is so transparent, can't men see through her?

10   But the quality of the seductress that is irresistible to men is her combination of vulnerability and willfulness. She has a passionate energy, an infectious appetite for life (Scarlett's favorite expletive is "great balls of fire"), but she trades on her helplessness. Probably men are flattered, but not fooled. They secretly admire her strength, which is, paradoxically, so unfeminine. One lover complains, with relish, that she cut her teeth on his heart.

11   Scarlett is ruthless, self-absorbed and manipulative. As the film makes clear, war brings out the best in her—her indomitable will to survive. She lies, cheats, and even steals her sister's fiancé to keep the family estate intact. At war's end, knowing there will be a building boom, she sets up her own lumber business and is as brutal as any man, replacing slave labor with that of convicts on starvation rations.

12   But while the Don Juan is often admired by other men for his swordsmanship (that old metaphor for sexual conquest), the vamp is vilified by other women for throwing herself after men, for making a spectacle of herself, and so forth. She becomes an outsider, and the only one to whom she might be vulnerable is an outsider like herself.

13   In *Gone With the Wind*, Rhett Butler is the outsider, and Scarlett's twin. He says they're made for each other—they're both selfish and ruthless, but, as he once remarks, at least they have the guts to look life in the face.

14   The vamp, like the Don Juan, is always the basis for a cautionary tale and both must get their comeuppance. By the end of the film, Scarlett discovers she really loves Rhett Butler, but it's too late. His cavalier dismissal of her final plea to stay is the stuff of legend. And he's a smart man not to give in. To do so would be foolish. He knows Scarlett's misfortune is to love only the one who resists her. After all, he's a Don Juan himself.

15   These days we are less prescriptive in our notions of sexual propriety, and so the seducers and seductresses are not nearly so coy in their behavior. And anyway, at some point most of us play at erotic games of seduction and many of us are even promiscuous. But the game of sexual conquest can still involve a cautionary tale.

16   To play at sex hardens the heart. *Why can't I meet anyone who feels anything?* we say. *Why can't I meet anyone who responds?* Yet sometimes what we are meaning is the exact opposite: *Why can't I let myself go, and love?*

Glossary

acrimony: extreme bitterness of temper; ill feeling

archetype: (in Jungian psychology) an inherited primitive mental image

narcissist: anyone who has excessive interest in one's own appearance, comfort, abilities, importance, etc. (from the Greek mythological character Narcissus)

Tantalus: Greek mythological king doomed in the lower world to stand in water that always receded when he tried to drink it

supplicating: asking humbly and earnestly, as by prayer

incarnations: persons or things serving as the type or embodiment of a quality or concept

Comprehension Questions

1.   How does Sullivan define the word *narcissist*?

2.   What does the novelist Leon Whiteson say is the reason certain men have multiple lovers?

3.   Why are women, according to Sullivan, so attracted to Don Juan types?

Questions about Form

1. Reread the last paragraph of the piece. Is this an appropriate paragraph for the end? Why or why not?

2. *Gone with the Wind* is a very old movie (it was released in 1939, before most of the readers of this text were born). Why do you think Sullivan refers to it here?

Questions for Discussion

1. In paragraph 8, Sullivan refers to the many labels of the female version of Don Juan. Discuss what you think the relationship is between a *Doña Juana* and what you know of a *femme fatale*.

2. Despite the indisputable similarities between the characteristics of the Don Juan and those of the female counterpart, do you think the male of this type is still looked upon more positively than the female, as Sullivan suggests? Why or why not?

3. Based on the entry in the above glossary for *Tantalus*, what do you think Sullivan means when she refers to "Tantalus games"?

4. Consider the last paragraph of this piece.

   a) Is the problem that she refers to common today? Discuss.

   b) What is Sullivan suggesting is the answer to this problem? Do you agree? Explain.

Writing Ideas

1. Write a paragraph or essay of cause and effect discussing either the causes or the effects (not both) of being a Don Juan or Doña Juana (pick one).

2. Much of Sullivan's piece deals with the reasons for which the Don Juan/Doña Juana type of person makes the worst kind of dating or mating partner to have. Write a paragraph or essay on the reasons such a person would make an ideal dating or mating (pick one) partner, instead. If you have to add a sarcastic tone to your composition, so be it. On the other hand, if you believe such a person would, in fact, make an ideal partner, then, of course, there's no need for the sarcasm.

✦ ✦ ✦

Gadget-Savvy but Socially Inept?*

Sarah Boesveld

Newspaper reporter Sarah Boesveld has written for the *Globe and Mail,* the *Toronto Star* and the *National Post*. While with the *Globe and Mail*, she was in charge of the Money, Family, and Work beats. She also wrote for the Style, Travel, and Review sections. Her piece from the *Globe and Mail* that follows deals with the popular

---

*Sarah Boesveld, "Gadget-Savvy but Socially Inept? Tech May Be Altering Your Mind," *The Globe and Mail* (16 October 2008). © Globe and Mail. All rights reserved.

© Neustockimages/istockphoto

topic of technology, but with a less-than-popular angle: the negative impact of technology on our brains and our behaviour, and what we can do to combat it.

1   You've called your family for supper. Silence. You call again.

2   "I'll come after I beat this level," your son says.

3   "I just have a few important e-mails to send," your hubby says.

4   "Just let me finish chatting with my friends on IM," your daughter replies.

5   While dinner cools on the table, your family's brains are evolving faster than ever, rewiring and building new **neural** pathways to respond to technology but leaving those wired for in-person chit-chat to fester, says Gary Small in his new book *iBrain: Surviving the Technological Alteration of the Modern Mind,* coauthored by his wife, Gigi Vorgan.

6   Dr. Small spoke with *The Globe and Mail* about how he feels technology is altering the physical makeup of our brains and changing the way we interact with one another.

7   *G&M*: **You say that as people become more tech-savvy, they risk becoming less able to have a proper face-to-face conversation. Are we fated to become social zombies?**

8   Dr. Small: I hope not. I think there's definitely evidence that when we spend more time with the technology we spend less time talking face-to-face. There's a very recent study finding young people who play video games were less able to recognize the emotional expression from a face—whether it was angry or happy. My answer is balance.

9   I say turn off the computers and the [personal digital assistants] at a certain time every night and enjoy your family, your friends.

10   *G&M*: **In iBrain, you compare Digital Natives and Digital Immigrants. Who are they?**

11   Dr. Small: Teenagers and young adults today would be considered Digital Natives. Digital Immigrants are those who come to [technology] later in life, who had more face-to-face human contact time growing up.

12   *G&M*: **What is the biggest difference you've seen in the brains of those born into a world of technology and those who've had to adapt?**

13   Dr. Small: As the brain ages, it goes through developmental steps. There's a process in young people of **pruning**, meaning that a lot of the neural networks are kind of pruned away, are never used. Sixty per cent of the brain **synapses** are pruned away during development. And the teenage brain is not as **empathetic**. Without the face-to-face time learning to read the subtle, **non-verbal** social cues, we are going to miss out on some of the empathy building that's traditionally learned during adolescence.

14   *G&M*: **How does clacking away on BlackBerrys or sitting in front of the computer for hours mess with the way our brains are wired?**

15   Dr. Small: Whether you're looking at a book page, whether you're looking at your computer screen or whether you're talking to your friend, there's stimulation that goes through the senses. A whole network of neural **circuits** and synapses are triggered. That leads to a complex array of neurochemical and electrical reactions in the brain. When we repeat an activity over and over again, specialized circuits develop and get stronger. The concern is if we're repeatedly doing an activity, those circuits will be strengthened, yet we will neglect others that may be important in our lives.

16   *G&M*: **You say the brain is evolving to respond to technology. How? And doesn't evolution take thousands of years and involve handing down genes through generations?**

17   Dr. Small: [The brain] does take time to truly evolve, but I think in terms of the concepts of who's going to adapt to this new technology, we're seeing an evolutionary change. Those people who are adept at figuring out the tools and working with it, they're going to do better. The Digital Natives in many ways are doing much better.

18   *G&M*: **So how can we control technology and not let it control us?**

19   Dr. Small: I think we're trying to help bridge the brain gap essentially by upgrading the technology skills of the Digital Immigrants and helping younger Digital Natives with their face-to-face contact skills. Think about when is it time to end the e-mail conversations and pick up the phone or walk down the hall and talk to your colleague face-to-face. I think having an appreciation of the differences is important. Also to take breaks and not just have contact with other people, but to be by yourself—to take walks outside, to converse, to try to balance your technology time with your offline time.

20   *G&M*: **How can you tell your social skills are failing because of tech-overload?**

21   Dr. Small: Ask a few questions, see if it is an issue for you. Do you tend to hide your technology use from others? Does it seem to interfere with your ordinary life? Do you miss it when you don't have it? I've had people call me, they check into a hotel in New York and they're in a panic because the server's down.

22   *G&M*: **So how can we adapt without throwing our computers out the window?**

23   Dr. Small: We need to first recognize that the technology train is here and it's moving forward rapidly. We each need to understand where we should focus our efforts to improve the quality of our lives, whether it's cutting back on our technology, improving our tech skills, [or] working a little harder to connect, offline or not.

Glossary

neural: of or relating to a nerve of the central nervous system

pruning: reducing the extent of something by cutting or removing unnecessary parts

synapses: points of contact between neurons, where nerve impulses are transmitted

empathetic: having the ability to share and understand another's feelings

non-verbal: not concerned with words

circuits: paths of electrical currents; distances or courses around things

Comprehension Questions

1. In what specific ways, according to the article, are people suffering as a result of having more technology in their lives?

2. What is the difference between "Digital Natives" and "Digital Immigrants," according to Dr. Small? How do their brains differ?

3. What is the connection between the effects of technology on our brains and our relationships with people?

Questions about Form

1. Is the question-and-answer format in this article effective? Why or why not?

2. Is the title effective? Why or why not? Would it have been more effective without the question mark? Explain.

Questions for Discussion

1. What do you think Boesveld means by the term "social zombie" in her first question to Dr. Small? What in the article causes you to draw your conclusion?

2. Dr. Small is quoted as saying that those who are more adept at working with technology are "going to do better." What do you think he means by this? Do you agree or disagree? Explain.

3. Dr. Small suggests in Paragraph 21 that if you tend to hide your technology use from others, this is a sign that your "social skills are failing." What do you think he means by this? What are examples of this in relation to texting or Facebook?

Writing Ideas

1. Using evidence from the article and your own experience, write a paragraph or essay discussing the ways in which technology has a negative impact on people's lives.

2. Interview a "Digital Immigrant" or someone who "survived" his or her teen years and early adulthood without the kinds of technology common to us today. Does your interviewee think he or she would have been happier with more technology during those years? Why or why not? Discuss your findings in a paragraph or essay.

◆ ◆ ◆

Selling Illusions*

Neil Bissoondath

Novelist, short story writer, and essayist Neil Bissoondath was born in Arima, Trinidad, in 1955, and now lives in Canada. The following piece is an excerpt from his book *Selling Illusions: The Cult of Multiculturalism in Canada*, published in 1994. As this piece indicates, Bissoondath exhibits some strong feelings about multiculturalism in Canada and how perhaps it's not what it is purported to be. In the following piece, he relates his experience as an 18-year-old who has just come to Canada to attend York University.

1   If the York University campus was a safe haven from which to discover the pleasures of Canada, . . . it was also the place where I first encountered reasons for unease.

2   York operates on a college system. New students choose, or are assigned to, one of the various colleges on the campus. Unfamiliar with the system, ignorant of the purposes behind the individual colleges, I allowed myself to be assigned to Bethune College.

3   Familiarity with the college brought a certain dismay. Bethune College, named in honour of **Dr. Norman Bethune,** is an institution devoted to Third World studies; it had a certain reputation for left-wing radicalism. The reason for my dismay was simple: my major was to be French language and literature. The bilingual Glendon College, my logical "home," was never mentioned. I can only assume that I was enrolled at Bethune in part because I had come from a Third World country and in part because my adviser assumed that I would be most comfortable in an environment where a high percentage of students were, like me, non-white. It was an assuredly benign assumption, one made with the best of intentions, but also with no regard to my personal beliefs or intellectual interests. My adviser, then, had looked at me through the lens of her own stereotype and guided me according to the presumed comforts of "sticking with your own."

4   Although I was not at first aware of it, the concept of "sticking with your own" was just then in vogue at York. This became clear the moment you entered the main cafeteria at Central Square in the massive concrete bunker of the Ross Building. It was large and brashly lit, institutional in character, a place for feeding oneself rather than enjoying a meal. I remember it as a loud and busy place,

*From *Selling Illusions* by Neil Bissoondath. Copyright © Neil Bissoondath, 1994, 2002. Reprinted by permission of Penguin Group (Canada), a Division of Pearson Canada Inc. and the author.

brash with the sounds of trays and cutlery roughly handled, of a multitude of voices blended into a steady roar.

5   And yet, it seemed a benign atmosphere, friendly in an impersonal way. The controlled chaos offered an anonymity that would ease the task of inserting oneself, of fitting in. Or so it seemed at first.

6   Chaos is always subtly ordered, and it did not require a very discerning eye to decode the chaos of the Central Square cafeteria. Indeed, a map could be drawn, various sections coloured in to denote defined areas. To highlight, for instance, the table at which Chinese students congregated behind a wall of Cantonese; or the tables over in the corner protected by the raucous enthusiasm of West Indian accents; or the table more subtly framed by **yarmulkes** and Star of David pendants.

7   To approach any of these tables was to intrude on a clannish exclusivity. It was to challenge the unofficially designated territory of tables parcelled out so that each group, whether racially, culturally or religiously defined, could enjoy its little enclave, its own little "homeland," so to speak, protected by unspoken **prerogatives**.

8   The idea of "sticking with your own" was reinforced by various student organizations, many of which were financially assisted by the university. Controversy arose at one point when an application for membership in the Black Students' Federation was received from a student—a writer for the campus newspaper, as it turned out—whose skin colour seemed to disqualify him. Questions arose: Was being black a prerequisite for belonging to the Black Students' Federation? Or was a commitment to the issues raised by the association sufficient justification for belonging? Just how relevant was skin colour, how relevant cultural background, how relevant political belief?

9   A hint of the complexity of the question may be discerned in a story once told to me by a friend. One afternoon, he stopped in at his favourite coffee house in Toronto's Kensington Market, a small place brightly decorated in the tropical style. It featured reggae music and the rich Blue Mountain coffee from Jamaica. As he sipped his coffee, he eavesdropped on a conversation at the table behind him, three young men, evidently musicians, discussing their next gig. My friend understood little of what was said—their thick Jamaican accents made their words **undecipherable**—but he enjoyed listening to their speech in the same way that he enjoyed the sounds of reggae. Cup empty, he rose to leave. On his way out he glanced at the men and with delight saw, as he put it, "one black guy with dreadlocks and two white guys with blond hair and blue eyes." An encounter, then, with the wickedness of history. He left the coffee house thrilled at abandoning the wreckage of a stereotype.

10   The issue at York was eventually settled by the decision to admit the white student to the Federation—not on the grounds that race was irrelevant but that, as an organization financially assisted by the university, it had to respect the university's regulations prohibiting discrimination on the grounds of race and colour. I did not belong to the Federation, but the resolution was pleasing anyway, even though there was a tincture of discomfort at the way in which it had come about: through technicality, and not through the application of principle. None of the real questions had been grappled with, none answered.

11   Questions of segregation and **exclusivity** kept raising their heads. One day a Jewish friend invited me to join him for coffee in the Jewish Students' Federation lounge. I was reluctant—the lounge seemed to me governed by even stronger proscriptions than the table in the cafeteria—but he insisted. As he fixed us each a coffee, he said in a voice clearly intended for others in the room that I should feel free to help myself from the coffee-machine at any time. And then he added in strained tones that the lounge, provided by the university, was open to all: I was to ignore anyone who tried to stop me. It was in this way that he sought to make me part of unsuspected **internecine** tensions, while publicly declaring his own position.

12   The issues made me wary: I neither joined the Black Students' Federation nor revisited the Jewish Students' Federation lounge. I learned instead to keep my distance from the tables that would have welcomed me not as an individual but as an individual of a certain skin colour, with a certain accent, with a certain assumed cultural outlook—the tables that would have welcomed me not for who I was and for what I could do but for *what* I was and for what they presumed I represented. I had not come here, I decided, in order to join a ghetto.

13   Alone in a new land, I faced inevitable questions. Questions about my past and my present, about the land left behind and the land newly found, about the nature of this society and my place in it. At eighteen, about to embark on a new life, I felt these to be weighty issues.

14   For many people at those cafeteria tables, though, these were questions of no great importance. They were almost aggressive in dismissing any discomfort they might have experienced by flaunting the only government policy that seemed to arouse no resentment: Canada as a multicultural land. Officially. Legally. Here, they insisted, you did not have to change. Here you could—indeed, it was your duty to—remain what you were. None of this American melting-pot nonsense, none of this remaking yourself to fit your new circumstances: you did not have to adjust to the society, the society was obligated to accommodate itself to you.

15   An attractive proposal, then, a policy that excused much and required little effort. And yet I found myself not easily seduced.

16   The problem was that I had come in search of a new life and a new way of looking at the world, "to expand my horizons" (to use a cliché) from the narrow perspectives of my youth in Trinidad. I had no desire to transport here life as I had known it: this seemed to me particularly onerous baggage with which to burden one's shoulders. Beyond this, though, the very act of emigration had already changed me. I was no longer the same person who had boarded the aircraft in Trinidad bound for Toronto: I had brought with me not the attitudes of the tourist but those of someone embarking on an adventure that would forever change his life. This alone was a kind of psychological revolution.

17   Multiculturalism, as perceived by those at whom it was most explicitly aimed, left me with a certain measure of discomfort.

18   At the end of my first university year, I returned to Trinidad to visit my parents. It wasn't long before I was impatient to get back to Toronto. This had to do in part with the realization that, even after so short a time, old friends had become new strangers, and that old places had remained simply old places.

More importantly, though, the desire to return had to do with me and with the life I had begun constructing in my adopted city. I relished the freedom this life offered, the liberation of the anonymity of the big city. I had made new friends—some of them from among "my own kind," some not—and had found all the books, magazines and films denied me in Trinidad. I had, for the first time in my life, found a place other than my parents' house that I wished to call home: a place where I could be myself.

19   Sharing this with those who wished me to bolster their ethnic bastion in Toronto made me distinctly unpopular. I was seen as a kind of traitor, unwilling to play the game by indulging in a life best described as "Caribbean North." If there was any **alienation**, it came not from the society at large but from those who saw themselves as the front-line practitioners of multiculturalism. By establishing cultural and racial exclusivity, they were doing their bit to preserve the multicultural character of the country, while I, seeking to go beyond the confines of my cultural heritage, was seen as acting counter to those interests.

20   To put it succinctly, they coveted the segregated tables of the cafeteria, while I sought a place at tables that would accommodate a greater variety.

Glossary

Dr. Norman Bethune: a Canadian surgeon and international humanitarian revered in China for his heroic and selfless treatment of the wounded in that country's struggle for a republic; he died of blood poisoning in 1939

yarmulkes: skullcaps often worn by male Jews, especially during prayer and religious functions

prerogatives: exclusive rights or privileges

undecipherable: unable to be understood

exclusivity: the act of shutting out

internecine: of or relating to a struggle within a nation, an organization, or a group

alienation: feeling estranged from one's social environment

Comprehension Questions

1. What does Bissoondath mean by what he refers to as the "homeland" in paragraph 7? Why does he not want to join the "homelands"?

2. Why does Bissoondath think he was assigned to Bethune College?

3. What was really happening, according to Bissoondath, when his Jewish friend served him a coffee in the Jewish Students' Federation lounge?

4. What is the story told to Bissoondath by his friend who visited Toronto's Kensington Market? What is the meaning of it? How does it support Bissoondath's overall thesis?

Questions about Form

1. What does Bissoondath include in this piece that helps you to identify with his concerns?

2. What is the setting of Bissoondath's essay? Does this help to make the piece more effective? Why or why not?

3. What is the author doing in the last paragraph of this piece? Is it effective? Why or why not?

Questions for Discussion

1. Do "homelands," as Bissoondath would define them, exist at your school? What do you think are the reasons they exist there? Do they do more harm than good, as Bissoondath suggests?

2. Do you generally "stick" with people "of your own kind"? From your own experience, what are the advantages and disadvantages of this behaviour?

3. Are there clubs at your school that seem exclusive to people of a certain skin colour, religion, or culture? Would they refuse to accept a student who wanted to join if this student didn't seem to "belong"? Is this a violation of human rights law?

4. Judging only by this essay, what would you say is the author's attitude toward multiculturalism in this country? Do you agree with it? Why or why not?

5. Do you think Canadians in general are less racist than Americans? Why or why not? What in this article by Bissoondath supports your answer?

Writing Ideas

1. In a paragraph or essay, argue whether you think multiculturalism, the way it is promoted at your school, contributes to or combats racism.

2. In a paragraph or essay, argue whether or not a club should be able to offer exclusivity to people of only one skin colour, one culture, or one religion.

3. Imagine you are creating your own college/university social club. In view of Bissoondath's concerns, what would the basic guidelines regarding membership of your new club be? Support them in a paragraph or essay.

4. Identify a social club that seems to be exclusive to a particular race, religion, or culture. Write a paragraph or essay supporting or criticizing this perception of exclusivity.

◆ ◆ ◆

Lessons of Love from Stories of Old

Gary Lipschutz

Ideas we have about love are often harmful. According to the author of this argumentative essay, we get some of these ideas from the popular misinterpretations of stories—stories we've known and embraced since childhood. The stories themselves might have a great deal of wisdom to offer, but, unfortunately, these stories often are misinterpreted by a society that is generally lazy and materialistic. And the result is damage in our lives around the whole issue of love. In this essay, written in 2003, Lipschutz, who teaches English and mythology at Toronto's Centennial College, not only blames "external sources" (religious organizations, businesses, the media, etc.) for this damage, but also those among us who listen to them. Most tragic, he says, is that these misinterpretations too often defy what is in our own hearts.

1   Why is it that the very thing so many people want so badly is the one thing they never seem to find? Why is it that people, young and old, spend so much time on chat lines, so much money on dating services and so much energy obsessing over the "perfect" love and/or marriage? Why is it that the success rate of getting these things is pretty low?

2   Well, did it ever occur to you that our ideas about love are often unrealistic? We may get some of them from movies, from TV sitcoms, and worse, I dare say, from so-called reality TV shows such as *The Bachelor* or *Joe Millionaire* (a title that, in itself, suggests less-than-virtuous values). How often do we ask why the media seem to sell the idea that fashion, sex appeal and money are the most important parts of any relationship?

3   One reason for these false and damaging ideas is **commercialism**. Large businesses spend inordinate amounts of money on research into the human psyche. They know that "sex sells." They know that in their appeal to the sexual urges of a person, especially the person within a certain age range, they are more likely to exert influence over the consumer's buying choices. But is there an adverse if **inadvertent** effect as well? Do these ads in any way cause us to go after certain things in relationships that are inaccessible, things that have absolutely nothing to do with love and therefore things that do not contribute to the staying power of a relationship?

4   Advertisements and "reality" TV shows are not the only things brainwashing us. We've all grown up with certain stories: stories from religious scripture, fairy tales such as "Sleeping Beauty" and "Cinderella" and Shakespearean plays such as *Romeo and Juliet*. Most of us are familiar with the latest cinematic rendition of *Titanic*, especially the love story in it that took place between Jack and Rose.

5   Why are such stories so predominant in our lives? They help to maintain our hopes and dreams when it comes to the very thing we want the most: love, no, the perfect love. But the problem is they probably cause more harm than good, even if the intentions of those who make them up are honourable. The problem is not the stories themselves. The problem lies in the interpretation of these stories. Let's look at a classic example of misinterpretation of the story "Sleeping Beauty."

6   Everyone knows more or less what happens in "Sleeping Beauty," regardless of the version to which one was exposed. *A king and queen give birth to a daughter after many years of trying. Upon the girl's birth, the king is so overjoyed, he decides to hold a great feast to which he invites many people. There are 13 wise women in his kingdom, but the king only invites 12 because*

Courtesy of Jock MacRae

he had only 12 golden plates from which they could eat. To get revenge for not being invited, the thirteenth "wise" (and scornful) woman arrives at the feast and cries out, "In her fifteenth year, the princess shall prick herself with a spindle and fall down dead!"

7   By the time this thirteenth wise woman had cursed the princess, 11 wise women who were invited had given gifts to the princess, but the twelfth had not yet spoken. Although she could not undo the evil spell, she could, however, soften it with a wish: "The princess shall not die," she said. "Instead, she shall fall into a deep sleep for one hundred years."

8   Of course, it's the following part, more than any other, for which the whole story is known and loved:

9   *After the princess's 100-year slumber was over, a prince approaches the sleeping beauty and kisses her lips. She awakens, smiles at him fondly, and they, of course, marry each other and live happily ever after.*

10   Before discussing the interpretation of "Sleeping Beauty," it's first necessary to note the difference between an interpretation that is literal and one that is

symbolic. Understanding the difference may result in a very different way of understanding not only "Sleeping Beauty," but also most other stories regardless of their source.

11   People who take things **literally** take what is spoken or written at face value. Even when it comes to religious scripture, Joseph Campbell, world-renowned mythologist, says that most of us belong to two schools of thought: in one school, there are those who believe the stories of religious scripture are true because they're believers of the miraculous; yes, Moses parted the Red Sea with his hands, or yes, Jesus raised Lazarus from the dead simply because the scriptural texts say so. And in the second school of thought, there are those who do not believe in these types of miracles simply because they are unrealistic. In other words, the difference as to whether people "believe" in scripture or not seems to depend on what they believe has literally happened two or three thousand years ago. Whether they believe in miracles or not, most people take these stories literally.

12   What if a third situation were possible? Those who study mythology may realize that myth (including religious stories) is not meant to be interpreted literally, but symbolically. In other words, things that are spoken or written might be meant to represent ideas, usually relating to some aspect of our humanity, that are otherwise difficult to understand. In fact, originally, the word *myth* did not mean "falsehood" the way it does today. The word *myth* referred to (and still does for those who are educated in the area) a story about the divine mysteries of life, thus the letters "MY. . ." suggesting MYstery *mysterion* or **MYstical.** In this context, the body of mythology is not just about Greek gods and Celtic wizards, but also heroes such as Moses of the Old Testament and Jesus of the New and, by extension, ALL of the characters of stories in every religion of the world, bar none. All such stories shed light on the mystery of humanity. They all include characters of the divine. Symbolically speaking, it could be argued that Moses represents every person in the world who eventually gets called by a higher power to do something heroic and can succeed against insurmountable odds if the holy deed is faced with a great deal of courage and conviction. Did Moses actually part the Red Sea? Only those who are literalists care, not to mention those who are bent on insisting their religion is superior to all others. The difference between "our" truth and "their" truth is what unfortunately causes **acrimony** among the religions of the world. Many present-day wars are testimony to this unfortunate side of our human nature.

13   What if the messages of these divine stories, regardless of whether we relegate them to myth, religion or fairy tales, are the same? Undeniably, regardless of interpretation, they all seem to have certain messages in common: Arrogance and selfishness are bad. Humility and sacrifice are good. Treat your neighbour as yourself. (And don't forget, your neighbour might be of a different skin colour or religious background or social class—a detail that too often gets lost in people's interpretations, sometimes for evil reasons.) Be fair and kind to people. Don't kill people (unless you are 100 per cent sure your killing them is in self-defence). Don't lie because, as psychiatrist and prolific author M. Scott Peck (famous for

his book called *The Road Less Traveled*) says in his book *People of the Lie*, the lie is the very root of human evil. Judge a person by her or his character and not on the basis of how much money he makes or how intelligent he is or how beautiful she is on the outside. And one's character, to quote the wizard in *Harry Potter and the Chamber of Secrets*, is determined not by a person's abilities but by her or his choices. Wouldn't the world be a better place if we all recognized that all these stories are telling us not only the same things, but that the important things in life are things universal to human consciousness? Doesn't it make more sense to concentrate on our similarities rather than our differences? Is religion meant to unite or divide us? Is the answer not obvious?

14   And what about Sleeping Beauty's never-ending naptime? Bruno Bettelheim, famous child psychologist and psychological interpreter of children's literature, said that what's important among other things is what Sleeping Beauty's 100-year slumber symbolizes or represents. Why, for that matter, is the 100-year sleep important at all? Literally speaking, nobody sleeps for 100 years. Then this part of the story has no meaning, right? Wrong! It has a world of meaning if it's interpreted symbolically. A cigar, symbolically speaking, is never a cigar. The 100-year sleep, it could be argued, should be the focal point of the story. The title, after all, is "*Sleeping* Beauty."

15   A more prevalent reason for ignoring the significance of the centennial snooze is that it seems to have nothing to do with the message of this story that most people desperately want to cling to: that a woman must be rescued by a man. (The first time I shot down the "rescuing" message of "Sleeping Beauty" in a class I was teaching, a young female student stormed out of the room in angry protest and promptly proceeded to drop my course.) Too many of us think, or at least hope, the rescuing part is realistic because we're basically selfish (or chauvinistic if we're male) and lazy. Too many women want to be "rescued," and too many men think they have to do the "rescuing." And that, to too many men, means making lots of money and perhaps getting a hair transplant or wearing thousand-dollar suits because if you don't look like a prince and you don't own a white horse (in modern-day terms, an expensive car and/or a condo), Sleeping Beauty won't even look at you, much less ride off with you into the sunset.

16   If the wedding of Prince Charles and Princess Diana seemed like a "fairy tale," their lives together certainly did not. Why did Sleeping Beauty and her prince get to ride off into the sunset, while Princess Diana and her lover (a lover other than her dashing prince) died a violent death? Why did a life for the world's favourite royal start out as a fairy tale and end up in a fiery and fatal car crash? Wasn't Diana meant to be "rescued" by her charming (not to mention, rich) prince?

17   If Sleeping Beauty doesn't look at you because you don't dress fashionably or you don't have a full head of hair or you don't have a nice car and condo, she's not worth your time because these things have absolutely nothing to do with love. She may be attracted to you for your sense of style, your hair, or your money, and she may feel like she's being "saved" from poverty, or her parents, or both, but she will only stay with you until she finds a richer or better-looking prince or

until you lose your money or, better yet, until you leave her first when you finally realize what your "princess's values" really are.

18   The 100-year slumber, according to Bettelheim, represents a stage in a person's life (not just a female's) during which she must develop her own mind away from her parents and away from her friends. Call it mental and emotional downtime or a physical or inner journey to "find oneself," an accounting of the soul, whatever you wish. The point is, too often young people make the biggest mistakes in their lives because they don't listen to an inner voice. It's much easier to "take the path of least resistance" and do what your parents tell you in order to make them happy. It's easier to follow your friends' advice; after all, they have your best interests in mind, right? Actually they probably don't, even if they don't realize it themselves. Thomas Hobbes, a 17th-century social theorist, said that people are basically selfish. And chances are we haven't gotten less selfish in the last 400 years. If anything, with more affluence in our lives, with the Internet and other types of "instantly gratifying technology" at our fingertips, we're more selfish than ever. So when we tell our friends what they should do, we're actually telling them what WE want them to do. If we were real friends, we'd try to find out what they want and then support them unconditionally.

19   When Sleeping Beauty wakes up from her 100-year slumber, she's grown. She hasn't grown old physically, of course. If she had, Prince Charming would not be kissing her, right? But how else has she grown? Having spent the time BY herself, she's learned ABOUT herself. She's "slept," which might symbolize she's spent time understanding her **unconscious**, the voice inside, the voice we tend to hear when we turn off the cell phone, the TV and the computer—the noise and chatter we hear every day. Technology makes it even more difficult than ever before to shut out the noise. For this reason, the message of the 100-year sleep in "Sleeping Beauty" becomes more relevant today than ever. We all desperately need this downtime, this distance from the noise, if we're ever going to know what our own hearts are saying. There are two problems, as I see it. First, we don't take the time or make the effort to challenge our assumptions of the interpretations of most stories, especially ones with which we've grown up. Second, even if we did, and even if people did understand what Bettelheim was trying to say, shutting out the noise of our cell phones, the TV and our computers would still be too difficult, the usual excuse made by spiritually lazy and unawakened people.

20   "Sleeping Beauty," simply put, is not about a princess being "rescued" by a prince; it's about the importance of a **spiritual awakening**. After all, the story is called "Sleeping Beauty" (becoming beautiful from self-knowledge), not "The Poor Girl Who Turns into a Princess Because She Gets Rescued by a Rich Man." Don't forget Diana wasn't even poor to begin with. And secondly, if she were "rescued," one would think she'd live to see forty.

21   When Sleeping Beauty awakes, having learned who she is and what she really wants, she is then, and only then, able to *recognize* the right man for her. The prince doesn't rescue her; she saves her own soul by choosing the man she is meant to be with because she now knows who that man is, and she has the courage to go after him regardless of what her friends or family might say or do. To her,

Gary Lipschutz   *Lessons of Love from Stories of Old*

this right man *becomes* her prince. This prince will look handsome and rich not because he's got model-good looks and drives a Jaguar or BMW but because to her, the princess who now knows what's right for herself, the man whom she has recognized as the right one LOOKS handsome, and he SEEMS rich, but in non-material ways. That, after all, is the story of *Titanic*. Rose saved her own soul when she dumped the rich, handsome fiancé (the one her mother wanted her to marry) and made the commitment to love a penniless man whom she had just met. She *knew* he was her soulmate. Nobody else could tell her this, certainly not her mother. Those who take the time to learn about themselves and follow their own hearts once they realize what their hearts are saying—it is they who have grown up. It is they who have lived their own authentic lives. It is they who are rich.

Glossary

commercialism: emphasis on financial profit as a measure of worth

inadvertent: unintentional

literally: taking what is spoken or written at face value, without symbolic interpretation

mystical: of spiritual truth beyond human understanding

acrimony: bitter disagreement, hostility

unconscious: part of the mind of which we are unaware, but which is largely responsible for our emotions, behaviour, etc.

spiritual awakening: new awareness of the importance of soul as opposed to physical things

Comprehension Questions

1. What ideas, according to the author, do most people have about love?

2. What causes people to have these ideas?

3. How do most people interpret "Sleeping Beauty"?

4. What is different about Bruno Bettelheim's interpretation of "Sleeping Beauty"?

5. Why did the author's student walk out of his class in anger?

6. What does the author mean by the last sentence in the essay: "It is they who are rich"?

Questions about Form

1. What does the author do to make this essay effective?

2. What are the intended audience and purpose of this essay?

3. Why do you think the author mentions the movie *Titanic*?

4. Why are paragraphs 6, 7, and 9 largely in italics?

Questions for Discussion

1. What is the more believable fairy tale in our society, "Sleeping Beauty" or "Beauty and the Beast"? Why?

2. What is your definition of the perfect love?

3. Where do you think your idea of this definition (in your answer to question 2) comes from?

4. Do you think the perfect love according to your definition exists?

5. Compare this essay to "Don Juan/Doña Juana" (starting on page 385) by Rosemary Sullivan. What do the two pieces have in common? How do they differ?

6. Woody Allen, a very controversial film director/actor on the celebrity love scene (because of his marriage to Soon-Yi Previn, the adopted daughter of his former partner, Mia Farrow), once interviewed a seemingly happy couple on the street in one of his movies. He asked to what they attributed their happiness as a couple. The male of the couple responded that they were both superficial: they both loved talking about fashion and other materialistic interests that they had in common. Do you think Woody Allen is saying these two people are likely to stay happy as a couple? Do you agree with him? Why or why not?

Writing Ideas

1. In a paragraph or essay, explain where people get their ideas of love.

2. In a paragraph or essay, identify the story that you believe best illustrates your ideas about love, and explain why.

3. What are the most important things in a relationship? What often attracts us first to the one we want to date? Why do the answers to these questions often cause trouble later on? Based on your answers to the above questions, write a paragraph or essay in which you discuss the reasons behind the breakdown of many relationships.

◆ ◆ ◆

A Tough Approach that Might Work*

James C. Morton

A lawyer, legal educator, and author, James C. Morton has written more than 25 legal texts as well as numerous papers and articles. He is Past President of the Ontario Bar Association and a long-time human rights and community activist. He's served as a Governor for the Canadian International Peace Project, Counsel for the Canadian Somali Congress, and Legal Counsel (pro bono) for Artists Against Racism, a registered charity fighting racial and religious prejudice. In this piece published in the *Ottawa Citizen* on October 13, 2008, Morton argues that tough punishment is not the solution to the common problem of chronic offences in the area of petty theft.

*Source: James Morton, "A Tough Approach that Might Work," *The Ottawa Citizen* (13 October 2008). Reprinted by permission of the author.

© iQoncept/Shutterstock

1   In a season of tough talk on crime, I would like to propose a challenge to our political leaders. In this country, one group of criminals commits a disproportionate number of crimes that we could easily reduce with more coercive sentencing. However, our usual form of **coercion**—imprisonment—doesn't work for them. They need a different kind of sentence. But to make that happen—and to significantly reduce the number of crimes they commit—would require a degree of will and wisdom that our legislators can't seem to muster.

2   The legal system refers to these men—they are almost all men—as **chronic** offenders. What everyone knows—but the justice system doesn't acknowledge—is that they are also drug addicts, hooked on heroin or crack cocaine. They steal not for gain but to support their addiction, to pay for their next fix.

3   This has nothing to do with getting high. For an addict, the point is to avoid the effects of withdrawal—in the case of heroin, including cramps and muscle spasms, fever, cold sweats and goose bumps (hence the phrase "cold turkey"), insomnia, vomiting, diarrhea and a condition called "itchy blood," which can cause compulsive scratching so severe that it leads to open sores. For addicts, drug use is not a lifestyle choice that's easy to change. Many have been addicted for their entire adult lives, and as a result have spent half their lives behind bars, serving dozens of sentences for minor crimes. These are the "revolving door" criminals that some critics point to—arrested, tried, sentenced to a few weeks or months, then dumped back out on the street, only to be arrested, tried and convicted again a few weeks later.

4   Canada has hundreds of criminals like that, mainly in the larger cities. Vancouver alone recently identified 379. According to a report by the Vancouver Police Department, the vast majority were addicted to drugs or alcohol. Many also suffer from a mental disorder, generally untreated. In the five years between 2001 and 2006, Vancouver's few hundred chronic offenders, as a group, were

responsible for 26,755 police contacts—more than 5,000 contacts per year, 14 a day. The costs are staggering. Arrests, prosecutions and incarcerations end up costing some $20,000 per criminal per month—per month! There has to be a better way.

5   Punishment alone is not it, though, for a couple of reasons. For one, the idea of punishing criminals is based at least partly on the concept of specific **deterrence**. You steal, we lock you up. Applied most strongly to property crimes—which is what these offenders mainly commit—specific deterrence assumes that the criminal is a rational actor who will consider: Is it worth it? And in fact, specific deterrence often works; many offenders really do stop committing crimes after fairly short jail sentences. But not addicts.

6   The problem is the presumption of a rational actor. That is exactly what we do not have with drug addicts, who do not—usually cannot—stop to consider the likely punishment for a crime they are about to commit. They see only the escape from the more immediate and dire punishments of drug **deprivation**. By comparison, the threat of being caught and thrown in jail is nothing.

7   As well, because chronic offenders tend to commit minor crimes and draw short sentences—say, 30 to 90 days for theft—their lives shift constantly between jail and the streets.

8   We could use longer sentences to "warehouse" chronic offenders—the American "three strikes and you're out" approach. But long-term imprisonment would be a very high-cost way to deal with what is really a public health issue.

9   And there's the **crux** of the problem. The criminal justice system is not designed to treat addicts. While prisons do provide some drug treatment, it is almost always short-term and underfunded. And these offenders, with their short sentences, rarely get even that. The voluntary drug treatment programs offered by the public health system seldom work for them either, because kicking an addiction is extremely unpleasant and requires willpower and usually some money, neither of which street addicts have.

10   Clearly, Canadians need more protection from chronic offenders than we are now getting. While their crimes may be petty, their victims number in the thousands. And those victims are left not only with a monetary loss, but also with a lingering fear that affects their sense of personal safety and their trust in the criminal justice system. But blaming that system, as many do, misses the point—which is our failure as a society to deal with severe drug and alcohol addiction.

11   With chronic offenders, the first step is to recognize that what we have is an issue of both criminal law and public health. The next step is to require addicted offenders to undergo serious, long-term drug treatment.

12   Canada's experience with mandatory drug treatment is quite limited. In the late 1970s, British Columbia passed legislation under which heroin addicts could be compelled to take part in an intensive government-funded treatment program. The Supreme Court of Canada upheld the statute but the provincial legislature ultimately repealed it, concerned about civil liberties. (This was the time of *One Flew Over the Cuckoo's Nest*.)

13   These days, Vancouver's Downtown Community Court tackles street crime by taking guilty pleas and moving the accused into treatment as part of their sentencing, but only with their consent, which misses the point.

14   We're less constrained with juvenile offenders. Since 1996, Alberta law has required minors with an apparent alcohol or drug addiction to participate, with or without their consent, in an assessment and treatment program. Saskatchewan and Manitoba have similar legislation and even allow parents of drug-addicted children to ask a court to require treatment, whether or not the child is in trouble with the law.

15   Although the research is scant, mandatory treatment does appear to have about the same success rate as voluntary treatment. A 1970s American study looked at the effectiveness of methadone maintenance treatment for those who entered the program under high, moderate or no coercion and found no significant difference in outcomes for the three groups.

16   Given the costs of incarceration—not counting the costs to future victims—paying for mandatory drug treatment for them hardly seems an issue, even if it only works some of the time. As for whether mandatory treatment is somehow inhumane, how humane is it to sentence these addicts to punishments we know don't work and then dump them back on the street no better than before?

17   More than costs or moral qualms, though, the main obstacle to mandatory drug treatment for addicted offenders is probably institutional. Both the justice system and the health system have entrenched groups with turf to protect: prisons, parole boards, hospitals. Collaboration would mean breaching walls; even with good intentions, a mandatory treatment program would raise irksome issues such as which ministry pays, health or justice, and which is responsible. But don't we elect our leaders to solve such problems?

18   The question is not whether we will be soft on crime but whether we can be smart about crime. Crime in the real world is not an exciting TV show. Crime has real costs and victims. Politics aside, Canadians generally—and victims of crime specifically—deserve evidence-based criminal justice policies that actually reduce crime. Our challenge is to make the tough choices that move beyond "tough on crime" **rhetoric** and produce real change.

Glossary

coercion: the act of persuading or restraining a person by force

chronic: persisting for a long time

deterrence: discouragement of someone from doing something

deprivation: the denial of something considered to be a necessity

crux: a difficult matter; a puzzle

rhetoric: language designed to persuade or impress (often with an implication of insincerity or exaggeration)

Comprehension Questions

1.   In your own words, and in one sentence, what is the author's main opinion in this article?

2. Describe thoroughly what Morton refers to as the "revolving door" criminal discussed in the article.

3. What, specifically, is the cost of dealing with the type of criminal discussed in this article?

4. What does Morton mean by the "rational actor" when it comes to offenders? How does this contrast with the "chronic" offender?

5. What does the author mean by "regular punishment," and why does it not work for the type of criminal discussed in this article?

6. What does the author suggest as a solution for dealing with the particular offender discussed in his article?

7. What practical steps, according to the author, need to be taken in order to implement his suggested solution?

Questions about Form

1. Morton uses first-person references (*I, we* and *our*) throughout his article. Is this an effective use or not? Explain.

2. In the first sentence of the last paragraph, Morton juxtaposes the cliché "soft on crime" with his term "smart about crime." How effective is this juxtaposition? Explain.

Questions for Discussion

1. Mental health problems have always been stigmatized within society. Do you think that if the judicial system begins to focus more on mental health, we will see a reduction of petty crime, as the author suggests?

2. In the last paragraph, Morton writes, "Our challenge is to make the tough choices that move beyond 'tough on crime' rhetoric and produce real change." What do you think the author means by this? Do you agree or disagree? Explain.

3. Morton describes the general challenges to the solution he suggests as relating to lack of public funding and to logistical complications given the short sentences usually served by this class of offenders. In your opinion, are these challenges insurmountable? Explain.

Writing Ideas

1. If it is true that most thefts are committed by drug addicts who are avoiding withdrawal, why do you think society is so slow to first discover, and then effectively deal with, the problem? Write a paragraph or an essay outlining your reasons.

2. Considering the author's argument as to what the problem is, write a paragraph or an essay in which you point out other solutions (or parts of the solution) that the author has not discussed.

3. To what extent does the problem of addiction relate to crimes committed across the country other than the kind of petty theft described here for which police are constantly arresting offenders? Would the same solution that Morton suggests be relevant to those crimes? Explain in a paragraph or an essay.

♦ ♦ ♦

How to Quit Putting Things Off*

Julia McKinnell

How many times have you thought that if you had just spent more time working at something and less time procrastinating, you could have achieved better results? Well, you're clearly not alone. It seems almost everyone procrastinates on occasion, but how does one combat procrastination? Contributing editor to *Maclean's* magazine Julia McKinnell looks to a Calgary professor's book for the solution to this time-wasting practice.

1   People confess to procrastination and then laugh it off, like the 900,000 members of the Facebook group, "I was doing homework; then I ended up on Facebook." For many, though, procrastination isn't funny. Look at the poet Samuel Coleridge, writes Piers Steel, the Calgary professor who's becoming known internationally for his insights on procrastination, in his new book *The Procrastination Equation: How to Stop Putting Things off and Start Getting Stuff Done*. The poet spent 25 years writing the poem **Kubla Khan**. His excuses were legendary. For other people, Steel writes, the pain of procrastination "is about diets postponed, late-night scrambles to finish projects and disappointed looks from the people who depend on you."

2   The good news is that techniques for treating procrastination exist. "They are scientifically proven. It's not a question of will they work. They're **vetted**," Steel tells *Maclean's*. "I was one of the first guinea pigs for this."

© photos.com

*Julia McKinnell, "How to Quit Putting Things Off." Reprinted by permission of Julia McKinnell.

3   Steel knows that procrastination is not the by-product of perfectionism, as it was once believed. The theory that "we delay because we are perfectionists anxious about living up to sky-high standards" feels good, he writes, but doesn't pan out. "Neat, orderly and efficient perfectionists don't tend to dilly-dally." Laziness isn't the problem either, he says. The truly lazy person thinks, "I don't want to do this. You can force me to do it but I have no desire to do it." The procrastinator, on the other hand, wants to do the work, "yet finds when the moment of action comes, they keep putting it off."

4   To treat procrastination, it helps to know that impulsiveness or "wanting it all now" is the main source of it, he writes; "Showing self-control or delaying gratification is difficult for those of us who are impulsive. We just don't have much ability to endure short-term pain for long-term gain."

5   Past failures and "learned helplessness" also lead to procrastination. Steel gives the example in the book of Eddie, an underperforming salesman. "After a series of attempts that all resulted in failure, Eddie began to expect failure even before he started." The problem is, "if you start believing your goals aren't achievable, you stop effectively pursuing them."

6   To combat the problem, create a new "spiral of success," he suggests. "If you can't run a mile, then run a block. Stop when you've done that and the next time try two blocks. Nobody has to know about your small successes; keep them as your own happy little secret." Steel writes that "personal stories of triumph can bolster people's spirits for years. 'I did it!' translates into 'I can do it.'"

7   Still, don't be overly confident, he warns. The overconfident "tend to discount problems," often underestimating how long a task will take. "As Freud puts it, we need to activate the reality principle. This entails imagining what could go wrong and how you would prevent or **mitigate** potential pitfalls."

8   It's wise to anticipate temptation. "If you can anticipate powerful temptations, you can act in advance to ward them off." Steel gives the example of Ulysses from Homer's ***Odyssey***. The goddess Circe warns Ulysses to guard against the lure of the Sirens. If his men hear the singing of the Sirens, these beautiful naked women will distract them and the men will become enthralled, and blissfully starve to death. Circe tells Ulysses to fill his men's ears with wax to make them deaf. It works and he sails safely past temptation.

9   For solutions to modern temptations such as sleeping in, Stell cites such gizmos as an alarm clock called SnuzNLuz. "Every time you press the snooze button, it donates 10 or more dollars to your most detested charity; a little extra sleep comes at the cost of your assisting groups that represent the antithesis of your political position, sexual orientation or environmental stance."

10   "Quick tip," he tells *Maclean's*. "If you want to address procrastination, find out when your power hours are, when your **circadian rhythm** pops, and try to reserve your hardest work for then. For most people that's 10 to 2. A lot of people use that time for meetings and emails, and that's sad, really. That's when you could've got most of your entire day done."

Glossary

Kubla Khan: a poem by Samuel Taylor Coleridge completed in 1797 but left unpublished until 1816

vetted: made a careful and critical examination of (a work, scheme, etc.)

mitigate: make less intense or severe

Odyssey: a major ancient Greek epic poem, attributed to Homer, that tells the story of the warrior Ulysses' long sea voyage home after the Trojan War

circadian rhythm: the cyclical twenty-four-hour period of human biological activity

Comprehension Questions

1. Specifically identify the differences between the lazy person and the procrastinator.

2. According to the article, what are the ways to fight procrastination?

Questions about Form

1. Why do you think the author includes the examples of Samuel Coleridge's *Kubla Khan* and Homer's *Odyssey*?

2. Why is Facebook mentioned so early in the first paragraph of the reading? Is this an effective way to begin the article? Why or why not?

Questions for Discussion

1. How does today's widespread practice of multitasking contribute toward procrastination?

2. In many *Fortune 500* companies today, cell phones are being banned at the boardroom door because of accusations of lack of focus. What is the connection, if any, between today's technology craze and the tendency toward procrastination?

3. Facebook is being blamed in the article for much of the procrastination that takes place today. Would you agree? Explain.

4. Aside from the suggestions in the reading for treating procrastination, what in the past has worked for you that you would suggest to others? Explain.

Writing Ideas

1. Are people more likely to procrastinate today more than ever? Write a paragraph or an essay outlining reasons for your answer.

2. The author suggests various reasons why people procrastinate. Which one do you agree with the most? Write a paragraph or an essay in which you provide reasons for your answer.

3. Do you agree with Piers Steel's advice on how to overcome the tendency to put things off? In a paragraph or an essay, explain why or why not.

✦ ✦ ✦

Till Fraud Do Us Part*

Cameron Ainsworth-Vincze

For some, it is just a matter of time before they enter into the institution of marriage. For others, as wonderful as the prospect seems in some respects, marriage is utterly feared. Fuelling this fear in Canada today is the growing incidence of fraudulent marriage. *Maclean's* writer Cameron Ainsworth-Vincze gives us a glimpse into this type of desecration of what is still, for many, a holy institution.

1 Navdeep Dhillon left her Abbotsford, B.C., home in April 2004 along with her family and travelled to India for a moment she had long waited for. After selecting a traditional red dress with her mother and cousins in her native province of Punjab, Dhillon exchanged wedding vows in an arranged marriage with a man she had never met but with whom she expected to share the rest of her life in Canada. Three weeks later she returned to Abbotsford, where the 29-year-old works as a computer technician, and submitted a sponsorship application form along with a $1,525 immigration fee to enable her new husband to gain entry into Canada.

2 Five months later, Dhillon's husband, who had been recommended by relatives, arrived. But Dhillon's dream of a happy marriage quickly turned into a nightmare when, she says, he told her he had only wed her to immigrate to Canada, and then disappeared without a trace. "I can't really explain what's happening with me. It's really hard to tolerate," she says. "I never had any suspicion he was going to do that to me." But Dhillon's story is not a unique one. Increasing numbers of Canadians are becoming victims

© iofoto/Shutterstock

*Cameron Ainsworth-Vincze, "Till Fraud Do Us Part," *Macleans*, (24 July 2006). Reprinted by permission of the author.

of **sham** marriages, sometimes being financially drained by the devious acts of foreigners who used them to enter the country. To make matters worse, Ottawa requires Canadians to support their spouses for a period of up to three years, and if a sponsored spouse receives any government assistance during that time, their provincial government is permitted to pursue repayment.

3   Dhillon believes her husband, luckily, has a job and has received no government assistance. But her family put forward a $20,000 **dowry**, not a penny of which has been returned. Dhillon doesn't even know where the man is currently living. Her family has tried contacting his family in India, but they keep disconnecting the phone. He has applied for a divorce, but Dhillon wants the marriage **annulled** and the government to deport him back to India. "If it doesn't do that, it means they are promoting fraud marriage," she says. "And people will do it over and over again."

4   To combat escalating incidents of sham marriages, the Vancouver-based Canadian Marriage Fraud Victim Society is petitioning Ottawa to change the Immigration Act to deter foreign spouses from using Canadians to obtain residency with the objective of leaving them once they reach Canadian soil. "We are suggesting they must live together or the divorce shouldn't be **sanctioned** earlier than three years," says society spokesman Krishan Bector. "They won't get married simply to come to Canada, but for life-long companionship. This is what marriage is all about."

5   New Democrat MLA Raj Chouhan, however, believes such a change would do more harm than good. "There is no quick fix," he says. "It's an issue that requires all of us to discuss, debate and then come up with some kind of suggestion." There will likely be people willing to live through three years of a sham marriage to stay in Canada; Chouhan fears that could force a woman to suffer a possibly abusive relationship for that time. "She will be just like a slave," he says.

6   To find a viable solution, Chouhan is spearheading a campaign to inform communities about fraud marriages, and he is raising the issue in the provincial legislature. He also believes it is essential to construct a support network for victims. "We need to let them know they are not alone," he says. "Public awareness is so essential for people to understand." But Dhillon hopes some type of legislation is passed soon so that others are protected from the pain she lives with. "I am really afraid now. I can't even trust in men."

Glossary

sham: false; pretended

dowry: property that a woman brings to her husband in marriage

annulled: made no longer binding under the law

sanctioned: ratified by authority; authorized

Comprehension Questions

1. What, in your own words, is the thesis of this article?

2. What did Dhillon lose as a result of her experience?

3. What are the suggested solutions in the article for preventing the type of fraud described in this piece?

Questions about Form

1. Why do you think the author starts his article by referring to a particular person's experience?

2. Is the title powerful? Why or why not? Discuss.

Questions for Discussion

1. What can parents do to prevent this type of thing from happening to their daughter?

2. According to New Democrat MLA Raj Chouhan, the policy change the Vancouver-based Canadian Marriage Fraud Victim Society is suggesting is a bad one. What policy do you think the government should adopt?

3. Read "Lessons of Love from Stories of Old" (beginning on page 396) by Gary Lipschutz. What is similar between that article and this one? Why does materialism often get in the way of a good marriage?

Writing Ideas

1. Write a paragraph or essay on how an arranged marriage should be managed given the situation described in the article.

2. In a paragraph or essay, argue for or against the traditional notion of the "dowry." Remember, you might want to argue that another culture has its own version of the "dowry." Explain this briefly before you state your thesis. Remember to give logical reasons in support of the stand you take.

◆ ◆ ◆

Unit V **Appendices**

Appendix A Distinguishing between Words Often Confused

Words That Sound Alike

allowed (*verb*)   permitted
aloud (*adv.*)   out loud

> Examples:
> The boy was finally allowed to stay up late.
> Her question was stated aloud for all to hear.

altar (*noun*)   an elevated place or table for religious rites
alter (*verb*)   to change or adjust

> Examples:
> The altar was decorated for the church service.
> If you alter the plans, they won't work out.

aural (*adj.*)   having to do with the ear or hearing
oral (*adj.*)   having to do with the mouth or speech

> Examples:
> I have poor aural skills because I won't listen.
> The history of the First Nations is kept alive through their oral traditions.

brake (*verb*)   to stop
    (*noun*)   a device used for slowing or stopping
break (*verb*)   to smash, crack, or come apart
    (*noun*)   a crack, severing; an interruption, change

> Examples:
> Apply the brake when you want to stop.
> You'll have to break the lock to get in.
> Give me a break!

capital (*adj.*)   chief; major; fatal
      (*noun*)   leading city; money
capitol (*noun*)   a building in which a U.S. state legislature assembles

> Examples:
> Ottawa is the capital of Canada.
> The capitol building for the New York state legislature is in Albany.

chord (*noun*)   three or more musical tones sounded together;
                  harmony
cord (*noun*)   a small rope of twisted strands; any ropelike structure;
                  a unit of cut fuel wood

> Examples:
> Many guitar chords are easy to play.
> A strong cord is needed to tie the bundle together.

close (*verb*)   to shut
clothes (*noun*)   garments
cloth (*noun*)   fabric; a piece of material

> Examples:
> Close the door and keep the cold out.
> T-shirts are our favourite type of summer clothes.
> His coat was made of cloth, not leather.

coarse (*adj.*)   rough; not fine; common or of inferior quality
course (*noun*)   direction or path of something moving; part of a meal;
                  a school subject

> Examples:
> Coarse sandpaper is used to make a rough finish.
> One course I'm taking this year is English grammar.

complement (*noun*)   something that completes or makes up a whole
        (*verb*)   to complete; to supplement, enhance
compliment (*noun*)   an expression of praise
        (*verb*)   to give praise

> Examples:
> A blue blazer complements grey slacks.
> Good work deserves a compliment.

complementary (*adj.*)   complementing, often completing a pair or group of
                  things that go together
complimentary (*adj.*)   expressing a compliment; given free as a favour

> Examples:
> With the textbook, he assigned the complementary study guide.
> I have complimentary tickets to the game.

fair (*adj.*)	unbiased; light colour; free of clouds; promising; lovely
(*noun*)	an exhibition; regional event; market
fare (*noun*)	a charge for transportation; food
(*verb*)	get along; do

Examples:
A pink sunset means a fair day will follow.
The train fare is increasing yearly.

flour (*noun*)	the powder produced by grinding a grain
flower (*noun*)	a blossom of a plant
(*verb*)	to blossom

Examples:
Wheat flour is used to make bread.
Tulips flower in early spring.

for (*prep.*)	directed to; in the amount of; on behalf of; to the extent of
(*conj.*)	because
four (*noun, adj.*)	number
forty (*adj.*)	Notice that this number is spelled differently from *four*, *fourteen*, or *twenty-four*.
fore (*noun, adj.*)	situated near the front

Examples:
This gift is for you.
There are four people in attendance.
His ideas came to the fore at work.

forth (*adv.*)	onward in time, place, or order
fourth (*noun, adj.*)	number

Examples:
Go forth from this place.
She is fourth in line for tickets.

forward (*verb*)	to send on to another address
(*adj.*)	bold; progressive
(*adv.*)	moving toward the front
foreword (*noun*)	introduction to a book; preface

Examples:
Move forward so you can hear the speaker.
The foreword to a book is sometimes called the preface.

grate (*verb*)	to shred; to annoy or irritate
(*noun*)	a metal grill
grateful (*adj.*)	appreciative
great (*adj.*)	large; significant; excellent; powerful; skillful; first-rate

Examples:
Her negative attitude grates on my nerves.
Winning the prize was a great achievement.

it's	contraction of *it is*
its	possessive form of *it*

Examples:
It's a nice day today.
The bush has all of its new buds.

knew (*verb*)	past tense *of know*
new (*adj.*)	not old

Examples:
The student knew the correct answer.
His new car is this year's model.

know (*verb*)	to understand
no (*adv.*)	a negative response
(*adj.*)	not any; not one

Examples:
You would know the work if you'd study.
Having no money means that you are poor.

pain (*noun*)	suffering
pane (*noun*)	a panel of glass

Examples:
A cut finger can cause a lot of pain.
Windows contain panes of glass.

passed (*verb*)	the past tense of to *pass*—to move ahead
past (*noun*)	time before the present
(*prep.*)	beyond
(*adj.*)	no longer current

Examples:
I passed the exam and moved to the next grade.
I was past the exit before I noticed that I had missed it.

patience (*noun*)	calm endurance; tolerant understanding
patients (*noun*)	persons under medical treatment

Examples:
Waiting for someone usually takes patience.
Patients in hospitals often are very ill.

peace (*noun*)	absence of war, calm
piece (*noun*)	a portion, a part

Examples:

Peace came when the war was over.

His piece of cake was huge.

plain (*adj.*)   simple; ordinary; unattractive; clear

    (*noun*)   a flat, treeless land region

plane (*noun*)   an aircraft; a flat, level surface; a carpenter's tool for levelling wood; a level of development

Examples:

The flat plain stretched for miles without a tree.

I used a plane to make the wood smooth.

presence (*noun*)   the state of being present; a person's manner

presents (*noun*)   gifts

    (*verb*)   (third person singular) to introduce; to give a gift

Examples:

The presence of the teacher kept the students quiet.

Presents are given on birthdays.

principal (*adj.*)   most important; chief; main

    (*noun*)   the head of a school; a sum of money

principle (*noun*)   rule or standard

Examples:

The principal rule is the most important guideline.

There are principles of conduct to be followed at school.

rain (*noun, verb*)   water falling to earth in drops

reign (*noun, verb*)   a period of rule for a king or queen

rein (*noun*)   a strap attached to a bridle, used to control a horse

Examples:

A good rain will soak the crops.

The monarch's reign extended for many years.

To control a horse, learn how to use the reins.

raise (*verb*)   to move upward; to awaken; to increase; to collect

    (*noun*)   an increase in salary

rays (*noun*)   thin lines or beams of radiation

raze (*verb*)   to tear down or demolish

Examples:

A raise in pay often rewards good work.

The sun's rays contain harmful radiation.

The old building was razed to the ground.

sight (*noun*)   the ability to see; a view

site (*noun*)   the plot of land where something is located; the place of an event

cite (*verb*)   to quote as an authority or example

> **Examples:**
> Some people with perfect sight don't see clearly.
> The opera house's site is between two theatres.
> I can cite my grammar text as my authority.

stair (*noun*)	one of a flight of steps
stare (*noun, verb*)	a fixed gaze; to look at insistently

> **Examples:**
> Each stair climbed brings you farther up the steps.
> A steady gaze can be considered a stare.

stake (*noun*)	a post sharpened at one end to drive into the ground; a financial share
(*verb*)	to attach or support; to set limits with a stake
steak (*noun*)	a cut of meat, usually beef

> **Examples:**
> My stake in the profits amounted to a quarter share.
> I like my steak well done and thick.

stationary (*adj.*)	standing still
stationery (*noun*)	writing paper and envelopes

> **Examples:**
> Anything that is stationary does not move.
> Stationery can be written upon.

they're	contraction of *they are*
their	possessive
there	at that place

> **Examples:**
> They're a happy couple.
> This antique is their prized possession.
> I'll meet you over there, behind the store.

to (*prep.*)	in a direction toward
to (+ *verb*)	the infinitive form of a verb
too (*adv.*)	also; excessively; very
two (*noun*)	number

> **Examples:**
> Go to school.
> To see is to believe.
> I, too, am going to the party.
> Two is one more than one.

vain (*adj.*)	conceited; unsuccessful
vane (*noun*)	a plate of wood or metal, often in the shape of a rooster, that pivots to indicate the direction of the wind; the weblike part of a feather

vein *(noun)* a blood vessel; the branching framework of a leaf; an occurrence of an ore; a strip of colour; a streak; a transient attitude

Examples:
A vain person spends a lot of time in front of a mirror.
The vane on the roof tells the wind direction.
Veins in your body contain blood.

waist *(noun)* the middle portion of a body, garment, or object
waste *(verb)* to use thoughtlessly or carelessly
   (noun) objects discarded as useless

Examples:
A belt around your waist holds your pants up.
Excess packaging contains much waste.

wait *(verb)* to remain inactive
weight *(noun)* the measure of the heaviness of an object

Examples:
Remain here and wait for my arrival.
My weight goes up every time I eat.

ware *(noun)* an article of commerce
wear *(verb)* to have on
   (noun) deterioration as a result of use
where *(adv.)* at or in what place

Examples:
You can sell your wares at the flea market.
What clothes will you wear?
He asked where the museum could be found.

weather *(noun)* atmospheric conditions
whether *(conj.)* if it is the case that

Examples:
The weather report calls for rain.
She will go whether I go or not.

whole *(adj.)* complete
hole *(noun)* an opening

Examples:
A pie is whole before it is sliced and served.
Holes in the road need to be filled in.

who's contraction of *who is*
whose possessive

wood (*noun*)   the tough tissue from trees
would (*verb*)   past tense of *will*

Examples:
Most paper is made from wood fibre.
He would go, he said, if he could find a ride.

write (*verb*)   to form letters and words; to compose
right (*adj.*)   conforming to justice, law, or morality; correct; toward a conservative political point of view
     (*noun*)   that which is just, morally good, legal, or proper; a direction; a political group whose policies are conservative
     (*adv.*)   directly; well; completely; immediately
rite (*noun*)   a traditional, solemn, and often religious ceremony

Examples:
Write a letter to your aunt.
You should always try to do what is right.
Last rites were said over the dying person.

yoke (*noun*)   a harness fastening two or more animals together; a form of bondage
yolk (*noun*)   the yellow of an egg

Examples:
Animals in a team are joined by a yoke.
Some diners like their eggs cooked without the yolks broken.

you're   contraction of *you are*
your   possessive

Examples:
You're my best friend.
Take your gift to the party.

Words That Sound or Look Almost Alike

Some words are often confused with other words that sound or look almost the same. Learning to spell these words correctly involves a careful study of pronunciations along with meanings.

	Pronunciation	Meaning
accept	*a* as in *pat*	*verb*: to receive; to admit; to regard as true or right
except	the first *e* as in *pet*	*prep.*: other than; but; only

Examples:
I accepted the parcel from the courier.
Everyone was there except the two of us.

access	*a* as in *pat*	*noun*: a means of approaching; the right to enter or make use of
excess	the first *e* as in *pet*	*noun*: a quantity or amount beyond what is required

Examples:
Access to the files will provide you with information.
Overeating is an unnecessary excess.

advice	Pronounce *-ice* like the word *ice*.	*noun:* opinion as to what should be done about a problem
advise	Pronounce *-ise* like *eyes*. the word	*verb:* to suggest; to counsel

Examples:
My best advice is to accept the offer.
I advise you to do what is right.

affect	*a* as in *about*	*verb*: to influence
effect	the first *e* as the *e* in *pet* or *i* in *pit*	*noun*: result *verb*: to bring about a result

Examples:
I can affect his decision with my advice.
The effect of the rain was to cancel the game.

allusion	*a* as in *about*	*noun*: an indirect reference
illusion	the first *i* as in *pit*	*noun*: a mistaken concept or belief

Examples:
An allusion was made to my great intelligence.
It is an illusion to think you will get rich without working.

breath	*ea* as the *e* in pet	*noun*: the air that is inhaled or exhaled in breathing
breathe	the *ea* as the *e* in *be*	*verb*: to inhale and exhale air

Examples:
You can see your breath on the window on a cold day.
Breathe deeply and inhale the clean country air.

clothes	*o* as the *oe* in *toe*	*noun*: garments; wearing apparel
cloths	*o* as the *aw* in *paw*	*noun*: pieces of fabric

Examples:

The clothes you are wearing are fashionable.

Pieces of cloth can be torn from the fabric to make rags.

conscience	kŏn′ shəns (two syllables)	*noun:* recognition of right and wrong
conscientious	kŏn shē en′ shəs (four syllables)	*adj.:* careful; thorough
conscious	kŏn′ shəs (two syllables)	*adj.:* awake; aware of one's own existence

Examples:

My conscience told me to do the right thing.

I conscientiously performed my duty to the best of my ability.

She was conscious of the fact that he was behind her.

costume	*o* as in *pot*, *u* as the *u* in *you*	*noun:* a special style of dress for a particular occasion
custom	*u* as in *cut*, *o* as in *gallop*	*noun:* a common tradition

Examples:

The costume he wore reflected his Ukrainian heritage.

It is our custom to wash our hands before eating.

council **counsel** }	*ou* as in *out*	*noun:* a group that governs *verb:* to give advice *noun:* a lawyer; advice
consul	*o* as in *pot*	*noun:* a governmental official in the foreign service

Examples:

The town council passed a by-law.

Good counsel is advice well received.

Canada has a consul in many foreign countries.

desert	di zurt′ *i* as in *pit*	*verb:* to abandon *noun:* something deserved (often plural)
	dez′ ert the first *e* as in *pet*	*noun:* barren land
dessert	di zurt′ *i* as in *pit*	*noun:* last part of a meal, often a sweet

Examples:

The desert is usually a hot, arid place.

Our family usually eats dessert following dinner.

He got his just deserts.

diner	*i* as the *ie* in *pie*	*noun*: a person eating dinner; a restaurant with a long counter and booths
dinner	*i* as in *pit*	*noun*: chief meal of the day

Examples:
A diner is a place where meals are served.
Dinner is usually eaten in the early evening.

emigrate **emigrant** }	*e* as in *pet*	*noun*: someone who leaves a country to settle in another country
immigrate **immigrant** }	the first *i* as in *pit*	*verb*: to come into a country *noun*: someone who enters a country to settle there

Examples:
Many people decided to emigrate from Ireland during the famine.
Immigrants to our country bring valuable skills.

farther	*a* as in *father*	*adj., adv.*: greater physical or measurable distance
further	*u* as in *urge*	*adj., adv.*: greater mental distance; more distant in time or degree; additional

Examples:
Montreal is farther than Toronto from Windsor.
We drew further apart in our approach to the problem.

local	lo' kəl *a* as in *about*	*adj.*: relating or peculiar to a place
locale	lo kal' *a* as in *pat*	*noun*: a place, scene, or setting, as of a novel

Examples:
Everyone here goes to the local school on the next block.
Our town was the locale for a movie.

moral	mor' al *a* as in *about*	*adj.*: a sense of right and wrong *noun*: the lesson of a story, fable, or event
morale	mo ral' *a* as in *pat*	*noun*: the attitude or spirit of a person or group of people

Examples:
The moral of the story taught us never to cheat.
Their morale was shown by their enthusiasm for their jobs.

personal	per′ son al	*adj.*: pertaining to a particular person
personnel	per son nel′	*noun*: the people employed by an organization; an administrative division of an organization concerned with the employees

Examples:
The matter is a personal one between him and me.
Most of the plant's personnel were laid off.

precede	the first *e* as the *i* in *pit*	*verb*: to come before
proceed	the *o* as the *oe* in *toe*	*verb*: to continue

Examples:
You go first and precede me down the hall.
Proceed with the story you started yesterday.

quiet	qui′ et *i* as the *ie* in *pie*, *e* as in *pet*	*adj.*: silent *noun*: silence
quit	*i* as in *pit*	*verb*: to give up; to stop
quite	*i* as the *ie* in *pie*; the *e* is silent	*adv.*: somewhat; completely; truly

Examples:
It was a quiet night when no sound could be heard.
Quit what you are doing and start something else.
It is quite true that I am guilty.

receipt	the first *e* as the *i* in *pit*, *ei* as in the *e* in *be*; the *p* is silent	*noun*: a bill marked as paid; the act of receiving something *verb*: to mark as paid
recipe	the first *e* as in *pet*, the *i* like the *a* in *about* the final *e* as in *be*	*noun*: a formula for preparing a mixture, especially in cooking

Examples:
The receipt for the dinner was marked "paid."
The recipe calls for more chocolate in the cookies.

special	spĕsh′ əl	*adj.*: exceptional; distinctive
especially	Notice the extra syllable at the beginning.	*adv.*: particularly

Examples:
She was a special person, one of a kind.
It is especially important to file an income tax return.

than	*a* as in *pat*	*conj.*: used to make a comparison
then	*e* as in *pet*	*adv.*: at that time; in that case

> Examples:
> She is smarter than I am.
> It was then that I made up my mind.

thorough	the first *o* as the *u* in *urge*, *ou* as the *oe* in *toe*	*adj.*: all that is needed; fully done
though	*ou* as the *oe* in *toe*	*conj.*: despite the fact
thought	*ou* as the *aw* in *paw*	*verb*: past tense of to think
through	*ou* as the *oo* in boot	*prep.* used to indicate entrance at one side and exit from the other; finished
threw	sounds like *through*	*verb*: past tense of to throw

Note: *Thru* is only an informal spelling for the word *through*. Do not use it in formal writing.

> Examples:
> The thorough investigation found a hidden clue.
> It's not true, though, that I told a lie.
> He thought of the answer before he spoke.
> Go through that exit to get outside.
> He threw the ball as far as he could.

Words That Sound or Look Almost Alike: sit/set; rise/raise; lie/lay

These six verbs are among the most troublesome in English because each is similar in sound, spelling, and meaning to another verb. Since they are all irregular verbs, students must be careful to learn to spell the principal parts correctly. The key to learning how to use the verbs *sit*, *rise*, and *lie* is to remember that these are actions the subject can do without any help; no other person or thing has to be included in the sentence. When you use the verbs *set*, *raise*, and *lay* in a sentence, the actions of these verbs are done to other persons or objects; these persons or things have to be included directly in the sentence. For example, when you use the verb to sit, all you need is a subject and a form of the verb:

> I sit.

However, when you use the verb to *set*, you need a subject, a form of the verb, and an object.

> Examples:
> I set the glass on the table.

The subject *I* and the verb *set* are followed by the object *glass*, which is what the subject set on the table.

	sit: to take a sitting position *never* takes an object	**set:** to place something into position *always* takes an object	

Present:	I *sit*.	I *set the glass* down.
Present participle:	I *am sitting*.	I *am setting the glass* down.
Past:	I *sat*.	I *set the glass* down.
Past participle:	I *have sat*.	I *have set the glass* down.

	rise: to stand up; to move upward *never* takes an object	**raise:** to make something move up or grow; *always* takes an object	

Present:	I *rise*.	I *raise the flag*.
Present participle:	The sun *is rising*.	I *am raising the flag*.
Past:	He *rose* at eight o'clock.	I *raised the flag*.
Past participle:	I *have risen early* today.	I *have raised the flag*.

The verbs *lie* and *lay* are easily confused because two of their principal parts have the same spelling. It takes concentration to learn to use these two verbs correctly.

	lie: to recline *never* takes an object	**lay:** to put; *always* takes an object	

Present:	I *lie* down.	I *lay the pen down*.
Present participle:	I *am lying* down.	I *am laying the pen* down.
Past:	Yesterday I *lay* down.	I *laid the pen* down.
Past participle:	I *have lain* down.	I *have laid the pen* down.

- The verb *lie* can also be a regular verb meaning "to tell an untruth." The principal parts of this verb are *lie, lying, lied, has lied*.

Words That Sound or Look Almost Alike: choose/chose; lose/loose; lead/led; die/dye

These verbs are often misspelled because there is confusion about how to spell the vowel sounds of the verbs. Study the spelling of the principal parts below.

Present	**Present Participle**	**Past**	**Past Participle**
choose	choosing	chose	has chosen
lose	losing	lost	has lost
lead	leading	led	has led
die	dying	died	has died

Notes:

- *Loose* is an adjective meaning "not tightly fitted." Remember, it rhymes with *goose*.
- *Lead* can also be a noun meaning a bluish-grey metal. Remember, it rhymes with *head*.
- *Dye* is another verb meaning "to colour." Its principal parts are *dye, dyeing, dyed, has dyed.*

Words That Sound or Look Almost Alike: use/used; suppose/supposed

To use means to bring or put into service; to make use of.

> **Present:** I *use* my brother's bike to get to school.
> **Past:** Yesterday I *used* my father's car.

Use to means *to have as a custom* or *regular practice* in the past. It usually occurs in its past form, *used to*:

> I *used to* take the bus downtown, but now I get a ride with my neighbour.

Note, however, that in expressions with the auxiliary *did*, you use the present form:

> Did you *use to* take the bus?

A form of to be + used to means to be familiar with or accustomed to.

> I *am used to* walking to school.

To *suppose* means to *guess*.

> **Present:** I *suppose* he is trying.
> **Past:** I *supposed* he was trying.

A form of to be + supposed to means ought to or should.

> Waiters *are supposed to* be courteous.

Many people have difficulty knowing when to choose *used* and *supposed* in their writing because in speaking, the final *d* is often not clearly heard.

> **Incorrect:** I am *suppose to* be in school today.
> **Correct:** I am *supposed to* be in school today.

Appendix B Solving Spelling Problems

Learning to Spell Commonly Mispronounced Words

Several common English words are often mispronounced or pronounced in such a way that the result is incorrect spelling. Below are sixty common words that are often misspelled. As you study them, be careful to spell each of the underlined syllables correctly.

I. Common Omission of Vowels

1. Do not omit the underlined syllable with the *a*:

acciden<u>tal</u>ly	liter<u>a</u>ture
basi<u>cal</u>ly	mini<u>a</u>ture
bound<u>a</u>ry	sep<u>a</u>rate
ex<u>tra</u>ordinary	temper<u>a</u>ment
inciden<u>tal</u>ly	temper<u>a</u>ture

2. Do not omit the underlined syllable with the *e*:

consid<u>e</u>rable	math<u>e</u>matics
diff<u>e</u>rence	num<u>e</u>rous
fun<u>e</u>ral	scen<u>e</u>ry
int<u>e</u>resting	

   However, notice the following words in which the *e* is omitted:

disaster	*becomes*	disastrous
enter	*becomes*	entrance
hinder	*becomes*	hindrance
hunger	*becomes*	hungry
launder	*becomes*	laundry
monster	*becomes*	monstrous
remember	*becomes*	remembrance

3. Do not omit the underlined syllable with the *i*:

aspirin   family   similar

4. Do not omit the underlined syllable with the o:

chocolate   humorous
environment   laboratory
favourite   sophomore

5. Do not omit the underlined syllable with the *u*:

luxury
accuracy

6. Do not omit the underlined syllable with the *y*:

studying

II. Common Omission of Consonants

1. *b*   5. *n*
   probably   government
2. *c*   6. *r*
   arctic   February
3. *d*   library
   candidate   surprise
   handkerchief   7. *t*
   handsome   authentic
   supposed to   identical
   used to   identity
4. *g*   partner
   recognize   promptly
          quantity

III. Common Addition of a Syllable

Do not add unnecessary syllables (e.g., athelete):

athlete
athletic

IV. Common Transposition of Letters

Do not transpose the underlined letters:

perform   prefer
persuade   tragedy

Practice **Identifying the Correct Spelling**

Circle the correct spelling for each of the following words. Check your answers against those in the Answer Key on page 463.

1.	separate	seprate	seperate
2.	probably	probaly	probly
3.	ardic	arctic	artic
4.	surprise	saprize	surprise
5.	tragedy	tradgedy	trajedy
6.	quantity	quantidy	quanity
7.	litrature	literature	literture
8.	hungery	hungary	hungry
9.	handsome	hansome	handsom
10.	favourite	faverite	favrite
11.	nucular	nuclear	nuclar

Learning to Spell *ie* and *ei* Words

Use this rhyme to help you remember how to spell most *ie* and *ei* words:

> *i* before *e*
> except after *c*
> or when sounded like *a*
> as in *neighbour* or *weigh*.

i before *e*

The majority of all the *ie* and *ei* words use *ie*.

> believe
> chief
> friend
> shriek
> yield

except after *c*

> ceiling
> conceit
> conceive
> receipt
> receive

or when sounded like *a*

> beige
> eight
> reins
> sleigh
> vein

Once you have learned the rhyme, concentrate on learning the following groups of words that are the exceptions to this rhyme.

caffeine	leisure	ancient
codeine	seize	conscience
protein	seizure	efficient
		sufficient

neither	counterfeit
either	Fahrenheit
	foreign
sheik	height
stein	
their	
weird	

Practice Choosing *ie* or *ei*

Choose the correct combination of *ie* or *ei* for the following words. Check your answers against those in the Answer Key on page 463.

1. sl_____gh
2. bel_____ve
3. s_____ge
4. v_____l
5. l_____sure

6. dec_____t
7. n_____ce
8. w_____ght
9. prot_____n
10. anc_____nt

Plural Nouns

Almost all nouns are made plural simply by adding *s* to the singular form:

girl	*becomes*	girls
dinner	*becomes*	dinners

However, each of the following groups of words has its own special rule for forming the plural.

1. Words ending in *y*:

In words ending in *y* preceded by a *consonant*, change the *y* to *i* and add *es*.

lady	*becomes*	ladies
ceremony	*becomes*	ceremonies

Words ending in *y* preceded by a *vowel* form their plurals in the regular way, by just adding *s*.

day	*becomes*	days
monkey	*becomes*	monkeys
valley	*becomes*	valleys

2. Words ending in *o*:

Most words ending in *o* preceded by a consonant add *es* to form the plural.

echo	*becomes*	echoes
hero	*becomes*	heroes
potato	*becomes*	potatoes

However, musical terms or names of musical instruments (which derive from Italian) add only *s*.

piano	*becomes*	pianos
solo	*becomes*	solos
soprano	*becomes*	sopranos

Words ending in *o* preceded by a *vowel* add *s*.

patio	*becomes*	patios
radio	*becomes*	radios
rodeo	*becomes*	rodeos

Some words ending in *o* may form their plural by adding *s* or *es*.

memento	*becomes*	mementos	*or*	mementoes
pinto	*becomes*	pintos	*or*	pintoes
zero	*becomes*	zeros	*or*	zeroes

If you are uncertain about the plural ending of a word ending in *o*, it is best to use the dictionary. The dictionary gives all the endings of irregular plurals. If no plural form is given, you know the word will form its plural in the regular way, by adding only *s*.

3. Words ending in *ch, sh, s, x,* and *z*:

For words ending in *ch, sh, s, x,* and *z*, add *es*.

> witches
> dishes
> dresses
> taxes
> buzzes

4. Words ending in *fe* or *f*:

Some words ending in *fe* or *f* change the *f* to *v* and add *es*. You can hear the change from the *f* sound to the *v* sound in the plural.

wife	*becomes*	wives
leaf	*becomes*	leaves

Other words ending in *f* or *ef* keep the *f* and just add *s*.

sheriff	*becomes*	sheriffs
belief	*becomes*	beliefs

Again, you can hear that the *f* sound is kept in the plural. Some words can form their plural either way. If so, the dictionary will give the preferred way first.

5. Foreign words:

Some words borrowed from other languages keep the plurals from those languages to form the plural in English.

alga	*becomes*	algae
alumna	*becomes*	alumnae
alumnus	*becomes*	alumni
crisis	*becomes*	crises
phenomenon	*becomes*	phenomena

6. Compound nouns:

Compound nouns make their plurals by putting the *s* on the end of the main word.

brother-in-law	*becomes*	brothers-in-law
passer-by	*becomes*	passers-by

7. Irregular plurals:

Some nouns in English have irregular plurals.

Singular	Plural
child	children
deer	deer
foot	feet
goose	geese
man, woman	men, women
moose	moose
mouse	mice
ox	oxen
sheep	sheep
tooth	teeth

 Practice **Forming the Plurals of Nouns**

Using the rules you have learned, make the following words plural. Check your answers against those in the Answer Key on pages 463–464.

1. puppy   _____

2. mother-in-law   _____

3. tooth   _____

4. cameo   _____

5. phenomenon   _____

6. loaf   _____

7. match   _____

8. mix   _____

9. enemy   _____

10. bag   _____

Prefixes and Suffixes

Like everything else in this world, words had to begin somewhere. Many English words come from (had their *roots* in) other languages; others were created to describe something new. For example, modern English has many roots in Old English, ancient Greek, and Latin. For example:

Roots and Derivatives

Old English

akr	a field, acre
foda	food, fodder
haelan	to heal, health
war	defence, war

Latin

audio	to hear, audience
dignus	dignity, worth
clarus	clear, clarify
nomen	name

Greek

angelos	angel
gramma	a letter
kosmos	the world
logos	word

Prefixes and suffixes can be added to the roots of words to alter the meaning of the words or to create new words with new meanings. A **prefix** is a word or part of a word placed before the root of a word, and a **suffix** is placed after the root. As is the case with root words, the English language derives many of its prefixes and suffixes from Latin and Greek. For example:

Some Latin Prefixes

ante-	before
contra-	against
extra-	beyond
in-	in, into
non-	not
post-	after
pro-	before
super-	above

Some Greek Prefixes

ampli-	on both sides
anti-	opposite
auto-	self
hemi-	half
hyper-	over, above
mono-	alone, single
para-	beside
pro-	before

Some Latin Suffixes		**Some Greek Suffixes**	
-ary	belonging to	*-ic*	pertaining to
-ess	feminine of	*-ism*	act, state, condition
-et, ette	denoting diminution	*-ist*	a doer
-ty	quality, state, condition		

Here are some examples of English words with prefixes and suffixes added:

anti	+	biotic	=	antibiotic
benefit	+	ary	=	beneficiary
communist	+	ism	=	communism
hemi	+	sphere	=	hemisphere
host	+	ess	=	hostess
in	+	dispensable	=	indispensable
pro	+	claim	=	proclaim

Adding a prefix or, especially, a suffix may change the spelling of the original root word. Consult the basic spelling rules on the following pages for tips on spelling words that include prefixes and suffixes.

Should the Final Consonant Be Doubled?

The answer to the question of whether a final consonant should be doubled involves the most complicated spelling rule. However, the rule is well worth learning because once you know it, you will suddenly be able to spell thousands of words correctly.

In order to understand the rule, remember first the difference between vowels (*a, e, i, o, u*, and sometimes *y*) and consonants (all the other letters in the alphabet). The problem in spelling occurs when you want to add an ending that begins with a vowel, such as *-ed, -er, -est,* or *-ing*. Sometimes a word will double the last letter before adding an ending:

> trap + ing = trapping The fur traders spent their time tra*pp*ing animals.

Sometimes the word will *not* double the last letter before adding the ending:

> turn + er = turner He dropped the pancake tur*n*er.

How do you know when to double the final consonant?

> **Rule for Doubling One-Syllable Words**
> Double the final consonant of a one-syllable word when adding an ending that begins with a vowel only if the last three letters of the word are a consonant-vowel-consonant combination.

Since *rap* in the word *trap* is a consonant-vowel-consonant combination, this one-syllable word will double the final consonant when adding an ending beginning with a vowel. Since the last three letters *urn* in the word *turn* are a vowel-consonant-consonant combination, this one-syllable word does not double the final consonant when adding an ending beginning with a vowel.

Note that in words with *qu* like *quit* or *quiz*, you should think of the *qu* as a consonant (he *u* does have a consonant *w* sound): *quit* + *ing* = quitting.

Rule for Doubling the Consonant in Words of More Than One Syllable

For words of more than one syllable, the rule adds more condition: if the first syllable is accented in the newly formed word, you do not double the final consonant.

pre fer′ + ed = pre ferred′

but

pre fer′ + ence = pref′ er ence

(The accent has changed to the first syllable.)

Practice Doubling the Consonant?

For each of the following one-syllable words, determine whether or not the word will double the final consonant when adding an ending beginning with a vowel. The first two are done for you. Check your answers against those in the Answer Key on page 464.

One-Syllable Word	Consonant-Vowel-Consonant Combination?	Double?	Add *-ing* Ending
drag	yes	yes	dragging
drain	no	no	draining
slip			
crack			
broil			
win			

Try these two-syllable words:

con *trol′* + ing   =   _____

fe′ *ver* + ish   =   _____

For each of the following words of more than one syllable, determine whether or not the word will double the final consonant when adding an ending beginning with a vowel.

com pel′ + ed   =   _____

dif′ *fer* + ence   =   _____

be ginn′ + ing   =   _____

Doubling the Final Consonant When Adding Endings That Begin with Vowels

Decide whether or not to double the final consonant when adding the endings to the following words. Check your answers against those in the Answer Key on page 464.

	Word		Ending		New Word
1.	bit	+	en	=	_____
2.	oc cur′	+	ence	=	_____
3.	wa′ ver	+	ing	=	_____
4.	pre fer′	+	ed	=	_____
5.	pre′ fer	+	ence	=	_____
6.	thin	+	er	=	_____
7.	trans fers′	+	ed	=	_____
8.	sail	+	ing	=	_____
9.	pro pel′	+	ent	=	_____
10.	o mit′	+	ed	=	_____

Words Ending in –y

1. When a *y* at the end of a word is preceded by a consonant, change *y* to *i* and add the ending.

carry	+	er	=	carrier
merry	+	ment	=	merriment
funny	+	er	=	_____
pretty	+	ness	=	_____
vary	+	es	=	_____

Exceptions: Do not change the *y* to *i* if the ending starts with an *i*. Few English words have two *i*'s together.

study	+	ing	=	studying (not studiing)
ready	+	ing	=	_____

Some long words drop the *y* when adding the ending. You can hear that the *y* syllable is missing when you pronounce the word correctly.

military	+	ism	=	militarism
accompany	+	ist	=	_____

2. When *y* at the end of a word is preceded by a vowel, do not change the *y* when adding the ending. Simply add the ending.

survey	+	s	=	surveys
enjoy	+	ment	=	_____

Practice **Adding Endings to Words That End in -y**

Add endings to the following words, being sure to change the *y* to *i* whenever necessary. Check your answers against those in the Answer Key on page 464.

Word	Ending		New Word
1. key	+ s	=	_____
2. lonely	+ ness	=	_____
3. cry	+ ing	=	_____
4. cry	+ s	=	_____
5. pray	+ er	=	_____
6. employ	+ ment	=	_____
7. monkey	+ ing	=	_____
8. beauty	+ ful	=	_____
9. theory	+ es	=	_____
10. ceremony	+ al	=	_____

Is It One Word or Two?

There is often confusion about whether certain word combinations should be joined together to form compound words. Study the following groups of words to avoid this common confusion.

These words are always written as one word:

another	everything	playroom
bathroom	grandmother	schoolteacher
bedroom	nearby	southeast, northwest, etc.
bookkeeper	nevertheless	workplace
cannot	newspaper	yourself
downstairs		

These words are always written as two words:

a lot	high school
all right	living room
dining room	no one
good night	

These words are written as one or two words depending on their use:

all ready (*pronoun + adj.*)   completely prepared
already (*adv.*)   previously; before

all together (*pronoun + adj.*)   in a group
altogether (*adv.*)   completely

all ways (*adj. + noun*)	every road or path
always (*adverb*)	on every occasion
any one (*adj. + pronoun*)	one person or thing in a specific group
anyone (*indef. pronoun*)	any person at all
every day (*adj. + noun*)	e.g., I do my chores every day.
everyday (*one-word adj. placed before a noun*)	e.g., I do my everyday chores.
every one (*adj. + pronoun*)	every person or thing in a specific group
everyone (*indef. pronoun*)	all of the people
may be (*verb*)	might be
maybe (*adv.*)	perhaps

 Practice One Word or Two?

Fill in the blank in each of the following sentences by choosing the correct word or words to complete that sentence. Check your answers against those in the Answer Key on page 464.

1. The blue rug looks beautiful in the white _____.
   (bed room, bedroom)

2. The room is usually occupied by our _____ but she is not here right now. (grandmother, grand mother)

3. She has _____ left for a winter vacation.
   (all ready, already)

4. Last night we all called her and _____ we sang "Happy Birthday" over the phone. (all together, altogether)

5. We _____ remember her birthday, no matter where we are.
   (all ways, always)

6. _____ likes to be remembered on special days, particularly a birthday.
   (Every one, Everyone)

7. Next year, _____ all the members of the family will be able to
   (may be, maybe)
   celebrate her birthday with us.

8. If she _____ come to us, we will drive up and surprise her.
   (cannot, can not)

9. Most families have members who do not live _____.
   (near by, nearby)

10. _____, we can keep in touch by letter, phone, or visits.
    (Never the less, Nevertheless)

Word List 1: Silent Letters

b	**h**	**p**	**w**
climb	exhibit	pneumonia	answer
crumb	rhetproc	psychology	
debt	rhythm		
doubt	school	**s**	
sibtle		aisle	
	l	debris	
c	colonel	island	
indict			
	n	**t**	
d	autumn	depot	
knowledge	column	listen	
Wednesday	condemn	mortgage	

Word List 2: Double Letters

accidentally	exaggerate	questionnaire
accommodate	finally	recommend
across	guarantee	sheriff
address	harass	succeed
annual	necessary	success
apparently	occasionally	suggest
arrangement	omission	summarize
committee	possession	tomorrow
embarrass	preferred	written *but* writing

Word List 3: *-able* or *-ible*

-able

Usually, when you begin with a complete word, the ending is *-able*.

acceptable
agreeable

- These words keep the *e* when adding the ending:

    peaceable   manageable
    noticeable   knowledgeable

- These words drop the e when adding the ending:

    conceivable   dispensable
    desirable   imaginable

-ible

Usually, if you start with a root that is not a word, the ending is *-ible*.

audible	illegible	possible
compatible	incredible	sensible
eligible	permissible	susceptible
feasible	plausible	tangible

Word List 4: *de-* or *di-*

de-	**di-**
decide	dilemma
decision	dilute
delinquent	discipline
descend	discuss
describe	disease
despair	disguise
despicable	dispense
despise	dispute
despite	dissent
despondent	divide
destructive	divine
develop	division
device	

Word List 5: The *-er* Sound

Most words ending with the *-er* sound are spelled with *-er*, as in the words *prisoner*, *customer*, and *hunger*. Words that are exceptions to this should be learned carefully.

-ar

beggar	dollar	polar
burglar	grammar	similar
calendar	pillar	vulgar
collar		

-or

actor	emperor	professor
author	governor	sailor
bachelor	motor	scissors
doctor		

-our	**-re**	**-ur**	**-yr**
humour	centre	murmur	martyr
labour	litre		
neighbour	theatre		

Word List 6: *-ance* or *-ence*

Most words with the *-ence* sound at the end are spelled *-ence*. Here are a few examples:

audience	insistence
correspondence	intelligence
excellence	licence (noun)
existence	presence
independence	reference

Learn these exceptions:

-ance

		-ense
allowance	nuisance	license (verb)
ambulance	observance	
appearance	resistance	**-eance**
assistance	significance	vengeance
attendance	tolerance	
balance		
deliverance		
dominance		
guidance		
ignorance		

Word List 7: Problems with *s, c, z, x,* and *k*

absence	criticize	medicine
alcohol	ecstasy	muscle
analyze/analyse	emphasize	prejudice
auxiliary	especially	recede
awkward	exceed	sincerely
biscuit	exercise	supersede
complexion	fascinate	vacillate
concede	magazine	vicious
consensus		

Word List 8: Twenty-Four Demons

acquire	courageous	occurred
argument	extremely	occurrence
benefit	frightening	privilege
cafeteria	grateful	ridiculous
category	inoculate	secretary
cemetery	lightning	truly
conquer	ninety	until
corroborate	ninth	village

Appendix C Irregular Verbs

Principal Parts of Irregular Verbs

Simple Form	Past Form	Past Participle
1. All three principal parts are the same.		
beat	beat	beat or beaten
bet	bet	bet
burst	burst	burst
cast	cast	cast
cost	cost	cost
cut	cut	cut
fit	fit	fit
hit	hit	hit
hurt	hurt	hurt
let	let	let
put	put	put
quit	quit	quit
read	*read	*read
rid	rid	rid
set	set	set
shut	shut	shut
split	split	split
spread	spread	spread
wet	wet	wet
2. The past form and past participle are the same.		
bend	bent	bent
lend	lent	lent

*Pronunciation changes.

Simple Form	Past Form	Past Participle
send	sent	sent
spend	spent	spent
build	built	built
creep	crept	crept
feel	felt	felt
keep	kept	kept
sleep	slept	slept
sweep	swept	swept
deal	dealt	dealt
mean	meant	meant
leave	left	left
bleed	bled	bled
feed	fed	fed
flee	fled	fled
lead	led	led
speed	sped	sped
cling	clung	clung
dig	dug	dug
spin	spun	spun
stick	stuck	stuck
sting	stung	stung
strike	struck	struck
swing	swung	swung
wring	wrung	wrung
win	won	won
lay (to put)	laid	laid
pay	paid	paid
say	said	said
sell	sold	sold
tell	told	told
bind	bound	bound
find	found	found
grind	ground	ground
wind	wound	wound
bring	brought	brought
buy	bought	bought
fight	fought	fought

Simple Form	Past Form	Past Participle
find	found	found
think	thought	thought
seek	sought	sought
catch	caught	caught
teach	taught	taught
have	had	had
sit	sat	sat
hear	heard	heard
hold	held	held
shoot	shot	shot
stand	stood	stood

3. All forms are different.

draw	drew	drawn
fall	fell	fallen
shake	shook	shaken
take	took	taken
bear	bore	borne
swear	swore	sworn
tear	tore	torn
wear	wore	worn
blow	blew	blown
fly	flew	flown
grow	grew	grown
know	knew	known
throw	threw	thrown
begin	began	begun
drink	drank	drunk
ring	rang	rung
shrink	shrank	shrunk
sing	sang	sung
sink	sank	sunk
spring	sprang	sprung
swim	swam	swum
bite	bit	bitten (or bit)
hide	hid	hidden (or hid)
drive	drove	driven

Simple Form	Past Form	Past Participle
ride	rode	ridden
stride	strode	stridden
rise	rose	risen
write	wrote	written
dive	dove	dived
break	broke	broken
freeze	froze	frozen
speak	spoke	spoken
steal	stole	stolen
weave	wove	woven
get	got	gotten
forget	forgot	forgotten
choose	chose	chosen
give	gave	given
forgive	forgave	forgiven
forbid	forbade	forbidden
do	did	done
eat	ate	eaten
go	went	gone
lie (to recline)	lay	lain
see	saw	seen

Practice Irregular Verbs

Supply the past form or the past participle for each verb in parentheses. Check your answers against those in the Answer Key on page 464.

1. We _____ four trout in the stream.
   (to catch)

2. I shouldn't have _____ my gloves on the counter.
   (to lay)

3. The audience _____ when the singer attempted the high notes.
   (to flee)

4. The pipe _____ yesterday; we are waiting for a plumber.
   (to burst)

5. He has _____ aimlessly around the city for several hours.
   (to ride)

6. The firefighters _____ down the ladder.
   (to slide)

7. The elevator _____ quickly to the tenth floor.
   (to rise)
8. She had _____ her job because of her medical condition.
   (to quit)
9. It was clear he had _____ about our agreement.
   (to forget)
10. He had washed and _____ out all his clothes in the bathtub.
    (to wring)

Appendix D **Answer Key to Practices**

Unit I: Grammar

Chapter 2: Recognizing Subjects and Verbs

Finding the Subject of a Sentence

PRACTICE (p. 16)

1. The <u>plane</u> landed.
2. <u>Michelle Bates</u> gathered her bags.
3. <u>She</u> was so excited.
4. Strange <u>sounds</u> filled her ears.
5. A <u>mother</u> and her three <u>children</u> shared a lunch.
6. The battered red <u>taxi</u> idled outside.
7. A light <u>rain</u> had fallen recently.

Finding Hidden Subjects

PRACTICE (p. 21)

1. (<u>You</u>) look ~~at a map of South America~~.
2. Where is the ancient <u>city</u> ~~of Chan Chan~~?
3. Here ~~on the coastal desert of northern Peru~~ stand the <u>remains</u> ~~of this city of the kings~~.
4. <u>Chan Chan</u>, ~~once the fabulously wealthy centre of the Chimor~~, is situated ~~in one of the driest, bleakest regions in the world~~.
5. <u>It</u> was the largest pre-Columbian city ~~in South America~~.
6. ~~In the ruins of this city~~, <u>scientists</u> have found fragments to piece together the mystery ~~of the past~~.
7. How could this <u>civilization</u> have survived this hostile environment and become so advanced?

Finding Action Verbs

PRACTICE (p. 22)

1. Some <u>people</u> (collect) very strange objects. (present)
2. One <u>man</u> (saved) the fortunes ~~from fortune cookies~~. (past)
3. A <u>group</u> of people ~~in Alberta~~ often (met) to discuss their spark plug collections. (past)
4. <u>People</u> ~~in Brandon~~ (will gather) many types ~~of barbed wire~~. (future)
5. <u>Collectors</u> (take) pride ~~in the possession of unusual items~~. (present)
6. A <u>collection</u>, ~~like odd rocks or unique automobiles~~, (will let) a person express his or her individuality. (future)
7. <u>Collections</u> (keep) us entertained ~~from childhood to old age~~. (present)

Chapter Review Exercises

Finding Subjects and Verbs in Simple Sentences

PRACTICE (p. 25)

1. <u>Mother</u> and <u>Dad</u> always (blame) me ~~for any trouble with my sister~~.
2. My <u>sister</u>, ~~the most popular girl in her class~~, (is) two years older than I.
3. Yesterday, ~~for instance~~, <u>she</u> (was trying on) her new graduation dress.
4. Helpfully, <u>I</u> (took out) her new shoes and purse ~~for her~~.

5. <u>Margaret</u> instantly (became) furious ~~with me~~.
6. I (was) only (sharing) Margaret's excitement ~~about her new clothes~~.

Chapter 3: Solving Verb Problems

Correcting Unnecessary Shifts in Verb Tense

PRACTICE 1 (p. 33)

Answers will vary. These are sample answers.

1. After I complete that writing course, I will take the required history course.
2. In the beginning of the movie, the action was slow; by the end, I was sitting on the edge of my seat.
3. The textbook gives the rules for writing a works cited page, but it doesn't explain how to use parenthetical references.
4. I was walking in the park when all of a sudden I saw her running toward me.
5. The encyclopedia gave several pages of information about astronomy, but it didn't give anything about black holes.
6. The invitation requested that Juan be at the ceremony and that he attend the banquet as well.
7. That website gives you excellent information, but it is too cluttered.

PRACTICE 2 (p. 34)

Doctor Norman Bethune <u>grew</u> up in Gravenhurst, Ontario. He was educated in Toronto and <u>served</u> as a stretcher bearer in World War I. He contracted tuberculosis and thereafter <u>devoted</u> himself to helping other victims of the disease when he <u>practised</u> surgery in Montreal. He also <u>invented</u> or redesigned twelve medical and surgical instruments. Bethune travelled to Russia in 1935, joined the Communist Party, and <u>went</u> to Spain in 1936, where he organized the first mobile blood transfusion service during the Spanish Civil War. After returning to Canada, he shortly left for overseas again, this time to China, where he helped the Chinese Communists in their fight against Japan. "Spain and China," he <u>wrote</u>, "are part of the same battle." While there, he contracted an infection and died. Mao's essay "In Memory of Norman Bethune," prescribed reading during China's Cultural Revolution, urges all Communists to follow Bethune's example of

selfless dedication to others. Bethune is the best-known Canadian to the Chinese, and many Chinese visit his Canadian birthplace.

Using the Correct Tense

PRACTICE (p. 35)

1. have stopped
2. would have
3. will buy
4. had never been
5. liked
6. will soon be
7. is

Choosing the Right Voice

PRACTICE (p. 40)

1. The Canadian health minister made no policy or funding announcements at the International AIDS Conference in Toronto.
   The active is more appropriate. Others did make policy announcements. Knowing who didn't is important.
2. Microsoft founder Bill Gates gave $650 million (U.S.) to the war against HIV/AIDS.
   The passive is probably just as appropriate as the active here. Bill Gates is famous throughout the world, but the amount that he gave is extraordinary, also.
3. Zimbabwe's foreign minister was allowed into Canada for the international conference despite a ban on visits by senior officials from that country.
   The passive is more appropriate. The doer of the action would be Canadian authorities—too insignificant to even mention. The subject in this sentence, Zimbabwe's foreign minister, is the centre of the controversy here.
4. Former U.S. president Bill Clinton told the audience that a lot of mistakes were made during his presidency, but underfunding AIDS research was not one of them.
   The active is more appropriate. Former U.S. President Bill Clinton is more well known than anyone at this conference, even Bill Gates.
5. Twenty-two thousand delegates and 8000 journalists, exhibitors, volunteers, and staff attended the International AIDS Conference in 2006.

Both active and passive are equally appropriate. The number of attendees is massive, but the event itself is worthy of attention.

6. Many at the conference discussed in great detail the impact that poverty has on HIV and AIDS in developing countries.

   The passive is more appropriate. The topic of discussion is more important than the general population that discussed it. Also, the sentence using active voice above sounds awkward.

7. The importance of the role of media in spreading the word about HIV/AIDS was stressed by actor and activist Richard Gere.

   The active voice is more appropriate. Richard Gere is a celebrity activist. What he said matters less than the fact that he is at the conference in the first place.

Chapter Review Exercises

Solving Problems with Verbs

PRACTICE (p. 42)

1. He ought not to drive so fast. *or* He shouldn't drive so fast.
2. It is essential that Lynn take her dog to the vet.
3. I wish I were a chef.
4. She sang for a huge crowd Saturday night.
5. I was shaken up by the accident. *or* The accident shook me up.
6. The skiers climbed the hill.
7. My father asked me last night to help him build a deck.

Chapter 4: Subject-Verb Agreement

Making the Subject and Verb Agree

PRACTICE 1 (p. 45)

1. cycles
2. amazes
3. vary
4. cheer
5. hope

PRACTICE 2 (p. 46)

1. are
2. move
3. move
4. are
5. are

PRACTICE 3 (p. 47)

1. is
2. has
3. is
4. specifies
5. is
6. are
7. is

PRACTICE 4 (p. 48)

1. is
2. was
3. seem
4. takes
5. has

PRACTICE 5 (p. 48)

1. are
2. is
3. are
4. are
5. is

PRACTICE 6 (p. 49)

1. are
2. are
3. has
4. have
5. claps

PRACTICE 7 (p. 49)

1. do
2. were
3. does
4. do
5. were

Chapter Review Exercises

PRACTICE 1 (p. 50)

1. doesn't
2. were
3. doesn't
4. Were
5. doesn't

PRACTICE 2 (p. 50)

1. price, has
2. decision, requires
3. She, doesn't
4. guide or security guard, sees
5. committee, agrees
6. Potato chips and cola, are
7. One, is

Chapter 5: Coordination and Subordination

Recognizing the Comma and Coordinating Conjunction

PRACTICE (p. 55)

1. The <u>audience</u> <u>was packed</u> into the room ⟨ , for ⟩ this <u>was</u> a man with an international reputation.
2. He <u>could have told</u> about all his successes ⟨ , but ⟩ instead <u>he</u> <u>spoke</u> about his disappointments.

3. His <u>words</u> <u>were</u> electric (, so) the <u>crowd</u> <u>was</u> attentive.

4. I <u>should have brought</u> a tape recorder (, or) at least I <u>should have taken</u> notes.

Recognizing the Semicolon, Adverbial Conjunction, and Comma

PRACTICE 1 (p. 58)

1. The <u>restaurant</u> <u>is</u> always too crowded on Saturdays (; nevertheless,) it <u>serves</u> the best food in town.

2. The <u>land</u> <u>was</u> not for sale (; however,) the <u>house</u> <u>could be rented</u>.

3. The <u>lawsuit</u> <u>cost</u> the company several million dollars (; consequently,) the <u>company</u> <u>went</u> out of business a short time later.

4. The <u>doctor</u> <u>told</u> him to lose weight (; furthermore,) she <u>insisted</u> he also stop smoking.

Combining Sentences Using Adverbial Conjunctions

PRACTICE 2 (p. 59)

Answers will vary. These are sample answers.

1. People once preferred to write with a pen or pencil; however, the computer has now become a favourite writing tool.

2. Computers provide a powerful way to create and store pieces of writing; furthermore, they make the editing process fast and efficient.

3. Computers have revolutionized today's offices; consequently, no modern business is without them.

4. Computers have become relatively inexpensive; accordingly, most people own a computer.

5. Many children know more about computers than many adults; moreover, many children are teaching adults how to operate computers.

6. Professional writers have become enthusiastic about the use of computers; nonetheless, there are still some writers who will use only a ballpoint pen.

7. We have many technological aids for writing; nevertheless, let us not forget that the source of all our ideas is the human brain.

Recognizing Dependent and Independent Clauses

PRACTICE 1 (p. 64)

| 1. DC | 3. IC | 5. IC | 7. DC |
| 2. DC | 4. DC | 6. DC | |

Combining Sentences Using Subordination

PRACTICE 2 (p. 65)

Answers will vary. These are sample answers.

1. While he was eating breakfast, the results of the election came over the radio.

2. Simon gave up his plan to launch a dot-com company because he felt it was too risky.

3. I will see my teacher tonight, as she is speaking at the university this evening.

4. The designer hoped for a promotion, although not one person in the department was promoted last year.

5. Since the designer hoped for a promotion, she made sure all her work was done accurately and on time.

Combining Sentences Using a Relative Pronoun

PRACTICE (p. 68)

Answers will vary. These are sample answers.

1. The chemistry lab that I attend is two hours long.

2. The student assistant who is standing by the door is very knowledgeable.

3. The equipment that was purchased last year will make possible some important new research.

Recognizing Restrictive and Nonrestrictive Clauses

PRACTICE (p. 69)

1. Canada's first census, which was taken in 1667, showed 3215 non-Native inhabitants in 668 families.

2. Most of the families who lived near the St. Lawrence River were French Canadians.

3. By the time of Confederation, the population of the country had risen to 3 463 000, which was an increase of 1077 percent over 200 years.

4. If the population of Canada, which is about 30 000 000 persons now, increases by a similar

percentage over the next 150 or so years, we'll have a population of 280 200 000 by the year 2167.

5. Where do you think we will we put everyone who lives in Canada then?

Chapter Review Exercises

Combining Sentences Using Coordination and Subordination

PRACTICE (p. 71)

Answers will vary. This is a sample paragraph.

The wind is strong; the waves are choppy and growing larger. I paddle my kayak harder, but my arms are getting tired. As the energy drains from them, they grow limp and heavy. The other side of the harbour seems distant. The glow of the setting sun is behind me, spreading orange and purple fingers across the sky. The wall of rocks that lies offshore picks up the last light of the setting sun, becoming a silver beacon. I focus on that wall and paddle harder. The sea smashes against my bow, pushing me away from shore. As flecks of spray hit my face, I taste the salt on my lips. With that taste of the sea, the beauty of the sea and shore strikes me. I am distracted from my labour and absorbed by the world around me. As my kayak finally glides past the rocks to the sheltered beach beyond, I am exhilarated and exhausted.

Chapter 6: Correcting Fragments

PRACTICE 1 (p. 77)

1. a. Add a subject
2. b. Add a verb
3. c. Add a subject and a verb
4. b. Add a verb
5. b. Add a verb
6. a. Add a subject
7. d. Add or delete words to express a complete thought.

Turning Fragments into Sentences

PRACTICE 2 (p. 79)

Answers will vary. These are sample answers.

1. The otter returned to the river.
2. A bird on the oak branch sang.

3. The river flowed between the island and the mainland.
4. The hawk, in a soaring motion, flew into the sky.
5. The fishing boats on the lake glided over the water.
6. The loon dropped like a stone into the water.
7. Because the fisherman put the net away, the fish were safe at last.

PRACTICE 3 (p. 79)

1. As long as it's a windy day, we'll be able to fly the kite.
2. Into the forest, armed with a machine gun, the fugitive dashed.
3. complete
4. The college student jogged along a deserted and dusty road.
5. The meadow below is where the deer and the antelope play.
6. The groundhog was run over by three different cars.
7. complete

Identifying Phrases

PRACTICE 1 (p. 81)

1. infinitive
2. infinitive
3. prepositional
4. prepositional
5. noun
6. noun
7. prepositional

PRACTICE 2 (p. 82)

1. prepositional
2. infinitive
3. prepositional
4. noun
5. verb
6. prepositional
7. infinitive
8. verb
9. infinitive
10. prepositional

Correcting the Fragment That Contains a Participle

PRACTICE 1 (p. 83)

Answers will vary. These are sample answers.

1. a. He is climbing in the Rockies.
   b. He climbs in the Rockies.
   c. Climbing in the Rockies, he left his stereo behind.
   d. Climbing in the Rockies is the thing to do.

2. a. He is playing video games.

b. He plays video games.

c. Playing video games, he didn't hear the robbers.

d. Playing video games is time-consuming.

3. a. She is going clubbing on Tuesdays.

b. She goes clubbing on Tuesdays.

c. Going clubbing on Tuesdays, she met her best friend.

d. Going clubbing on Tuesdays is tiring.

Recognizing the Fragment

PRACTICE 2 (p. 84)

1. complete	**6.** fragment
2. fragment	**7.** complete
3. fragment	**8.** fragment
4. fragment	**9.** fragment
5. complete	**10.** fragment

Editing for Fragments

PRACTICE 3 (p. 85)

Fragments:

Which took the game to 5–3 for Italy.

But 10 minutes before the end of extra time.

For head-butting Marco Materazzi.

And had insulted both his mother and his sister.

Partying with abandon.

Because he didn't take the moral high road.

While millions of fans watched his every move.

Sample corrected paragraph (answers will vary):

Soccer's World Cup in 2006 was won by Italy for the first time in 24 years, but it is public disgrace for which the game will be remembered by the world. By half time, the final game between Italy and France was tied 1–1. After 120 minutes, the game was still tied. The final victory depended on the penalty shootout, which took the game to 5–3 for Italy. But 10 minutes before the end of extra time, France's illustrious captain, Zinedine Zidane, was expelled for head-butting Marco Materazzi. Apparently, Marco had called him a terrorist and had insulted both his mother and his sister. Was this a deliberate, desperate, and cheap attempt to achieve final victory in what had become a gruelling final game? Celebrations by Italians around the world were unstoppable. They partied with abandon. But soccer scandal continues to loom over the Italian team. Zinedine Zidane exited from his last World Cup under an umbrella of shame because he didn't take the moral high road while millions of fans watched his every move.

Chapter 7: Correcting Run-Ons

Correcting Run-Ons

PRACTICE 1 (p. 91)

Answers will vary. These are sample answers.

1. Simple: (a) Five-year-old Davie asked Grandpa for an iPod for his birthday. He started crying because Grandpa didn't know what that was.

Compound: (b) Five-year-old Davie asked Grandpa for an iPod for his birthday, but he started crying because Grandpa didn't know what that was.

(c) Five-year-old Davie asked Grandpa for an iPod for his birthday; however, he started crying because Grandpa didn't know what that was.

Complex: (d) When five-year-old Davie asked Grandpa for an iPod for his birthday, he started crying because Grandpa didn't know what that was.

2. Simple: (a) Many people are opposed to gambling in all its forms. They will not even buy a lottery ticket.

Compound: (b) Many people are opposed to gambling in all its forms, so they will not even buy a lottery ticket.

(c) Many people are opposed to gambling in all its forms; indeed, they will not even buy a lottery ticket.

Complex: (d) Since many people are opposed to gambling in all its forms, they will not even buy a lottery ticket.

3. Simple: (a) Hockey may be Canada's national sport. The game can be quite brutal.

Compound: (b) Hockey may be Canada's national sport, but the game can be quite brutal.

(c) Hockey may be Canada's national sport; however, the game can be quite brutal.

Complex: (d) Although the game can be quite brutal, hockey may be Canada's national sport.

4. Simple: (a) Many young people manage to travel. They find ways to do it cheaply.
   Compound: (b) Many young people manage to travel, for they find ways to do it cheaply.
   (c) Many young people manage to travel; they find ways to do it cheaply.
   Complex: (d) Many young people manage to travel because they find ways to do it cheaply.

5. Simple: (a) The need for a proper diet is important in any health program. All the junk food on the grocery shelves makes it hard to be consistent.
   Compound: (b) The need for a proper diet is important in any health program, yet all the junk food on the grocery shelves makes it hard to be consistent.
   (c) The need for a proper diet is important in any health program; however, all the junk food on the grocery shelves makes it hard to be consistent.
   Complex: (d) Even though the need for a proper diet is important in any health program, all the junk food on the grocery shelves makes it hard to be consistent.

PRACTICE 2 (p. 94)

Answers will vary. These are sample answers.

1. Simple: The airline has begun its new route to the islands. Everyone is looking forward to flying there.
   Compound: The airline has begun its new route to the islands, so everyone is looking forward to flying there.
   The airline has begun its new route to the islands; consequently, everyone is looking forward to flying there.
   Complex: Ever since the airline began its new route to the islands, everyone has been looking forward to flying there.

2. Simple: The movie begins at nine o'clock. Let's have dinner before the show.
   Compound: The movie begins at nine o'clock, so let's have dinner before the show.
   The movie begins at nine o'clock; therefore, let's have dinner before the show.
   Complex: Since the movie begins at nine o'clock, let's have dinner before the show.

3. Simple: The studio audience screamed at the contestant. They wanted her to try for the big prize.

Compound: The studio audience screamed at the contestant, for they wanted her to try for the big prize.
The studio audience screamed at the contestant; they wanted her to try for the big prize.
Complex: The studio audience screamed at the contestant because they wanted her to try for the big prize.

4. Simple: Maya needs new shoes. She is running in the marathon.
   Compound: Maya needs new shoes, for she is running in the marathon.
   Maya needs new shoes; she is running in the marathon.
   Complex: Since she is running in the marathon, Maya needs new shoes.

5. Simple: My actor friend grabbed my arm. She wanted to tell me about her new part in the movie.
   Compound: My actor friend grabbed my arm; she wanted to tell me about her new part in the movie.
   My actor friend grabbed my arm, for she wanted to tell me about her new part in the movie.
   Complex: My actor friend grabbed my arm because she wanted to tell me about her new part in the movie.

Editing for Run-Ons

PRACTICE 3 (p. 96)

Every sentence in the paragraph is a run-on sentence. Sample corrected paragraph (answers will vary):

Mythology is the study of myths, and myths are known as the oldest form of literature. The oldest myths are creation myths. Cultures from around the world have their own creation myths. All of them are amazingly similar despite the vast geographical distances between these cultures and the fact that there are no known ways in which communication could have taken place between certain ones. Details of these myths change from one culture to the next; however, various themes of the myths remain the same. For example, although characters (most of the time, but not all of the time) take on new names from one culture to another, every culture refers to the existence of a creator. Also, the number of gods differs from one mythology to another; nevertheless, every mythology has at least one god or one heroic figure in it. All in all, myths are incredible stories that, in many cases, have lasted thousands of years. No matter where they come from and what they are about, they bear striking similarities from one culture to another, and they all share a wisdom about something that never changes: our human nature.

PRACTICE 4 (p. 96)

Every sentence in the paragraph is a run-on sentence. Sample corrected paragraph (answers will vary):

Sigmund Freud and Carl G. Jung were both psychiatrists who have had a great deal of influence on the study of psychology to this day. For example, each psychiatrist is famous for his own model of the human psyche. In Freud's model, there are three main parts. They are the ego, the id, and the superego. In Jung's model, there are also three main parts: the conscious, the personal unconscious, and the collective unconscious. Freud (Jung's teacher and subsequent collaborator until they parted due to a major disagreement in 1912) and Jung both believed that dreams come from the unconscious part of our psyche (for Freud, this meant the id and superego); nevertheless, they disagreed a great deal in the area of dream interpretation.

Chapter 8: Parallel Structure

Making Sentences Parallel

PRACTICE 1 (p. 101)

1. dirty
2. sewing her own clothes
3. willingly explain material more than once

PRACTICE 2 (p. 101)

Answers will vary. These are sample answers.

1. Winter in Edmonton is very windy and bitterly cold.
2. I would prefer fixing an old car to watching television.
3. Alex is a talented athlete, a top student, and even a generous friend.
4. The apartment is crowded and dark.

5. The dancer is slender and graceful.
6. The trees were tall and leafy.
7. My friend loves to play chess, to read science fiction, and to work out at the gym.

PRACTICE 3 (p. 102)

Answers will vary. These are sample answers.

1. The dog had to choose between jumping over the fence or digging a hole underneath it.
2. She was great at swimming, canoeing, and rock climbing.
3. As I looked down the city street, I could see the soft lights from restaurant windows, I could hear the mellow sounds of a nightclub band, and I could sense the carefree moods of people walking by.
4. The singers have been on several road tours, have recorded for two record companies, and have expressed a desire to make a movie someday.
5. They would rather order a pizza than eat home cooking.
6. I explained to the teacher that my car had broken down, my books had been stolen, and my assignment pad had been left at home.
7. That night the prisoner was sick, discouraged, and lonely.

Chapter 9: Pronouns

Chapter Review Exercises

Making Pronouns and Antecedents Agree

PRACTICE (p. 114)

Answers will vary. These are sample answers.

1. The father mailed his son's high school yearbook to him.
2. No one wants his or her income reduced.
3. When a company fails to update its equipment, it often pays a price in the long run.
4. Graduates today have many more options open to them than ever before.
5. Everybody knows his or her own strengths best.
6. All the soccer players put effort into their game.
7. If the campers want to eat quickly, they should help themselves.

Chapter 10: Modifiers: Misplaced and Dangling

Chapter Review Exercises

Revising Misplaced or Dangling Modifiers

PRACTICE (p. 120)

Answers will vary. These are sample answers.

1. Wearing his tuxedo, Victor fed the dog.
2. While we were visiting the Vancouver Aquarium, the otters entertained us.
3. The toddler that ate her breakfast started singing cheerily.
4. A band that we had heard earlier was playing in the park.
5. After running over the hill, I noticed that the farm was visible in the valley below.
6. The truck, which was broken down on the highway, caused a traffic jam for kilometres.
7. I saw three spiders hanging from the ceiling in my bedroom.

Chapter 11: Punctuation

Insert Necessary Commas

PRACTICE 1 (p. 123)

1. Problems with the water supply of Canada, the United States, Europe, and other parts of the world are growing.
2. Water is colourless, tasteless, odourless, and free of calories.
3. You will use on an average day 90 L of water for flushing, 120 L for bathing and washing clothes, and 95 L for other uses.
4. It took 450 L of water to create the eggs you ate for breakfast, 13 250 L to obtain the steak you might eat for dinner, and over 200 000 L to produce the steel used to make your car.
5. The English–Wabigoon river system runs through Grassy Narrows, Ontario, and had become polluted with mercury.

PRACTICE 2 (p. 124)

1. The most overused bodies of water are our rivers, but they continue to serve us daily.

2. Canadian cities often developed next to rivers, and industries followed soon after in the same locations.
3. The people of the industrial age can try to clean the water they use, or they can watch pollution take over.
4. The Great Lakes are showing signs of renewal, yet the struggle against pollution in them must continue.
5. Most people have not been educated about the dangerous state of our water supply, nor are all our members of Parliament fully aware of the problem.

PRACTICE 3 (p. 125)

1. A total solar eclipse, when the moon's shadow blots out the sun completely, is an outstanding cosmic event.
2. Once you see your first solar eclipse, you start looking forward to the next one.
3. However, witnessing this spectacle takes planning and the ability to travel to the best viewing spots.
4. In eastern Turkey, on August 11, 1999, a crowd of astronomers and "eclipse chasers" watched the last total eclipse of the millennium.
5. At the moment of totality, people cheered, clapped, and even cried.

PRACTICE 4 (p. 127)

1. Natural disasters, I believe, have not been historically significant.
2. They have, however, significantly affected the lives of many Canadians.
3. Canada's worst coal-mine disaster, at Hillcrest, Alberta, occurred on June 19, 1914.
4. In Springhill, Nova Scotia, furthermore, 424 persons were killed in the mines between 1881 and 1969.
5. Avalanches, storms, and floods, which are natural disasters, have also made their marks on the face of our country.

PRACTICE 5 (p. 127)

1. Honey, I hope you're not planning to wear that hat.
2. I wonder, Samir, if the game has been cancelled.
3. Dad, could I borrow five dollars?

4. Can you help me, Doctor?

5. Ayesha, is that you?

PRACTICE 6 (p. 128)

1. "I'm innocent," he cried, "of all charges against me."

2. He mumbled, "I won't incriminate myself."

3. "I was told," the defendant explained, "to answer every question."

4. "This court," the judge announced, "will be adjourned."

5. "The jury," said Al Tarvin of *The Star*, "was hand-picked."

PRACTICE 7 (p. 128)

1. Kicking, the child was carried off to bed.

2. To Maria, Suzuki was the boss from hell.

3. When you can, come and visit us.

4. Whoever that is, is going to be surprised.

5. Skin cancer seldom kills, doctors say.

Using the Apostrophe

PRACTICE 1 (p. 132)

1. boys'
2. their
3. Moses's or Moses'
4. Antony and Maria's
5. nobody's
6. his
7. 1700's or 1700s
8. It's
9. Vancouver's
10. Wendy's

PRACTICE 2 (p. 132)

1. Cherry's
2. geese's
3. Carol's and Tess's
4. somebody's
5. hers
6. two's
7. can't

Insert Necessary Quotation Marks

PRACTICE 1 (p. 135)

1. "The Hot House" is one of the stories contained in Rosemary Sullivan's *More Stories by Canadian Women*.

2. Nellie McClung said, "I'll never believe I'm dead until I see it in the papers."

3. no quotation marks needed

4. To "diss" is a slang term meaning to show disrespect.

5. She read the article "Whiz Kids" in The Review.

Using Semicolons

PRACTICE 2 (p. 135)

1. One of the best ways to remember a vacation is to take numerous photos; one of the best ways to recall the contents of a book is to take notes.

2. The problem of street crime must be solved; otherwise, the number of vigilantes will increase.

3. The meal was composed of bruschetta, an appetizer; roast duck, the house specialty; and lemon mousse, a tart dessert.

4. The bank president was very cordial; however, he would not approve the loan.

5. New methods of production are being used in the factories of Japan; eventually they will be common in this country as well.

Using Colons

PRACTICE 3 (p. 137)

1. Two Canadian-born comedians have achieved great success in the United States: Jim Carrey and Mike Myers.

2. The official has one major flaw in his personality: greed.

3. no colons needed

4. The college offers four courses in English literature: Romantic Poetry, Shakespeare's Plays, The British Short Story, and The Modern Novel.

5. Arriving at 6:15 in the morning, Marlene brought me a sausage-and-cheese pizza, some ginger ale, and a litre of ice cream.

Using Dashes or Parentheses

PRACTICE (p. 139)

1. Herbert Simon is—and I don't think this is an exaggeration—a genius.

2. George Eliot (her real name was Mary Ann Evans) wrote Silas Marner.

3. You should—in fact I insist—see a doctor.

4. Health Canada's website has suggestions to help smokers quit (visit www.infotobacco.com).

5. Mass media (television, radio, movies, magazines, and newspapers) are able to transmit information over a wide range and to a large number of people.

Chapter Review Exercises

Punctuation Overview

PRACTICE 1 (p. 139)

1. To measure crime, sociologists have used three different techniques: official statistics, victimization surveys, and self-report studies.
2. "David" is one of the best-loved poems of Earle Birney.
3. That show uses one thing I hate: a laugh track.
4. Farley Mowat has written numerous books for adults; however, he also writes very popular books for children.
5. Tuberculosis (also known as consumption) has been nearly eliminated by medical science.
6. The Victorian period (1837–1901) saw a rapid expansion in industry.
7. He told me—I remember the day—that he would never give up.

PRACTICE 2 (p. 140)

1. Many young people have two feelings about science and technology: awe and fear.
2. Mr. Doyle, the realtor; Mrs. Tong, the bank officer; and Ivan Petroff, the lawyer, are the three people to help work out the real-estate transaction.
3. The book was entitled *English Literature: The Victorian Age.*
4. "My computer," she said, "has been crashing all day."
5. She brought a bathing suit, a towel, sunglasses, and several books to the beach. (no colon after brought)
6. The meeting to discuss a pay increase—I'll believe it when I see it—has been rescheduled for Friday.
7. The complex lab experiment has these two major problems: too many difficult calculations and too many variables.

Chapter 12: Capitalization

Capitalization

PRACTICE (p. 145)

1. Italian
2. Canadian Rockies

3. Bible
4. University of Alberta
5. Hallowe'en
6. Bell Canada, Friday, Winnipeg, Manitoba
7. Cobalt-60, Canadian, Dr. Donald Green
8. Why
9. Canadian Auto Workers
10. *Women of the Klondike*, North

Chapter 13: Unit I Review: Using All You Have Learned

Identifying Parts of Speech

PRACTICE 1 (p. 148)

2. constant: adjective modifying the noun source
3. of: preposition, which starts the prepositional phrase of creativity and inspiration
4. and: coordinating conjunction (one of the FANBOYS) joining two items
5. him: pronoun in the objective case
6. inspired: action verb in the past tense
7. throughout: preposition, which starts the prepositional phrase throughout his life
8. his: possessive adjective modifying the noun ideas
9. was: helping verb to be in the past tense
10. when: subordinate conjunction that begins a dependent clause
11. often: adverb modifying the past tense verb led
12. the: definite article
13. right: adjective modifying the noun direction
14. had: past tense of the irregular action verb to have
15. impending: adjective modifying the noun death
16. become: past participle of the irregular action verb to become
17. a: indefinite article
18. symbol: common noun
19. properly: adverb modifying the verb understood
20. only: adverb modifying from his inner experiences
21. outer: adjective modifying the noun world
22. for: preposition, which begins the prepositional phrase for him
23. he: pronoun in the subjective case
24. could: modal auxiliary (helping verb)
25. happenings: common abstract noun

Editing Sentences for Errors

PRACTICE 2 (p. 148)

These are sample answers. There is more than one way to correct many of these sentences.

1. Roma (also known as Gypsies or Romany Gypsies) now are living in many countries of the world.
2. The international community of scientists agrees that these Roma originally came from India thousands of years ago.
3. After the original Roma people left India, they went to Persia; there they divided into groups.
4. One branch of Roma went west to Europe, while the other group decided to go east.
5. In the Middle Ages . . . Little Egypt.
6. C
7. Today, Roma families may be found from Canada to Chile, living much as their ancestors did thousands of years ago.

PRACTICE 3 (p. 149)

These are sample answers. There is more than one way to correct many of these sentences below.

1. The laser beam, a miracle of modern science, already has many practical uses in today's world.
2. Laser beams are narrow, highly concentrated beams of light that burn brighter than the light of the sun.
3. Scientists have found many possible military uses for the laser, but they are hoping these can be converted into constructive uses.
4. C
5. The possibility of making a laser was first described in 1958, and two years later, in California, the first laser beam was created.
6. Since they are so precise, laser beams are used in medicine to help make a specific diagnosis and to perform operations such as repairing delicate retinas and removing cancerous tumours.
7. The future uses of the laser seem endless, and it is up to us to decide whether we want to use this invention for war or for peaceful purposes.

Unit II: The Writing Process

Chapter 15: The Paragraph

Finding the Topic Sentence of a Paragraph

PRACTICE (p. 171)

1. Love is a crazy, complicated affair, made trickier by the tangle of superstitions that go along with it.
2. The brain is one of the most remarkable organs, a part of the body that we have only begun to investigate.

Finding the Topic in the Topic Sentence

PRACTICE (p. 171)

1. Remodelling an old house
2. College work and high school work
3. A well-made suit
4. Growing up near a museum
5. My favourite room in the house
6. A student who goes to school full-time and also works part-time
7. The expense of skiing
8. The change that had come over my friend
9. Current tax laws
10. Greek restaurants

Finding the Controlling Idea

PRACTICE (p. 172)

1. T: vigorous exercise CI: reduces stress
2. T: St. John's and Corner Brook CI: differ
3. T: wonder foods CI: less than wonderful
4. T: athletic scholarships available to women CI: numbers increasing
5. T: caffeine CI: adverse effects
6. T: Madame Benoît CI: amusing personality
7. T: computers CI: will make newspapers obsolete

Avoid Restating the Topic Sentence

PRACTICE (p. 182)

1. a. SD   b. R   c. SD   d. SD
2. a. SD   b. SD   c. R   d. SD

Chapter 16: The Essay

Recognizing the Thesis Statement

PRACTICE (p. 195)

1. thesis
2. title
3. fact
4. thesis

5. title
6. fact
7. fact

Unit III: Writing Strategies

Chapter 21: Narration

Coherence: Placing Details in Order of Time Sequence

PRACTICE (p. 257)

2. 4, 5, 1, 6, 2, 3

Chapter 22: Description

Coherence: Putting Details in Spatial Order

PRACTICE (p. 269)

1. 4, 2, 3, 1, 5
2. 2, 3, 1, 4

Chapter 23: Process

Coherence: Order in Logical Sequence

PRACTICE (p. 278)

7, 5, 1, 8, 2, 6, 3, 9, 4

Chapter 24: Comparison and/or Contrast

Evaluating the Two-Part Topic

PRACTICE (p. 288)

Answers could vary depending on the purpose of the paragraph.

3. too broad
4. suitable

5. too broad
6. too broad

Recognizing the Two Methods

PRACTICE (p. 291)

1. block; differences
2. point-by-point; similarities

Chapter 27: Cause and Effect

Looking for the Causal Relationship

PRACTICE 1 (p. 317)

1. T
2. C
3. T
4. C
5. C
6. T
7. C

Separating the Cause from the Effect

PRACTICE 2 (p. 318)

1. a. C   b. C   c. E   d. E   e. C   f. E
2. a. C   b. C   c. E   d. E   e. C   f. C

Unit V: Appendices

Appendix B: Solving Spelling Problems

Identifying the Correct Spelling

PRACTICE (p. 433)

1. separate
2. probably
3. arctic
4. surprise
5. tragedy
6. quantity

7. literature
8. hungry
9. handsome
10. favourite
11. nuclear

Choosing *ie* or *ei*

PRACTICE (p. 434)

1. sleigh
2. believe
3. siege
4. veil
5. leisure

6. deceit
7. niece
8. weight
9. protein
10. ancient

Forming the Plurals of Nouns

PRACTICE (pp. 436–437)

1. puppies
2. mothers-in-law
3. teeth
7. matches
8. mixes

4. cameos
5. phenomena
6. loaves
9. enemies
10. bags

Doubling the Consonant?

PRACTICE (p. 439)

slip: yes, yes, slipping

crack: no, no, cracking

broil: no, no, broiling

win: yes, yes, winning

control: controlling

fever: feverish

compel: compelled

differ: difference

begin: beginning

Doubling the Final Consonant When Adding Endings That Begin with Vowels?

PRACTICE (p. 440)

1. bitten
2. occurrence
3. wavering
4. preferred
5. preference
6. thinner
7. transferred
8. sailing
9. propellent
10. omitted

Adding Endings to Words That End in -y

PRACTICE (p. 441)

1. keys
2. loneliness
3. crying
4. cries

5. prayer
6. employment
7. monkeying
8. beautiful
9. theories
10. ceremonial

One Word or Two?

PRACTICE (p. 442)

1. bedroom
2. grandmother
3. already
4. all together
5. always
6. Everyone
7. maybe
8. cannot
9. nearby
10. Nevertheless

Appendix C: Irregular Verbs

Irregular Verbs

PRACTICE (p. 449)

1. caught
2. laid
3. fled
4. burst
5. ridden
6. slid
7. rose
8. quit
9. forgotten
10. wrung

Index

Lipschutz, Gary, "Lessons of Love from Stories of Old," 396–397
List
  colon, 136
  comma, 123
  semicolon, 135
Literary research essay, 226–227
local, locale, 426
Logic, 316–317
Longer quotation, 230, 231
lose, loose, 429–430
"Lost Salt Gift of Blood, The" (MacLeod), 270
"Love Hurts" (Yuen), 200, 302–304
Lycos, 228

Main supporting sentence, 176–178
Mapping, 159
may be, maybe, 442
McKinnell, Julia, "How to Quit Putting Things Off," 408
"Meaning of Myth, The" (model paragraph), 299
Misplaced modifier, 118–119
Missing antecedent, 113
MLA. *See* Modern Language Association (MLA)
Modal auxiliary verb, 6, 7, 24, 42
Modern Language Association (MLA) format, 238–241
  electronic sources, 239, 240–241
  end documentation, 239–241, 250
  headers, 238
  internal documentation, 238–239
  parenthetical references, 238–239
  sample research paper, 249–250
  title page, 238
  when used, 233
  Works Cited list, 239–241, 250
Modifier, 117–121
  awkwardness, 119
  common modifiers, 119
  dangling, 119–120
  defined, 118
  misplaced, 118–119
  proximity to word it modifies, 118
  squinting, 119
mono-, 437
Months of year, 143
Moola, Faisal (with David Suzuki), "No Great Sacrifice," 352
moral, morale, 426
Moral Philosophy for Modern Life (Falikowski), 344
Morton, James C., "A Tough Approach That Might Work," 403
"Mother Fortress" (model paragraph), 270–271
Mustafa, Naheed, "My Body Is My Own Business," 364–366

"My Body Is My Own Business" (Mustafa), 364–366
myth, 298–299

Narration, 254–263
  defined, 254
  making a point, 255
  model essay, 261–262
  model paragraph, 256–257, 260
  narrative essay, 260
  placing details in sequence, 256
  choosing important events (step 3), 258
  making a list of events (step 2), 258
  ordering events chronologically (step 4), 258
  putting sentences in standard paragraph form (step 7), 259
  writing a concluding statement (step 6), 259
  writing a topic sentence for narration (step 1), 258
  writing one sentence per event (step 5), 258
neither . . . nor, 48
new, knew, 419
"Nice and Neighbourly?" (model paragraph), 306–307
no, know, 419
"No Great Sacrifice" (Suzuki/Moola), 352–354
non-, 437
none, 47
Nonfiction readings. *See* Readings (authors); Readings (titles)
Nonrestrictive clause, 69, 127
Nonrestrictive word, etc., 126
not only . . . but also, 48
Noun
  abstract, 4
  common, 3, 14
  concrete, 4
  countable, 4
  group, 49
  non-countable, 4
  plurals, 434–437
  proper, 3, 14
Noun phrase, 81
Number
  comma, 128
  hyphen, 138

Object, 4, 15
Objective case, 107
Oft-confused words, 416–430
  choose/close, lose/loose, lead/led, die/dye, 429–430
  sit/set, rise/raise, lie/lag, 428–429
  use/used, suppose/supposed, 430

words that sound alike, 416–423
words that sound/look almost alike, 423
oral, aural, 416
"Other Family, The" (Bannerji), 380–385
Outlining, 162
Overused words, 266–267

pain, pane, 419
para-, 437
Paragraph, 168–187
  concluding sentence, 185–186
  controlling idea, 172–175
  defined, 168
  essay, and, 190–191
  format, 168–169
  length, 226
  sample outline format, 186–187
  supporting detail. *See* Supporting detail
  topic sentence, 169–172
  types, 170
Parallel structure, 99–105
  defined, 99
  list—parallel clauses, 100
  list—same kind of phrase, 100
  list—same part of speech, 100
Paraphrasing, 220–222. *See also* Summarizing and paraphrasing
Parentheses, 138–139
Parenthetical references, 238–239
Participial phrase, 82, 83
Parts of speech
  adjective, 5, 14
  adverb, 7, 25
  article, 9–10
  conjunction. *See* Conjunction
  interjection, 9
  noun. *See* Noun
  preposition, 7–8, 18
  pronoun. *See* Pronoun
  verb. *See* Verb
passed, past, 419
Passive euthanasia, 344
Passive voice, 38–40
Past form (verb), 29–31, 446–449
Past participle (verb), 29–31, 446–449
Past perfect tense, 36, 37
patience, patients, 419
peace, piece, 419–420
Perfect tense, 36–37
personal, personnel, 427
Personal definitions, 297
Personal pronoun, 5, 107
Persuasion, 161, 329
Persuasive appeals, 330
Phrase, 81
Pianissimo, Donald, "Whose Choice Is It, Anyway?" 322–323